Viktor Savchenko

Free Will in Civil Law

A Ukrainian Perspective

With a foreword by Thomas Douglas

UKRAINIAN VOICES

Collected by Andreas Umland

99 *Daria Antsybor, Michel Bouchard*
Memeing War
The Digital Folklore Memetic Mirror of Contemporary Ukrainian Culture and Society
ISBN 978-3-8382-2040-6

100 *Sergiy Korsunsky*
The Age of Revisionism
International Relations in Times of War, Uncertainty, and Insecurity
ISBN 978-3-8382-2023-9

101 *Olena Bogatyrenko (ed.)*
Was bedeutete Russlands Besetzung der Krim?
Zwölf Frauen berichten, wie sie 2014 den Beginn des Russisch-Ukrainischen Krieges erlebten
Übersetzt von Hermann Haushahn
ISBN 978-3-8382-2292-9

102 *Alla Prokhovnik-Raphique*
Whispers of Survival
War, Trauma, and the Making of Civilian Rescuers
With a foreword by Sarah Adams
ISBN 978-3-8382-2114-4

103 *Maryna Starodubska*
Ukraine Layer by Layer
Freedom and Friction in a Frontier Society
With a foreword by Natalka Cmoc
ISBN 978-3-8382-2117-5

The book series "Ukrainian Voices" publishes English- and German-language monographs, edited volumes, document collections, and anthologies of articles authored and composed by Ukrainian politicians, intellectuals, activists, officials, researchers, and diplomats. The series' aim is to introduce Western and other audiences to Ukrainian explorations, deliberations and interpretations of historic and current, domestic, and international affairs. The purpose of these books is to make non-Ukrainian readers familiar with how some prominent Ukrainians approach, view and assess their country's development and position in the world. The series was founded, and the volumes are collected by Andreas Umland, Dr. phil. (FU Berlin), Ph. D. (Cambridge), Associate Professor of Politics at the Kyiv-Mohyla Academy and an Analyst in the Stockholm Centre for Eastern European Studies at the Swedish Institute of International Affairs.

Viktor Savchenko

FREE WILL IN CIVIL LAW

A Ukrainian Perspective

With a foreword by Thomas Douglas

ibidem
Verlag

Bibliografische Information der Deutschen Nationalbibliothek
Die Deutsche Nationalbibliothek verzeichnet diese Publikation in der Deutschen Nationalbibliografie; detaillierte bibliografische Daten sind im Internet über http://dnb.d-nb.de abrufbar.

Bibliographic information published by the Deutsche Nationalbibliothek
The Deutsche Nationalbibliothek lists this publication in the Deutsche Nationalbibliografie; detailed bibliographic data are available on the Internet at http://dnb.d-nb.de.

ISBN (Print): 978-3-8382-2133-5
ISBN (E-Book [PDF]): 978-3-8382-8133-9

Leuschnerstraße 40
30457 Hannover
Germany / Deutschland
info@ibidem.eu

Printed in the EU

Contents

Foreword

It is a pleasure to introduce this monograph by Dr. Viktor Savchenko, which is the culmination of research that he conducted during his time at the Uehiro Oxford Institute.

When Viktor joined the University of Oxford as a British Academy Fellow, I have had the privilege of serving as his academic mentor. During this period, I have seen his work evolve into an ambitious synthesis that touches on many different areas of law and also begins to bridge a significant divide between philosophy and civil law.

The timely publication of *Free Will in Civil Law: A Ukrainian Perspective* meets a growing global interest in Ukraine. While international attention often focuses on geopolitics, this book shifts the perspective toward the country's intellectual traditions, offering a sophisticated analysis of how free will is applied in Ukrainian law.

Savchenko's research addresses a significant gap in existing scholarship. While the philosophical debate over free will is vast, it often remains detached from the practicalities of private law. Conversely, legal scholarship sometimes treats free will as a merely procedural matter. This monograph unites these perspectives by examining the methodological principles for recognising freedom of the will across a broad spectrum of legal relations.

By examining how freedom of the will operates within different areas, Savchenko provides more than just legal commentary. He offers a window into the values of a legal system striving to align with European standards while maintaining its unique scholarly voice.

At a time when Ukraine's European future is being forged, understanding its legal and philosophical perspectives is more important than ever. This book makes a substantial contribution to that understanding, and I highly recommend it to scholars of law, philosophy, and Eastern European studies alike.

Professor Thomas Douglas
Uehiro Oxford Institute
University of Oxford

Introduction

This monograph is the first comprehensive study of the theoretical and practical problems of free will in civil law, with in-depth attention to the legal system of Ukraine. The work provides a thorough analysis of new ideas and contemporary international legal trends concerning the subject. The relevance of this research is underscored by the central importance of free will to all fields and institutions of civil law. This principle determines the logic and scope of the study, each section of which offers a detailed analysis of the significance of free will for a specific area of civil law. The study demonstrates how an understanding of this concept affects the resolution of contemporary challenges in civil law, analysing the relationship between free will, personal integrity, and compliance with legal requirements.

This monograph will be of value to academics, lecturers, doctoral candidates, students, legal practitioners, and the general public.

Civil law is based on constructs and principles that stem from the foundational ideas of the nature of law itself. It is fundamentally based on normatively enshrined principles, namely: (1) the inadmissibility of arbitrary interference in a person's private life; (2) the inadmissibility of the deprivation of property rights, except in cases established by law; (3) freedom of contract; (4) freedom of entrepreneurial activity not prohibited by law; (5) judicial protection of civil rights and interests; (6) the principles of justice, good faith, and reasonableness.

The essence of these principles suggests they are united by a profound legal idea: the concept of free will. Indeed, the notion of human freedom in action and decision-making underlies the entirety of civil law.

Free will is of central importance to all fields and institutions of civil law, a fact that determines the logic and relevance of this study. Each section, therefore, provides a detailed analysis of the significance of free will for a particular sub-branch of civil law. Furthermore, we demonstrate how understanding the legal nature of free will impacts the resolution of contemporary problems in civil law. It finds undeniable reflection in personal non-property rights, in the right of ownership and property rights in the property of others, in the law of obligations, and in intellectual property and inheritance law.

Free will is the basis of civil legal relations, which are founded on the principles of dispositivity and autonomy of the will. Violations of these principles are grounds for declaring transactions invalid, classifying vitiating factors, and exempting from civil liability.

Despite this, legislation contains no formal definition of free will, nor does it delineate its boundaries and principles. Likewise, legal doctrine has not yet defined its concept or its place within the legal system.

Nevertheless, the concept of free will is applied across all areas of civil law, influencing the development of legislation and the formation of legal values, acting as a tacit benchmark for law-making. This study is primarily based on the Civil Code of Ukraine of 2003, which remained the governing legislation at the time of writing (early 2026). However, the relevance of the theoretical framework presented here extends well beyond existing legislation. On January 22, 2026, a new draft of the Civil Code was registered in the Verkhovna Rada of Ukraine. Notably, this prospective legislation closely aligns with the expanded concept of free will advanced in this monograph. The author submitted proposals regarding these issues to the Parliament, and the Verkhovna Rada has officially acknowledged the importance of this research for the ongoing legislative reform. Consequently, this work offers both an analysis of the established legal framework and a theoretical foundation for the future of Ukrainian civil law.

An analysis of civil legislation confirms the absence of direct normative contradictions to this legal idea. This provides grounds to assert that the concept of free will is fundamental to the entire branch of civil law and requires a deep and comprehensive analysis.

Some studies have addressed individual issues of free will in the context of legal philosophy, civil law, and criminal law. Still, modern scientific research has primarily focused on specific principles and institutions. This subject has been addressed by scholars such as Ronald Dworkin (in his work on abortion and euthanasia), David McGoldrick (on the International Covenant on Civil and Political Rights), Lauri Hannikainen (on peremptory norms), Paul Gordon Lauren (on the evolution of human rights), and Johannes Morsink (on the origins of the Universal Declaration). H. L. A. Hart developed a doctrinal "Will Theory," which was countered by the "Interest Theory" proposed by Jeremy Bentham and Rudolf von Jhering. However, these scholars focused primarily on human rights without paying sufficient attention to civil law. More recently, Visa Kurki has investigated free will in the context of legal personhood.

Despite its fundamental importance, a comprehensive study of free will within civil law has not yet been conducted. Given its central role and the aforementioned lack of extensive research, the need for such an inquiry is clear.

The author expresses his gratitude to his academic supervisor, Professor Roman Maydanyk, Academician of the National Academy of Legal Sciences of Ukraine; to the reviewers for their objective assessment of the text; to Professor Tetyana Kaganovska, Rector of V.N. Karazin Kharkiv National University; Professor Vitaliy Seryogin, Dean of the Faculty of Law; and Olena Ustymenko, Head of the Department of Civil Law Disciplines, for their assistance in writing and publishing this monograph. The author is also grateful to Professor Thomas Douglas, Director of Research at the Uehiro Oxford Institute, for invaluable advice and discussions; and to his grandparents, parents, wife, children, and family for their inspiration, support, and understanding.

The author extends special gratitude to Balliol College, University of Oxford, its Master and Fellows, and the British Academy for their comprehensive support of this research.

Published for the first time in English, this book is a revised and updated translation of a monograph previously released in Ukrainian, which has received prestigious awards, including:

1. The Best Publication of 2024 from the National Academy of Sciences of Higher Education of Ukraine;

2. Winner of the III National Competition of Scientific and Educational Publications on Law, Security, and European Integration for the Best Monograph of 2024.

1. Methodological Principles of Recognition of Free Will as the Genesis of Legal Understanding

1.1. Historical and Philosophical Analysis of Free Will as the Genesis of Legal Understanding

Law is the foundation of a civilised society, because it allows us to distinguish between order and chaos, system and disorder. Historically, the primary purpose of law has been the regulation of social relations, a fundamental idea that remains unchanged.

The relevance of a historical and philosophical analysis of free will as the origin of legal understanding is underscored by the foundational works of G. W. F. Hegel. He was the first to conclude that the starting point of law is will, therefore, freedom constitutes its substance and concept, and the system of law is the kingdom of realised freedom (De Caro and Putnam 2020). Philosophical and legal scholarship indicates that the will represents the transformation of subjectivity into objectivity. It is the unity of theoretical consciousness and practical activity, the efficacy of objectified consciousness, and the purposeful regulation of behavior aimed at reshaping reality (Blikhar 2015, 150).

To fully explore this issue, it is necessary to examine the understanding of free will throughout various periods: in the philosophy of Antiquity, the Middle Ages, and the Renaissance; in the doctrines of the Modern Age and classical German philosophy; in 20th-century Western philosophy; and in contemporary Ukrainian philosophy. Such an analysis will allow us to trace the shifting paradigms in the understanding of free will across different historical epochs and to assess its profound impact on the development of law.

The philosophy of antiquity laid the foundations for the understanding of free will, as well as basic legal concepts. Confirmation of this can be seen in the works of Jaspers, who noted that the West is familiar with the idea of political freedom. In Greece, he argued, a form of freedom existed—albeit briefly—that arose nowhere else. This community of free people withstood the pressures of universal despotism and totalising organization. In doing so, the polis established the foundations for the entire Western conception of liberty, encompassing both the reality of freedom and its ideals (Jaspers 2000).

Aristotle defined philosophy as the process of "thinking about thinking"—the development of thought aimed at self-knowledge and, simultaneously, knowledge of the external world. He argued that without this self-awareness, a person possesses a slavish consciousness, becoming a mere executor of another's will in their motivational impulses. Therefore, the central question of philosophy is not the relationship between matter and consciousness, but that between will and reason. Aristotle posited that the will is not inherently rational from birth; it must be cultivated to become so (Zhadko and Bidzilia 2019). The relevance of these ideas will become apparent later in our discussion of the connection between free will and civil capacity, the scope of a minor's free will, and other related issues.

Ancient times produced a great number of legal philosophers who explored the fundamental ideas of law.

The ancient world produced a great number of legal philosophers who explored the fundamental ideas of law. The flourishing of slave-owning democracy spurred the development of views on personal autonomy and choice. At the same time, the belief in an inexorable fate (*fatum*) that guides individuals and limits their free will persisted. The relationship between free will and predestination has been a recurring theme throughout human history, reflected in the works of leading scientists, philosophers, theologians, and lawyers.

For example, the Stoics are well-known, particularly the concept of fate, which is higher than the gods and is the embodiment of immutable cosmic laws. According to common understanding, fate is a predetermined, unavoidable destiny — a mysterious force that dictates the course of all existence (*Slovnyk ukrains'koi movy* [Dictionary of the Ukrainian Language] 1979, 10:570). Antiquity proclaimed the immensity of fate, yet it did not assert that individuals must obey the will of the gods in all circumstances (Potsiurko 2018, 2). These two approaches formed a single philosophy wherein individuals should act according to the dictates of fate but retain the autonomy to decide whether to accept them.

Thus, the initial understanding of free will presupposed the existence of fate alongside freedom of action. Socrates emphasised the existence of an inner voice (*daemon*) that a person hears throughout life and which helps him make choices.

The Cynics paid particular attention to the issue of free will. The founder of the Cynic school is considered to be Antisthenes, a student of Socrates, who linked free will with knowledge and volitional actions (Prince 2020). Free will came to be understood through *ataraxia* (tranquillity) and the rejection of external dependencies, especially fate.

Plato continued to develop Socrates' ideas about free will. In his works, the concept of the need to recognize the existence of three kinds of being is traced: eternal ideas, concrete things that change, and the space in which things exist. Plato divided the soul into three principles: the rational, the spirited (affective), and the irrational (appetitive). Free will is aimed at subjugating the irrational parts of the soul by the sensible part. According to the philosopher's ideas, the soul is not endowed with valid free will and is subject to the world of ideas. He also interpreted freedom itself as a person's responsibility to the state in which they live (Cooper 1997).

Aristotle considered free will to be relevant only for free people. This was explained by the lack of enslaved people's right to dispose of even their own lives, and therefore, enslaved people had no free will and the ability to make legal decisions. Aristotle also considered freedom as an opportunity to participate in power with others alternately and influence the formation of the state will (Aristotle 2003, 66–69). However, Aristotle did not analyse free will in its pure form, distinguishing only between voluntary (conscious) and involuntary (unconscious) actions. He believed that the self acts as the rational cause of voluntary actions, whereas involuntary actions occur spontaneously, without a conscious goal, or are caused by external circumstances that one cannot resist (Gunderman 2006). Aristotle defined *entelecheia* as the inner striving for a goal and perfection,—that which actualises what is otherwise merely potential, such as the force that makes a flower grow from a seed (The Editors of Encyclopaedia Britannica 1998).

Aristotle's ideas on free will can be summarised as follows: human freedom is manifested in actions aimed at achieving virtue, which is possible only when reason aligns with the senses. He also used the term of *proairesis*, which can be defined as a rational choice or deliberated desire (Sorabji 2007).

Somewhat different views are found in the philosophical treatises of Cicero. One must agree with G. Striker, who highlights the eclecticism of Cicero's philosophy and his attempt to create a distinctly Roman philosophy befitting the greatness of his state and satisfying the spiritual needs of its people (Striker 2022). Cicero's idea of free will stems from his analysis of the soul and mind. He noted that the mind—with its memory, thought, and imagination—allows a person to preserve the past, foresee the future, and comprehend the present. This capacity, he argued, is divine and can only come from God; therefore, the nature of the soul is something special, distinct from the physical world we know (Cicero 2010).

In his understanding of free will, Cicero included the idea that there is something in the soul that is independent of fate and foresight, thanks to which a person is endowed with the ability to think independently, make decisions and be responsible for them. He explained this with the thesis that a soul that feels itself moving also feels that it moves by its own power, not by an external one (Cherevko 2022).

Cicero's views on free will, seen through the prism of passions and desires, were progressive for his time. M. V. Vidryhan summarises Cicero's concept by noting that desire and joy arise from our understanding of the good; what seems good becomes a goal to be achieved. Desire, taking hold of a person, becomes the driving force for action. When the goal is achieved, the person rejoices. Thus, will is a stable and rational desire or aspiration for the good. If this desire becomes overly agitated and irrational, it turns into lust and evil (Vydryhan 2019, 16). This is confirmed by Cicero's statement that, according to the laws of nature itself, all people are drawn to what is considered suitable for them, and the opposite is avoided; therefore, if the object seems reasonable, then nature itself commands us to achieve it. If this desire is stable and rational, the Stoics call it *boulesis*, and we call it will (Cicero 1991).

Summarising Cicero's ideas on free will: a creator or god, who is a free mind in continuous self-motion, stands behind the universe and animates human bodies with particles of its divine soul; the soul is an ideal phenomenon located in the head, possessing mental, volitional, and sensory properties; will is a stable and rational desire for the good; those who claim that fate and a primordial series of causes govern humanity deny free will; human freedom consists not in wanting for nothing or obeying no one, but in having the will to submit when necessary, to govern when it is a moral or state duty, and to resist succumbing to fate or other external circumstances while pursuing what is right and honorable, even in the face of great difficulties and dangers; humans experience various forms of freedom, including moral, religious, and political (Vydryhan 2019, 17).

The period of Antiquity was a great impetus for the development of philosophical and legal thought, in particular, by laying the foundation for the original concepts of free will. The ideas of its leading thinkers became the basis for later developments. For example, they inform the views of Erich Fromm, who argued that the only criterion for the realisation of freedom is the individual's active participation in determining their own destiny and the life of society—not just through the formal act of voting, but through their daily activities, work, and relationships with others (Fromm 2011).

The historical experience of Ancient Greece is valuable primarily because it accumulated a highly developed body of political-legal thought and state practice that remains relevant today. It is characteristic that prominent thinkers like Protagoras, Socrates, Plato, and Aristotle, who represented different approaches to the limits of individual freedom and state power, emerged during the classical period of Greek democracy. This revealed the direct link between political freedom and personal freedom, which could be realised through citizenship, individuality, and intellectual, artistic, or entrepreneurial pursuits (Vdovychyn 2013, 419–420).

The ideas of Antiquity regarding free will are also reflected in the works of Quintus Horatius Flaccus, who expressed an ambivalent attitude toward social criticism in his satires and poetic invectives (Tarrant 2020). While acknowledging the omnipotence of Fortune, he maintained that individuals have the right to free choice and must bear responsibility for their actions. This constitutes the uniqueness of Horace's vision of fate's role in human life.

The ideas about free will, laid down in Antiquity, underwent their development in the Middle Ages and during the Renaissance. The Stoics had taken the first steps in distinguishing between foresight, fate, and their connection to free will, but it was in the Middle Ages that the concept of predictability and freedom was elaborated upon at the level of religion. The era was permeated with Christian influences, which interpreted free will as the ability to choose between good and evil and to act in accordance with Church teachings or to disregard them (Yaruniv 2018, 29). As a result, free will became understood through the norms of morality.

Medieval Christianity faced a dilemma: from the standpoint of reason, free will exists, meaning a person is responsible for their actions; from the perspective of faith, there is complete submission to the Divine will, which limits the ability to make independent decisions.

A special place in the transition from the views of Antiquity to Medieval Christianity is occupied by the ideas of Origen—a Greek Christian theologian, philosopher, and scholar (Holcomb 2018)—the founder of biblical philology and the author of the term "God-man" (The Oxford Handbook of the Epistemology of Theology 2017).

Origen paid considerable attention to the issue of free will, which he believed transforms depending on a person's actions. He argued that a person is born with complete free will, but it becomes limited with each act committed. As a result of their life, a person either retains full free will and is reborn or loses it and merges with God, leading to a complete transformation of their free will (Kantzer 2012). These views bear a resemblance to the concepts of karma and reincarnation in Hinduism and Buddhism, although Origen had no direct connection to them.

The works of Aurelius Augustine were of great importance for understanding free will. His treatise *De libero arbitrio* (On Free Choice of the Will) deserves special attention, as he focuses on the relationship between human and divine will. He emphasised that everything created by God is to some extent involved in absolute goodness - the All-Good God: after all, the Almighty, carrying out creation, depicted in the created a certain measure, weight and order, laying down an extraterrestrial image and meaning. To this extent, good is inherent in nature, in people, in society. He noted that any nature that can become better is good (Bagnall 2012). Thus, Augustine deepened the idea of theodicy, acknowledging the influence of God on human will and the impossibility of evil existing without good.

At the same time, Augustine explicitly recognized the active power of the will, locating it at the very center of human psychology. In his analysis of the mind, he argued that the will is not merely a moral capacity but a fundamental element of all cognition, inseparable from memory and intellect. Illustrating this interdependence, he wrote:

> I remember that I have memory, understanding, and will; and I understand that I understand, will, and remember; and I will that I will, understand, and remember. (Augustine 2002, 58)

By introducing this theory, Augustine posited that the will is the unifying force that directs attention and actualises thought. This inherent capacity for volition is what made the theological narrative of human freedom possible. For instance, Augustine maintained that Adam was created with a truly free will; had God not endowed him with this capacity, Adam's breaking of the covenants would have been meaningless—an act of divine orchestration rather than a genuine, tragic choice of his own volition.

As M. Potsyurko summarises, in his early works, Augustine held that reason and wisdom are a worthy path to a blessed life, which entails the liberation of the soul from bodily defilement and living in accordance with the soul's rational part. He emphasised that free decision is not subject to natural causality and that divine providence does not eliminate the autonomy of the will (Potsiurko 2018, 174). Later, he adopted a fideistic position, affirming the imperfection of human reason in matters of faith and advocating for complete reliance on Divine grace (a conviction Augustine held during the anti-Pelagian polemic) (Ibid.).

Similar ideas can be found in the writings of Boethius, who emphasised that man is endowed with reason and the ability to distinguish what to desire from what to avoid. He argued that if there were no free will, there would be no point in rewarding the good and punishing the wicked, as these outcomes would not be the result of free choice (Boethius 1999).

Further development of ideas about free will can be seen in the works of Thomas Aquinas, who defined man's striving for freedom as his characteristic feature. He emphasised that man is endowed with a rational soul and free will, and because of this, he chooses his actions and is responsible for them. Reason is recognized as the basis for free will and dominates it. Using a logical method, Aquinas concluded that freedom of choice is necessary; without it, concepts like sin and virtue, punishment and reward, could not exist. However, a person can only be free if the source of their free will is reality and if their intellect accurately reflects objective necessity (Aquinas, *Opera omnia*).

Aquinas's views were refined in the religious mysticism of Bernard of Clairvaux, who defined freedom as the soul's ability to follow its own will, independent of external coercion. Clairvaux attributed the presence of evil in human life to free will, born of original sin (Claraevallensis 1620). An analysis of his selected works reveals three types of freedom in his concept. The first distinguishes man as a unique creature with a mind and soul, a freedom endowed by nature. The second is freedom from sin, called the 'freedom of grace'. The third, the freedom from suffering or the freedom of life, gives a person the ability to overcome their desires and sins (Clairvaux 1987). Thus, Clairvaux speaks of free will as the capacity to make decisions through a struggle between reason and sin. If the religious component is removed, it becomes clear that modern conceptions of free will are based on similar principles.

The religious constants of the Middle Ages began to take on a progressive form with the advent of the Renaissance and the start of the Reformation. This was based on Giordano Bruno's idea of freedom of thought and the right to doubt religious dogmas. Bruno's ideas continued the concepts of his predecessor, Pico della Mirandola, who posited that free will gives man the ability to either ascend to God or become a slave to his passions, distinguishing humanity from other creatures (Copenhaver 2022).

At the same time, the Reformation gave rise to new theological approaches to free will. Martin Luther emphasised the impossibility of a rational theodicy, arguing that a person's salvation is not linked to their purposeful actions. He reasoned that only a person completely disappointed in themselves ceases to choose and instead waits for God to act, thereby having the chance for future happiness. The highest form of faith, he argued, is to believe that God is merciful even when He saves few and condemns many, and to consider Him just when, by His own will, He makes us worthy of condemnation (Potsiurko 2018, 176). The views of Francisco Suárez are also of great importance; he speaks of God's influence on human actions only in cases where *gratia efficiens* (effective grace) can occur without restricting human freedom (Suárez 2011). These ideas became the basis for the theory of Congruism.

In summary, for Antiquity, the understanding of free will was tied to the existence of fate. In the Middle Ages, the Augustinian dilemma arose between acknowledging free will and complete submission to the will of God. The Reformation emphasised a fatalism that precluded free will, while the Renaissance prioritised the autonomy of the human will alongside the divine. Although the approaches of medieval philosophers often reflected a deterministic, theocentric position, they contradicted the classical evangelical tradition and were later completely reinterpreted.

Ideas about the autonomy of human free will evolved in the philosophy of the Modern Age. The rational determinist approach to the will is linked to the theories of Thomas Hobbes, Baruch Spinoza, Immanuel Kant, Johann Gottlieb Fichte, and G. W. F. Hegel.

Hobbes developed a fundamental concept of free will that became the basis for numerous doctrines, including theories of relative derivation and rational choice (Boudon 2003). He justified free will based on the conviction that any object is free if its essential nature contains no obstacles to its movement when acting according to its internal laws (Johnson 2020). A flame, for instance, spreads in various directions but is not endowed with a will to determine its path. Thus, free will exists within the real possibility of choosing one's behavior. A person has the freedom to walk, but if they have no legs, they are physically unable to do so, and their free will is limited. Human actions arising from the will are free, yet they are also necessary, as they are caused by factors independent of the subject. Like all other natural phenomena, human actions are subject to the universal law of mechanical necessity, which is nonetheless compatible with freedom (Holden 2023).

René Descartes attributed the will to the thinking world of man, emphasising the existence of free will as the ability to decide for oneself what to agree with and what to reject (Descartes 1985).

Classical German philosophy fostered a deep understanding of free will not only through the lens of philosophy but also from the perspective of law. Kant asserted a direct link between legal freedom and the rationality of the will, which, based on a formal, universally rational principle, is alone capable of ensuring the moral quality of actions. Reason, according to Kant, is subject to its own legislation and is thus autonomous and self-legislating (Brovko 2007, 44).

Kant argued that the problem of free will is of a transcendental nature and therefore cannot be understood by physiology or psychology. The concept of freedom, he claimed, is one of the inevitable problems of pure reason and the cornerstone of the entire edifice of transcendental philosophy (Schneewind 2002). Kant paid considerable attention to this issue, starting with his first work, *Principiorum primorum cognitionis metaphysicae nova dilucidatio*. His understanding of free will can be summarised as its perception as practical reason, once again proclaiming the inseparability of free will from the capacity for free thought and decision-making.

Kant finds the manifestation of free will in the meaning that a person ascribes to their actions. If a person were indifferent in their choices, their actions would be random, marking the end of all freedom (Brown, Nardin and Rengger 2002). These ideas later evolved into the metaphysical concept of transcendental freedom. In his *Critique of Pure Reason*, Kant defined free will as something that can manifest independently of sensory impulses (Kant 2007).

The relationship between free will and law is a distinct aspect of his philosophy. Kant thoroughly substantiated the independence of the will from any law except the moral law (Kant 2007). From this, one can conclude that external factors, such as positive law, cannot limit the internal component of free will, as only one's own reason serves as its measure. This can be illustrated in civil law: legislation mandates a written form for real estate sales contracts, yet parties, aware of this, knowingly conclude the contract orally. For instance, instead of a car sales contract, they execute a power of attorney. The external influence of the law failed to compel compliance. Free will allowed the parties to consciously violate the law's norms. Formally, the parties achieved their goal (one receives money, the other gains possession and use of the property), but legally, their actions are not recognized as a transfer of ownership.

When parties comply with the law, they also do so at their own discretion, guided by moral norms. This study will further argue that the law does, in fact, limit free will through its norms, compelling parties to make decisions within its framework. On this issue, Kant's theory is more philosophical than practical-legal, as from a normative standpoint, transactions that violate legal requirements (e.g., defects of form or will) are deemed invalid.

One of Kant's key theses is the compatibility of free will with the necessity that exists in nature, where free will is understood as the independence of the will from causes external to the subject (or reason). This view can be defined as a form of compatibilism, albeit a special kind, as compatibilists typically define free will in a way that does not presuppose independence from external factors. Kant inextricably linked free will with moral responsibility, which suggests his support for compatibilism as an opposition to causal determinism.

To define free will as the genesis of legal understanding, it is necessary to note Kant's concept of the autonomy of the will, where he endowed the will with the property of establishing laws for itself. This approach correlates with the modern principle of freedom of contract, which allows parties to create their own contractual norms. However, the laws a person's will establishes for itself cannot alter positive legal norms. As the real estate example illustrates, the parties' decision to disregard a regulatory requirement is free and conscious, but it does not create the intended legal relationship. Thus, the parties' free will cannot change the norms of law and must be subordinate to them. In this case, free will manifests in the decision to comply with the regulatory imperative or not.

An opposing understanding of free will can be found in the works of Hegel. While Kant viewed free will through individual human actions, Hegel emphasised a socio-political understanding.

Hegel's thesis that the starting point of law is the free will, that freedom is its substance, and that the system of law is the "realm of realised freedom" is classic (Hegel 2000, 24). It was Hegel who placed free will at the foundation of the understanding of law, emphasising the impossibility of law's existence without it. Today, this idea is central to the system of natural law.

As Nataliia Brovko notes, the dialectic of free will generates a system of forms and degrees of law, which leads to the ambiguity of the concept of law in Hegelian philosophy. It is used in several primary meanings: law as freedom (idea of law), law as a specific degree and form of freedom (particular law), and law as statute (positive law). All stages of the development of the objective spirit are determined by the idea of freedom, and this sphere itself is the realisation of freedom in the forms, methods, and institutions of human coexistence (Brovko 2007, 36).

Hegel emphasised that a person who is not conscious of their freedom cannot possess free will, and that only a thinking intellect is truly endowed with it. Based on this, one might assume that an incapacitated person cannot have free will, and question its existence in someone under the influence of alcohol or drugs.

Another representative of classical German philosophy, Friedrich Schelling, shifted the understanding of free will by transforming the concepts of reason's scope and free causality. He based free will on human decision-making, emphasising that every person acts only according to their own will, never against it (Dews 2023).

In turn, Hermann Cohen entered into a polemic with Kant's ideas, proposing to abolish the concept of free will and use autonomy instead. Autonomy in Cohen's philosophy carries a different meaning than in Kant's. It is not legislation given by a metaphysical self, but legislation through which the moral self first emerges – not as a given, but as a pure task. The concept of autonomy is similar to free will in that both allow actions to be attributed to a moral subject. Cohen writes of responsibility as one of the developmental stages of the concept of autonomy (Cohen 1919).

Ludwig Feuerbach advanced this problem as far as a materialist who had not yet overcome a contemplative approach to cognition could go (Feuerbach 1986). His ideas about free will were detailed through his understanding of criminal law and were predicated on the existence of free will, as a person independently decides to commit a crime. He emphasised that only a person who has freely committed a crime can be held accountable. Of significant importance was the idea of not holding a person criminally liable if they, guided by their free will, voluntarily refrain from committing a crime. Today, however, the timing of such a refusal is crucial for the legal qualification of the act, distinguishing between a completed crime, an attempted crime, and a situation where a person intended but did not even begin to commit the crime. It is in the latter case, where a free refusal occurs at a stage that cannot even be classified as an attempt, that Feuerbach's idea is most relevant.

The most complete and theoretically finished concept of the will as the first principle of being was formulated in the 19th century by Arthur Schopenhauer. According to his philosophy, in the phenomenon of objectification, the will is not so much the cause as the very essence of being (Hannan 2009). Within the ontological general will, a series of objectifications of varying levels arise, initially without a rational observer (Schopenhauer 1995). Prudka notes that Schopenhauer was primarily interested in the inner world of the individual, without aligning their behavior with social factors. Consequently, everything related to society was of secondary importance to him, leading to shortcomings in his concept of freedom, which he considered in isolation from society and disconnected from its moral and historical foundations (Prudka 2019, 65).

It is impossible to discuss free will as the genesis of legal understanding without mentioning the ideas of John Locke. He argued that only a person who has reason and acts according to its dictates can be free; there can be no freedom where there is no thought (Locke 1824). In his views, we again see support for the direct link between free will and reason as its primary enabling mechanism. Gottfried Wilhelm Leibniz, in turn, developed Locke's ideas, introducing the notion that mental activity is determined, but not necessarily through compulsion or a mechanical push.

Leibniz applied the principle of pre-established harmony to the problem of free will (Leibniz 2017). He refused to accept that every human action is predictable but fell into his own dilemma: if everything is based on harmony, endowing humans with free will would lead to chaos and destroy that harmony. He, therefore, concluded that freedom is the self-activity of a rational subject, guided by increasingly well-founded motives. The more motivated, rational actions we perform, the more freedom we attain.

Leibniz distinguished between actual and legal freedom. Legal freedom reflects the existing laws of a state, and its measure for each person is normatively defined (Parkin and Stanton 2013). The purpose of legal norms is to establish the formal boundaries of free will. Leibniz held that actual freedom manifests as freedom of action (the ability to decide what to do and how) and is therefore linked to an individual's material, social, and physical state (Look 2021). For example, a wealthy person has a greater degree of free will than a poor one because they have more opportunities for its realisation. This concept reveals similarities between the views of Leibniz, Spinoza, and Locke.

The views of Modern Age philosophers on free will can be summarised by the position of Karl Marx, who viewed freedom in relation to law. For him, freedom is defined by law, which should protect it but also establishes its limits and methods of implementation. He defined laws as general norms of behavior in which freedom acquires an impersonal, theoretical existence, independent of the arbitrariness of any single individual (Vidal et al. 2018).

The philosophical concepts of the Modern Age attempted to explain the nature of free will by linking it to empirical knowledge, which later raised doubts among rationalist metaphysicians and empiricists, who developed their own concepts in the 20th century.

Friedrich Nietzsche developed Schopenhauer's ideas on free will and presented his own vision in works such as *Thus Spoke Zarathustra, Beyond Good and Evil,* and *On the Genealogy of Morality*. His understanding was linked to the concept of the will to power and reflected the influence of antagonism and the voluntarist views of his predecessors, resulting in an incomplete concept of the relationship between free will and necessity (Acampora 2013).

Emmanuel Mounier spoke of the danger of understanding free will merely as freedom of choice, as this would render it incapable of making a choice due to insufficient impulse and would foster a culture of indecision or unprincipledness, which he saw as a spiritual disease of modern thought. Mounier highly valued psychoanalysis but disagreed with its claims that morality, art, and religion arise from subconscious animal drives. Instead, he argued that the unconscious allows a person to communicate with a higher reality (De Tavernier 2009, 362).

Martin Heidegger, in his seminal work *Being and Time*, argued that anxiety (*Angst*) is a foundation for free will (Velkley 2011). Karl Jaspers refined this position, considering free will in relation to cognition, internal law, and arbitrariness. Jaspers derived his understanding of free will through its necessary connection with guilt. In The Question of German Guilt, the philosopher discusses freedom as the overcoming of arbitrariness and the impossibility of exercising a purely divine or evil will, writing about freedom of decision, law, and the realisation of existence (Jaspers 2000).

Jean-Paul Sartre proposed an original theory of free will, identifying it with absolute freedom in his work *Being and Nothingness* (Sartre 2021). He argued that because every human possesses reason, free will—the ability to choose one's actions—is inherent in everyone. Thus, free will is again reduced to the ability to make decisions based on one's own subjective convictions.

Special attention should be paid to the libertarian interpretation of free will, particularly the fundamental works of Robert Kane, who contrasted ancient determinism with a genuine understanding of free will. Kane argued that the kind of free will we truly care about—the one that makes us the "true creators" of our actions—emerges during conscious deliberation. This deliberation is caused by indeterministic processes that are neither counter-causal nor purely random; it is the indeterminate result of the effort of will we experience when choosing between alternative courses of action (De Caro and Putnam 2020).

Correlating free will with the right to make decisions, Kane introduced the concept of a splintered will, which manifests in the inability to choose between two equally rational options based on previously formed motives, character traits, and experiences (Waller 2003). The philosopher insisted that personality-shaping actions occur at difficult moments in life when we are torn between conflicting views on what we should do and who we should become. At such times, the tension and uncertainty in our minds are reflected in a certain indeterminacy within the neural processes themselves, excited by the conflict in our wills (Mele 2017). In effect, Kane's theory suggests that, possessing free will, a person can make opposing decisions in similar situations.

The ideas of European thinkers on free will also found a place in the views of Soviet and Ukrainian philosophers. The interpretation of free will was established in the works of the Westernisers of the mid-19th century, who believed that self-awareness and an understanding of free will came to the Slavs later than to Europeans. Comparing the development of Western European and Slavic tribes, they noted that the Germanic peoples were the first to be inspired by a deep sense of individuality, whereas the Slavic peoples represented a qualitatively new phenomenon. The latter's family-oriented way of life did not cultivate the sense of separateness and focus that compels a person to draw a line between themselves and others (Sheiko, Kolodii and Ilchenko 2018, 49).

Agreeing with Sheiko, Kolodiy and Ilchenko, it should be noted that the methodology for comprehending the essence of free will requires holistic knowledge – an organic connection of empirical, rational-theoretical, and intuitive-religious cognition. In this respect, both the Westernisers and the Slavophiles demonstrate a dependence on creating a synthetic theory of knowledge to resolve the question of freedom and necessity (Sheiko, Kolodii and Ilchenko 2018, 57).

Pyotr Chaadaev addressed the concept of free will through the prism of the relationship between freedom and necessity. He noted that man is endowed with consciousness and free will, making him a bearer of the social world. Free will exists independently to a certain extent, and strict providentialism is absent; however, true freedom must ultimately strive to comprehend and reunite with the eternal freedom of (Sheiko and Kolodii 2019, 30).

Concluding this historical and philosophical analysis, the definition of free will has evolved from Antiquity to the present day and has ultimately been reflected in legal norms. In Antiquity, free will was inextricably linked with fate. The Middle Ages produced several different concepts, but all were closely tied to divinity, giving rise to the Augustinian dilemma of recognising free will or complete submission to God's will. The Reformation emphasised a fatalism that precluded free will, while the Renaissance prioritised the autonomy of the human will alongside the divine. Although the approaches of medieval philosophers often reflected a deterministic, theocentric position, they contradicted the classical evangelical tradition and were later completely reinterpreted.

In the philosophy of the Modern Age, free will was recognized as an indisputable property of the human mind, necessary for self-awareness. At the same time, it was not considered absolute, due to its limitations by legal and moral norms. In subsequent theories, human autonomy increasingly moved away from determinism, taking the form of the possibility of free decision-making. The modern understanding of free will is grounded in the ideas of natural law.

The study of past philosophical concepts is of great importance for shaping and clarifying the content of modern philosophical paradigms (Sheiko and Ilchenko 2023, 9). Of course, the number of scholars who have studied free will is far greater than those mentioned in this study. However, the analysis conducted is sufficient to affirm the evolution of views on free will and its undeniable influence on law. This makes further research into the legal nature of free will a relevant and urgent task.

1.2 The Legal Nature of Free Will

The concept of free will has a significant impact on civil law, which is founded on the principles of dispositivity and autonomy of the will. Violations of these principles can serve as grounds for declaring transactions invalid or exempting individuals from liability, making the concept of fundamental importance for all areas of civil law. However, legislation does not contain a definition of free will, nor does it delineate its boundaries and principles.

The issue of free will has been studied by scholars globally, all of whom recognize its importance in legal science. To begin with, it is appropriate to turn again to the concept of G.W.F. Hegel, who laid the foundation for the modern legal understanding of free will. Hegel begins his definition by criticising slavery, emphasising that an enslaved person does not know their essence, infinity, or freedom; they do not know themselves as an essence, which means they do not think of themselves (Hegel 2000, 39).

The very existence of a person in slavery is also connected with will. This can be explained by the fact that even a person who is entirely subject to the will of another and has no rights still makes an independent decision to remain in such a state. For example, an enslaved person independently chooses the path of servitude or finds an opportunity to change their condition—even through suicide, as a manifestation of free will. Hegel emphasised that when we speak only of the will as such, without defining it as a will that is free in and for itself, we are speaking only of a disposition toward freedom, or of a natural and finite will, and therefore not of a truly free will. In a genuinely free will, the truly infinite is endowed with reality and presence (Hegel 2000, 40).

By substantiating the personal freedom of the individual as the embodiment of the universal freedom of their will, Hegel proclaims the inalienability of the individual and considers slavery and serfdom to be states of alienated liberty, which are unjust and must be overcome. According to his views, the enslaved person's absolute right to freedom is inherent in the very nature of things (Brovko 2007, 50).

The main idea of Hegel, which became the foundation for further understanding of will, is to recognize human activity, its choices, and decision-making as a manifestation of free will.

The issue of free will is also relevant to the Ukrainian intellectual tradition, which can be traced in the works of Dontsov (*Nationalism*), Dragomanov (*The Path to Freedom*), Kistyakivskyi (*In Defense of the Law*), Pavlyk (*The Slavery of Women*), and others. Zhvania emphasizes that even in the works of Taras Shevchenko and Lesia Ukrainka, the combination of the idea of free will with reason and the ability to make a conscious choice can be traced. Illustrating this opinion, he notes:

> Life for an internally free individual always involves situations that require an active choice between good and evil... in the lyric-epic works of Taras Shevchenko and Lesia Ukrainka, there are heroes whose actions are the result of a conscious choice... and heroes whose actions depend on emotions and passions... in the works of both artists, one can read the statement that every person is capable of pacifying passions and of self-mastery... that is, every person, guided by will, can improve himself... which is the possibility of free will, elevating a person to the level of a creator, since he himself creates the world of his inner self. (Zhvaniia 2009, 127)

We should agree with the conclusions of Lebid-Hrebeniuk, who identifies the following stages in the evolution of free will:

1. Hagiographic tradition: Any specific person (such as Prince Volodymyr, Saints Boris and Gleb, or Theodosius of the Caves) realizes their own freedom of choice within the limits of the absolute freedom of God's will.
2. Moral law: The moral law is given to man by God as an a priori given, forming the basis of ethical behavior.

3. The Baroque era: A transition occurs from a God outside man to a God inside him, which leads to a partial subjectivization of free will.
4. Modern literature: Free will is understood as a special internal state of man, when he realizes his own will at the behest of an internal (and self-established) moral imperative (Lebid-Hrebeniuk 2009, 38).

Later, Ivan Sechenov introduced the concept of will into the scientific paradigm as the active component of reason and moral feeling (Lebid-Hrebeniuk 2009, 102). His understanding of free will was based on a person's ability to act freely in accordance with their thoughts and desires, as well as contrary to them; therefore, the will must mediate between the reflexes of the brain and actions. For there to be no conflict between free will and law, they must be based on the same moral principles. This is a profound understanding of the role of free will and its significance for law. If a person consciously violates contractual norms defined by civil legislation, then their understanding of what is right contradicts legal norms. In this case, a conflict arises between an individual's will and the public will of the state, as expressed in regulatory acts. This is why we should discuss the dynamism of civil law and its ongoing development.

Civil law norms emerge in response to existing social relations. We are observing the rapid growth of civil legal relations and the emergence of new legal structures, including novel types of contracts. Today, we must create relevant civil law norms that are consistent with the free will already exercised by participants in these legal relations. Otherwise, the parties will attempt to circumvent current legislation through its existing gaps. This can be seen today in the example of virtual assets (digital property), the circulation of which is carried out through grey markets, the number of which is growing as new types of objects that can be qualified as virtual property constantly appear (Nekit 2019, 41).

The understanding of law as the value of ordered human freedom was criticised by K. Yu. Herman, who emphasised that such a position contradicts the tenets of legal positivism. Representatives of this school speak of the inadmissibility of determining the value of law through its connection with the triad of natural-law values, being satisfied only with such characteristics as general obligation, normativity, and formal certainty (Herman 2015, 118).

Modern scientists pay special attention to the relationship between law and free will. For instance, Bogdan Kistyakivskyi speaks of the essence of law as human freedom—not just any freedom, but a freedom that is defined and secured in a certain way. Because freedom is a property and form of life inherent in a person, reflecting their desire for self-expression and self-realisation, it does not mean that freedom is the possibility of doing anything (Sikach 1999, 225). Here, we see the concept of free will in a person, which allows them to make decisions and perform actions freely, but only within the framework of established law.

Volodymyr Shkoda considered law as a combination of will and reason, recognising its auxiliary function in making correct decisions (Shkoda, 1997).

As can be seen, the understanding of free will is closely related to the idea of freedom. Therefore, it is necessary to define this concept to understand free will in civil law studies.

The academic understanding of freedom is often reduced to its definition as the absence of political and economic oppression or restrictions in the socio-political life of a class or society as a whole; will (*Slovnyk ukrains'koi movy* [Dictionary of the Ukrainian Language] 1978, 9:98).

Freedom is defined as life or existence without dependence on anyone; the ability to behave at one's own discretion; the ability to act without obstacles and prohibitions in any field; the ability to express one's will as a subject, conscious of the laws of nature and society; ease, the absence of difficulties in anything ("*Svoboda*" [Freedom] n.d.-c).

In the *Philosophical Encyclopedic Dictionary*, freedom is defined as a special way of determining spiritual reality, since spirituality is a specific property of human existence. Freedom directly manifests itself in human life, which is the interaction of spiritual (conscious and unconscious) and natural (physical and biological) factors ("*Svoboda*" [Freedom] n.d.-a). Freedom is the awareness of the permissible limits of human behavior, which depend on the specific situation of human existence (individual and social) and, in this regard, is the awareness of necessity. The defining characteristics of freedom as a spiritual phenomenon are choice (since the spiritual space is a pluralistic field of possibilities) and responsibility (the correlate of necessity in the sphere of the spirit). Freedom as a cognised necessity (fatalistic freedom) is only formal (degenerate, deprived of its essential features) ("*Svoboda*" [Freedom] n.d.-a).

In the *Dictionary of Synonyms of the Ukrainian Language*, freedom is generally recognized as a synonym for will, meaning the absence of restrictions on someone in something ("*Svoboda*" [Freedom] n.d.-b).

In the Legal Encyclopedia, freedom in law is associated not only with the subject's responsibility for their actions, which implies their free will, but also with the measure of responsibility. The requirement of justice necessitates establishing this measure of responsibility for an act, and a fair verdict establishes the measure of punishment (Shemshuchenko 2003, 516).

To summarise, we can conclude that the academic understanding of freedom boils down to recognising it as the ability to make decisions freely, without dependence on external factors.

Freedom is generally understood by most scientists as the ability to make choices. O. O. Punda defines freedom as the possibility of a person's manifestation of will in combination with the awareness of the laws of nature and society and his ability to act in accordance with his own goals and interests, based on the knowledge of objective necessity (reality) (Punda 2006, 12).

L. Yarmol and S. Vandeo consider freedom through its internal and external aspects. Internal freedom is regarded as a person's independence from the interference of law in their aspirations for freedom in thoughts, beliefs, and conscience; therefore, it is inappropriate to regulate the internal freedom of a person by law. The external aspect of freedom is manifested in a person's actions and inaction (Yarmol and Vando 2015, 253).

In their study, they conclude that freedom is a natural feature and, at the same time, a necessity for a person, embodying self-sufficiency and individuality. The peculiarity of freedom lies in its contradictory nature. If it is unlimited, it eliminates itself, which is why the law becomes the main expression and form of its embodiment (Yarmol and Vando 2015, 256). O. P. Donchenko, in the study of freedom as a category of law, substantiates that freedom as a form of creative self-realisation of the individual is a formal and substantive category of modern Ukrainian law, which is based on the dynamic unity of natural law and positivist principles (Donchenko 2010, 5). It is argued that freedom as a legal category is one of the ways of manifesting freedom as an existential characteristic of human existence and consists in the individual's desire not only to find a connection with and realisation of the world in themself but also to ensure congruence with the world and other people. It is also substantiated that the epistemological function of freedom is the knowledge of law through freedom and its definition as a measure of freedom, which creates conditions for the optimal harmonisation of social relations (Donchenko 2010, 6).

V. Zhadko and P. Bidzilya suggest starting from the fact that freedom is not just a perceived necessity, but a means for developing freedom of thought (Zhadko and Bidzilia 2019, 4). This refers us to current research on the right to freedom of thought and opinion, conducted by scholars such as Marc Blitz and Jan Bublitz (2021). In this relationship, the issue of determining the priority between law and freedom is recognized as central. On the one hand, law exists to implement freedoms, and human freedom should have a higher character than the law. Law exists to protect people's freedoms and freedom in general.

N.I. Brovko notes that human freedom, in dialectical unity with the responsibility for one's own actions, is a fundamental legal value, the source of which is the nature of man as a being capable of choosing his goals and means to achieve them. The embodiment of this is the freedom of the individual in its personal dimension and the corresponding natural law (Brovko 2010, 7).

However, freedom cannot go beyond the limits established by law—the freedom of an individual ends where the liberty of another person begins. In some instances, the law limits a person's freedom and rights. Law and free will are inextricably linked and form a vector for each other's development. Thus, free will outlines the paradigm in which law should develop, and law outlines the limits of free will and the conditions for its implementation.

In turn, various works reveal the understanding of freedom as the law of autonomy, encompassing the ability to make self-commitments and govern oneself, which forms the basis for the existence of law. Law appeared to regulate relations, formalising the norms of morality and rules of conduct adopted in society, and became an extension of freedom. The primary tasks assigned to it could not exist without the concept of freedom. In the context of civil law, we can provide the following example: a person collected shells on the shore and made a necklace from them, which they then exchanged for apples. All of this is a manifestation of civil law constructions, including property rights and barter agreements. These constructions would be impossible without freedom. The above statement is complemented by the idea of dividing freedom into internal and external aspects. Thus, internal freedom is connected to a person's moral values, and external freedom is established by law. Internal freedom remains a personal matter for a person as long as it complies with the legally defined limits of external freedom. At the moment when a person violates the norms of law, there is a need to determine their guilt, and this cannot be done without encroaching upon the limits of their internal freedom (Emerson, Pattison, and Poole 2020).

The above reflects the doctrinal understanding of freedom as the ability to choose and make decisions that may or may not comply with the norms of law. However, in the legislation of Ukraine and international acts, the construction "rights and freedoms of man and citizen" is established. The word 'freedom' is found in five thousand regulatory legal acts, but typically in the context of the fundamental constitutional freedoms of man and citizen. Normatively enshrined freedoms reflect natural human rights, which have the highest legal protection and form the foundation of the entire legal system, guiding the development of legislation. This leads to one of the key principles of law—the principle of freedom. In general, the principle of freedom allows for the possibility of choosing a variant of behavior within the limits of the law's norms.

The basis of human freedoms is the idea developed by the Sophists concerning the division of law into natural and positive law. Natural law is considered to be derived from the natural order of things—from the order of the universe and the nature of man. Positive law is artificial, created by people and devoted to the interests of an artificial formation such as the state (Danylyan 2009). Through natural law, its norms and principles, individual legal consciousness connects its existence with universal, general fundamentals of being; through positive law, it connects its existence with a specific state and its institutions (Danylyan 2009).

O. O. Volodina rightly notes that freedom is a right inherent in every person from birth and constitutes the most important good and condition for the normal development of the individual and society. The right of the individual to physical freedom and inviolability is the core of any system of government that defines itself by the rule of law (Volodina 2005). This approach aligns with the natural-law understanding of freedom and builds upon the classical ideas of Plato, Aristotle, Kant, and Hegel.

The conclusions of S. F. Denysov and G. O. Zubov, which generalize the legal understanding of freedom, are logical:

1. In national law and legislation, freedom is a measure of the possible behavior of a subject of social relations and is the opposite of duty, which is a measure of the proper behavior of a subject.
2. Legal freedom does not have a precise mechanism for implementation; it corresponds to the responsibility to refrain from committing any actions that violate this freedom (Denysov and Zubov 2016, 11).

Speaking about the connection between law and freedom, the following theses can be distinguished: law outlines the normative boundaries of freedom; law is based on freedom and recognizes its social value; the idea of freedom is reflected in legal institutions and principles; and law protects freedom.

Returning to the normative understanding of freedom, it is necessary to refer to the Constitution of Ukraine, which stipulates that the legal order in Ukraine is based on the principles according to which no one can be forced to do something that is not provided for by law (*Konstytutsiia Ukrainy* [Constitution of Ukraine] 1996, art. 19). This norm gives rise to a dualism in the boundaries of freedom. On the one hand, it is the freedom to dispose of one's subjective rights and fulfill obligations, reflecting the fundamental principle that everything not prohibited by law is permitted. On the other hand, it concerns the clear observance of legal norms by the state and its bodies, according to the principle that only what is stipulated in the law is permitted.

We can agree with N.V. Fedina that society is interested in preserving the freedom of all participants in social interaction and thus carries out the norming and formalisation of liberty based on a general scale and equal measure (where everyone is free to the same extent, and the freedom of one person is limited by the freedom of another). This forms legal regulation. To ensure the freedom of participants in social communication, the law organises it based on the principle of formal equality, abstracting from the initial differences characteristic of people and formally recognising them as equal and free subjects (Fedina 2015, 74).

Analysis of Article 19 of the Constitution of Ukraine provides grounds to assert responsibility for violating the legal concept of freedom. The constitutional prohibition of coercion should be interpreted as the inadmissibility of illegal actions of one party toward another in relations between citizens, as well as between citizens and state and local government bodies, and among state bodies themselves (the state and its bodies cannot force other entities to act in a manner different than that provided for by the Constitution and laws of Ukraine) (Tatsiy and Petryshyn 2011, 140).

It should also be agreed that coercion for the purpose of committing unlawful actions can relate both to the use of subjective rights (e.g., inducing a citizen against their will to join a political party) and to the performance of legal obligations (e.g., forcing a state body to adopt an illegal act) (Tatsiy and Petryshyn 2011, 141). Violation of the legal idea of free will is of fundamental importance for civil legal relations and can, for example, become a basis for declaring a transaction invalid due to vitiating factors.

Thus, the constitutional understanding of freedom is achieved by providing a person with the ability to behave in a certain way and by prohibiting coercion, except in cases provided for by law. Herman notes that freedom, which is not given the form of a legal norm, should be defined and enshrined in legislation at the level of a principle (not a right) as a higher goal on which the law is based. This reveals and specifies the individual's ability to freely express their will within the framework of the existing legal system (Herman 2015, 121).

However, as will be proven later, free will is the foundation for the principles of civil law, its sub-branches, and institutions. Agreeing with the position of Herman would lead to proclaiming free will as the principle on which other principles of law are based, making it a super-principle. With this in mind, we believe that free will extends beyond the understanding of a principle and takes the form of a legal concept, which is manifested in the principles of autonomy, pluralism, tolerance, and the inviolability of human rights, among others.

The legal idea is the most general, abstract expression of the essence of law, its project or task (regulatory idea); it constitutes the ideal aspect of the existence of law, its form (in the Aristotelian sense) (Danylyan 2017, 140).

The global nature of the legal idea of free will is confirmed by its manifestation throughout all of law. Without the concept of free will, the rule of law is compromised, human rights are suppressed, political (electoral) rights are absent, a fair judicial system loses its meaning, democratic societies cannot exist, and, ultimately, modern liberal states and supranational values lose their mechanisms of implementation. This brings the legal concept of free will closer to the idea of human rights (Hague Convention for the Protection of Cultural Property in the Event of Armed Conflict, 1954), justice, and other fundamental values, which, according to N. Simmonds, are normative standards governing what we should do, regardless of what current practices and institutions may require (Simmonds 2008).

Just as human rights, in their most fundamental sense, are considered as transcendent moral principles on which positive law is based (Howard 1993), so the idea of free will becomes a superstructure—a paradigm that determines the vector of law development and is formed as an imperative.

By analogy with the justifications of the good faith imperative by D. Pavlenko (Pavlenko 2008, 16), it can be determined that the imperative of free will formulates the behavior of participants in legal relations and indicates the connection between civil law and natural law, since the application of free will is a necessary element and a prerequisite for the normal development of society, regardless of its enshrinement in legislation.

However, despite the fundamental importance of free will, the legislator does not single it out as a norm or principle, and there is no such concept in regulatory acts. But, as we will see later, the idea of free will permeates the entire regulatory framework and supranational legislation and is reflected in court decisions. A.J. Colbert defines such an attitude to free will as clues that should not be ignored if we are serious about the value of the rule of law (Kolber 2016).

The concept of free will is fragmented across legal systems and norms, yet it is not embodied as a separate institution, principle, or norm. This may be due to the interdisciplinary nature and global scope of this idea, which complicates its normative consolidation, as well as the absence of a well-formed and established concept. And although free will has a transcendent basis, it is immanent to law, as confirmed by its significant manifestation in legal science and practice.

Free will in civil law is a legal idea that, in the absence of direct normative consolidation, is embodied through ideologemes. And although such idea-norms do not contain a direct reference to free will, they reflect its essence, using concepts such as voluntariness, by consent, free expression of will, prohibition of coercion, and at will.

Given that a definition of free will in civil law has not yet been fully established in legal scholarship or practice, the author proposes the following concept for discussion:

> Free will is a fundamental element of civil legal ideology. It reflects an individual's capacity to consciously, freely, and independently make decisions regarding their participation in civil legal relations. This includes the power to perform acts or omissions, exercise subjective rights, fulfilll obligations, and bear legal liability. Ultimately, this concept serves as the foundation for the formation of civil law principles and institutions.

R. R. Eman proves that an idea must fulfilll its function if it is to be valid. Since reality is the standard of knowledge, a theoretical notion must correspond to reality to fulfill its function. If it did not conform to reality, it would not lead to knowledge. The reality of an idea is the basis of its validity, as it makes it possible to fulfill its function (Ehman 1961, 225). For a comprehensive understanding of free will as a legal concept, it is necessary to establish its tasks, which will confirm its validity.

The following functions of free will as a legal idea can be distinguished: law-making and regulatory.

The law-making function involves influencing the vector of norm-setting and shaping legal consciousness. Although free will is not directly enshrined in regulatory acts, it is, in fact, reflected through other legal principles, institutions, and norms. As will be demonstrated in the following sections of the monograph, the concept of free will is incorporated into all sub-branches of civil law, thereby influencing the development of legislation and the formation of value orientations within the law, serving as a latent criterion for norm-setting. An analysis of current civil legislation confirms the absence of direct normative opposition to the legal concept of free will.

The regulatory function consists of creating regulatory requirements that presuppose the use of free will to participate in civil legal relations. The conditions of voluntariness, consent of the parties, free expression of will, and prohibition of coercion confirm this.

The legal functions of free will can be supplemented by psychological ones, including incentive and inhibitory mechanisms. The incentive function ensures the fulfillment of duties and the performance of actions. If a person does not have a pressing need to act but is aware of the need to perform an action, the will creates an auxiliary incentive, altering the meaning of the action and causing experiences associated with its intended consequences (Varii 2009, 152). In civil law, an example can be given when a party does not want to fulfill contractual obligations. Still, the will induces them to do so, motivating them with the threat of legal responsibility. The inhibitory function, on the contrary, is aimed at deterring unlawful behavior. A person can inhibit the emergence of undesirable motives and actions (Varii 2009, 152). In civil law, this function is invoked when a considers refusing to comply with regulatory rules.

The practical application of the above functions is actualised in the context of each sub-branch of civil law, which will be shown below. However, we can already conclude that the performance of these tasks by free will as a legal concept indicates its validity and soundness.

The aforementioned determines the logic of this study, as each section involves determining the meaning of free will for a separate sub-branch of civil law. In addition, we demonstrate how understanding the legal nature of free will impacts the resolution of current civil law issues. Today, there is no established list of such problems, as each scholar places their own emphasis. With this in mind, in each section, we analyse the meaning of free will in relation to solving current issues, drawing on the views of leading scientists who have attempted to generalize them.

In international law, free will is reflected as a legal idea. In particular, the right of every person to liberty and personal integrity, the prohibition of slavery, and the prohibition of arbitrary arrest and detention are proclaimed in the International Covenant on Civil and Political Rights (art. 9) and in the Universal Declaration of Human Rights (art. 3). It is separately proclaimed that all human beings are born free and equal in dignity and rights, and that they are endowed with reason and conscience and must act toward one another in a spirit of fraternity.

The most formulated embodiment of the legal idea of free will in international law is the principle of autonomy of will (*lex voluntatis*).

Lex voluntatis refers to the ability of private international law subjects, who are subject to different jurisdictions, to determine at their own will which law of a country will govern their legal relations. This idea is in stark contrast to domestic disputes, in which the parties are subject to the local legal system. Party autonomy—the power of the parties to a contract to choose the law of a particular country to govern their relations—enhances certainty and predictability and recognizes that the parties may be in the best position to determine which set of legal principles is most appropriate for their legal relationship (Hague Conference on Private International Law 2015).

There are different approaches to understanding the principle of autonomy of will, including viewing it as a conflict of law principle or a special legal institution (Pohoretska 2014, 253). However, in the context of studying free will, the main idea of this principle is the possibility for the parties to go beyond the limits of actual jurisdiction by opposing their interests to national norms. Thus, the parties may be citizens of countries A and B, sign an agreement in country B (actual jurisdiction), but determine that the law of country D governs their relations. This is confirmed by numerous court cases, such as *Penn v. Lord Baltimore, Peninsular and Oriental Steam Navigation Co v. Shand, Lloyd v. Guibert, Bell v. Kennedy, Godard v. Grey, Schibsby v. Westenholz, and Phillips v. Eyre*, among others (Micklitz 2015). The law of most states provides for unlimited and unconditional autonomy of the parties' will regarding the choice of applicable law (Vasylchenko 2007).

However, the principle of autonomy of will is not absolute, as parties cannot conclude an international contract without first determining a jurisdiction. Having defined it, they must comply with the chosen national legislation. Also, as L. Khasneziri notes, when concluding and performing a contract, the parties cannot violate either the rights of third parties or the interests of society as a whole. This limitation is known as the public order clause (Hasneziri 2023, 146). This makes it possible to understand the principle of autonomy of will as an extension of the principle of freedom of contract, according to which the parties independently determine the content and conditions of contractual relations, but within the limits set by law.

Freedom of contract can be considered either as the leading economic principle underlying all markets – the market vision – or as a moral principle based on the will of individuals – the voluntarist vision of contractual autonomy (Whittaker 2011). And while English law is based on the concept of contractual autonomy, which is seen as an instrument to promote free trade and means the freedom to voluntarily participate in economic transactions without any risk of legal interference, French law is based on the concept of *l'autonomie de la volonté* (autonomy of the will) and the political concept of *volonté générale* (general will) (Merrett, Mitchell and Day 2023). According to N. O'Connor, this demonstrates interference with the freedom of contract as a political counter-project to the concept of contractual autonomy outlined in the Civil Code, which characterises French law as rational and political (O'Connor 2019).

In general, the principle of autonomy of will is an exception to the general rules, and its necessity stems from the need to regulate international commercial relations. If, in the hierarchical subordination of will, the state (public) will prevails over the private will, then in the context of lex voluntatis, the private will plays a dominant role. However, even in such a case, having chosen the jurisdiction of a particular country, the parties fall under the prevailing public will. The principle of autonomy of will is perhaps the only case of direct implementation of the legal idea of free will in the legislation of Ukraine, which is reflected in the Law of Ukraine "On International Private Law" (*Pro mizhnarodne pryvatne pravo* [On Private International Law] 2005, art. 1, para. 1, cl. 5).

Although this approach is atypical for legal regulation, in international and foreign regulatory acts, the concept of choice of law is used instead of autonomy of will, which reflects the freedom of individual will (Meng 2014, 41).

As a result of the analysis, we emphasise that the principle of autonomy of will in private international law is a normative embodiment of the broader concept of free will. While these terms are closely related and often complementary, they are not identical. Free will is a fundamental philosophical issue regarding the presence or absence of cause-and-effect relationships (determinism) and the internal capacity to make decisions.

In contrast, autonomy of will is a more specific concept utilised in legal and ethical contexts; it denotes the capacity to act according to one's own convictions without external interference. This distinction is illustrated by the example of an open window: free will is the inherent ability to decide whether to open a window or not; autonomy of will is the right to execute that decision at one's own discretion, free from external hindrance. Furthermore, it is important to note that the concept of autonomy is dynamic, varying across cultural and historical contexts. In some philosophical systems, free will is even viewed as an illusion, whereas autonomy of will is recognized as a necessary social construct.

Summing up the intermediate conclusions, it should be stated that freedom consists in the possibility of any expression of will that does not harm others and the common good. In other words, legal freedom is limited by the rights and freedoms of other people, the principles of morality, and the interests of general well-being, solely for its establishment and real provision (Herman 2015, 121).

For a more detailed understanding of the legal nature of free will, it is advisable to interpret the term 'will' as the second part of the phrase 'free will.'

The Ukrainian dictionary contains several definitions of the term will:

1. As a function of the human psyche, consisting primarily of power over oneself, control of one's actions, and conscious regulation of one's behavior.
2. As the right to dispose of something at one's discretion.
3. As the absence of restrictions, privilege, freedom, and independence ("*Volia*" [Will] 2019).

The current legislation does not establish a direct definition of will, instead using it as an established and understood term. This approach is questionable because the concept of will is fundamental to a significant number of issues in both criminal and civil law.

In criminal law, will is a mandatory element in determining whether an act is socially dangerous. A person's will affects the form of guilt and can be categorized into the following types:

1. Direct intent (material component): A person desires the occurrence of socially dangerous consequences.
2. Direct intent (formal component): A person desires to commit a socially dangerous act.
3. Indirect intent (material component): A person does not desire but consciously allows or is indifferent to the occurrence of the consequences.
4. Alternative-specific intent (volitional element): A person desires or consciously allows the occurrence of any of the possible consequences.
5. Unspecified intent: A person desires, knowingly allows, or is indifferent to the consequences.
6. Criminal recklessness (material component): A person does not desire or allow the consequences to occur, counting on certain circumstances to prevent them.
7. Criminal negligence: A person is unaware of the possible consequences but should have been aware of and foreseen them; or, a person does not understand the possible consequences despite a duty to do so.

The volitional element in these forms of culpability serves as the boundary between different degrees of criminal responsibility, as it reflects the internal relationship between the subject's free will and the resulting social harm.In all these cases, the person's will is of a different nature, but it is of key importance for the qualification of a socially dangerous act. The absence of will is the basis for recognising a person as insane.

In addition, criminal law provides for punishment in the form of restriction of liberty, deprivation of liberty, and life imprisonment. Each of these sanctions operates on the concept of will but does not define its interpretation, which presumably differs from the understanding of free will.

The Criminal Code of Ukraine only specifies the essence of each specific punishment.

1. Restriction of liberty: Consists in keeping a person in open-type penal institutions without isolation from society under conditions of supervision with mandatory involvement of the convict in labor (*Kryminal'nyi kodeks Ukrainy* [Criminal Code of Ukraine] 2001, art. 61).
2. Deprivation of liberty for a specific period: Consists in isolating the convict and placing them for a specific period in a closed-type penal institution (Ibid., art. 63).
3. Life imprisonment: Is established for the commission of especially grave crimes and is applied only in cases specifically provided for by the Criminal Code, if the court does not consider it possible to apply deprivation of liberty for a specific period (Ibid., art. 64).

The content of these norms suggests that their purpose is to restrict rights and create coercion. That is, before the application of these sanctions, a person's will consists in the ability to do everything that is not prohibited by law. After the application of sanctions, the person is limited in their choice of possible behavior and is subject to mandatory coercion (such as performing labour).

The concept of will is of particular importance in civil law, particularly due to its impact on a person's legal capacity. Here, it is appropriate to distinguish between freedom, will, civil capacity, and legal personality.

The ability to have civil rights and obligations (civil legal capacity) is possessed by all natural persons. The civil legal capacity of a natural person arises at the moment of their birth, and in cases established by law, the interests of a conceived but not yet born child are protected. In certain cases established by law, the ability to exercise certain civil rights and assume corresponding obligations may be associated with the natural person reaching a specific age.

The civil legal capacity of a natural person ceases at the moment of their death (*Tsyvil'nyi kodeks Ukrainy* [the Civil Code of Ukraine] 2003, art. 25). All natural persons are equal in the ability to have civil rights and obligations. A natural person has all personal non-property rights established by the Constitution and the

Civil Code of Ukraine and is capable of having all property rights established by the Civil Code and other laws (Ibid., art. 26).

A natural person who is aware of the significance of their actions and can control them has civil capacity.

Civil capacity is an individual's ability to acquire civil rights for themself through their actions and independently exercise them, as well as the ability to create civil obligations for themself, independently fulfill them, and bear responsibility in case of non-performance (Ibid., art. 30). An individual who has not reached the age of fourteen (a minor) has the right to independently perform small household transactions and exercise personal non-property rights to the results of intellectual and creative activity protected by law (Ibid., art. 31).

In addition, an individual aged fourteen to eighteen (a minor) has the right to: (1) independently dispose of their earnings, scholarship, or other income; (2) independently exercise rights to the results of intellectual and creative activity protected by law; (3) be a participant (founder) of legal entities, unless prohibited by law or the constituent documents of the legal entity; (4) independently conclude a bank deposit (account) agreement and manage the funds (Ibid., art. 32).

A natural person who has reached the age of eighteen (majority) has full civil capacity. If a natural person who has not reached the age of majority marries, they acquire full civil capacity from the moment of marriage registration. If the marriage is terminated before they reach the age of majority, the full civil capacity is preserved. If the marriage is recognized as invalid for reasons not related to the unlawful behavior of the minor, the full civil capacity is also preserved (Ibid., art. 34).

Full civil capacity may be granted to an individual who has reached the age of sixteen and works under an employment contract, as well as to a minor who is registered as the mother or father of a child, or who has reached sixteen and wishes to engage in entrepreneurial activity (Ibid., art. 35).

As we can see, civil legal capacity and civil capacity are closely related to the concepts of freedom and will, but they are not identical.

O. O. Kovalenko proposes defining will in law as free will, which corresponds to all the essential characteristics of law and thus differs from arbitrary will. Will is the driving force of aspiration and desire (Kovalenko 2017, 119).

I. I. Kachala gives a similar position, understanding by will not only a physical quality but also the right not to be forced to do what is not provided for by law, and to be free in choosing one's behavior and having the right to develop one's personality (provided that the rights and freedoms of others are not violated), as well as the guaranteed possibility of realising stipulated constitutional rights and freedoms (Kachala 2010, 250). Such a definition broadly outlines the concept of freedom but seems to be an eclectic combination of the concepts of freedom, will, and legal capacity.

When generalizing the points discussed above, the following distinction between key legal concepts becomes clear:

1. Freedom in law: The possibility of behavior not prohibited by law and the absence of coercion, except in cases specifically provided for by legislation.
2. Will in law: The ability to control one's actions and their external manifestation, alongside the conscious regulation of one's behavior, which is not limited solely to legally defined possibilities.
3. Civil legal capacity: The normatively defined possibility of a person to be the bearer of subjective rights and obligations.
4. Civil capacity: The legal ability of a person to exercise their rights through their own actions and to bear corresponding obligations.

This conceptual differentiation allows for a more nuanced understanding of the subject's autonomy within the legal field, where "freedom" and "will" provide the philosophical and psychological basis, while "legal capacity" and "capacity" provide the formal-legal framework for activity.

Active and passive forms characterise these concepts. Freedom and legal capacity should be considered passive, as they only provide for the possibility of specific behavior or potential participation in legal relations. Will and civil capacity are active—they represent the use of one's rights and opportunities. Just as will is the active use of freedom, so civil capacity is the active application of legal capacity. However, will and freedom lose their meaning without each other. Will without freedom allows for making decisions, but without the opportunity to implement them. Conversely, freedom without will is the opportunity to implement decisions, but without the ability to freely make them.

Having determined the distinction between the concepts of freedom, will, civil capacity and legal capacity, we can evaluate the concept of free will itself.

In a broad sense, free will is often reduced to the question of whether a person is free to make their own decisions or if they are predetermined. It could be assumed that for civil law, free will should be considered as meaningful actions or inaction aimed at participating in civil legal relations. However, such an understanding does not fully reveal the essence of the legal concept.

The previous section of the monograph examined the understanding of free will in detail at different historical stages. Today, free will is typically understood from the standpoints of determinism, compatibilism, incompatibilism, libertarianism, and the theory of moral responsibility.

Determinism claims that free will is based on the causal connection of phenomena. Theological determinism is based on the construction "if God foresaw that I would act in a certain way, then I must act in that way," but admits the unresolved question of "whether God necessarily knows in advance that I will act in a certain way" (Lucas 1970). Biological determinism claims that the current state of human societies is a specific result of biological forces and the biological nature of the human species; all deterministic theories describe a particular model of society that corresponds to socio-economic biases (Dialogue 1976).

In biological determinism, free will is linked to genes, which is why we do not make decisions independently, because we are limited by the genes embedded in us. The application of deterministic theories to the legal understanding of free will would lead to a legal collapse, as external influences could be used to explain any human action. Such an approach in civil law would make it possible to always justify a person's actions or inaction by the impact of external factors that made a personal decision impossible. As a result, this could render civil law constructions impossible, constantly raising issues of exemption from liability, force majeure, and even the very essence of freedom of contract and equality between the parties. Therefore, one cannot agree with the deterministic approach to understanding free will in civil law.

At the same time, some theories view determinism not as a forced model of behavior, but as a partially imperceptible sequence of events that lead to decision-making. Such a statement arises when a person concludes a deal under the influence of neuromarketing technologies, raising questions about the independence of the buyer's decision-making.

In compatibilist theories, on the other hand, the compatibility of determinism and free will is asserted. Free will in classical compatibilism is reduced to a person's ability to do whatever they want. Thomas Hobbes supplements this statement by clarifying that liberty refers to the agent rather than the faculty of will itself. He argues that a person is free when they encounter no external obstacles to acting on their desires. Hobbes states:

> From the use of the word free-will, no liberty can be inferred of the will, desire, or inclination, but the liberty of the man; which consisteth in this, that he finds no stop, in doing what he has the will, desire, or inclination to doe. (Hobbes 1996, 262)

The *Stanford Encyclopedia of Philosophy* questions the view of classical compatibilism, recognising it as requiring improvement. It states that various mental illnesses can force a person to act as they want without hindrance, but intuitively it seems they do not act of their own free will ("Compatibilism" 2024). For example, a person suffering from a form of psychosis that causes hallucinations may act as they please without hindrance, but they can hardly be said to act of their own free will (Ibid.).

This statement is complemented by the position that a person loses free will when subjected to violence. For example, when a person enters into a transaction under duress or enters into a marriage against their will, there is a violation of free will. This approach is already considered close to the normative one, as violating free will in these cases would have significant legal consequences. This situation also occurs in criminal law, in particular when someone is deprived of free will through rape, murder, theft, or other forms of violence. In these cases, free will is denied not because the past causally determines the future, but because the aggressor deprives the victim of their desires or the right to choose an action. The aggressor forces the victim, and, according to compatibilists, this is precisely what denies her free will. Thus, what matters is that the individual's choice was the result of their own desires and preferences, and not imposed by some external (or internal) force.

Some views of compatibilists are closely aligned with the modern legal understanding of free will. One should agree with D. K. Dennett, who in his works proclaims the idea that the existence of free will is substantiated by the fact that a person can act contrary to what is expected of them (Dennett 2007, 155). The correctness of this statement can be illustrated with an example. In Article 743 of the Civil Code of Ukraine, the mandatory written form of an annuity contract is imperatively fixed. When the parties intentionally violate this norm and conclude an agreement in violation of the requirements for its form, we can speak of a manifestation of their free will (although such a transaction will be null and void). If free will did not exist, people would always act within the limits of the law, without violating it.

A somewhat different perspective on the understanding of free will is presented in the theory of incompatibilism. For instance, D. Pereboom writes in his works about the incompatibility of free will with determinism (Pereboom 2001). Pereboom, as a researcher of consciousness and physicalism, believes that actions subject to ethical assessment are actually causally determined, which contradicts the existence of free will and, accordingly, excludes the moral and legal responsibility of the subject (Ibid.). The basis of this theory is the denial of external influence and causality on human decision-making. A person is proclaimed to make all decisions independently and acts as *causa sui*. Free will, as the possibility of choosing more than one course of action, is supported by the concept of libertarianism.

As we can see, different approaches to understanding freedom cannot be entirely relevant for understanding free will from the position of civil law. We can agree with V. I. Tymoshenko, who claims that unconditional adherence to any one of the above directions will yield one-sided ideas about free will. In contrast, the synthetic unification of the methodological approaches used by different directions makes it possible to recreate a holistic picture of the results achieved by philosophical, political, and legal thought in understanding the issue of free will and determinism, and to determine the directions for further research (Tymoshenko 2007, 235).

Modern legal doctrine also pays close attention to the study of free will, recognizing its fundamental importance. For example, O. P. Donchenko substantiates the following conclusions:

1. Law is a measure of freedom, which, in the legal sense, is a form of self-determination for participants in legal relations regarding the choice of goals and methods of achieving them.
2. It is a form whose content is a set of specific legal rights of a person and a citizen, thanks to which freedom becomes more defined.
3. The principle "everything is permitted that is not prohibited by law" implies the expression of freedom, since the latter finds its maximum general expression as a general rule (Donchenko 2009, 49).

This perspective emphasizes that legal freedom is not an abstract void, but a structured space where individuals exercise their will within a framework of clearly defined rights and prohibitions.

It can be concluded that philosophy understands free will as an internal component of reason and consciousness. At the same time, jurisprudence focuses on the active, external manifestation of free will in the form of the expression of will. The legal understanding of free will is closely related to a person's ability to be aware of their actions and inaction, to understand their consequences, and to provide an assessment.

Erich Fromm suggests considering free will through several distinct understandings:

1. Natural (non-normative): The ability to make decisions based on one's own will.
2. Positive (normative): Making decisions in accordance with one's own will and based on normative prescriptions.
3. Real (actual): The guaranteed probability of making decisions in accordance with one's own will and based on normative prescriptions (Fromm 2011).

Based on this, we can speak of a legal understanding of free will as the ability to make decisions that is normatively guaranteed and limited. Internal free will correlates with the inviolability of the right to freedom of thought and is not subject to restrictions; however, the external manifestation of free will through the expression of will is limited by legal prescriptions.

Some academics define free will in terms of its distinction from the social freedom of a citizen and the spiritual freedom of an individual. Thus, free will is understood as the possibility of conscious choice in life, making one's own decisions, determining life priorities, and organising one's life; social freedom of a citizen is considered as human rights in society and the state, regulated by laws; and spiritual freedom is understood through the Christian definition of freedom of the spirit from slavery to sin and sinful passions (from passions and wrong habits, for example, from anger, impatience, condemnation, greed, envy, etc.) (Denysov and Zubov 2016, 7).

There is also a purely formal-legal understanding of free will as the absence of external coercion, which was supported by Harald Höffding (1902). Here, the critical understanding is that only the will of another person is recognized as external coercion. That is, the norms of legislation, decisions of courts or state bodies are not the coercion that makes free will impossible. If this position were the opposite, we would have to discuss the deterministic absence of free will in general. In that case, each norm of legislation to a certain extent acts as a form of coercion, and given that a person's life is always subject to the legal field, we would have to argue for the constant primacy of law that renders free will impossible.

V. S. Blihar provides a comprehensive philosophical and legal analysis of free will, offering the following conclusions:

1. Two-dimensionality of free will: The concept assumes both an internal dimension (where human freedom is manifested in the faculty of will) and an external dimension, which expresses the conditions of human existence, including legal frameworks.
2. Methodological interpretation: Interpreting free will as the ability to choose decisions based on legal knowledge allows for the perception of free will in the context of choosing behavior and understanding the conditions under which such behavior is justified or condemned.
3. Fundamental necessity: The problem of free will is central to legal philosophy; denying its existence would render law itself meaningless and superfluous, as law presupposes a subject capable of choice.
4. Law as a product of will: Law logically arises from freedom and is inherently directed toward human free will, serving as a direct product of that will (Blihar 2015, 151).

These conclusions emphasize that free will is not merely a psychological attribute but the very ontological foundation upon which the entire structure of law and legal responsibility is built. M. I. Yaruniv offers his own definition:

> Human free will is the ability to realise and bear responsibility for the choices of one's actions, which can be expressed as random forms of behavior caused by a consistent and substantiated system of qualitatively objective regularities. (Yaruniv 2018, 22)

Yaruniv connects the axiological-normative justification of human free will with several factors:

1. Awareness of choice: The awareness of the possibility of one's own choice through natural will and the desire for change.

2. Self-isolation and state influence: Attempts to isolate one's self; understanding the value of personal natural free will; and the significant role of the state in imposing legal restrictions on human actions, which influences the awareness of responsibility.
3. Inherent value: The value of human free will, inherent in its natural beginning as a human personality (Yaruniv 2018, 22).

These factors demonstrate that free will is not only a subjective psychological state but also a socially and legally conditioned value that matures through the interaction between the individual and the state's normative framework.

Summarising the above, we can conclude that free will is a legal concept that forms the essence of civil law, serves as the basis for civil legal relations, determines the possibility of choosing one's behavior, and performs the function of autonomy for the subject of law.

The concept and place of free will in civil law are based on the following fundamental theses:

1. Fundamental legal idea and autonomy: Free will in civil law is a fundamental legal idea that expresses the autonomy of a person's will and is manifested in various institutions. However, it is not absolute and can be limited by the norms of law, morality, public interest, and the interests of others. The free will of one person cannot limit the rights and freedoms of another, provided that such restrictions are lawful, justified, and proportionate.
2. Relationship to legal principles: Free will is closely related to the principles of civil law and serves as the basis for the implementation of rights and freedoms. It is a broader concept than a specific legal principle or institution, acting as an overarching idea that influences their formulation and functioning.

3. Reflective manifestation: Free will is a legal idea that is not always directly enshrined in regulatory legal acts. Instead, it is reflected through the content of legal institutions and the principles that are built upon it.

The idea of free will reflects the essence of civil legal relations, which are based on the principles of dispositivity, free expression of will, freedom, equality, etc. This justifies the need for a thorough examination of the relationship between free will and the principles of civil law.

1.3. Manifestation of Free Will in the Principles of Civil Law

Civil law is a set of legal norms that regulate property and related non-property relations based on legal equality, autonomy of will, and property independence of their participants (Mazur 2006, 5). It is generally recognized that the functioning of all legal institutions and the entire spectrum of social relations depends on civil law. The basis of civil law is the fundamental principles upon which the entire system of this branch of law is founded.

The study of the principles of civil law has received considerable attention in numerous scientific works; however, a thorough analysis of the importance of free will as the foundation of these principles has not yet been conducted.

As noted by O. V. Basai, the principles of civil law are foundational provisions, shaped by legal consciousness, that reflect the objective laws of development and needs of society. They exist on several planes: first, as legal ideas produced by legal science and social practice, which constitute the basis of society's legal views; second, as general provisions enshrined in Article 3 of the Civil Code of Ukraine, which follow from the content of other norms and form the basis for the legal regulation of civil relations (Basai 2018, 68).

The understanding of civil law principles has undergone evolutionary stages. As Y. Nosyk summarises, the current state of research on the principles of civil law in Ukraine, while exhibiting features of succession from Soviet-era studies, reveals striking changes in views. The most noticeable differences are manifested in a departure from formal positivism and an orientation toward the ideas of natural law. These universal values underlie inalienable human rights and the basic concepts of private law (Nosik 2021, 87).

The principles of civil law are primarily based on the natural law concept, which explains the fundamental meaning of free will. Determining its connection with these principles allows us to understand the mechanisms of its implementation. This is particularly significant given that any right, freedom, or legitimate interest has value only if it can be implemented and protected (Zudikhin 2011a, 1), particularly by restoring the right, protecting interests, and applying measures of influence, including liability, to the offender (Zudikhin 2011c, 407).

I. O. Kharitonov proposes a definition:

> Legal principles are starting ideas that express the most important laws and foundations of a given type of state and law, are of the same order as the essence of law and constitute its main features, are distinguished by universality, higher imperativeness and general significance, and correspond to the objective necessity of building and strengthening the social order. (Kharytonov, 2008, 7)

I. A. Biriukov and Yu. O. Zaika define the principles of civil law as the basic foundations that embody the fundamental, most characteristic features of this law, which can be directly applied in the regulation of civil legal relations (Biriukov and Zaika 2006, 10).

The principles of law constitute a paradigm, a vector in which law develops. Therefore, it can be assumed that confirming the inseparable relationship between free will and the principles of civil law will prove the fundamental importance of free will for all of civil law.

I. O. Michurin notes that the principles of civil law are the most global ideas and fundamental provisions, according to which the holistic legal regulation of personal non-property and property relations is carried out (Michurin 2010, 8).

The civil legislation of Ukraine does not contain a definition of principles (*pryntsypy*), and the Civil Code of Ukraine generally uses the term general principles (*zahalni zasady*). The theoretical distinction between these terms has a doctrinal basis, but an in-depth study of this is not the purpose of this monograph. N. Yu. Golubeva defines general principles of civil law as principles already established in legislation, while legal principles should comprehend the fundamental concepts of civil law (Holubieva 2008b, 19). However, since the concepts are very close in meaning, we will not focus on their distinction.

Therefore, as a working definition, we propose to agree with the understanding of legal principles as the starting ideas of law's existence, which express its most important regularities and foundations, are of the same order as its essence, are distinguished by universality and higher imperativeness, and correspond to the objective necessity of building and strengthening a particular social order (Kolodii 1999, 19).

The relationship between the principles of civil law and free will can be considered in the context of the interplay between natural freedom and legal principles. A. M. Kolodii emphasizes that the natural freedom of a person cannot manifest itself directly as a legal right to freedom; it can only form specific requirements. Based on these requirements, a corresponding idea of freedom is formed, which serves as the prototype of the legal state of freedom until it is embodied in a legal form such as a principle, a subjective right, or a component of the method of legal regulation (Kolodii 1998, 176).

To acquire a legal character, the requirements arising from the natural state of freedom must be determined by the economic and political level of development of society and the social opportunities that provide a particular way of life for a person (Zahorui 2017, 225). By analogy, it is possible to assume the existence of free will beyond its normative consolidation in the principles of civil law. This provides reason to argue for the existence of free will regardless of its formal enshrinement. However, after undergoing normative reflection, free will finds its place in the principles, ideas, institutions, and norms of civil law.

The doctrine of private law distinguishes the following principles: (1) autonomy of will; (2) voluntariness; (3) legal equality; (4)

legal protection of private interest; (5) coordination; (6) general permission (Kolodii 1998, 176); (7) dispositivity (Chubokha 2013); and (8) stability of civil relations (Shyshka 2004, 96), among others.

Some authors supplement this list with the principles of individual civil law institutions (Kosenko 2006; Andrianov 2005; Holubieva 2008a). In particular, they highlight:

1. Principles of performance of obligations: Proper performance, real performance, impossibility of unilateral refusal, business cooperation, and economy.
2. Principles of civil liability: Inevitability of liability and liability for fault.
3. Principles of copyright: Freedom of creativity, national treatment, independence of protection, and automatic protection.
4. Principles of securing the performance of obligations: For instance, the principle of publicity.

However, the above-mentioned doctrinal principles are not fully reflected in legislation. Article 3 of the Civil Code of Ukraine (*Tsyvil'nyi kodeks Ukrainy* [Civil Code of Ukraine] 2003, art. 3) clearly outlines the general principles of civil legislation:

1. Inadmissibility of arbitrary interference in a person's private life.
2. Inadmissibility of deprivation of property rights, except in cases established by the Constitution of Ukraine and law.
3. Freedom of contract.
4. Freedom of entrepreneurial activity that is not prohibited by law.
5. Judicial protection of civil rights and interests.
6. Justice, good faith, and reasonableness.

This statutory list represents the formal-legal boundaries within which free will must operate, providing a normative framework that balances individual autonomy with social and legal order.

These principles are explicitly enshrined because they are directly formulated in a legal norm. Given their primary status as principles of civil law, it is these provisions specified in Article 3 of the Civil Code of Ukraine that should be considered the normatively defined principles for which free will serves as the basis. The validity of the thesis about the fundamental importance of free will for the principles of civil law should be verified through an analysis of the relationship between free will and each of these explicitly enshrined principles.

First, the connection between free will and the principle of inadmissibility of arbitrary interference in a person's private life is unambiguous. The content of this principle is the subjective right of a person to a private life, supplemented by a prohibition on its violation. It follows from this principle that state authorities, local self-government bodies, and any other persons should not interfere in the private affairs of civil law subjects if they act in accordance with the law.

The principle of inadmissibility of arbitrary interference in a person's private life is multidimensional and corresponds to numerous civil and constitutional rights. In particular, Article 32 of the Constitution of Ukraine (Konstytutsiia Ukrainy [Constitution of Ukraine] 1996, art. 32) stipulates that:

1. Non-interference: No one may be subjected to interference in their personal and family life, except in cases provided for by the Constitution.
2. Information control: The collection, storage, use, and dissemination of confidential information about a person without their consent is not allowed, except in cases specified by law and only in the interests of national security, economic well-being, and human rights.
3. Right to access: Every citizen has the right to access information about themselves held by state and local government bodies, institutions, and organizations that is not a state or other legally protected secret.
4. Judicial protection: Everyone is guaranteed judicial protection of the right to refute inaccurate information about themselves and their family members, the right to demand

> the removal of any information, and the right to compensation for damages caused by the collection, storage, use, and dissemination of such inaccurate information.

Other articles of the Basic Law and other sources of civil law contain numerous rights that continue the idea of the inviolability of private life. In particular, the Civil Code of Ukraine identifies several personal non-property rights that are natural human rights based on this principle. The relationship between free will and personal non-property rights will be examined in detail in the second section of this research.

As we can see, the recognition of a person's private life and the prohibition of arbitrary interference with it runs like a red thread through all legislation. But private life is a historical category and emerged as a holistic object of legal protection only from the end of the 19th century. Before that, the law did not protect private life as a whole, but only some of its individual manifestations, primarily housing and correspondence (Basai 2013).

Throughout its development, the right to private life has expanded and gained increasing importance. Today, private life is understood as a special part of the private sphere of human life, consisting of various relationships, phenomena, and events that do not have public significance and are determined and regulated by the person themself based on social conditions, guaranteed and protected by law from unlawful interference (Bobryk 2004, 6).

The indissoluble connection between free will and the right to private life becomes clear from the definition proposed by R. A. Maydanyk. Thus, private life is an attempt by people to freely choose under what circumstances and to what extent they will reveal themselves, their attitudes, and their behavior to others. Private life is a key value that strengthens dignity, a fundamental right, and an expectation of every person (Maydanyk 2012). It is logical that the exercise of the right to private life is impossible without the use of free will, as the prospect of free choice is based upon it.

Confirmation of this conclusion can be seen in the thesis of I. O. Kharitonov, who defines the principle of inadmissibility of arbitrary interference in a person's personal life as a requirement for ensuring personal freedom, which is sometimes called personal sovereignty, putting into this concept the ability of an individual to determine the type and nature of behavior, place in society and in the system of civil relations at his own will (Kharytonov 2008, 10).

The combination of this principle and free will should be justified by the thesis that law governs the external relations of one person's liberty with respect to the freedom of others, while morality governs a person's internal motivations (Yefremova 2011, 258). Similarly, a distinction should be made between this principle and personal non-property law. The principle of inadmissibility of arbitrary interference is based on the freedom of one person in relation to the freedom of another. Another person or body, guided by free will, cannot arbitrarily interfere in the personal life of any person. At the same time, the right to a private life is an absolute, personal non-property right that ensures the social existence of an individual. From this perspective, free will is more closely related to a person's internal motivations. Thus, we must distinguish between the principle of non-interference and the right to a private life.

Therefore, free will is the foundation for both the principle of inadmissibility of arbitrary interference in private life and for the personal non-property right to a private life. However, they are not identical, and the manifestation of free will in them is different.

As V. Borisova correctly notes, the norms of civil law are always aimed at ensuring the private interests of participants in civil relations; therefore, no one, except for cases provided for by law, can arbitrarily interfere in private affairs. In particular, the secrecy of health status, personal life and correspondence are protected by Articles 286, 301, and 306 of the Civil Code of Ukraine. The inadmissibility of arbitrary interference in private affairs means a ban not only for public entities but even for parents (for example, to influence a capable person regarding the disposal of their income) (Borysova 2017, 71).

The very concept of private life and its connection with free will will be considered later. But for now, it should be determined that the principle of non-interference in private life means that no legal norms should contain the possibility of interference by other persons or bodies in a person's private sphere.

The importance of this principle is proclaimed in Article 12 of the Universal Declaration of Human Rights:

> No one shall be subjected to arbitrary interference with his privacy, family, home or correspondence, nor to attacks upon his honor and reputation. Everyone has the right to the protection of the law against such interference or attacks. (Universal Declaration of Human Rights 1948, art. 12)

The principle of non-interference in personal life manifests in various aspects. As V. Syvukhin rightly suggests, this principle provides for the following possibilities:

1. Organizational autonomy: Choosing legal means and methods to satisfy one's own needs in organizing personal and family life.
2. Negative obligation: Demanding non-interference from other persons.
3. Legal protection: Appealing to state authorities to protect violated rights in cases of unlawful interference or in the event of applying self-defense measures.
4. Social enjoyment: Using social benefits, such as a private and family life (Syvukhin 2007, 6).

In the broadest sense, the content of this right includes the following possibilities:

1. Prohibitory function: Prohibiting interference in personal and family life, except in cases provided for by the Constitution.
2. Consensual control: Granting consent to the collection, storage, use, and dissemination of confidential information, except in cases provided for by law.
3. Access to personal data: Accessing information about oneself held by state and local government bodies that does not constitute a state or other protected secret.
4. Right to refutation: Refuting false information about oneself and one's family through legal protection.

5. Restorative measures: Demanding the removal of false information through judicial protection.
6. Compensatory claims: Compensating for damages caused by the collection, storage, use, and dissemination of false information (Ibid.).

A violation of any of the above elements would constitute an infringement of the civil law principle of non-interference in private life. By establishing this principle at the heart of the Civil Code, the legislator proclaimed its significance and the impossibility of creating norms that would violate it.

The principle of non-interference in private life implies a ban on other persons, state authorities, and local self-government bodies from interfering in a person's private life and the exercise of their subjective civil rights. In other words, this is a ban on interference in the process of exercising free will. Understanding the principle from this angle somewhat alters its established meaning and reveals its relationship with free will.

However, this principle is not absolute, as intervention is permitted in cases where it is not perceived as arbitrary.

Interference with private life, and therefore the restriction of free will, is permissible if it is carried out to ensure due recognition and respect for the rights and freedoms of others, as well as compliance with the norms of morality, public order, and general welfare (Maydanyk 2012). A vivid example is the possibility of violating this principle by entering a person's home without their consent.

This is provided for in Civil Code of Ukraine, which stipulates that in urgent cases related to saving lives and property or the direct prosecution of persons suspected of committing a crime, the law may establish a different procedure for entering a person's home or other property, and for conducting inspections and searches (*Tsyvil'nyi kodeks Ukrainy* [Civil Code of Ukraine] 2003, art. 231 para. 3).

Of particular importance is the violation of this principle through the unscrupulous dissemination of information about a person's private affairs. The collection, storage, use, and dissemination of information about personal life, as well as information that violates personal and family secrets, the secrecy of correspondence, telephone conversations, and other messages without the consent of the interested person, is not permitted. Persons who have gained access to information about citizens in the course of performing their official duties are liable under the law for violating confidentiality. The Civil Code of Ukraine stipulates that the circumstances of an individual's personal life may be disclosed by other persons only if they constitute an offense, as confirmed by a court judgment, decision, or resolution of an administrative body (Ibid., art. 293).

The Unified State Register of Court Decisions contains hundreds of cases involving violations of this principle, which have led to harm to honor, dignity, and business reputation. As an illustrative example, we can cite the case of the Zboriv District Court of the Ternopil region, dated February 12, 2020, No. 599/2491/19. The plaintiff filed a lawsuit for the protection of honor, dignity, and business reputation, as well as the refutation of inaccurate information and compensation for moral damage and legal costs. The plaintiff justified their claims by citing videos, texts, and articles posted on Facebook and YouTube, which were false and harmed their business reputation. The posted information created a negative impression and attitude toward the plaintiff as a negligent owner and an unfriendly neighbor. The comments to the video contained false information and a distortion of facts, discrediting their business reputation. This information, statements, and comments contained calls for physical violence, harassment of the plaintiff and his relatives, and formed a negative attitude toward him among citizens. The court ruled that the defendant was obligated to refute the false information in the same manner in which it was disseminated and to recover from him UAH 15,689.40 (for moral damage, legal aid costs, and court fees) (*Rishennia Zborivs'koho raionnoho sudu Ternopils'koi oblasti* [Decision of the Zboriv District Court of Ternopil Oblast] 2020).

In this example, two vectors of the application of free will can be seen. The defendant, acting of their own free will, disseminated information about the plaintiff. However, such actions violated the principle of inadmissibility of arbitrary interference in a person's private life. On the other hand, the plaintiff, guided by their own free will, first committed actions about which the defendant spread information, and then, again guided by free will, filed a lawsuit.

As we can see, free will is manifested in the application of the principle of inadmissibility of arbitrary interference in a person's private life. This principle asserts the protection of free will as it is applied in the private sphere. At the same time, this principle limits the free will of other participants in legal relations by prohibiting arbitrary interference.

A similar construction can be traced in other principles of civil law. Thus, the principle of inadmissibility of deprivation of property rights, except in cases specified by law, is also based on free will. This principle is aimed at protecting a subjective civil right, which, as enshrined in Article 321 of the Civil Code of Ukraine, is inviolable. Article 41 of the Constitution of Ukraine also declares the prohibition of unlawful deprivation of property rights. The forced alienation of private property may be carried out only in exceptional cases for reasons of public necessity, in accordance with the law and subject to prior and full compensation for its value. The forced alienation of such objects with subsequent full compensation is permitted only in conditions of war or a state of emergency.

Article 1 of the Protocol to the Convention for the Protection of Human Rights and Fundamental Freedoms also guarantees the protection of property rights, stating that "every natural or legal person is entitled to the peaceful enjoyment of his possessions. No one shall be deprived of his possessions except in the public interest and subject to the conditions provided for by law and by the general principles of international law" (Council of Europe 1952, art. 1).

However, it should be borne in mind that this position applies only to a person's existing property, and not to the right to acquire property, as the right to inherit property is not a property right until it becomes contested (European Court of Human Rights, 1979).

The principle of inadmissibility of deprivation of property rights is a fundamental concept for protecting civil legal relations based on the possession, use, and disposal of property.

The right of ownership is a person's right to things (property), which they exercise in accordance with the law and independently of the will of other persons. The owner possesses, uses, and disposes of their property at their own discretion and can perform any lawful actions on it. Without delving into the controversy surrounding the content of property rights, it is evident that free will is the basis for the owner to possess, use, and dispose of property belonging to them at their own discretion and in their own interests.

It is through this triad of powers that one can see the relationship between free will and the principle of inadmissibility of deprivation of property rights. In accordance with this principle, civil law norms provide owners with the possibility of stable (permanent) exercise of ownership powers and legal protection against actions involving the unjustified deprivation of property. This should be considered a legal means of establishing respect for and the inviolability of property rights (Maydanyk 2012). The relationship between free will and the law of obligations, specifically the emergence and termination of property rights, as well as the rights of possession, use, and disposal, will be examined in detail in the following sections of the monograph.

The next principle of civil law based on free will is the principle of freedom of contract, which provides a practical means to determine the content of an agreement. Freedom of contract, as a principle of civil law, acts as a guiding force for all contractual relations, laying down their philosophy and logic.

In addition, the violation of freedom of contract leads to the conclusion of a transaction that does not reflect the valid will of one or more parties (Aleksii 2019, 59).

The essence of the principle of freedom of contract manifests in the following legal possibilities:

1. Atypical contracts: To conclude a contract that is not explicitly provided for by acts of civil legislation, provided it complies with the general principles of civil law.
2. Gap-filling: To regulate relations within a contract that is provided for by civil legislation, even if such relations are not specifically regulated by those acts.

3. Derogation from statutes: To depart from the provisions of acts of civil legislation and regulate relations at one's own discretion, unless such derogation is expressly prohibited by law (*Tsyvil'nyi kodeks Ukrainy* [Civil Code of Ukraine] 2003, art. 6).

This principle serves as a cornerstone of private law autonomy, allowing parties to tailor their legal relationships to their specific needs while remaining within the broader framework of justice and reasonableness.

In fact, this principle creates a limitless field for contractual relations, giving parties the right to apply existing contract types at their own discretion and to create their own structures. In practice, this leads to the emergence of hybrid agreements for the provision of services, the performance of works, and other purposes. This approach is absolutely justified because civil relations are developing faster than their legislative regulation. As an example, we can cite the long-established e-commerce and cryptocurrency markets, which are still not sufficiently regulated by specific rules.

Free will in the principle of freedom of contract is the idea by which parties enter into contractual relations and create new rights and obligations toward each other. At the same time, free will is a mandatory criterion for recognising the legality of a contract under this principle. After all, the creation of such relations through the violation of free will—under the influence of deception, coercion, etc.—is grounds for recognising the transaction as invalid.

There are cases of conditional coercion when a party enters into a relationship under conditions that restrict the principle of freedom of contract. This issue is investigated in detail in O. V. Basai's dissertation, and the connection between such cases and free will will be analysed in the relevant section of this study. However, such situations are associated with the presence of a weaker party to the contract. Depending on the circumstances, this may be an individual consumer, a creditor, or a person entering into a relationship with an entity holding a monopoly position in the market, among others (Basai 2014, 20). In consumer contracts, freedom of contract is limited in favor of the weaker party by preventing unfair terms, a practice also reflected in international legal acts, such as the *Model Rules of European Private Law*, which deny the emergence of obligations from an unfair term.

Very closely related to the above is the principle of freedom of entrepreneurial activity that is not prohibited by law. This principle corresponds to the personal non-property right of an individual to choose an occupation. Applying the concept of free will, a person independently chooses a professional activity, including entrepreneurship.

The Constitution of Ukraine (*Konstytutsiia Ukrainy* [Constitution of Ukraine] 1996, art. 43) guarantees the right of every individual to engage in entrepreneurial activity and labor, establishing the following framework:

1. Freedom of Labor: Everyone has the right to work, including the opportunity to earn a living through work they freely choose or to which they freely agree.
2. State Support: The state creates conditions for citizens to fully exercise their right to work, guarantees equal opportunities, and implements vocational training and retraining programs.
3. Prohibition of Forced Labor: The use of forced labor is prohibited, with specific exceptions for military or alternative service, work under a court sentence, or during martial law and states of emergency.
4. Working Conditions and Wages: Everyone has the right to proper, safe, and healthy working conditions, and to wages no lower than the legal minimum.
5. Special Protections: The use of women and minors in work hazardous to their health is prohibited; furthermore, protection against unlawful dismissal and the right to timely payment are guaranteed by law.

The Law of Ukraine "On Foreign Economic Activity" defines economic activity as any activity—including entrepreneurial—related to the production and exchange of tangible and intangible goods (*Pro zovnishn'oekonomichnu diial'nist'* [On Foreign Economic Activity] 1991, art. 1).

Previously, in the now-repealed Commercial Code of Ukraine, economic activity was understood as the activity of business entities in the sphere of social production, aimed at the manufacture and sale of products, performance of work, or provision of services of a value nature that have price certainty (*Hospodars'kyi kodeks Ukrainy* [Commercial Code of Ukraine] 2003, art. 3).

The principle of freedom of entrepreneurial activity is an intersectoral principle that determines the legal regulation of relations involving entrepreneurs. The opportunity to engage in such activity is conditioned by the right to a free choice of occupation, which allows defining freedom of entrepreneurship as the free exercise of this activity and the option to undertake it or not (Basai 2014, 20).

Before the Commercial Code of Ukraine was invalidated, freedom of entrepreneurial activity was defined as a core principle of business, alongside several other pillars:

1. Economic Diversity: Ensuring economic diversity and equal protection by the state for all business entities.
2. Free Movement and Social Orientation: The free movement of capital, goods, and services throughout Ukraine, subject to state regulation necessary for social orientation, fair competition, environmental protection, consumer rights, and national security.
3. National Production: The protection of the national producer.
4. Non-Interference: The prohibition of illegal interference by state authorities and their officials in economic relations (*Hospodars'kyi kodeks Ukrainy* [Commercial Code of Ukraine] 2003, art. 3, para. 1).

This framework illustrates the transition from a state-controlled economy to a market-based system where "freedom" is balanced by the social responsibilities of the state.

The normative definition of entrepreneurial activity was also previously based on the concept of free will. Thus, in Article 42 of the now-repealed the Commercial Code of Ukraine, entrepreneurship was defined as an independent, initiative-driven, systematic, and at one's own risk economic activity carried out by business entities to achieve financial and social results and generate a profit (Ibid., art. 42).

Each of these features of entrepreneurial activity is also based on free will.

Independence is a state in which an entrepreneur can make unlimited decisions and independently carry out any activity that complies with current legislation. Guided by their own free will, entrepreneurs decide which activities to engage in and which decisions to make. The entirety of entrepreneurial activity is an implementation of the entrepreneur's free will. They independently determine prices, product ranges, suppliers, employees, and the form of taxation, among other factors. Even the type and content of contracts are chosen independently, based on the principle of freedom of contract.

Initiative is a logical continuation of the above. It is based on the manifestation of ingenuity and individual abilities in the process of activity, which is impossible without free will, because every decision made by an entrepreneur is a manifestation of their personal skills.

Systematicity refers to the constant, non-periodic, and long-term nature of economic activity, which reflects its professional nature and is defined as the exercise of the right to choose the type of activity. Systematicity allows us to distinguish entrepreneurial activity from a hobby. The decision to systematically engage in entrepreneurial activity is also a manifestation of free will, as it cannot be forced.

The risky nature of entrepreneurial activity implies the presence of two key elements: the potential for making a profit and the possibility of incurring losses. Obtaining a profit (income) is the purpose of the activity, as its results are sold for a fee in the market. Thus, entrepreneurial activity is a way of earning money at one's own risk. It is the set of decisions made independently by the entrepreneur, under the guidance of their own will, that leads to either profits or losses.

The final requirement is state registration as a business entity. If a person decides to start a business but does not register it as prescribed by law, this is done voluntarily, as a manifestation of their free will. Similarly, the decision to start a legal business must be a conscious, considered decision based on free will.

If we turn to the previous norms of the now-repealed Commercial Code, we can see that the above position was specified in the principles of entrepreneurship: (1) free choice of the type of entrepreneurial activity; (2) independent formation of the direction of activity, choice of suppliers and consumers, and attraction of resources; (3) free hiring of employees; (4) economic calculation and risk; (5) free disposal of profits; (6) independent implementation of foreign economic activity (Ibid., art. 44).

As we can see, the principle of freedom of entrepreneurial activity is based on the idea of free will, which is detailed by its characteristics and its own principles.

As noted by O. V. Basai, freedom of entrepreneurship is manifested in the freedom to dispose of one's abilities to work, in the freedom to choose a type of activity or profession, freedom from unfair competition and monopolistic activity, as well as in the general freedom to do everything that is not prohibited by law. At the same time, the exercise of entrepreneurs' rights is, on the one hand, ensured, and on the other, limited by the state, taking into account objective public interests (Basai 2014, 21). This definition is correct but requires clarification in view of the issues of free will.

Given the above, it is logical to define free will in entrepreneurial activity as the ability to engage in private activities aimed at making a profit, at one's own will, at one's own discretion, independently, proactively, systematically, and at one's own risk.

All the outlined principles and free will in general would have no meaning without the principle of judicial protection of civil rights and interests. This thesis is confirmed by M. V. Sydorenko, who concludes that judicial protection is the only principle of civil legislation that directly indicates the jurisdictional form of protection for the rights and interests of participants in civil relations and ensures the implementation of all other principles (Sydorenko 2012, 4).

Regardless of the circumstances, the court cannot deny justice if a citizen of Ukraine, a foreigner, or a stateless person believes that their rights and freedoms have been violated, obstacles have been created to their exercise, or there are other infringements (Koroied and Kryshtof 2015, 23). The opportunity to apply to court to protect rights and freedoms is guaranteed by the Constitution of Ukraine. According to the Decision of the Constitutional Court of Ukraine of May 23, 2001, No. 6-rp/2001, the right to judicial protection is one of the fundamental inalienable rights and freedoms (*Rishennia Konstytutsiinoho Sudu Ukrainy* [Decision of the Constitutional Court of Ukraine] 2001).

The possibility of applying to court is also provided for in the Civil Procedure Code of Ukraine as the right to seek protection, according to which every person has the right to apply to court for the protection of their violated, unrecognized, or disputed rights, freedoms, or interests (*Tsyvil'nyi protsesual'nyi kodeks Ukrainy* [Civil Procedure Code of Ukraine] 2004, art. 3).

The judicial protection of civil rights and interests is implemented through specific legal mechanisms. According to the Civil Code of Ukraine (*Tsyvil'nyi kodeks Ukrainy* [Civil Code of Ukraine] 2003, art. 16), the court may protect civil rights and interests by:

1. Recognition and Validity: Recognition of a right or recognition of a transaction as invalid.
2. Restoration and Performance: Termination of an action that violates a right, restoration of the situation existing before the violation, or forced performance of an obligation in kind.
3. Legal Relationships: Changing or terminating a legal relationship.
4. Damages and Compensation: Compensation for losses, property damage, or moral (non-property) damage.
5. Administrative Legality: Recognition of the decisions, actions, or inaction of a state or local government body as illegal.

Regarding the theoretical framework of these remedies, O. V. Zudykhin argues that the right to appeal for protection is inextricably linked with subjective substantive law in two primary respects: (1) it arises only upon a violation of a subjective right or when this right is challenged by others; and (2) the nature of the claim for protection is determined by the nature of the violated or challenged substantive right (Zudykhin 2011b, 74).

This underscores the vital connection between free will and judicial protection. When a subjective right rooted in free will is compromised—for instance, through unlawful state interference in entrepreneurial activity—the principle of judicial protection serves as the primary mechanism to preserve that will. Ultimately, the essence of preserving a right lies in removing obstacles to its exercise, thereby restoring the autonomy of the subject.

However, judicial protection is not the only way to ensure one's rights and interests, as legislation provides for the possibility of protection by the President of Ukraine, state authorities, a notary, and self-defense. When exercising these rights, free will manifests as the ability to independently decide how a person wants to protect—or not to protect at all—their rights and interests. A person's failure to exercise the right to protection is not a basis for terminating a violated civil right, except in cases established by law.

Therefore, free will is of great importance for the principle of judicial protection and is implemented in two ways:

1. When a subjective civil right based on free will is violated (i.e., an appeal to the court to protect the very manifestation of free will).
2. When a person, guided by free will, decides to protect or not protect their rights and interests, as well as when choosing the form of such protection.

The last of the explicitly enshrined principles of civil law is the principle of justice, good faith, and reasonableness. In European private law, this is traditionally recognized not as a set of three principles, but as a single principle (*Treu und Glauben* in German; *bona fides* in French), which is manifested in the unity of three interconnected components (Maydanyk 2012). In Ukraine, it is precisely the triad of these elements that forms a single enshrined principle. Moreover, Ukraine is the only post-Soviet state to have outlined this triad for regulating civil legal relations, recognising good faith as an internal criterion, and justice and reasonableness as external, objective measures of the quality of law (Maydanyk 2012).

The Civil Code of Ukraine does not define the concepts of good faith, justice, and reasonableness. Nonetheless, an analysis of its provisions (in particular, art. 12, para. 5; art. 13; and art. 23, para. 3) indicates that through these categories, the law establishes the limits for the exercise of civil rights, thereby preventing their abuse (Borysova et al. 2007, 73).

Let us consider the manifestation of free will in each element of this principle.

The principle of good faith enables the incorporation of moral and ethical considerations into civil law. According to the most widely held opinion, the category of good faith is determined by ethical and moral categories. At the same time, the inclusion of the so-called objective criterion of ignorance of specific facts in the category of good faith allows us to speak of its non-identity with the category of morality (Valihura 2020a, 12).

In modern academic doctrine, good faith is primarily understood as honest behavior, the honest conduct of affairs, business decency, and compliance with ethical standards accepted in society, as well as the actual honesty of a person. Academic agree that legislators traditionally use the concept of good faith to describe the boundaries of lawful behavior and, thus, to determine the limits of the possible exercise of civil rights (Kuzmenko 2023). Building on this thesis, it can be argued that the principle of good faith governs the conditions for the exercise of free will, which must be implemented in accordance with moral and legal norms. In their combination, free will and the principle of good faith create rules for participation in civil legal relations. That is, the principle of good faith stipulates that to enter into legal relations, one must be guided by the norms of legislation, without violating them, and the goal must align with the goal specified in the Civil Code.

For example, when parties conclude a gift agreement for real estate instead of a sale agreement to reduce the tax burden, they act in violation of the principle of good faith. The manifestation of free will here takes the form of a conscious decision to violate the law and conclude a fictitious transaction.

As an example of a violation of this principle, Yu. M. Aleksashina cites a case where one party finds an error in a contract sent by the other party that unconditionally changes the contract in their favor; it would be in good faith to notify the sender of such an error and redo the contract (Aleksashyna 2012). If this becomes known, the other party will be able to challenge such a transaction, referring to the conscious decision of the party who, guided by their own free will, decided not to report the error. However, proving the other party's knowledge of these circumstances will be difficult.

According to N. S. Kuznetsova, within the framework of an obligation, the principle of good faith is specified as a general obligation, which implies the need for: (1) each party to do everything that will mutually facilitate the fulfillment of the obligation and to avoid what may complicate it; (2) to avoid violating the rights of the other party; (3) to genuinely do everything necessary together to fulfill the terms of the contract; (4) to provide the necessary information on the implementation of initial actions (Kuznietsova 2003, 13).

The principle of good faith creates a prohibition on unfair relations between parties, even if they have agreed to them and included them in the contract. Confirmation of this can be found in the Resolution of the Supreme Economic Court of Ukraine No. 5021/1197/2011, which recognized as unfair the terms of a contract for legal services that stipulated a monthly payment of UAH 30,000—regardless of whether services were provided—as the agreement did not specify the volume or frequency of these services at all. The court found this could serve as a tool for implementing a fictitious bankruptcy procedure (*Postanova Vyshchoho hospodars'koho sudu Ukrainy* [Resolution of the Supreme Economic Court of Ukraine] 2012).

Separately, the requirements of good faith are specified in Council Directive 93/13/EEC of April 5, 1993, on unfair terms in consumer contracts. A contract term that was not individually negotiated is recognized as unfair if, in violation of the requirement of good faith, it causes a significant imbalance in the parties' rights and obligations to the detriment of the consumer. If a term is recognized as unfair, it does not create rights or obligations for the consumer and is invalid, while the contract remains valid without the unfair term (Council Directive 93/13/EEC 1993). The legal consequence will be the possibility of challenging the contract clause in court.

Good faith as a condition of civil relations is fully disclosed in the German Civil Code. Any legal act that contradicts accepted standards of good conduct is recognized as invalid in Germany, as is any act by which a person takes advantage of the need, weakness, or inexperience of another to force them to promise or agree to provide property interests that significantly exceed the value of what is offered (*Bürgerliches Gesetzbuch* [German Civil Code] 1896, § 138). Section 242 of the German Civil Code establishes the obligation to perform contracts in good faith. The interpretation of a contract must also be carried out taking into account good faith (*Bürgerliches Gesetzbuch* [German Civil Code] 1896, § 157). Similar norms can be seen in the Civil Code of Ukraine.

On the one hand, good faith is an obligation, the violation of which allows for the challenge of a transaction; on the other, it can be considered a mistake. Some scholars suggest understanding good faith in the subjective sense as an innocent mistake by the subject regarding the illegality of their behavior. In contrast, bad faith is understood as knowledge of their illegality, as well as inexcusable ignorance of it (Basai 2014, 22). In an objective sense, good faith reflects the idea of morality and is aimed at ensuring the balance of private interests between the parties (Basai 2014, 22).

Free will manifests itself in this principle in two ways. The first is when a party or parties knowingly observe or violate this principle. The second is when someone unknowingly makes a mistake that violates good faith. In practice, regardless of the circumstances, a violation of the doctrine of good faith is grounds for challenging the transaction. However, proof of an intentional breach can affect the scope of civil liability and compensation.

Free will, in the principle of good faith, is the need for a conscious and free choice of conscientious and honest behavior by participants in legal relations when performing their duties and exercising their subjective rights.

The concept of justice is very multifaceted, but it is not defined in the Civil Code of Ukraine.

The *Cambridge Dictionary* defines justice as the system of laws in a country that governs the judicial process and determines punishments, as well as the condition of being morally right ("Justice" 2015).

The *Oxford English Dictionary* defines justice as upholding what is right through the exercise of authority and the imposition of deserved rewards or punishments ("Justice" 2014).

Yu. A. Tobota has generalized the doctrinal understanding of the principle of justice in civil law, identifying four primary variants of its interpretation:

1. Normative Adequacy: The definition of the scope and limits of the exercise and protection of civil rights and interests in a manner adequate to an individual's compliance with legal requirements.
2. Moral and Ethical Compliance: The alignment of a subject's behavior with the dominant moral and ethical norms within society.
3. Evaluative Normative Comparison: An evaluative concept manifested through the comparison between a specific action and its resulting legal consequence.
4. Proportionality and Balance: The concept of equality of proportions, focusing on the proportionality of chosen legal means to the intended goal (Tobota 2020, 43).

This multifaceted approach demonstrates that justice in civil law is not a static rule but a dynamic instrument that balances individual behavior with social ethics and legal consequences.

In conclusion, we can agree that justice in civil law is a property determined by the good faith and reasonableness of participants, which determines the nature of the relationship between them or the correlation of certain phenomena within civil law (in particular, rights and obligations) and is associated with the possibility of applying civil liability measures proportional to the nature of the offense committed (Tobota 2020, 51).

In civil law, justice is embedded in its norms. The provisions of such norms describe actions recognized as unlawful according to society's moral standards, and the sanctions provide for civil liability for their commission (Basai 2018, 92). Free will is the basis for the principle of justice because it serves as a measure for understanding the legal nature of the behavior of participants in legal relations. It is free will that allows us to determine the presence of intent and negligence, awareness, and the level of understanding when making decisions. The principle of justice is based on how the parties, exercising their free will, dispose of their subjective rights and fulfill their obligations. Applying the principle of justice, we must necessarily find out whether free will was exercised or if there was a mistake or other factors that limited it.

Reasonableness as a principle of civil law is based on the idea that reasonable actions should be understood as actions that a person with a standard, average level of intelligence, knowledge, and life experience would perform (Aleksashyna 2012, 91). The principle of reasonableness performs an interpretative, supplementary, and corrective function in private law, because interpreting, supplementing, and correcting legal norms is possible only where it is permitted, where the norms are dispositive (Otradnova 2009b, 370).

The principle of reasonableness is applied in two forms: as a mandatory element for all legal relations and as a way of regulating specific situations. These forms lack a clear, normative definition. In the absence of clearly prescribed obligations to act or refrain from acting, the legality of a person's behavior should be based on the concept of reasonableness – the actions of a normal, average person in a specific situation (Otradnova 2009a). Thus, the Civil Code of Ukraine contains norms that directly address the application of this principle.

Article 12 of the Civil Code of Ukraine states that if the law establishes the legal consequences of an individual's unconscionable or unreasonable exercise of their right, it is presumed that the individual's behavior is in good faith and reasonable, unless otherwise established by the court (*Tsyvil'nyi kodeks Ukrainy* [Civil Code of Ukraine] 2003, art. 12).

Article 23 of the Civil Code of Ukraine states that, when determining the amount of compensation, the court must proceed from what monetary compensation would be necessary for an average person to compensate for their moral damage in a specific situation (Ibid., art. 23).

Article 122 of the Civil Code of Ukraine stipulates that in the event of a dispute between participants in a general partnership, the authority to manage the affairs of the partnership granted to one or more participants may be terminated by the court at the request of other participants if there are sufficient grounds, in particular as a result of a gross violation by an authorised participant of their duties or the discovery of their inability to manage affairs reasonably (Ibid., art. 122).

Article 1193 of the Civil Code of Ukraine stipulates the application of the principle of reasonableness when the court decides to reduce the amount of compensation for damage caused, taking into account the financial condition of the individual who caused it (Ibid., art. 1193).

Article 846 of the Civil Code of Ukraine refers to reasonable terms: where the contract does not establish terms for the performance of work, the contractor is obliged to perform the work, and the customer has the right to demand its performance within reasonable terms, in accordance with the essence of the obligation, the nature and volume of work, and business customs (Ibid., art. 846).

Article 1232 of the Civil Code of Ukraine states that heirs are obliged to reimburse reasonable expenses incurred by one of them or another person for the maintenance, care, treatment, and burial of the testator (Ibid., art. 1232).

There are other examples, but as we can see, the principle of reasonableness involves taking actions conditioned by the standard, established perception of a particular situation. In this context, free will is recognized as a fundamental condition for the application of this principle.

The legislation provides for a presumption of reasonableness regarding the actions of a participant in a legal relationship; therefore, we must assume that any actions proceed from this principle. At the same time, the boundaries and grounds for determining reasonableness are not defined by regulations, which complicates the process of qualifying a subject's behavior.

In civil law, the concepts of "reasonable term" and "reasonable fee" are essential for balancing the interests of parties. As S. Rusu and M. Stefanchuk note, the court should be guided by several key criteria when interpreting these categories:

1. Determination of a Reasonable Fee: The court should base its assessment on an amount that approximately corresponds to the market value of a similar product or service.
2. Establishment of a Reasonable Term: This should be based on the period necessary to perform specific actions under ordinary conditions, considering the standard practice in the relevant field.
3. Economic and Technical Indicators:
   For reasonable price: It is necessary to take into account cost price, normal income, and other relevant financial indicators.
   For reasonable term: Consideration must be given to technological processes and the time required for logistics, production, or the provision of services (Rusu and Stefanchuk 2003, 55).

This objective approach to reasonableness ensures that legal obligations are performed in a manner that is both economically viable and practically feasible, preventing arbitrary interpretations of contractual terms.

Let's consider an example. The parties have concluded a contract for services that must be provided within a reasonable time. To determine this, we need to know how long it usually takes to deliver such services. Only a violation of the maximum time will be considered unreasonable. That is, if a specific hairdressing service is typically provided in 2 hours, then providing it in 5 hours will be regarded as an unreasonable time. However, such frames are purely subjective, as it is unclear how to draw the line of reasonableness when the service is provided in 2 hours and 20 minutes or 4 hours and 5 minutes. The ability to clearly determine the moment of violation is subjective.

Taking this into account, one can trace the manifestation of free will in this principle. Thus, a party, guided by the principle of reasonableness and free will, independently determines the limits of reasonableness. Let us consider a contract of carriage. The carrier can provide a service in 1 hour, or they can drive slowly and provide the same service in 3 hours. This will depend on their decision and the totality of their actions, which serve as a manifestation of their free will.

It should be agreed that the principle of reasonableness is more fully understood in the Anglo-Saxon legal system. This is due to the possibility of using judicial precedent to demonstrate the performance of similar duties in other cases, which allows for the justification of reasonableness.

Simply put, the principle of reasonableness allows us to consider specific legal relations through the prism of stability and "normality" for similar cases. Since the principle is subjective in nature, free will within it allows for a more adequate qualification of a specific case, particularly through understanding the presence or absence of intent.

At the same time, we should consider this principle as an element of the triad of justice, good faith, and reasonableness.

As we can see from the analysis, free will is manifested in all principles of civil law. It serves as a basis without which their application is impossible. However, the list of principles in Article 3 of the Civil Code of Ukraine is not exhaustive, and an analysis of other norms reveals additional tenets of civil law that are also based on free will.

Article 1 of the Civil Code of Ukraine enshrines the principles of legal equality, free expression of will, and property independence of participants in civil relations.

The principle of legal equality is based on the idea that participants in civil legal relations have the same opportunity to have rights and obligations, and their relationship is horizontal, not vertical. No subject has an advantage over another, and one manifestation of this is that the same legal norms apply to relations between individuals and between legal entities, the state, etc. At the same time, the legislation provides exceptions, specifically imposing stricter requirements on professional participants in civil transactions and granting additional rights to consumers (Holubieva 2007, 283).

This principle ensures the same level of free will for participants in civil legal relations. From this, it can be concluded that the parties have the same opportunities to exercise their free will, which may be equally limited by their legal status or by separate legislative norms. Thus, the level of free will of one minor is recognized as equal to that of all other minors. At the same time, the opportunities for the exercise of a minor's free will will be less than those of an adult. Similarly, the presence of a special legal status expands the opportunities for exercising free will.

For example, a person performs a therapeutic massage for which they receive monetary compensation. This will be a manifestation of free will in the form of concluding a corresponding contract for services. If the person has the special legal status of a doctor, such actions will be considered the provision of medical services. If the person is not a doctor, the actions should be regarded as non-medical services. In both cases, performing the massage will be a manifestation of free will.

Another example is when a person performs a surgical intervention. Carrying it out as a manifestation of free will by a person who is not a doctor will be an illegal medical activity. Performing the same actions by a doctor will be the provision of medical services. Thus, the presence of a special status expands the possibilities for the legal manifestation of free will.

Therefore, the principle of equality in civil law provides for the same level of free will for participants with the same legal status, as well as an equal opportunity to change their legal status, thereby expanding the possibilities for the lawful manifestation of their free will.

The principle of free expression of will is an absolute manifestation of free will. Within the practice of jurisprudence, the free expression of will is characterized by the following features:

1. External Manifestation: It is a normatively prescribed external manifestation of the will of capable subjects, which creates legal consequences.
2. Status as a Legal Fact: It is a type of legal fact and can take the form of either lawful or unlawful actions.
3. Modality of Action: It can be carried out through active behavior or inaction (silence).
4. Methods of Expression: Legal significance can be attributed not only to direct expression of will but also to indirect (conclusive) expression.
5. Qualitative Requirements: The expression of will must be conscious, free, genuine, and adhere to a particular prescribed form (Volkova and Okhota 2017).

This distinction ensures that the law protects not just the abstract "thought" of a person, but the specific, objective manifestation of that thought that interacts with the rights of others and the legal order.

The fact that the expression of will must be conscious, free (unforced), and genuine is a direct extension of the idea of free will as the basis of the principles of civil law.

Free expression of will is essential for the exercise of absolute rights, in contract law, and for the institution of civil liability; therefore, its connection with free will will be explored in more detail below.

The principle of property independence of participants in personal non-property and property relations is also based on free will. This principle allows individuals to own, use, and dispose of their property at their own discretion and maintains the separation of one person's property from another's, thereby upholding the principle of the inviolability of private property.

The principle of property independence is implemented through participation in property relations that arise regarding the ownership or use of property—tangible and intangible goods that have the economic form of a commodity. Civil law regulates only that part of property relations based on the legal equality of participants, autonomy of will, their property independence, and which have a property-value character, involving mutual assessment by participants of the quantity and quality of labour for the material good (Belo 2019, 91).

The connection of free will with this principle is the same as with the principle of the inviolability of private property. Therefore, it should only be noted that the implementation of the principle of property independence can be considered legitimate only when it is based on free will.

Some scholars also identify other principles of civil law, such as the principle of dispositivity (Chubokha 2013, 299) and the stability of civil relations (Shyshka 2004, 96), among others.

In conclusion, it should be noted that civil legislation proclaims the inviolability of the free will of a participant in civil legal relations, which is clearly reflected in the principles of civil law. Free will is manifested in all principles of civil law, without which their implementation becomes impossible. Free will is manifested when applying the principle of inadmissibility of arbitrary interference in a person's private life. On the one hand, this principle proclaims the protection of free will as it is applied in the private sphere. On the other hand, this principle limits the free will of other participants by prohibiting arbitrary interference. The relationship between free will and the principle of inadmissibility of deprivation of property rights should be understood through the triad of possession, use, and disposal. Good faith possession arises as a manifestation of free will, in the context that a person consciously enters into legal relations and their will is directed to the lawful acquisition of rights, not to the acquisition of a thing from a non-owner, which they did not know and should not have known. In the case of use, free will will have the same manifestation as in possession, depending on whether the use is lawful or not. Disposal occurs as a manifestation of free will because only the owner has the right to choose the legal fate of the property.

Exceptions are cases of forced alienation as a sanction for a criminal offense or under exceptional circumstances. Free will in the principle of freedom of contract acts as a mechanism through which the parties enter into contractual relations and create new rights and obligations. At the same time, free will in this principle acts as a mandatory criterion for recognising the legality of the contract. The principle of freedom of entrepreneurial activity is based on the idea of free will, which is detailed by its features and its own principles. Free will is the basis for the principle of judicial protection.

It is implemented in two formats: (1) when a subjective civil right based on free will is violated (i.e., an appeal to court to protect the manifestation of free will itself); (2) when a person, guided by free will, decides to protect or not protect their rights and interests, and chooses the form of such protection.

Free will, in the principle of good faith, requires conscious, free, conscientious, and honest behavior from participants in legal relations. Free will is the basis for the principle of justice because it serves as a measure for understanding the legal nature of participants' behavior. It is free will that allows us to determine the presence of intent and negligence, awareness, and the level of understanding when making decisions. The principle of equality ensures that participants with the same legal status are afforded the same level of free will, as well as an equal opportunity to change their legal status, thereby expanding the possibilities for the lawful manifestation of their free will. The principle of free expression of will is an absolute manifestation of free will because it must be conscious, free, and genuine, which makes it a direct continuation of the idea of free will as the basis of the principles of civil law.

Conclusions

1. The understanding of free will has evolved from Antiquity to the present day, ultimately finding its reflection in legal norms. In Antiquity, free will was inextricably linked to fate. The Middle Ages produced several concepts—all closely tied to divinity—which gave rise to the Augustinian dilemma of recognizing free will versus complete submission to the will of God. The Reformation emphasized a fatalism that precluded free will,

whereas the Renaissance stressed the autonomy of the human will alongside the divine. The modern understanding of free will is based on the ideas of natural law but is also reflected in positive law through the principles and norms enshrined in civil legislation.

2. External factors—such as positive law—cannot limit the internal component of free will, as only one's own reason is its measure. This becomes especially relevant in civil law: although legislation mandates a written form for real estate sales contracts, parties, aware of this, may consciously conclude the agreement orally. In this case, the external influence of the law could not compel compliance with its norms. Free will gave the parties the ability to consciously violate the standards of civil law. Conversely, when parties comply with regulatory requirements, they also do so at their own discretion and by their own decision.
3. The academic understanding of freedom in civil law is often reduced to its recognition as the ability to make decisions without dependence on external factors. However, we believe that a complete absence of external influence on the will of participants in civil legal relations is impossible. Such relations necessarily involve the negotiation of contract terms and the exercise of rights only within the limits determined by law or by the parties' agreement.
4. Civil law and free will are inextricably linked and form a vector for each other's development. The concept of free will and the need for its external expression form a set of ideas that determine the general direction of civil law's development—which, in turn, defines the boundaries of free will and the conditions for its implementation.
5. Free will is the basis for all civil legal relations (regardless of whether its manifestation is necessary for all participants), determines the freedom to participate in those relations and to independently define their content, and performs the function of autonomy for the subject of law.
6. The legal idea of free will in civil law is a part of its legal ideology. It reflects a person's ability to consciously, freely, and in-

dependently make and implement decisions regarding participation in civil legal relations—through actions or inaction, the exercise of subjective rights, and the fulfilllment of obligations—as well as the ability to bear legal responsibility for them. It serves as the foundation for the formation of civil law, its principles, and its institutions.

7. The natural law nature of free will in civil law suggests the possibility of its existence beyond normative reflection in legal principles, in the form of a prototype of the legal state of freedom. This provides grounds to argue for the existence of free will regardless of its formal enshrinement. However, after undergoing normative reflection, free will finds its place within the principles and institutions of civil law, within the framework of legal positivism.
8. Free will is manifested in the application of the principle of inadmissibility of arbitrary interference in a person's private life. The essence of this principle involves the protection of free will as a component of a protected subjective right exercised in the private sphere. On the other hand, this principle limits the free will of other participants by prohibiting arbitrary interference; directing one's own will to carry out such interference is unlawful.
9. The relationship between free will and the principle of inadmissibility of deprivation of property rights should be understood, in particular, through the prohibition of restrictive influence on the powers of the property owner. Even in the case of arbitrary deprivation of the right to possession, use, or disposal, there is an unlawful restriction on the owner's ability to exercise their free will, because making it impossible to exercise even one of the elements of property rights leads to the frustration of that right.
10. In the principle of freedom of contract, free will determines the ability of the parties to enter into contractual relations and to create new rights and obligations. Regardless of its internal (will) or external form (expression of will), free will in this principle is a mandatory condition for recognizing the legality of a contract. Its conclusion under the influence of mistake, duress,

or other such factors is grounds for declaring the transaction invalid.

11. Free will within the principle of freedom of entrepreneurial activity determines the ability to engage in private activities aimed at making a profit at one's own discretion, independently, proactively, systematically, and at one's own risk. The principle of freedom of entrepreneurial activity is based on the idea of free will and is detailed by the features and principles that characterize it.
12. Free will within the principle of judicial protection of civil rights and interests is realized in two forms: (1) when a subjective civil right based on free will is violated, prompting an appeal to the court to protect the very manifestation of free will; and (2) when a person, guided by free will, decides whether to protect their rights and interests, and chooses the form of such protection.
13. Free will within the principle of good faith is the necessity for a conscious and free choice of conscientious and honest behavior by participants in legal relations when performing duties and exercising subjective rights.
14. Free will within the principle of justice serves as a measure for understanding the legal nature of the behavior of participants in legal relations. It is free will that makes it possible to determine the presence of intent or negligence, awareness, and the level of information when making decisions. The principle of justice is based on how the parties, exercising their free will, use their subjective rights and fulfilll their obligations. When applying the principle of justice, we must determine whether free will (in both its internal and external forms) was properly exercised or whether there was a mistake or other vitiating factors.
15. Due to the subjective nature of the principle of reasonableness, free will allows for a more adequate qualification of a specific case, particularly through an understanding of the presence or absence of intent. The principle of reasonableness allows us to consider specific legal relations through the prism of established norms and "normality" in the absence of sufficient legal regulation, for instance, when determining a reasonable time,

reducing the amount of compensation for damages, or in cases of inability to reasonably conduct business affairs.

16. The principle of legal equality provides for the same scope of free will for participants in civil legal relations who have the same opportunities for its implementation in accordance with their legal status (general, special, or individual). For example, a doctor has a special legal status that endows them with special rights, providing additional ways to exercise their free will. A patient also has a special legal status, but the scope of their free will and the methods of its implementation differ from those of the doctor due to their different rights. Thus, the scope of free will and the methods of its implementation may differ for participants with different legal statuses, which does not contradict the principle of legal equality.
17. The principle of free expression of will, on which civil relations are based, is an absolute manifestation of free will, because the expression of will must be conscious, free (unforced), and genuine, which is a direct embodiment of the idea of free will in civil law.
18. The implementation of the principle of property independence can be considered legitimate only when it is based on free will. This principle provides for the ability to own, use, and dispose of one's property at one's own discretion and proclaims the separation of one person's property from another's, continuing the ideas of the principle of the inviolability of private property.

2. Free Will in Personal Non-Property Rights of a Natural Person

2.1. The Role of Free Will in Personal Non-Property Rights that Ensure the Natural Existence of an Individual

As has been demonstrated, free will is the basis of the principles of civil law. The principles outlined in the previous chapter lay the foundation for civil legal relations, which cannot exist without the institution of personal non-property rights. This institution is the embodiment of free will, as it is based on the ability to freely determine one's behavior in the sphere of private life at one's own discretion (*Tsyvil'nyi kodeks Ukrainy* [Civil Code of Ukraine] 2003, art. 271). Therefore, for a comprehensive study of free will in civil law, it is necessary to identify its connection with absolute rights. To do this, we must establish the concept of absolute rights, identify the role of free will in the personal non-property rights that ensure an individual's natural existence and are possessed for life, and outline the meaning of free will in the personal non-property rights that ensure an individual's social existence.

One of the controversial issues in civil law is the differentiation between absolute rights and personal non-property rights, which are not identical concepts. Their precise distinction is not defined by legislation or legal doctrine.

Absolute rights are subjective rights where the right-holder is opposed by an indefinite and unlimited number of obligated persons. The obligation consists of refraining from actions that violate these absolute rights. Such rights are the basis of any democratic state under the rule of law and are recognized as inviolable and protected by law ("*Absoliutni prava*" [Absolute Rights] 2019). They are rights of a subject against which any other person is always obliged to refrain from infringing actions; they are fundamentally inviolable, and the law protects them against an unspecified circle of persons ("*Absoliutni prava*" [Absolute Rights] 2007).

If we proceed from the literal interpretation of the word "absolute" (from Latin *absolutus* - unconditional, complete, perfect, non-relative, unlimited), then absolute rights can indeed be defined as those that are unlimited, unchangeable, and unconditional (Slipchenko 2014, 68). Therefore, understanding absolute rights comes down to outlining their characteristic features, such as autonomy (independence from the will of other subjects), naturalness, and inviolability. Scholars propose considering absolute rights through two competing concepts: the "legal connection of a person with an object" and the "legal connection of persons in relation to an object." In the science of civil law, attempts are also made to reconcile these two opposing theories (Slipchenko 2014, 70).

Personal non-property rights are very close to the concept of absolute rights, as, at first glance, they are based on the same characteristics. However, they should not be conflated.

A personal non-property right is an absolute subjective right that belongs to every individual, is inseparable and inalienable from them, has no economic content, serves to individualise the person, arises at birth, and is held for life (Fediuk 2006, 7).

Both absolute and personal non-property rights are equally based on free will, but based on the definitions provided, their distinction is ambiguous. Today, two doctrinal approaches can be identified: (1) personal non-property legal relations represent an independent branch of absolute rights, alongside property and exclusive rights (Fediuk 2006, 7); (2) personal non-property legal relations are included in the group of exclusive legal relations and are a type of absolute right (Horyslavskyi 2003, 101).

As S. O. Slipchenko notes, such uncertainty is not acceptable because, unlike other issues related to legal relations, their classification has both theoretical and practical significance. The proper qualification of a specific type of legal relationship allows for the extension of the features of that category to it, a deeper understanding of its essence, the application of adequate legal constructions, the establishment of a proper place for the relevant norms, and their placement within certain civil law institutions (Slipchenko 2013, 9).

This issue is also a subject of controversy in foreign studies. In particular, it has been addressed by F. S. Kieff, A. Gewirth, M. W.

McConnell, R. B. Powell, J. L. Sax, and others. In general, it should be concluded that absolute rights form a separate category that includes property rights and personal non-property rights. Property rights are based on the principle of the inviolability of private property, which, as proven above, is founded on free will. Property rights are also closely related to personal non-property rights, particularly the right to the inviolability of one's home.

Absolute rights are based on the idea of a wide range of obligated persons who have a general duty to refrain from violating these rights. Personal non-property rights are a component of absolute rights. That is, they are specifically defined natural human rights to which a general duty of "inviolability" corresponds. Absolute rights are contrasted with relative rights, in which the right-holder is opposed by one or more specifically defined obligated persons. Traditionally, relative rights arise from the law of obligations; therefore, special attention will be paid to their connection with free will in the third chapter of this research.

Concluding this discourse, it is essential to consider the doctrinal distinction provided by I. O. Michurin, who clarifies the relationship between absolute and relative rights:

1. Doctrinal Definition: The scope of absolute rights is not clearly defined today, as the division of civil rights into absolute and relative remains more a matter of doctrine than a fixed categorization in civil legislation.
2. Breadth of Absolute Rights: Absolute rights are not limited to property; they encompass intellectual property rights, the right to a name, and other personal attributes.
3. Relativity in Personal Rights: Not all personal non-property rights are absolute. For instance, in family law, parental rights are considered relative, and relative civil rights extend beyond the law of obligations (Michurin 2018, 84).

The evidence suggests that absolute and personal non-property rights are not identical. While some personal non-property rights are absolute in nature, absolute rights can, in turn, encompass various personal non-property dimensions.

Having established the distinction between absolute and personal non-property rights, let us focus on the latter's connection with free will.

Having established this distinction, we turn to the connection between personal non-property rights and free will. These rights are fundamentally divided into two groups based on the human needs they satisfy (Chornoochenko 2000, 2):

1. Rights Ensuring Natural Existence
   These rights are inherent to the physical and biological essence of a human being:
   a. The right to life and health protection;
   b. The right to a safe environment;
   c. Freedom and personal inviolability.
2. Rights Ensuring Social Existence
   These rights facilitate the individual's interaction within society and the protection of their autonomy:
   a. Inviolability of personal and family life, including the secrecy of correspondence and other communications;
   b. Respect for dignity and honor;
   c. Inviolability of housing;
   d. Free choice of residence, freedom of movement, and freedom of creative activity (*Tsyvil'nyi kodeks Ukrainy* [Civil Code of Ukraine] 2003, art. 270).

The first category reveals the content of rights that ensure the natural existence of an individual. These include the right to life, to the elimination of dangers threatening life and health, to health care, to medical care, to information about one's health, to confidentiality about one's health, the rights of a person receiving inpatient treatment, the right to liberty, personal integrity, donation, family, guardianship or care, and to a safe environment. Each of these rights is based on free will, which will be demonstrated below by illustrating its role in each of them.

Personal non-property rights that ensure the natural existence of an individual are a set of powers naturally belonging to that person to own, use, and dispose of intangible goods. These rights are absolute in nature, determine a person's existence in the world (both biological and social), and do not require the person to be aware of the causal link between the properties of the good and the possibility of using it to satisfy their needs (Lisnicha 2007, 5).

Logically, all human rights would be meaningless without the right to life. Moreover, the emergence of free will is associated with the emergence of this right.

Article 3 of the Constitution of Ukraine declares that human life and health, honor and dignity, inviolability and security are recognized as the highest social values. The enshrinement of this norm at the heart of constitutional rights creates a vector according to which all legislation and civil legal relations declare the protection of the right to life.

The first international documents to recognize the right to life were the Universal Declaration of Human Rights and the European Convention for the Protection of Human Rights and Fundamental Freedoms, in which Article 2 states that everyone's right to life shall be protected by law and that no one shall be deprived of his life arbitrarily. However, these instruments define the right to life in a generalised form, and the relevant provisions are recognized as customary norms of international law that all states must adhere to; they are peremptory norms from which no derogation is permitted (Miroshnychenko 2005, 9).

Although the right to life is of fundamental importance, as reflected in both international and national law, it is not absolute. E. Wicks concludes that the right to life is shaped by two primary considerations:

1. Qualified Protection: The right to life is highly qualified, as its protection is subject to specific exceptions. These include the lawful use of the death penalty (where applicable) and the use of lethal force by state agents, provided such actions are both necessary and proportionate.
2. Limitations on Positive Obligations: Despite the increasing recognition of positive obligations under the right to life, any such obligations are subject to an implicit limitation of what is reasonable in the circumstances (Wicks 2012).

This interpretation suggests that the legal protection of life operates within a framework of necessity and reasonableness, balancing individual sanctity with the pragmatic requirements of state action and social order.

The right to life is a person's freedom to directly realise the opportunities they have as a member of the species *Homo sapiens* and to satisfy the essential biological, social, spiritual, and economic needs that are inseparable from the person, objectively determined by the level of human development, and which must be universal (Rohova 2006, 4).

There are three concepts regarding the emergence of the right to life: from the moment of birth, from the moment of conception, and in correlation with different stages of intrauterine development.

According to the Order of the Ministry of Health of Ukraine, a live birth is defined as the expulsion or extraction of a fetus from the mother's body which, after separation, breathes or shows any other signs of life—irrespective of the duration of the pregnancy.

A newborn is considered live-born if it exhibits at least one of the following signs: (1) Breathing; (2) Heartbeat; (3) Pulsation of the umbilical cord; (4)cDefinite movement of voluntary (skeletal) muscles (*Pro zatverdzhennia Instruktsii...* [On the Approval of the Instruction...] 2006, para. 1.2).

Furthermore, a newborn is specifically defined as a live-born child delivered after the 22nd week of pregnancy (Ibid., para. 2.5). These criteria are essential for establishing the legal status of a person and the subsequent protection of their rights, beginning from the moment of birth.

This approach is recognized as the only correct one from a legal standpoint because the right to life can only arise in a person who actually exists.

In this context, the question of the moment of the emergence of free will arises. If we associate it with conscious actions, the possibility of a newborn performing such actions is doubtful. The law does not enshrine a "right to free will"; it is outlined only as a requirement and an element of other rights or as a principle within other principles and legal relations. The logical conclusion is that free will emerges at birth, but its scope evolves with the development of an individual's capabilities. This approach allows us to compare the scope of free will with that of civil capacity. However, even within a specific level of capacity, the scope of free will can change. For example, a person is legally a minor from birth to age 14 and can participate in civil relations only within the limits of their capacity. During this time, their legal status remains unchanged, but their level of free will increases.

We could find confirmation of this in national legislation: (1) a minor has the right to independently perform minor household transactions that satisfy their everyday needs and correspond to their development; (2) a minor has the right to exercise personal non-property rights to the results of their intellectual and creative activity (*Tsyvil'nyi kodeks Ukrainy* [Civil Code of Ukraine] 2003, art. 31).

The ability to perform minor household transactions is directly related to the level of autonomy of will; the more mature and developed a person is, the greater the range of transactions they can participate in.

A newborn child cannot voluntarily participate in such transactions but is endowed with legal capacity. Guided by their own free will, a minor can exercise personal non-property rights to the results of their creative activity. For example, when a minor consciously says "goo goo" or draws a line on paper, one can raise the question of intellectual and creative activity. This is confirmed by the norm that the civil legal capacity of an individual arises at the moment of birth. Additionally, a minor can exercise their free will through legal representatives. When a child asks their parents to buy a toy, they do so as a manifestation of their free will. In turn, the parents, exercising their own free will, enter into a purchase and sale agreement in the interests of the minor. Another example is when a minor participates in a competition and wins a prize. In this case, through the manifestation of their own free will, the child becomes the owner of the property, creating new rights and obligations for themself.

It is logical to conclude that an individual's free will arises from the moment of birth, and its scope changes throughout life. It can increase due to intellectual development and changes in legal capacity and status, and decrease if legal capacity is limited, status changes, or a person is declared incapacitated.

At the same time, other concepts regarding the origin of the right to life exist. In particular, the idea that this right originates at the moment of conception is equated with the beginning of human life—religious culture is the primary supporter of this approach. However, even religious positions can be ambiguous. For example, *the Book of Genesis* states that God "breathed into his nostrils the breath of life" (*The Book of Genesis 2001*, 2:7). D. Novak considers this a convincing biblical argument for the position that only God can take a human life, since only God directly gave it (Novak 2007, 124). However, this verse can also be interpreted as supporting the view that the right to life arises at birth.

According to *Anatomy and Physiology* (Biga 2025, 1316), fetal development involves breathing movements, yet the fetus remains entirely dependent on the mother for gas exchange via the placenta. Prior to birth, the lungs are not functional for oxygen intake but are filled with fluid that must be expelled or absorbed (Biga 2025, 1318). The critical physiological milestone is the first breath, which inflates the lungs and begins independent life. Consequently, the thesis stated in *the Book of Genesis* must apply to a newborn child who begins to breathe on his own. The specific imagery of "breathing the breath of life into his nostrils" dictates a post-natal context, as this mechanism of receiving oxygen is impossible in utero where oxygenation occurs via the blood, not the airways. This distinction indirectly confirms the ambiguity of the religious concept by grounding it in the observable shift from placental reliance to independent breath.

At the same time, one can agree with B. V. Ostrovskaya that the beginning of a person's life *de jure* does not coincide with the beginning of their life *de facto*, which is a fatal error. A person as a biological being begins life (as an embryo) in the mother's womb from both a medical and a moral-ethical perspective. The fact of birth merely confirms their appearance in society but does not mark the beginning of their life (Ostrovska 2016, 143).

The first editions of the WMA Declaration on Therapeutic Abortion also emphasised respect for human life from the moment of conception (Declaration of Oslo on Therapeutic Abortion 1970, para 1).

However, in 2006, the Declaration was amended, and the first paragraph was revised to state: "The WMA requires the physician to have respect for human life" (Declaration of Oslo on Therapeutic Abortion 2006, para 1).

This updated version resolved the ethical-religious debate. However, some legal acts contain provisions that partially confirm the emergence of certain rights from conception. An example is the ability of a person conceived during the testator's lifetime to be an heir (*Tsyvil'nyi kodeks Ukrainy* [Civil Code of Ukraine] 2003, art. 1222). However, it is important to note that a live birth must occur for this right to be exercised, as this legal fact creates the real opportunity to participate in legal relations.

The third concept of the emergence of the right to life is associated with different stages of intrauterine development. Supporting this idea are medical criteria according to which even individuals born prematurely with a very low body weight are considered viable.

The preamble to the Declaration of the Rights of the Child states:

> The child, by reason of his physical and mental immaturity, needs special safeguards and care—including appropriate legal protection—before as well as after birthю (United Nations General Assembly 1959.

The obligation of such protection is associated with the first heartbeat at the 4th week of pregnancy, the registration of electrophysiological brain activity at the 6th week, reaction to pain stimuli, and so on. However, one cannot speak of conscious volitional actions of an unborn child as a manifestation of free will. While one can speak of certain conscious intrauterine movements, such a "child" cannot actually participate in civil legal relations; therefore, from the standpoint of civil law, they do not possess free will.Concluding this discourse, it should be stated that from a legal perspective, the right to life and free will arise only from the moment of birth.

As O. Kokhanovska notes, traditionally, the right to life was understood as the right to preserve life and was interpreted primarily as a rejection of war, the death penalty, and the establishment of rules for the use of weapons (Kokhanovska 2011, 7).

Free will can be manifested in the right to life through three of its aspects: (1) no one can be arbitrarily deprived of life; (2) the state has a duty to protect human life; (3) everyone has the right to protect their own life and health and that of others from unlawful encroachments.

First of all, free will is manifested in the prohibition of arbitrary deprivation of life. According to Article 6 of the International Covenant on Civil and Political Rights, this right is not absolute, as in certain cases defined by law, the deliberate termination of human life is permitted (International Covenant on Civil and Political Rights 1966, art. 6).

The right to life is also enshrined in the Universal Declaration of Human Rights: "Everyone has the right to life, liberty and security of person" (Universal Declaration of Human Rights, 1948, art. 3). It can be assumed that for countries where the death penalty and euthanasia are prohibited and life is declared the highest social value, the right to life is recognized as absolute. However, even in such a case, this right may be limited if the deprivation is not qualified as "arbitrary."

Arbitrary deprivation of life should be considered an action or inaction that led to the death of an individual in violation of the law. That is, in some cases, deprivation of life may be lawful. Let's consider several such grounds: the death penalty, abortion, euthanasia, and the actions of law enforcement and military personnel.

Ukraine has signed Protocol No. 6 to the European Convention for the Protection of Human Rights and Fundamental Freedoms, which establishes the complete abolition of the death penalty (Council of Europe 1983). For countries where the death penalty is applied, such deprivation of the right to life will be lawful. Even when it comes to depriving a person of their fundamental right, free will can play a role. For example, in the USA, under certain conditions, a convicted person can choose the method of execution. The list of execution methods in the USA was recently expanded and now includes lethal injection, the electric chair, lethal gas, or firing squad (Saakov 2020). This allows a person to exercise their free will for the last time to choose the method of their punishment, and even to have a "last wish."

Today, there is a trend toward the humanization of punishment and a reduction in the use of the death penalty. A study by Amnesty International in 2019 showed a 31% decrease in the use of the death penalty worldwide—reaching its lowest level in at least a decade (*"Doklad: Chislo smertnykh kaznei..."* [Report: The Number of Executions...] 2019). This trend continues. In 2020, 483 executions were reported worldwide, but this data does not include China, where it is believed thousands are executed annually (Holubov 2021). In the USA, where the death penalty is allowed, President Biden opposes it, and judicial practice shows that no federal death sentence has been carried out since 2003 (Saakov 2020). At the same time, the number of executions in Egypt has increased (Holubov 2021).

For Ukraine, the death penalty was historically an unpopular punishment. Even the *Ruska Pravda* did not provide for it, and attempts to introduce it in Kyivan Rus did not take root. In the society of that time, human life was valued, so most punishments were monetary fines. Despite the use of the term "execution" in legal acts, it should be noted that it meant only corporal punishment, not deprivation of life (Taranenko and Kolomiiets 2018, 89). For a long time, the highest, exceptional measure of punishment was exile—which did not exclude the death of the convicted, as the protection of the law did not extend to them. The systematic use of the death penalty in Ukraine began with the spread of the *Sudebnyk Kazimira IV* (1468) and *Lytovs'kyi statut* (1529).

The death penalty was provided for by the 1960 Criminal Code of Ukraine (*Kryminal'nyi kodeks Ukrainy* [Criminal Code of Ukraine] 1960, art. 24) for certain war crimes and for intentional murders under aggravating circumstances.

Upon gaining independence in 1991, Ukraine abolished the death penalty, and a moratorium on executions came into effect in 1995. The prohibition is based precisely on the protection of the human right to life. This is confirmed by a decision of the Constitutional Court of Ukraine, which states that life imprisonment is a less severe punishment compared to the death penalty—while ensuring the inalienable right to life of a person who has committed a particularly grave crime (*Rishennia Konstytutsiinoho Sudu Ukrainy* [Decision of the Constitutional Court of Ukraine] 2011a).

The basis for prohibiting the death penalty is also the fact that it represents a complete restriction of a person's will, leaving no possibility to reform one's behavior or influence one's own destiny. The use of the death penalty should be recognized as entirely contrary to the principle of free will.

Special attention should be paid to artificial termination of pregnancy as a bioethical issue related to the manifestation of free will and the restriction of the right to life.

The right to abortion should be considered from the perspective of the right to life and the right to medical care.

The connection between abortion and the right to life is the most controversial aspect, as it exists not only in the legal but also in the moral and ethical dimension. N. Hoerster argues that a rational discussion on the ethical and legal justification of abortion can only be conducted in the context of the right to life (Simon, 2000, p. 237).

Today, the legislation of different countries is divided into two camps: some prohibit abortions, while others allow them. Countries where abortions are completely banned include El Salvador, Nicaragua, Malta, the Philippines, the Vatican, and Poland. The main arguments for prohibition are moral-ethical norms and the protection of demographic interests.

Countries where abortion is permitted are divided into two categories. The first includes countries that limit abortions by indication, meaning termination is possible only for specific reasons, such as a threat to the mother's life or health, pregnancy resulting from a crime, severe genetic defects in the foetus, or social reasons. In Finland, Great Britain, India, and Japan, abortions are permitted only for such socio-economic reasons. In another large group of countries, abortions are allowed only to preserve life and health. In countries like Ukraine, France, and Switzerland, a woman can freely decide to terminate her pregnancy up to the 12th week.

In most cases, opponents of abortion emphasise the deprivation of the right to life of the embryo or foetus. This position has been reflected in national legislation, such as the Hungarian Law "On the Protection of Embryonic Life", which is justified by the lack of legal protection for the embryo when the law allows termination of pregnancy for reasons of a "crisis state" at the woman's decision (Jobbagyi 1994).

Regarding the status of the human embryo, O. A. Miroshnychenko concludes that:

1. Lack of absolute protection: Currently, the norms on the right to life, as applied by international and national human rights bodies, do not provide legal protection to the human embryo.
2. Specific restrictions: At the same time, individual states and international law have introduced prohibitions, such as those concerning the creation of embryos for commercial purposes or their preservation in vitro beyond a certain period (Miroshnychenko 2005, 12).

Ukrainian legislation establishes clear timeframes and conditions for the termination of pregnancy, balancing personal autonomy with state-defined limits. The Civil Code of Ukraine (*Tsyvil'nyi kodeks Ukrainy* [Civil Code of Ukraine] 2003, art. 281) stipulates that:

1. Up to twelve weeks: An abortion may be carried out at the woman's request.
2. Twelve to twenty-two weeks: An abortion may be performed only in cases established by law.
3. Beyond twelve weeks: The specific list of circumstances allowing for termination is strictly established by legislative acts.

These timeframes are further reinforced by the Fundamentals of Ukrainian Legislation on Health Protection (*Osnovy zakonodavstva...* [Fundamentals of the Legislation...] 1992, art. 50), which reiterates the same medical and legal boundaries.

However, the legislation regulates abortion not from the perspective of the right to life, but from the perspective of the right to medical care. That is, we are talking about different personal non-property rights.

Speaking about free will, we must understand that it is present only in the pregnant woman. As noted above, the embryo and foetus do not possess free will in the civil law sense. The right to life arises at birth; therefore, only the mother is considered a patient with personal non-property rights. In the issue of abortion, free will is exercised through the pregnant woman's right to medical care and right to life.

S. B. Buletsa states that Ukrainian legislation protects the interests of the human embryo, referring to it as a "person," not a "part" of the maternal organism. If, according to international and national legal acts, a human being in the mother's womb is recognized as a child, then all norms concerning the rights of children apply, including Article 6 of the Convention on the Rights of the Child, according to which every child has the right to life. Therefore, abortion should be equated with murder (Buletsa 2004, 586).

Even if one agrees with this position, the ability of an embryo or foetus to have free will and exercise its rights raises doubts. One can only assume a state obligation to protect the right to life of a future person, who will acquire free will after birth. Such views are reflected in the concept of the "right to be born." There is a concept that to establish proper guarantees of the right to life in this context, it is necessary, first, to legislatively limit the possibility of terminating pregnancy beyond 12 weeks to medical indications only, and second, to regulate this issue by law, not by a by-law (Cherviatsova 2013, 228).

It can be assumed that abortion constitutes an arbitrary violation of the right to life only when carried out in violation of the law. But even in such cases, we can only speak of the right to life of the patient, not of the embryo or foetus.

A different situation arises when it comes to the patient's right to medical care in the form of an abortion. In this case, free will manifests as the patient's conscious consent to medical intervention. The presence of free will is of fundamental importance here, serving as a guarantor of the legality of such intervention. For example, if a patient concluded a contract for medical services against her will, as a result of physical or mental pressure from another person, such as her spouse. In this case, there would be a vitiating factor (defect of will) and grounds to challenge the transaction.

Therefore, free will is of fundamental importance for legal relations concerning abortion, and only the provision of such services in violation of the law can be recognized as an arbitrary deprivation of the right to life.

The next form of arbitrary deprivation of the right to life is euthanasia, which is prohibited in Ukraine and is defined as the intentional acceleration of the death of an incurably ill person to end their suffering (*Osnovy zakonodavstva...* [Fundamentals of the Legislation...] 1992, art. 52, para. 3).

Euthanasia is divided into active—administering lethal drugs—and passive—withdrawing life-sustaining treatment. Countries where active euthanasia is allowed include the Netherlands, Belgium, Canada, and Spain. Countries that permit only passive euthanasia include Australia, the UK, France, and Germany. In most countries, euthanasia is prohibited.

The manifestation of free will depends on whether the euthanasia is voluntary or involuntary. Voluntary euthanasia is the application of lethal means at the request of an incurable patient who is aware of their actions and can control them. Involuntary euthanasia means causing death at the decision of family members, legal representatives, or public institutions (Alpers and Lo 1997). Voluntary euthanasia is a direct embodiment of free will, but consent given under the influence of drugs can call its voluntariness into question. Involuntary euthanasia is a manifestation of free will only if the patient gave prior, unequivocal consent while of sound mind.

It is essential to understand that euthanasia requires the coordinated will of the patient and the physician who assists. If a non-medical professional performs similar actions, it should be classified as assisted suicide. For example, if a relative of a terminally ill person purchases potent sedatives, knowing the person intends to use them to commit suicide, the relative may be considered to have assisted the suicide (NHS 2023).

The prohibition of euthanasia is based on the proclamation of human life as the highest social value and its inviolability. Therefore, regardless of the person's will, doctors must save a terminally ill patient. Even when a patient is in a coma and a return to a full life is impossible, their right to life is considered higher than their free will. As O. M. Pankiv and Y. I. Petrovsky rightly point out, in such a situation a person acquires a subjective right to life outside of their consciousness; it does not depend on their will. However, this right must be supplemented by the right to dispose of one's life, including its duration, which under certain circumstances may depend on the will and consciousness of a person (Pankiv and Petrovskyi 2007, 211). Judicial practice contains refutations of this position.

As B. Chan and M. Somerville point out, *Carter v. Canada* is likely to be among the most important decisions ever made by the Supreme Court of Canada. In a unanimous decision, all nine judges agreed that the absolute ban on "physician-assisted death" violated the Canadian Charter of Rights and Freedoms (Chan and Somerville 2016). This case was a significant impetus for the legalisation of euthanasia in Canada.

In 2011, G. Taylor—who had been diagnosed with amyotrophic lateral sclerosis—challenged the constitutionality of the prohibition on assisted suicide in the Criminal Code of Canada. The main argument was that the ban was discriminatory and violated the right to life, liberty, and security of the person (*Carter v. Canada* 2015). The ban on euthanasia is a severe restriction of free will and leads to additional suffering for the patient. In effect, the state unreasonably forces a terminally ill patient to wait for death, experience suffering, or seek other ways to end their life—such as suicide or help from relatives—which suppresses their honor and dignity.

The above refers us to the concept of the right to die. Normatively, such a right is not enshrined and essentially involves a renunciation of the right to life. In this issue, the definition of intent is central. Actions or inaction whose purpose is one's own death are considered a renunciation of the right to life.

If dangerous actions are not aimed at causing one's own death, their qualification should be different. For example, stunt performers put their lives in danger, and doctors conduct scientific experiments on themselves. The Geneva doctor J. Ponto tested a vaccine by allowing three vipers to bite him (Pankiv and Petrovskyi 2007, 211).

The manifestation of free will in these cases will depend on the goal. However, in any situation, doctors will be obliged to save a person's life. Even if a person makes constant suicide attempts of their own free will, the public interest in saving their life will be higher than their right to die. In other words, the personal non-property right to life is higher than free will.

In contrast to this concept, P. Tiensuu defines the right to life only as the right not to be killed (Tiensuu 2015). This position frames the right to life as a restriction on the will of another person to kill, intentionally or unintentionally.

Understanding the right to life as merely restrictive raises the question of the validity of prohibiting euthanasia and the right to suicide. This question arose in *Pretty v. United Kingdom* (European Court of Human Rights 2002) and was formulated by the Swiss Federal Court as "whether the European Convention on Human Rights grants mentally healthy persons, through the right to self-determination, the freedom to commit suicide and, consequently, impunity for the person who may assist for that purpose" (European Court of Human Rights 2011a).

Among the legally permitted grounds for restricting the right to life in Ukraine are the actions of law enforcement and military personnel.

The Law of Ukraine "On the National Police" provides for a list of police measures, defined as actions of a preventive or coercive nature that restrict certain human rights and are applied by police officers to ensure the implementation of their powers (*Pro Natsional'nu politsiiu* [On the National Police] 2015, art. 29, para. 1).

The law clearly provides for the possibility of restricting human rights and freedoms when implementing a police measure. A police measure must be lawful, necessary, proportionate, and effective. It is recognized as necessary if no other measure is possible or effective, and if it will cause the least harm. The actions of a police officer must also be proportional, ensuring that the harm caused does not exceed the good being protected.

Police measures are divided into preventive and coercive; coercive measures include the use of physical force, special means, and firearms. Each of these measures is regulated in detail by law, and in no case can their purpose be the deprivation of life.

Police officers may use physical force, including special combat techniques, to ensure their own safety and the safety of others, to prevent a crime, and to detain offenders.

According to the Law of Ukraine "On the National Police" (*Pro Natsional'nu politsiiu* [On the National Police] 2015, art. 45), police measures include: (1) handcuffs and other restraints; (2) rubber and plastic batons; (3) tear gas and irritants; (4) devices for forcibly stopping vehicles; (5) devices for destroying obstacles and forcibly opening premises; (6) electroshock devices; (7) special marking and dyeing agents; (8) flash-bang devices, as well as acoustic and microwave devices; (9) water cannons and armored vehicles; (10) devices for firing non-lethal rubber projectiles; (11) smoke-generating devices; and (12) the use of service dogs and horses.

When discussing restrictions on the right to life and, consequently, free will, the most severe measure of coercion is the use of firearms. A police officer is authorized to carry and use firearms only after appropriate special training. The use of firearms is allowed only in extreme cases (Ibid., art. 46):

1. Self-Defense: Repelling an attack on a police officer or their family;
2. Protection of Others: Protecting persons from a life-threatening attack;
3. Hostage Situations: Freeing hostages;

4. Property Protection: Repelling an attack on guarded objects;
5. Detention of Grave Offenders: Detaining a person caught committing a grave crime who is attempting to escape;
6. Armed Resistance: Detaining a person offering armed resistance or an armed individual threatening others;
7. Vehicle Interdiction: Stopping a vehicle by damaging it if the driver poses a threat to life or health.

A police officer is authorised to use a firearm only to inflict harm that is necessary and sufficient to immediately prevent or stop an armed attack, or if such an attack cannot be stopped by other means.

Thus, if a police officer uses a firearm under the conditions provided by law and this results in a fatal injury, it cannot be qualified as murder or abuse of power. The purpose of the officer's actions and the absence of intent are of fundamental importance; intentional murder will result in criminal liability. T. Wicks confirms that in some circumstances, the use of lethal force may be justified, but only if it can be considered reasonable (Wicks 2010).

Thus, intentional murder committed in excess of the limits of necessary defense, or by exceeding the measures required to detain an offender, is punishable by corrective labour, restriction of liberty, or imprisonment for up to two years (*Kryminal'nyi kodeks Ukrainy* [Criminal Code of Ukraine] 2001, art. 118).

A similar situation applies to the actions of military personnel. The peculiarity here lies in cases where a service member takes the life of a soldier on the opposing side. Such cases must be qualified taking into account international humanitarian law and the laws of war. This topic deserves a separate study, but it can be noted that the free will of the parties can be directly aimed at taking a life and will not be considered a criminal offense if international law is not violated. As I. Park notes, a state's primary obligations regarding the right to life do not cease during armed conflict but are adjusted by the requirements of international humanitarian law, such that a violation of the right to life occurs only when there is a violation of IHL regulating the use of lethal force (Park 2018).

The situation where death occurs as a result of a sports competition is debatable. For example, a boxer delivers a blow during a match that results in death or injury. Normatively, such actions could be qualified as manslaughter, battery, or grievous bodily harm. However, in practice, such events are qualified as accidents, and only when death occurs. This situation is also directly related to the issue of free will. The basis for this legal qualification is the absence of intent to cause fatal injury. This explains the practice of not holding athletes criminally liable. Numerous agreements between athletes and internal sports regulations serve as additional arguments, although there is no normative provision allowing civil law agreements to limit or clarify criminal law norms.

Summarizing the issue of prohibiting the arbitrary deprivation of life, it is necessary to cite Article 2 of the Convention for the Protection of Human Rights and Fundamental Freedoms.

Cases where the use of force may be deemed absolutely necessary—potentially leading to the deprivation of life—include: (1) in defense of any person from unlawful violence; (2) in order to effect a lawful arrest or to prevent the escape of a person lawfully detained; and (3) in action lawfully taken for the purpose of quelling a riot or insurrection (Council of Europe 1950, art. 2).

The European Court of Human Rights (ECtHR) and other international bodies consider proportionality, expediency, and absolute necessity to be the main criteria in the legal assessment of the use of force during a lawful arrest or to prevent escape (Tatsii and Petryshyn 2011, 189).

Free will can be manifested in the right to life through the state's duty to protect it. The case law of the ECtHR shows that the state's duty to guarantee the right to life should be understood to include taking adequate measures to ensure the safety of individuals and—in the event of serious injury or death—providing an effective independent judicial system capable of establishing facts, holding perpetrators accountable, and ensuring adequate compensation (European Court of Human Rights 2015).

The state's duty to protect human life has a dual meaning for free will. On the one hand, without a guaranteed right to life, the ability to exercise free will is called into question; on the other hand, the state's protective duty limits free will. For instance, a person does not have the right to refuse emergency care. In such a case, the state's duty to protect life and the public interest in saving it are considered higher than the individual's will to refuse medical care.

The duty of the state to protect human life is a multifaceted obligation that extends beyond mere non-interference. According to V. Ya. Tatsii and O. V. Petryshyn, this duty consists of the following essential elements:

1. Criminal Accountability: Establishing criminal liability for unlawful attacks on life.
2. Prohibition of Arbitrary Deprivation: Maintaining a strict legal ban on the arbitrary deprivation of life by state actors.
3. Extradition Safeguards: Prohibiting the extradition of a person to a state where they may face the death penalty.
4. Non-Refoulement: Prohibiting the expulsion of an individual to a state where their life would be under threat.
5. Preventative Infrastructure: Introducing organizational and legal means to protect the right to life, particularly in situations with a high probability of an absolute threat.
6. Self-Defense Guarantees: Implementing legal guarantees for individuals who protect their own life and health, or that of others, from unlawful encroachments (Tatsii and Petryshyn 2011, 187).

This framework ensures that the right to life is not merely a theoretical proclamation but a practical reality supported by the state's institutional and legal machinery.

The case law of the ECtHR shows instances where the state has failed to fulfilll its obligations to protect life. In *Gorovenky and Bugara v. Ukraine*, it was found that state authorities had failed to take sufficient measures to protect society from a specific individual they knew to be dangerous (European Court of Human Rights 2012). In *Gongadze v. Ukraine*, the authorities failed to fulfilll their positive obligation to protect a specific person from a known threat (European Court of Human Rights 2005). In *Kats and Others v. Ukraine*, it was established that adequate medical care was not provided to an HIV-infected person in custody (European Court of Human Rights 2008). In *Matushevskyi and Matushevska v. Ukraine*, a proper explanation for the death of a person in custody was not provided (European Court of Human Rights 2011b). In *Shchokin v. Ukraine*, the obligation to ensure the safety of prisoners was found to have been breached (European Court of Human Rights 2013b).

As we can see, the state's duty to protect human life has various manifestations. This duty is recognized as dominant over and limiting of free will. Regarding the state's positive obligation, the ECtHR emphasizes that Article 2 of the Convention obliges the state not only to refrain from intentionally and unlawfully taking a life but also to take appropriate measures to protect the lives of those within its jurisdiction (Kurylo 2017, 309). In the context of this duty, the issue of free will is more relevant for state officials who perform this duty. Their free will must be directed toward fulfillling these obligations. By protecting human life, they protect the ability to exercise free will.

Free will can be manifested in the right to life through the right to protect one's own life and health, and that of others, from unlawful encroachments. The right to self-defense is a measure of possible behavior granted and guaranteed by the state, which can be manifested in both intellectual and direct physical activity. It is carried out to uphold natural human rights as provided for by domestic and international norms and is based on the principles of law and other social norms that do not contradict universal rules of human coexistence (Horyslavskyi 2003).

To protect life and health, there is a normative possibility to choose any form of protection, both jurisdictional and non-jurisdictional, at one's own will. Based on the specific situation, a person independently decides how to protect their rights. Until the public interest becomes higher than the private interest, the free will in choosing the form of protection of the right to life will be limited only by the normative framework.

It is logical to attribute the right to life and the right to health to personal non-property rights that ensure the integrity of an individual, because a person's integrity, their free will, and their very existence stem from these fundamental rights. Moreover, the consequence of death is the termination of free will, and one's state of health can affect the scope of civil capacity and, consequently, the scope of free will.

It is normatively correct to use the term "health care," as the "right to health" is more of a doctrinal concept. The right to health should be recognized as comprehensive, consisting of the right to health care, medical care, information about one's health, confidentiality of health information, the right to donation, and the rights of a person receiving inpatient treatment. Let us consider the complex relationship of these rights with free will.

The rights to health and medical assistance are enshrined in several key international acts, which form the global basis for patient protection. These include the WMA Lisbon Declaration on the Rights of the Patient, the WHO Declaration on the Promotion of Patients' Rights in Europe, and the European Charter of Patients' Rights.

In the national context, Article 49 of the Constitution of Ukraine (*Konstytutsiia Ukrainy* [Constitution of Ukraine] 1996, art. 49) establishes the fundamental right to health care, medical care, and medical insurance through the following provisions:

1. State Financing: Health care is ensured by state financing of relevant programs.
2. Accessibility and Effectiveness: The state creates conditions for effective and accessible medical care for all citizens.
3. Free Medical Assistance: In state and municipal health care institutions, medical care is provided free of charge.
4. Network Stability: The existing network of such institutions cannot be reduced.
5. Institutional Diversity: The state promotes the development of medical institutions of all forms of ownership.

These constitutional guarantees reflect the state's positive obligation to ensure the physical and mental well-being of its citizens, providing a normative foundation for the exercise of free will in the context of personal health decisions.

The Civil Code of Ukraine states that an individual has the right to the protection of their health, which is ensured by the systematic activities of state and other organizations, as provided for by the Constitution and law (*Tsyvil'nyi kodeks Ukrainy* [Civil Code of Ukraine] 2003, art. 283).

Health care is a system of measures aimed at preserving and restoring physiological and psychological functions, optimal working capacity, and social activity of a person with the maximum biologically possible individual lifespan (*Osnovy zakonodavstva...* [Fundamentals of the Legislation...] 1992, art. 3).

Such measures are carried out by state and local government bodies, health care institutions, licensed individual entrepreneurs, medical and pharmaceutical workers, rehabilitation specialists, public associations, and citizens (Ibid.).

Article 6 of the Fundamentals of the Legislation of Ukraine on Health Care details the extensive scope of this right, declaring that every citizen is entitled to health care. This multifaceted right encompasses several distinct dimensions:

1. Socio-Economic and Environmental Conditions
    a. A standard of living necessary to maintain health (including food, clothing, housing, and medical care);
    b. A safe environment and sanitary-epidemiological well-being;
    c. Safe and healthy conditions for work, study, and daily life.
2. Medical Assistance and Patient Autonomy
    a. Qualified medical and rehabilitation care, which includes the free choice of a doctor, specialist, and treatment methods;
    b. Reliable and timely information about one's health status;
    c. The possibility of an independent medical examination;
    d. The right of an inpatient to have visitors, including a notary, lawyer, and clergy;
    e. Information regarding available telemedicine and telerehabilitation services.

3. Civic Participation and Protection of Rights
   a. Participation in the discussion of draft legislation and health care management;
   b. The ability to form public organizations;
   c. Legal protection from discrimination related to health status;
   d. Compensation for harm caused to health and the right to appeal unlawful decisions (Ibid., art. 6).

As the legislation notes, this list is not exhaustive, allowing for the further expansion of health-related protections as social and technological conditions evolve.

So, the right to health care is understood through a list of patient rights. However, several questions arise regarding the rights of foreigners to health care and the distinction between "medical care" and "medical services."

A detailed analysis of these issues leads to the following conclusions regarding the legal framework of health-related activities:

1. Dichotomy of Services and Works: Medical services represent a distinct object of civil legal relations and must be clearly distinguished from medical works. The primary criteria for this distinction are the specific purpose of the legal relationship and the ultimate form of its result.
2. Genus-Species Relationship: In a broad sense, "medical services" is a generic concept that encompasses "medical care." Medical care should be viewed as a specific type of medical service, characterized by the nuances of receiving free assistance within state and municipal institutions under special circumstances.
3. Functional Definition: Medical services are defined as the professional actions of a health care institution or a private practitioner aimed at either improving a patient's health or satisfying other legitimate needs through specialized medical intervention (Savchenko 2014, 7–9).

This classification allows for a more precise determination of the rights and obligations of the parties involved, particularly in cases where the boundary between a "service" and a "work" impacts the nature of legal liability.

The right to health care is inextricably linked to free will, which is manifested in issues of informed consent and refusal of medical care, as well as grounds for restricting free will.

Active health care begins with the provision of informed consent for medical intervention. As a general rule, informed consent is the consent of a patient or their legal representative, given based on complete and comprehensive information received from the attending physician, in an accessible form, about the purpose, nature, methods, probable risks, and possible consequences of the intervention (Lashkul, Sizintsova and Fershal 2013, 13). Informed consent is obtained freely, without threats, after providing the patient with adequate and understandable information about the diagnostic assessment, purpose, method, probable duration, expected benefits, alternative treatments, and possible pain, discomfort, and side effects (Sizintsova 2013, 267).

As we can see, medical intervention occurs based on the free will of the individual who decides to become a patient and gives consent. Such consent is characterised by mandatory elements that also stem from free will. The information must be complete and comprehensive, and consent must be voluntary and informed. The patient must receive full, reliable information and understand its meaning. We hereby declare a presumption that the patient has voluntarily manifested their free will to receive medical services. The doctor is obliged to convey all information correctly and ensure that the patient is fully aware of the situation and gives consent as a manifestation of their free will.

Violation of this obligation can result in significant legal consequences, from declaring the contract for medical services invalid to criminal liability. For example, placing a mentally sound person in a psychiatric institution is a criminal offense (*Kryminal'nyi kodeks Ukrainy* [Criminal Code of Ukraine] 2001, art. 151).

As we can see, the obligation to obtain informed consent is closely related to the personal non-property right to information about one's health. This right provides access to reliable and comprehensive information about one's health, including medical documents. In addition to the person themself, their parents, guardian, or trustee also have the right to information about the health of a child or ward. However, if an adult prohibits the disclosure of such information, their right to medical confidentiality will outweigh the parents' right to receive it. In some cases, the right to information may be limited if disclosure could worsen the patient's health or harm the treatment process. Without the right to medical information, a patient cannot fully exercise their free will when giving informed consent or refusing medical intervention.

Improper manifestation of free will may be grounds for a patient to challenge the quality of medical services. For example, in some countries, thirty per cent of lawsuits in spinal surgery are related to the improper documentation of the patient's informed consent (Makhni 2018). Interestingly, while the majority of medical lawsuits in Ukraine are resolved in favor of doctors due to the difficulty of proving substandard care, the practice regarding informed consent is different. It is the doctors who are obliged to verify the extent to which consent is informed, and therefore, they are responsible for protecting the patient's free will.

Healthcare is based on the principle of informed consent, which is an expression of the patient's free will. The realisation of the right to healthcare for children of different ages is achieved through a balanced system of decision-making that considers both the child's level of maturity and the responsibility of their legal representatives.

The legal regulation of this right for minors is complex; however, the existing notion of a conflict between the age for receiving information and the age for giving consent is mistaken. The key point is that Ukrainian legislation grants a patient the right to both receive medical information and give consent for medical intervention simultaneously from the age of 14. The right to consent (*Tsyvil'nyi kodeks Ukrainy* [Civil Code of Ukraine] 2003, art. 284; *Osnovy zakonodavstva...* [Fundamentals of the Legislation...] 1992, art. 43) would be ineffective without the right to the information necessary to make an informed decision. This approach is also consistent with the general principles of a child's right to receive age-appropriate information (*Pro okhoronu dytynstva* [On the Protection of Childhood] 2001, art. 9).

During this period, the role of legal representatives does not nullify but rather supplements the adolescent's rights. Normative acts, such as the Order of the Ministry of Health of Ukraine No. 382 (*Pro zatverdzhennia Tymchasovykh standartiv...* [On Approval of the Temporary Standards...] 2009, para. 1.3), regulate the procedure for providing care to this age group, establishing mechanisms for interaction between the doctor, the adolescent patient, and their parents, rather than "resolving" a non-existent conflict. A refusal by the parents is not given absolute priority, as this would negate the legal capacity granted to the adolescent in this sphere.

Therefore, providing medical care to a minor requires their personal informed consent as a mandatory condition for medical intervention. The will of the legal representatives does not limit but acts in parallel: their consent is also required, creating a system of dual protection for the patient's interests.

For a young child (under the age of 14), the situation is fundamentally different, as the right to consent is exercised by their legal representatives. They make decisions acting exclusively in the child's best interests and based on the doctor's recommendations.

The doctor's role in this system is not that of the 'final instance'. The doctor acts as an expert and a defender of the child's health. He or she is obliged to act in the child's interests, which includes the right to refuse to provide harmful interventions.

However, in the event of a critical disagreement—when legal representatives refuse life-saving treatment—the doctor does not make the decision unilaterally. Their duty is to apply to a court or to guardianship authorities. Thus, the true final authority that can override the will of the representatives to save a child is the state, in the person of the court.

In conclusion, instead of a simple hierarchy, there is a system of interaction and control, where rights and responsibilities are distributed among the patient (according to their age), their legal representatives, and the doctor, and in conflict situations, the court.

As Yu. Markov and A. Zhezher argue, the autonomy of a paediatric patient is not always realistic or legally acceptable, so parents provide "reasoned permission" for treatment. However, the goals of informed consent (protecting the patient's interests and including the family in decision-making) are similar for both paediatric and adult patients and are based on the same ethical principles (Markov and Zhezher 2019, 144).

Free will is essential in matters of refusing to exercise the personal non-property right to health care. In medicine, refusing a specific treatment can lead to a fatal outcome. However, treatment carried out without the consent of a mentally competent adult patient would constitute an interference with their physical integrity in a way that violates the right provided for in Article 8 of the *Convention for the Protection of Human Rights and Fundamental Freedoms* (Seniuta 2016, 16).

Every person has the right to refuse medical intervention. However, certain conditions must be met: the refusal must also be informed and voluntary. In this case, the same provisions apply as for consent—thus, the question of refusal by a minor arises. Representatives of the American Academy of Pediatrics emphasize the need to involve older children and adolescents in the process of giving informed consent or refusal (Lee et al. 2006; Duncan and Sawyer 2010).

A patient who has acquired full civil capacity and is aware of their actions has the right to refuse treatment. However, if a legal representative gives the refusal and it could have serious consequences for the patient, the doctor is obliged to inform the guardianship authorities (Sizintsova 2013, 268). This aligns with O. Babych's position that in such cases, there may be both compliance with the law and respect for the human right to receive medical care (Babych 2011). Notably, a patient can withdraw their refusal at any time; even after refusing treatment, they still have the right to pain and suffering relief (Buletsa 2012, 507).

So, in the matter of a minor patient's refusal of medical care, we again apply the triad mentioned above. It is established that only adults with full legal capacity who are aware of their actions have the right to refuse medical intervention *(Osnovy zakonodavstva...* [Fundamentals of the Legislation...] 1992, art. 43). Before the age of eighteen, a patient cannot refuse a medical service to which their legal representatives have agreed. In this case, the minor's refusal has no legal consequences for medical professionals, other than their obligation to act only in the patient's best interests. For example, if legal representatives order medical services that may cause unjustified harm to a minor's health (e.g., artificial lip augmentation), the patient cannot refuse them, and the doctor must independently determine the necessity and reasonableness of providing such services (Savchenko 2014, 97).

There are also many questions about a patient's awareness when they are in significant pain or under the influence of medication. This issue is most relevant in obstetric anaesthesia, which is characterised by a significant number of conflicts and legal gaps related to informed consent (Hoehner 2003).

Special attention should be paid to the refusal of medical intervention by a person who is unconscious, intoxicated, in shock, or in severe pain. This is justified by the fact that the primary condition for refusal is awareness of the consequences. When a person is in one of these states, their awareness, and therefore their free will, can be questioned. Furthermore, the law does not specify how medical professionals should determine when a person is making a conscious decision. For example, the level of alcohol intoxication at which a person's free will is so limited that refusal or consent is impossible is not clearly defined.

A separate category is cases where a person has no right to refuse medical care at all, and their free will is not taken into account. These are situations where there is a real threat to the patient's life and health. Consent to medical intervention is not required in urgent cases. However, the law does not provide a list of urgent cases that would allow for the restriction of free will to provide medical care without consent. Medical practice indicates that such cases are covered by emergency surgery (Stetsenko, Stetsenko and Seniuta 2008, 139).

The principle of informed consent is not absolute, particularly when individual autonomy conflicts with higher-order legal interests. O. Krylova identifies several primary grounds for providing medical care without a patient's consent:

1. Public Safety: When non-intervention poses a direct threat to the health of others.
2. Legal Incapacity: When the refusal is made by an incapacitated person or an individual whose state significantly impairs their ability to make reasoned decisions.
3. Life-Threatening Emergency: When a patient's condition threatens their life but simultaneously prevents them from providing consent.
4. Representative Unavailability: When it is impossible to obtain consent from legal representatives and any delay could lead to serious, irreversible consequences (Krylova 2006, 105).

Expanding on this framework, A. S. Dvornichenko summarizes that medical intervention without consent may be carried out in the following specific cases:

1. Imminent Danger: A real and present danger to life (distinguished from "scheduled" operations).
2. Principle of Necessity: The impossibility of minimizing the danger by any other legal means.
3. Objective Impossibility: The objective impossibility of obtaining consent from the patient or their authorized representatives.
4. Urgent Incapacity: Urgent cases where the patient's immediate physical or mental condition prevents them from expressing their will.
5. Epidemiological Safety: For individuals suffering from diseases that are dangerous to the public.
6. Mental Health Protection: For persons suffering from severe mental disorders that pose a risk to themselves or others.

7. Legal and Forensic Requirements: For persons who have committed socially dangerous acts, as well as during mandatory psychiatric examinations (Dvornichenko 2014, 34–36).

The grounds for medical intervention without consent can be divided into two categories: (1) when the patient's condition limits their free will; (2) when the public interest outweighs the patient's free will.

An example of the first category is when a patient is unconscious and cannot manifest free will. An example of the second category is when religious beliefs prohibit certain types of medical intervention. For instance, adherents of the Jehovah's Witnesses faith refuse blood transfusions. However, if a blood transfusion is necessary to save a life in an emergency, the patient's rights will be limited. In such a situation, medical care will be provided even if they refuse it. Here, we see the public interest in saving a life prevailing over free will.

The complex of rights related to health includes the personal non-property right to donation. It should be understood that the rights of the donor and the recipient are distinct personal non-property rights. The right to donation is the ability to transfer anatomical material, while the recipient's right is a personal non-property right to health care.

A donor is a person from whom anatomical material is taken during life or after death for transplantation or for the manufacture of bio-implants (*Osnovy zakonodavstva...* [Fundamentals of the Legislation...] 1992, art. 1). Transplantation is a special method of treatment consisting of transplanting an organ or other anatomical material from a human or animal to a recipient (Ibid.).

Free will manifests differently in this right depending on whether the donor is living or deceased.

A living donor of anatomical materials can only be a capable adult, except in cases provided for by law. Anatomical material can be removed from a capable adult only with their voluntary and informed written consent (*Pro zastosuvannia transplantatsii...* [On the Application of Transplantation...] 2018, art. 14). The condition of voluntariness and written consent is an expression of free will, confirming its mandatory nature for these legal relations. However, the limits of the donor's free will are determined by restrictions on who can be a recipient, age, health status, and other conditions. For example, it is prohibited to remove anatomical materials from living persons who are imprisoned, are foreigners illegally staying in Ukraine, suffer from severe mental disorders, have diseases that could be transmitted—to the recipient—have previously donated an organ, or are pregnant (Ibid., art. 14).

Some of these restrictions raise doubts. In particular, the ban on prisoners being donors is not sufficiently argued by the legislator. For example, the appropriateness of restricting the right of an imprisoned father to donate an organ to his child is questionable. It is believed that abolishing this restriction could protect the possibility of free will and help patients realise their right to health care.

A different procedure for realising the donor's free will applies when taking anatomical materials from deceased persons. Today, two legal models regulate this issue, both aimed at protecting a person's will during their lifetime. The first model is based on a presumption of general consent. The essence is the automatic consent of every person to posthumous donation. The individual's position is taken into account in that, during their lifetime, a person can prohibit any actions regarding their body, including refusing to be a donor (Shchyrba 2018, 27).

The second model is used in Ukraine and consists of obtaining consent for donation during one's lifetime, or obtaining consent from close relatives after death. Here, two options should be considered: when the person has given consent during their lifetime and when they have not. Regarding the first option, every capable adult has the right to provide written (or electronic) consent or refusal for the removal of anatomical materials from their body for transplantation after being declared brain dead (*Pro zastosuvannia transplantatsii...* [On the Application of Transplantation...] 2018, art. 16).

In this case, there is a direct manifestation of free will that formalises the person's choice. Such consent or refusal is absolute. If this consent or refusal is absent, a presumption of refusal arises.

However, even without prior consent, a decision can be made with the consent of the spouse or relatives who lived with the donor. It is believed that in this case, the representatives act in the interests of the deceased, expressing their presumed intentions. One could say they are expressing the will of the deceased, assuming they would have agreed to be a donor. Of course, this approach is subjective, but it aims to protect the interests and free will of the deceased.

In the case of deceased minors or incapacitated persons, anatomical materials may be taken with the consent of their legal representatives.

The legal nature of the manifestation of free will differs depending on whether the donor is living or deceased. In the first case, we speak of a manifestation of free will in the form of informed consent to transfer anatomical material. In the second, we speak of an officially recorded prior consent or refusal. Here, the manifestation of free will takes the form of an intention to be or not to be a donor after death. This is the realisation of free will and the exercise of the right to donate for the future.

The right to confidentiality of health information occupies a special place among personal non-property rights. According to the Law of Ukraine "On Information," data on a person's health is considered confidential (*Pro informatsiiu* [On Information] 1992, art. 11).

The Convention on Human Rights and Biomedicine recognizes information about a person's health as a component of the right to respect for private life (*Oviedo Convention on Human Rights and Biomedicine* 1997, art. 10).

The right to confidentiality of health information and medical secrecy should not be conflated, as they differ in their subject matter. The right to confidentiality of health is broader and imposes an obligation on an unspecified group of persons. Medical secrecy—which stems from the broader right to confidentiality—creates obligations only for specific subjects to maintain confidentiality regarding a patient's health information, even after their death (WMA 2018).

The manifestation of free will in these two rights also differs. The right to confidentiality of health is primarily related to a person's ability to independently decide how and what information about their health they want to share. This includes, for example, the prohibition on employers or educational institutions demanding such information. The patient alone decides whether to provide it, and a diagnosis is included on a sick leave certificate only at the patient's request.

Therefore, the right to confidentiality of health information is the ability to independently limit its content and form, as well as the circle of persons to whom it is provided, at one's own free will.

Medical secrecy is also protected by this right but has a different meaning.

Medical secrecy is all information obtained in the process of providing medical care that is not subject to disclosure, except in cases provided for by law, and which became known to medical workers or other persons in connection with their professional or official duties (Seniuta 2010, 262).

Medical secrecy is characterised by two main features: the presence of special subjects and special information.

The subjects of the obligation to maintain medical secrecy are not only doctors but a wide range of persons, including: (1) doctors of all specialisations; (2) other medical staff (nurses, laboratory technicians); (3) persons who received such information during their professional duties (e.g., HR employees who handle health certificates) (Matsegorin 2010, 156).

Special information includes the fact of seeking medical care, health status, diagnosis, pre-existing conditions, functional features of the body, bad habits, mental characteristics, property status, and other information obtained during a medical examination, including information about family and intimate life.

Legal liability is provided for the disclosure of medical secrecy. Article 145 of the Criminal Code of Ukraine provides for criminal liability for the intentional disclosure of medical secrecy by a person to whom it became known in connection with professional duties—if such an act caused serious consequences

(*Kryminal'nyi kodeks Ukrainy* [Criminal Code of Ukraine] 2001, art. 145).

According to Article 132, the disclosure by an official of information about an HIV test or other incurable infectious disease also entails criminal liability (Ibid., art. 132).

Furthermore, according to the Law of Ukraine on HIV/AIDS, people living with HIV have the right to compensation for damages related to the disclosure of their positive status (*Pro protydiu poshyrenniu khvorob... (VIL)* [On Countering the Spread of Diseases... (HIV)] 1991, art. 15).

Disclosure of medical information without a patient's consent is strictly regulated and permitted only in clearly established legal cases. The framework for such disclosure balances individual privacy with the interests of justice, public health, and family rights:

1. Judicial and Procedural Requirements
   Information may be disclosed during legal proceedings when such data is essential for the adjudication of a case (*Tsyvil'nyi protsesual'nyi kodeks Ukrainy* [Civil Procedure Code of Ukraine] 2004, art. 137). Similarly, law enforcement agencies may access treatment records from drug rehabilitation facilities if an individual is facing criminal or administrative liability (*Pro zakhody protydii nezakonnomu...* [On Measures to Counter Illicit...] 1995, art. 14, para. 5).
2. Rights of Family Members and Representatives
   a. Minors and Wards: Parents or guardians have the legal right to access health information regarding minor children (*Osnovy zakonodavstva...* [Fundamentals of the Legislation...] 1992, art. 39).
   b. Engaged Couples: Under family law, individuals planning to marry have a reciprocal right to be informed about each other's health status (*Simeinyi kodeks Ukrainy* [Family Code of Ukraine] 2002, art. 30).
   c. Post-Mortem Rights: In the event of death, family members are entitled to be present during investigations into the cause of death and to review the subsequent conclusions (*Tsyvil'nyi kodeks Ukrainy* [Civil Code of Ukraine] 2003, art. 285, para. 4).

3. Public Health and Social Protection
   a. Domestic Violence: Authorized bodies may request medical information in cases involving the prevention of and counteraction to domestic violence (*Pro zapobihannia ta protydiiu...* [On Prevention and Counteraction...] 2017, art. 9).
   b. Mental Health: Psychiatric data may be transferred without consent when necessary to organize urgent care for individuals with severe mental disorders (*Pro psykhiatrychnu dopomohu* [On Psychiatric Care] 2000, art. 6).
   c. Communicable Diseases (HIV): Information regarding HIV test results is strictly limited to the individual tested, their representatives, involved medical staff, or disclosures mandated by a court order (*Pro protydiiu poshyrenniu khvorob... (VIL)* [On Countering the Spread of Diseases... (HIV)] 1991, art. 13, para. 4).

Furthermore, healthcare professionals are bound by the obligation to ensure total patient anonymity when utilizing information that constitutes a medical secret for educational or research purposes.

In all the above cases, transferring information about a patient's health will not be considered a violation of medical secrecy. Thus, an individual has free will regarding decisions about the disclosure of their health information, but their free will may be limited in cases where a medical professional transfers information on legal grounds.

Personal non-property rights that ensure the integrity of an individual are intertwined with the right to eliminate a danger that threatens life and health, obligations arising from saving a person's health and life, and the conditions for eliminating such a threat.

The institution of creating a threat to an individual's life, health, or property is relatively new in Ukrainian civil law and was only normatively consolidated in 2003. Article 282 of the Civil Code of Ukraine (*Tsyvil'nyi kodeks Ukrainy* [Civil Code of Ukraine] 2003, art. 282) states that an individual has the right to demand the elimination of a danger created as a result of entrepreneurial or other activity that threatens life and health.

The application of this norm only to entrepreneurial activity is erroneous, as it applies to all types of activity. This personal non-property right is based on several factors: (1) the threat of danger to life and health; (2) the danger must be real; (3) the possibility of harmful consequences must depend on the activity of the person whose actions must be stopped; and 4) the danger must threaten legitimate rights and interests (Dzera et. al. 2011).

These norms establish the preventive nature of these rights, aiming to prevent negative consequences. The need to protect a right arises primarily in connection with unlawful behavior; however, Article 282 of the Civil Code of Ukraine emphasizes that protection can also occur in the event of a future threat of violation (Maliuha 2004, 145). N.P. Bondar classifies the personal non-property right to eliminate danger as a right whose preventive protection is carried out in court (Bondar 2015, 17).

However, it should be noted that the protection of this right is not limited to court and can take non-jurisdictional forms. For example, an individual can act in necessary self-defense against an attacker. Thus, of their own free will, a person protects their right to life and exercises the right to eliminate danger.

The right to preventive protection is exercised by the right-holder by identifying and preventing or stopping a real threat of violation of their subjective civil rights or interests (Ibid. 2015, 6).

The exercise of the right to eliminate danger is linked to various constitutional rights, particularly the right to a safe environment and to compensation for damage caused by its violation (*Konstytutsiia Ukrainy* [Constitution of Ukraine] 1996, art. 50).

Everyone is guaranteed the right to free access to and dissemination of information about the environment, food quality, and household goods. Therefore, when a person discovers a potentially harmful element in a food product, they decide, of their own free will, how to protect their right. They can simply not purchase the product, contact the manufacturer, or appeal to regulatory bodies or the court.

In the event of failure to eliminate a threat to life, health, or property, the interested person has the right to demand: (1) urgent measures to eliminate the threat; (2) compensation for damages; (3) prohibition of the activity that creates the threat (*Tsyvil'nyi kodeks Ukrainy* [Civil Code of Ukraine] 2003, art. 1164).

Next, we should consider the relationship between free will and the rights of an individual receiving inpatient treatment in a healthcare facility, specifically the right to liberty.

Let's define the concepts. An inpatient facility is a part of a hospital where the treatment and diagnostic process is continuous, and medical care is provided by doctors. Typically, patients with the most serious illnesses are treated in inpatient settings, requiring a comprehensive approach, complex methods, and constant medical supervision (Seniuta 2010, 464). Specific types include obstetric, day, home, medical, and psychiatric inpatient facilities.

While receiving inpatient treatment, a person is granted all the rights of a patient. However, these rights are expanded to include: (1) admission of other medical professionals; (2) admission of family members, guardians, or trustees; (3) admission of a notary and lawyer; (4) admission of clergy to perform religious services (*Tsyvil'nyi kodeks Ukrainy* [Civil Code of Ukraine] 2003, art. 287, para. 1; *Osnovy zakonodavstva...* [Fundamentals of the Legislation...] 1992, art. 6, cl. "k").

These rights are related to preventing the restriction of the patient's free will. It should also be emphasised that a patient has the right to refuse inpatient treatment at any time. Exceptions include cases where there is a threat to the patient's life and cases of compulsory treatment.

The grounds for compulsory treatment are clearly defined by law and must meet specific criteria: (1) the presence of elements of a crime in the offender's actions; (2) the presence of a disease in the offender that poses a danger to the health of others.

The conditions for applying compulsory treatment include: (1) a medical opinion confirming the disease; (2) a conviction for a crime; and (3) the absence of any of the criteria related to the grounds and conditions for compulsory treatment excludes its application (*Naukovo-praktychnyi komentar...* [Scientific and Practical Commentary...] 2009).

As we can see, compulsory treatment completely limits the patient's free will to refuse medical care and stems from the social danger of the patient's condition.

I. V. Zhuk argues that compulsory medical measures and treatment: (1) are truly compulsory, not violent; (2) have a dual legal and medical nature; (3) are not a form of criminal liability; (4) are not criminal punishment; (5) are not ordinary medical measures regulated by health legislation; 6) their use cannot be considered a violation of human and civil rights (Zhuk 2009, 8).

Sometimes patients experience significant restrictions on their free will while receiving inpatient treatment. For example, the rights of individuals receiving psychiatric care include: (1) communication with others, including a lawyer, without the presence of third parties; (2) notifying a person of their choice about the care; (3) access to media; (4) leisure and creative activities; (5) religious observance; (6) receiving visitors alone; (7) purchasing and using everyday items; (8) being alone (*Pro psykhiatrychnu dopomohu* [On Psychiatric Care] 2000, art. 25).

Failure to comply with these rights violates the free will of patients.

Patients undergoing addiction treatment often experience significant infringements on their free will and legal rights. V. P. Sharko conducted a detailed sociological and legal study at the Kyiv City Narcological Hospital "Sociotherapy," an institution providing medical and rehabilitation assistance to individuals with alcohol and drug addictions. The study revealed the following critical data regarding the state of patient rights:

1. Access to Information: Approximately 70% of respondents indicated that patients lack access to their own medical records.
2. Confidentiality and Safety: Almost one in seven respondents suspected a breach of medical confidentiality, while 16% suspected the misuse of medical drugs.

3. Personal Autonomy: One in four patients reported an inability to freely send and receive correspondence, and approximately half of the respondents were denied the possibility of receiving visitors.
4. Privacy Standards: A lack of privacy was highlighted by one-third of the doctors and half of the patients surveyed.
5. Institutional Environment: A significant number of respondents confirmed experiencing moral pressure from junior medical staff.
6. Legal Protection: Only one in three respondents believed that legal assistance was genuinely available within the institution.
7. General Sentiment: The majority of respondents emphasized an urgent need for the establishment of equal rights for patients (Sharko 2020, 71–73).

This study confirms that the free will of patients undergoing inpatient treatment is subject to unlawful restrictions, which is particularly relevant for specific patient categories. The personal non-property rights of an individual undergoing inpatient treatment are enshrined in legislation to protect their free will. But there are cases of restrictions.

This right is related to the personal non-property right to freedom and personal integrity. R. O. Stefanchuk summarizes the content of the right to freedom as follows: (1) freedom is a subjective civil right designed to ensure an individual's ability to freely determine their behavior; (2) an individual must be able to determine the scope of their freedom within the limits established by law and moral principles; (3) the right to freedom must create the opportunity to use that freedom within legal limits; (4) the right to freedom has legally stipulated limits, as uncontrolled freedom can turn into arbitrariness (Stefanchuk 2008, 369–370).

The right to freedom is a personal non-property right that consists in the ability to recognize an individual as the holder of the intangible good of personal freedom, the ability to freely determine one's behavior according to one's needs and interests within the law, and the ability to demand that others not violate this right (Ibid., 371).

However, the normative understanding of this right stems from the essence of personal non-property rights and determines that an individual has the right to freedom, and any forms of physical or mental pressure, including involving them in the use of alcohol or drugs, are prohibited (*Tsyvil'nyi kodeks Ukrainy* [Civil Code of Ukraine] 2003, art. 288).

The right to liberty as a personal non-property right provides for two types of prohibitions: (1) a prohibition on the deprivation or restriction of physical liberty, except in cases provided for by law; (2) a prohibition on coercion and pressure for an individual to make decisions.

The prohibition of physical deprivation or restriction of liberty is a cornerstone of democratic societies, declaring that no one may be deprived of their liberty except in specific, exhaustive cases and in accordance with a procedure prescribed by law.

According to the Convention for the Protection of Human Rights and Fundamental Freedoms (Council of Europe 1950, art. 5), lawful deprivation of liberty is limited to: (1) lawful imprisonment after conviction by a competent court; (2) lawful arrest or detention for non-compliance with a lawful court order or to ensure the fulfilllment of an obligation prescribed by law; (3) lawful arrest or detention based on reasonable suspicion of having committed an offense or when it is reasonably considered necessary to prevent the commission of an offense or fleeing after having done so; (4) the detention of a minor by lawful order for the purpose of educational supervision; (5) the lawful detention of persons for the prevention of the spreading of infectious diseases, or of persons of unsound mind, alcoholics, drug addicts, or vagrants; and (6) lawful arrest or detention of a person to prevent their unauthorized entry into the country or of a person against whom action is being taken with a view to deportation or extradition (Ibid.).

This list is exhaustive, meaning that any deprivation of liberty not falling under one of these specific sub-paragraphs constitutes a violation of the Convention, regardless of its compliance with national law..

All these measures are related to the restriction of free will due to public interest. As in cases of compulsory treatment, the restriction of the right to liberty should not deprive a person of their fundamental rights. Thus, persons deprived of liberty have the right to initiate proceedings in which a court can promptly establish the legality of their detention.

The second aspect of the right to freedom as a personal non-property right is the prohibition of coercion and pressure. The essence of this right lies in an individual's capacity to make decisions independently, which imposes a negative obligation on other participants to respect this autonomy and limits their ability to exert influence.

The Constitutional Court of Ukraine recognizes that the right to freedom constitutes a foundational pillar of the legal order through the following tenets:

1. Fundamental Value: Freedom is a fundamental value of a constitutional democracy and a vital prerequisite for a person's development and socialization.
2. Inalienable Choice: The right to freedom is an inalienable constitutional right that provides the ability to choose one's behavior for free and comprehensive development, to act independently, and to do everything that is not expressly prohibited by law.
3. External Autonomy: The right to freedom signifies that a person is free from external interference, with the exception of specific restrictions established by the Constitution and laws (*Rishennia Konstytutsiinoho Sudu Ukrainy* [Decision of the Constitutional Court of Ukraine] 2016).

As we can see, the right to freedom serves as the basis for other personal non-property rights. Additionally, the exercise of the right to freedom is a prerequisite for participation in contractual and other civil legal relations, where coercion is prohibited. This issue will be examined in more detail in the chapter on the fundamental role of free will in contract law.

From the above, it should be concluded that the personal non-property right to freedom is based on free will and manifests itself as a prohibition on the deprivation or restriction of physical liberty, except in cases provided by law, as well as a prohibition on coercion and pressure for an individual to make decisions.

The right to personal integrity flows from the right to liberty. One of its manifestations is the patient's right to informed consent or refusal of medical intervention. But the right to personal integrity is much broader.

As V. P. Grobova notes, the lack of a unified understanding of the content of personal inviolability leads to the fact that this institution is not fixed as a holistic system of norms, which causes duplication and contradictions in legal regulation and complicates the exercise of this right (Hrobova 2009, 97).

Article 289 of the Civil Code of Ukraine provides a general principle that an individual has the right to personal inviolability: (1) an individual may not be subjected to torture, cruel, inhuman, or degrading treatment or punishment; (2) physical punishment by parents, guardians, or educators of minors is not allowed; and (3) an individual has the right to dispose of their organs and other anatomical materials for scientific, medical, or educational purposes after death (*Tsyvil'nyi kodeks Ukrainy* [Civil Code of Ukraine] 2003, art. 289).

All these elements are aimed at protecting an individual's free will. This is confirmed by the fact that torture, cruel treatment, and physical punishment of children are direct threats to a person's free will. Such actions are a direct manifestation of illegal coercion, which completely contradicts the ideas of free will.

Although the right to personal integrity is not absolute and may be limited in cases specified by law (*Rishennia Konstytutsiinoho Sudu Ukrainy* [Decision of the Constitutional Court of Ukraine] 2011a), such restrictions must be carried out in compliance with constitutional guarantees (*Rishennia Velykoi palaty Konstytutsiinoho Sudu Ukrainy* [Decision of the Grand Chamber of the Constitutional Court of Ukraine] 2017).

The right to personal integrity requires protection from arbitrary restrictions, necessitating periodic judicial control over any deprivation of liberty. Consequently, certain constitutional values—particularly the inviolability of the person—require enhanced guarantees of their protection (*Rishennia Konstytutsiinoho Sudu Ukrainy* [Decision of the Constitutional Court of Ukraine] 2019).

However, after a detailed study, the Ukrainian Helsinki Human Rights Union concluded that current legislation contains serious unconstitutional restrictions on the right to liberty and requires immediate alignment with international and constitutional standards (*Analitychnyi ohliad prava...* [Analytical Review of the Right...] 2015).

O. V. Shvydkova concludes that the right to personal integrity is a complex legal institution that combines the norms of various branches of law to ensure a person's physical and mental integrity, the inviolability of their personal and family life, their honor and dignity, and the secrecy of their communications and home (Shvydkova 2006, 42). That is, in the opinion of the scholar, the right to personal integrity serves as the basis for some other personal non-property rights.

In combination with the right to liberty, the right to personal integrity means, first, the freedom of a person guaranteed by the state, which consists in providing them with a real opportunity to perform all actions they deem necessary for their personal existence and development, provided they do not contradict the law or violate the rights of others; second, personal security guaranteed by the state, which is expressed in protection from encroachments on their life, health, honor, and dignity, and in preventing unlawful interference with private and family life (Oliinyk 2006, 44). It should be agreed that the rights to liberty and personal integrity generalize the idea of enshrining free will in legislation. It can be said that the combination of these two rights personifies free will.

The US Declaration of Independence (1776) enshrines that all men are created equal and endowed by their Creator with certain inalienable rights—including Life, Liberty, and the pursuit of Happiness. As we can see, national and international legislation pays considerable attention to the right to liberty and security of person. It can be logically concluded that this is due to the urgent need to protect the free will of a person, which is the foundation of civil legal relations.

The right to a family and the right to custody or guardianship are also inextricably linked to free will.

A family is a group of people consisting of a man, a woman, children, and other close relatives who live together. A family consists of people who cohabit, share a common life, and have mutual rights and responsibilities. A married couple is considered a family, even if they do not live together for valid reasons. A child belongs to their parents' family even if they do not live with them. A family is created based on marriage, blood relationship, adoption, or other grounds not prohibited by law and not contrary to the moral principles of society (*Simeinyi kodeks Ukrainy* [Family Code of Ukraine] 2002, art. 3). Family members are recognized as individuals who permanently live together and run a common household, and are not necessarily close relatives. A mandatory condition is the fact of cohabitation, a joint household, shared expenses, and joint maintenance of the home (*Rishennia Konstytutsiinoho Sudu Ukrainy* [Decision of the Constitutional Court of Ukraine] 1999).

The right to a family comprises two key elements: the right to form a family and the right to live within a family.

The right to found a family is entirely based on free will. This is because a family arises only on two grounds: marriage or cohabitation with a shared life. Marriage is a family union of a woman and a man, registered with a state body (*Simeinyi kodeks Ukrainy* [Family Code of Ukraine] 2002, art. 21). The legislation directly establishes that marriage is based on the free consent of both a woman and a man (*Konstytutsiia Ukrainy* [Constitution of Ukraine] 1996, art. 51), and coercion into marriage is not allowed (*Simeinyi kodeks Ukrainy* [Family Code of Ukraine] 2002, art.24).

The principle of voluntariness of marriage provides for the possibility of concluding a marriage only with free, full, conscious, and informed consent. In the event of influence on the free expression of will, it provides legal protection against forced marriage by declaring it invalid. The principle of voluntariness also applies to de facto cohabitation and operates throughout the duration of the relationship, determining the state's obligation to guarantee the freedom to dissolve the marriage.

Therefore, marriage is the exercise of the right to a family only through the equal manifestation of free will by a man and a woman.

When the right to a family is realised through cohabitation, the will of the individuals to be considered a family is of fundamental importance. For example, friends or students living together will not automatically be considered a family. What is needed is the desire of these people to be one family and lead a common life. Even the cohabitation of a man and a woman and their self-recognition as a family is not a basis for the emergence of spousal rights and obligations without official marriage registration. In this case, they will be considered a family, but not spouses.

Only the free will of the participants in the legal relationship will determine their legal connection as a family. As we can see, the right to a family can be realised officially through marriage or through the conscious recognition of oneself as a family based on cohabitation. This approach is also aimed at protecting free will, as the law cannot force individuals to marry to exercise their right to a family.

At the same time, the procedure and conditions for registering a marriage are determined by law. The ban on marriage before the age of 18 (except in certain circumstances) can be seen as a restriction on the free will of a person who wishes to marry. However, this does not constitute a restriction of free will in the civil law sense, as the scope and limits of free will in this context are defined by normative permissions. The same applies to the desire to marry multiple people simultaneously or close relatives, which is prohibited by law.

The right to a family can be realised in other ways. A family can be created by a person who has given birth to a child, regardless of age (Ibid., art. 4). In this case, the level of legal capacity does not matter, as even a minor who has given birth becomes a mother and creates a new family. This right is absolute and cannot be limited. The exercise of the right to a family through childbirth is also possible only due to free will. This is justified by the fact that only a woman makes an independent decision to give birth. This is not about fertilisation, but about the decision to give birth. Even if fertilisation occurred against her free will (e.g., rape), the decision to give birth or have an abortion can only be made by the woman of her own free will. No coercion is allowed. Even after birth, parents can renounce their parental rights. If parents refuse to take their child from the maternity hospital, the right passes to grandparents or other relatives with permission from the guardianship authority. Accordingly, from the moment the parents or other relatives take the baby, the child's right to a family begins to be exercised, specifically the right to live in a family (Vovk 2021, 337).

The issue of the forced exercise of the right to a family requires special attention. It is understood that every child automatically exercises this right by virtue of their birth. A child belongs to their parents' family, and in this matter, their free will is not taken into account. Even if a child runs away from home or is placed in a boarding school, they still belong to their parents' family, even if they do not live with them.

A child can exercise the right to create a new family only after marriage or childbirth. Even a minor who has become a mother or father and who does not have the right to marry is considered to have exercised the right to create a family by giving birth and continues to exercise it as a member of that family (Syniehubov 2013, 372).

It remains unclear whether a minor can exercise the right to a family through cohabitation and leading a common life. The legislation does not specify the age at which such a right arises. The constitution only stipulates that parents are obligated to support their children until they reach adulthood (*Konstytutsiia Ukrainy* [Constitution of Ukraine] 1996, art. 51).

At the same time, legal representatives make decisions in the interests of their minor children. This raises the question of whether children and employees of a boarding school who live together and share a common life can be considered a family.

Therefore, the exercise of the right to a family occurs only under the condition of free will through marriage or cohabitation with the intention of being a family. The right of children to a family arises at birth and does not depend on their free will.

The right to a family gives rise to another personal non-property right. Thus, the right to guardianship or custody is provided for minors, as well as for individuals who have been recognized as incapacitated or whose civil capacity is limited (*Tsyvil'nyi kodeks Ukrainy* [Civil Code of Ukraine] 2003, art. 292).

Today, this issue is regulated by the Civil Code, the Family Code, and the Rules of Guardianship and Custody. Some scholars emphasise the need to adopt a separate Law "On Guardianship and Custody" to regulate these relations (Morozova 2011, 16).

The institution of guardianship and trusteeship is a system of separate legal norms within family law that regulates social relations related to the exercise of a minor child's right to the protection of their personal and property interests (Rudyi 2011, 207).

The right to guardianship or custody is related to free will through a person's ability to make decisions on this issue. Guardianship and custody are established to ensure the personal and property rights and interests of minors, as well as adults who, due to their health, are unable to exercise their rights and fulfill their obligations independently (*Tsyvil'nyi kodeks Ukrainy* [Civil Code of Ukraine] 2003, art. 55). Custody is established over minors who are orphans or deprived of parental care, and individuals whose civil capacity is limited (Ibid., art. 59).

Under the legal framework of Ukraine, the establishment of guardianship and custody serves as a protective measure for individuals who, due to age or health status, cannot fully exercise their rights and duties. According to the Civil Code of Ukraine, the court is responsible for appointing representatives in several distinct circumstances:

1. Incapacitated Persons: If an individual is judicially recognized as incapacitated, the court appoints a guardian.
2. Limited Civil Capacity: If an individual's civil capacity is judicially limited, a custodian is appointed.
3. Minors (Under 14): In cases where a child under the age of 14 is deprived of parental care, a guardian is appointed.
4. Adolescents (Aged 14 to 18): In cases where a minor between the ages of 14 and 18 is deprived of parental care, a custodian is appointed (Ibid., art. 60).

While the court holds primary jurisdiction in the aforementioned cases, the guardianship and trusteeship body (the administrative arm) also possesses the authority to establish these protections. However, this administrative path is only available in instances where the law does not explicitly mandate a judicial decree.

This dual system ensures that no individual is left without legal representation, balancing the rigorous oversight of the court with the administrative efficiency of local social services.

A person's free will has limited significance when guardianship and custody are established over them. This is based on the prevalence of the public interest, according to which the exercise of this right does not depend on the will of the ward. If a right is a measure of possible behavior, then the right to guardianship is an obligation to have one's personal and property rights and interests protected. A ward cannot refuse to be placed under guardianship or custody.

Exceptions include taking into account the wishes of a child upon reaching the age of ten when appointing a guardian, as well as when appointing a custodian over a capable adult who, due to health, cannot protect their own rights (in such a case, a custodian may be appointed only at their request). The ward may also initiate the procedure for dismissing the guardian or custodian.

Thus, Article 251 of the Family Code provides that a person may be relieved of their duties as a guardian or custodian if the relationship between them and the child hinders the exercise of guardianship or custody. The ward may independently report such a case of their own free will. Also, if the court has appointed a custodian, it may relieve them of their powers upon the application of the person under custody (*Simeinyi kodeks Ukrainy* [Family Code of Ukraine] 2002, art. 75).

The complete termination of guardianship does not depend on the ward's free will. It is terminated when a minor is transferred to their parents, when the ward reaches the age of fourteen, or when the civil capacity of an incapacitated individual is restored (*Tsyvil'nyi kodeks Ukrainy* [Civil Code of Ukraine] 2003, art. 76). The ward cannot influence any of these conditions.

A different situation concerns the termination of custody. Custody is terminated when an individual reaches the age of majority, when a minor marries, when a minor is granted full civil capacity, or when the civil capacity of an individual with limited capacity is restored (Ibid., art. 77). By their own free will, the ward can influence the occurrence of all these grounds, except for reaching the age of majority. For example, a person can, of their own free will, fulfill the conditions for marriage, emancipation (e.g., registering as an entrepreneur), or restoration of civil capacity (e.g., ceasing alcohol abuse).

Also, the ward may use free will to exercise rights that were not limited by the establishment of guardianship or custody. In particular, this applies to certain property rights, as wards are holders of subjective rights in relation to their guardians and custodians, and the latter have rights and obligations in relation to their wards and the guardianship authorities (Adakhovska 2012, 410).

A direct manifestation of free will is the ability of a person in need of assistance to apply for it. A capable individual who, due to health reasons, cannot independently exercise their rights and fulfill their duties, has the right to choose an assistant (*Tsyvil'nyi kodeks Ukrainy* [Civil Code of Ukraine] 2003, art. 78). In this case, free will is not restricted, and the assistant is endowed with an exhaustive range of rights and duties. In particular, the assistant has the right to receive pensions, alimony, wages, and correspondence belonging to the individual; to perform minor household transactions in their interest; and to represent them in state authorities and other organizations (Ibid., art. 78). Unlike a guardian or custodian, an assistant can be dismissed at any time at the request of the person they are assisting.

As we can see, the right to guardianship and care is not tied to the ward's free will but is aimed at ensuring their personal and property rights. At the same time, the ward retains free will in some matters and can influence the termination of custody or the replacement of their guardian or custodian.

This analysis of the relationship between personal non-property rights—those ensuring the natural existence of an individual—

and free will confirms that these concepts are fundamentally interconnected. Free will emerges at birth, and its scope evolves throughout an individual's life. Within this legal framework, rights function in three distinct ways: as prerequisites for free will, as limitations upon it, or as the primary mechanism for its implementation.

1. The Right to Life
   The right to life holds a higher status in the legal hierarchy than free will. It manifests through three essential aspects:
   a. Negative Obligation: The prohibition of arbitrary deprivation of life.
   b. Positive Obligation: The state's proactive duty to protect human life.
   c. Individual Agency: The right of every person to defend their own life and health.
2. Physical and Mental Integrity
   The legal idea of free will finds its most direct expression in the rights to health care and physical liberty:
   a. Healthcare Autonomy: Free will is realized through the doctrines of informed consent and the right to refuse medical care.
   b. Physical Liberty: The right to freedom acts as a dual prohibition—against the arbitrary deprivation of physical liberty and against any form of unlawful coercion.
   c. Personification of Will: The combination of the rights to freedom and personal integrity generalizes and personifies the legislative enshrinement of free will.
3. Social and Protective Dimensions of Will
   a. Family Rights: The right to a family is realized exclusively through the application of free will, specifically in the context of marriage or cohabitation.
   b. Protective Mechanisms: The right to guardianship and trusteeship is designed to safeguard the interests of those who, due to legal incapacity, cannot independently exercise their free will.

2.2. The Importance of Free Will in Personal Non-Property Rights that Ensure the Social Existence of an Individual

Free will is manifested in all personal non-property rights that ensure the natural existence of an individual, which are possessed for life. This suggests that the personal non-property rights ensuring an individual's social existence are also fundamentally based on the concept of free will.

Traditionally, this category includes a broad spectrum of protections essential for the development of the person in a social context:

1. Identity and Recognition: The right to a name (including its change and use), and the right to individuality.
2. Reputation and Dignity: The right to respect for dignity and honor, the right to respect for a deceased person, and the right to the inviolability of business reputation.
3. Privacy and Information: The right to a private life and its confidentiality; the right to information; the right to personal papers and their disposal; the right to access personal documents transferred to libraries or archives; and the right to the secrecy of correspondence.
4. Creative and Physical Autonomy: The right to the protection of one's interests during photo, film, television, and video recording; the right to freedom of creative activity; the right to freedom of movement and free choice of residence; and the right to choose one's occupation.

For a comprehensive understanding of free will in Civil Law, a deep analysis of the relationship between these specific rights and the exercise of autonomous decision-making is necessary. These rights do not merely protect the individual from interference; they provide the legal infrastructure through which free will is projected onto the social environment.

Summarising modern positions on the legal mechanism of these relations, S. O. Slipchenko distinguishes three groups: the proprietary concept (M. Malein, T. Lisnych, E. Petrov), the concept of exclusive rights (V. Dozortsev, V. Kolosov, M. Schwartz), and the concept of personal rights as an independent group of absolute rights (R. Stefanchuk, K. Horislavsky, L. Fedyuk, I. Nevzorov), and concludes that this group of rights still belongs to the exclusive category (Slipchenko 2012, 96). Traditionally, exclusive rights pertain to the institution of intellectual property. On the one hand, this institution and exclusive rights themselves reflect the ideas of free will. This is evident from the content of the official definition.

According to Article 1 of the Law of Ukraine "On Copyright and Related Rights," an exclusive right is a property right of a person who holds copyright and/or related rights to a work, performance, production, or broadcast, to use these objects exclusively and to grant or prohibit their use by others within the period established by law (*Pro avtors'ke pravo i sumizhni prava* [On Copyright and Related Rights] 2022, art. 1).

Thus, certain personal non-property rights that ensure social existence do indeed relate to intellectual property and exclusive rights. However, these do not include the right to choose an occupation, freedom of movement, and free choice of place of residence, among others. Therefore, it is more appropriate to understand this group of rights as an independent group of absolute rights.

In this context, it is essential to consider that these rights are characterised by two key features: intangibility and a lack of economic content. In turn, the latter feature is not an absolute characteristic of personal non-property rights that ensure social existence, and the property aspect of these relations is always dependent on and derived from their non-property nature (Slipchenko 2005, 15).

Many authors recognize the personal non-property rights that ensure an individual's social existence as a complex category that encompasses the inner personal feelings of each person; a person feels particular discomfort when these rights are violated (Naumenko 2014, 299). The range of rights included in this category plays a crucial role in an individual's social existence and is based on the manifestation of free will. To confirm this thesis, we will conduct an analytical examination of the relationship between each of these rights and free will.

One of the first rights that a person acquires at birth is the right to a name. This is understood as a legally granted measure of possible behavior, which consists of the ability of the right-holder to perform actions in their own name and to demand particular conduct from obligated persons (Molchanov 2009, 6).

This concept includes a given name, a patronymic, and a surname. In the Civil Code of Ukraine, the norms regulating the right to a name are very brief: (1) an individual has the right to a name; (2) an individual has the right to a transcribed record of their surname and given name in accordance with their national tradition; (3) in the event of a distortion of a name, it must be corrected; (4) if the distortion occurs in a document, the document is subject to replacement, and if in a mass medium, it must be corrected in the same medium (*Tsyvil'nyi kodeks Ukrainy* [Civil Code of Ukraine] 2003, art. 294).

This is based on the fact that the state registration of a name requires clear, logical, and balanced criteria, provided for at the legislative level, to serve as a primary basis for national identification worldwide (Sofinska 2014, 98).

Z. Romovska identifies the following elements within the right to a name: (1) the right to be named; (2) the right to be called by others as named by one's parents; (3) the right to resist any attempts to alter the name given by one's parents; (4) the right to apply to the relevant authorities to change the name given by one's parents (Romovska 2009).

Each of these elements constitutes a separate personal non-property right and has its own connection with free will.

The aforementioned norm only establishes the right to have a name, use its transcribed form, and be protected from its distortion. These rights arise at birth, and the right to a name itself is realised through legal representatives, without taking into account the free will of the subject of this right. The relationship between free will and the right to a name should be considered through its constituent elements. Thus, the right to a name is the legal possibility for an individual to: possess a name, change it, and use it in all spheres of activity; demand that all other persons refrain from its unlawful use; and resolve all issues related to its use by third parties (Portnov and Moskaliuk 2012, 42).

The first manifestation of this right is the ability to possess a name. The Convention on the Rights of the Child proclaims the child's right to a name from the moment of birth (United Nations General Assembly 1989, art. 7).

According to Article 144 of the Family Code of Ukraine, parents are required to register the birth of a child within one month. Failure to fulfilll this obligation is grounds for legal liability. The registration of a child's birth is carried out by the state civil status registration authority, which simultaneously determines the child's origin and assigns a surname, given name, and patronymic (*Simeinyi kodeks Ukrainy* [Family Code of Ukraine] 2002, art. 144).

Some scholars believe a conflict exists between the norms of the Family Code of Ukraine and the Convention on the Rights of the Child. This is justified by the fact that the national act allows for registration within one month, while the Convention proclaims the right to a name from birth. However, I do not consider this a conflict, as national legislation also establishes the emergence of the right to a name from birth, merely providing a specific period for its official registration.

The decision to choose a name rests entirely with the parents. It is they who, of their own free will, guided by their views and traditions, exercise the child's right to a name.

A child's given name is determined by the parents' consent. The given name of a child born to an unmarried woman, in the absence of voluntary recognition of paternity, is determined by the mother. If registration is carried out by another person, the name is assigned at their direction (*Pro zatverdzhennia Pravyl...* [On Approval of the Rules...] 2000, part III, para. 2).

A somewhat different situation arises with the surname and patronymic. If the parents have different surnames, the child is assigned the surname of the father or mother, or a double surname formed by combining them, with the parents' consent (Ibid., part III, para 21). In this case, the exercise of the right to a name is again based on the free will of the legal representatives.

A child's patronymic is assigned based on the father's given name. If the father has a double name, the patronymic is formed from one of them at the parents' choice (Ibid., part III, para 23).

At the parents' request, the patronymic may be formed in accordance with national traditions or not assigned at all. It is important that the patronymic of a child born to an unmarried woman, where paternity is not recognized, is determined by the given name of the person whom the mother has named as the father. In this case, only the woman's free will is at play. It should be recognized that this norm limits a man's rights and his free will. The man will be able to exercise his right to determine the child's patronymic only after being legally recognized as the father through a court.

In Ukraine, there are no norms that limit the range of permissible names. Therefore, parents have the right to choose any name for their child or even invent their own. However, it should be emphasised that parents act in the child's interests, which means the name given should not violate the child's other rights, such as the right to honor and dignity. Most scholars discuss violations of the principle of reasonableness during the exercise of the right to a name (Stefanchuk 2005a).

While the right to choose a name is a primary manifestation of parental free will, several countries have implemented specific legislative restrictions to protect the interests of the child or uphold public order. In these jurisdictions, parental autonomy is limited by the following criteria:

1. Sweden: Prohibition of names that may be deemed offensive or those that could cause discomfort to the bearer (Namnlag 1982).
2. Norway: Restrictions on names that refer to diseases, sexual terms, or profanity.
3. Germany: Requirement for names to be approved by a specialized state agency to ensure they do not harm the child's well-being.

4. Japan: Technical limitations where names must be composed of characters from a permitted list of 2,232 approved symbols (*Imena, iakymy ne mozhna nazyvaty maliukiv...* [Names that Cannot be Given to Babies...] 2018).
5. United States: State-level prohibitions against names containing numbers, ideograms, or obscenities (Larson 2011).

In all these instances, national legislation acts as a boundary to the parents' freedom of choice, prioritizing social norms and the protection of the child's identity over absolute parental discretion..

In conclusion, legal representatives exercise a child's right to a name in the child's interests and should be guided by this principle. A similar situation can be seen in other cases, such as when parents decide to baptise a child. This is not considered a restriction of the child's free will, as they may later change their religion. Similarly, they can exercise their free will regarding their name by changing it.

Therefore, the right to possess a name arises at birth and initially does not depend on the child's free will, as the name is chosen by legal representatives. An individual can later exercise their free will by deciding to change their name.

The Civil Code of Ukraine provides for the following grounds for changing a name: (1) at one's own discretion; (2) in the event of adoption, its annulment, or cancellation; (3) in the event of marriage registration, dissolution, or annulment (*Tsyvil'nyi kodeks Ukrainy* [Civil Code of Ukraine] 2003, art. 295).

In fact, the right to change one's name at one's own discretion supersedes all other grounds. An individual who has reached the age of sixteen has the right to change their surname, given name, and/or patronymic at their discretion. An individual who has reached fourteen may do so with parental consent. If a guardian has been appointed, their consent is required. Consent from only one parent is sufficient if the other is deceased, missing, incapacitated, or has been stripped of parental rights. If one parent objects, the dispute may be resolved by a guardianship authority or the court, taking into account the child's best interests (Ibid.). Thus, changing a name is an absolute manifestation of free will, where an individual independently decides to change their name to any other.

At the same time, R. Molchanov emphasizes the need to establish certain restrictions, suggesting that: (1) a name change must be due to a valid reason (e.g., dissonance, bad reputation); (2) frequent name changes should be prohibited (Molchanov 2014a, 156).

This position is insufficiently substantiated, and implementing such ideas could complicate the exercise of this personal non-property right and limit free will. The argument for a "valid reason" is subjective. The current legislation does not contain restrictions on the frequency of name changes, other than those inherent in the procedure itself (Molchanov, 2014b, p. 24).

Separately, the possibility of changing a name is provided for in the event of adoption. It is understood that in such cases, the person can express their own free will regarding the name change. For example, an adopted child has the right to keep or change their patronymic of their own free will.

Additionally, marriage, its dissolution, or its annulment can be grounds for a surname change. In these cases, a person can, of their own free will, decide to adopt the surname of their spouse. It is important that this right allows either spouse to take the other's surname.

The procedure for changing a name is clearly formalized and requires an application and several documents. State registration of a name change does not automatically entail changes to the civil status records of the person or their minor children, though certificates are reissued and previous ones are annulled (*Pro zatverdzhennia Poriadku rozhliadu...* [On Approval of the Procedure..] 2007, para. 13).

Special attention should be paid to the change of a child's surname by their parents. Here, we can distinguish cases that involve the child's free will from those that do not.

Cases where the child's free will is not taken into account include: (1) if both parents change their surname, the surname of a child under seven is also changed; (2) at the request of the parents, the surname of a child under fourteen may be changed to that of the other parent under certain circumstances (e.g., if one parent is deceased) (*Simeinyi kodeks Ukrainy* [Family Code of Ukraine] 2002, art. 148).

Cases where the child's free will is taken into account include: (1) if both parents change their surname, the surname of a child who has reached the age of seven is changed with their consent; (2) if one parent changes their surname, the child's surname may be changed with the consent of both parents and the child who has reached the age of seven (Ibid.).

For a long time, the practice of changing one's name limited the right to change one's patronymic. As V. O. Kozhevnikova emphasises, in contrast to the established limits for changing a name and surname, the right to change a patronymic was clearly limited, and such restrictions were unjustified and needed to be eliminated (Kozhevnykova 2018, 168).

The most famous precedent in this area is the case of *Garnaga v. Ukraine,* in which state authorities refused to change the applicant's patronymic. The applicant argued that living with her stepfather for a long time created a need for a closer legal bond—which is why she wished to change her patronymic after adopting his surname (European Court of Human Rights 2013a).

Furthermore, her biological father, whose name she bore as a patronymic, had not participated in her life, so there was no close family connection (Titko and Bozhuk 2020, 676). The ECtHR found that her right to change her name had been violated.

The right to change one's patronymic was significantly expanded by recent legislative updates. According to the amendments introduced in 2021, the procedure for considering applications was simplified to allow greater autonomy for individuals aged 14 and older (*Pro vnesennia zminy...* [On Amending Paragraph 3...] 2021).

Previously, a person over 14 could change their patronymic only if their father changed his name. Now, the right arises at 16 at their own will, or at 14 with parental consent. This change reflects the broader trend of aligning national family law with European human rights standards regarding the right to a name and identity.

In some cases, a refusal to change a name is possible. Grounds for refusal include if the applicant is under criminal investigation or administrative supervision, has an unexpunged criminal record, is wanted by foreign law enforcement, or has submitted false information (*Tsyvil'nyi kodeks Ukrainy* [Civil Code of Ukraine] 2003, art. 295). In such cases, we are talking about a restriction of free will due to the public interest.

S. I. Chornoochenko proposes granting individuals the right to challenge a name change decision in court if they have valid reasons against it, suggesting a one-year appeal period (Chornoochenko 2000, 7). However, this thesis is questionable. On the one hand, we declare that a person from a certain age has sufficient free will to change their name. On the other, we would be establishing that the free will of another person has greater legal force, which contradicts the principles of civil law.

From the right to a name emerges the personal non-property right to use a name. An individual has the right to use their name in all spheres of their activity (*Tsyvil'nyi kodeks Ukrainy* [Civil Code of Ukraine] 2003, art. 296).

Analysing this right, it is worth noting that it includes: the right to use one's name in all public relations (for a fee or free of charge), to disclose it, to permit or prohibit its disclosure, and to decide the fate of one's name (Cherepakha 2017, 353).

In effect, the right to use a name is an active form of the right to a name, which enables its independent use and creates obligations for others. It is aimed at identifying and individualising a natural person. The importance of individualization in law is primarily due to the fact that it recognizes a person's ability to be a participant in civil legal relations, as the legislator is interested in a clear differentiation of these participants (Stefanchuk 2008, 410).

At the same time, a name is not the only means of individualization; others are divided into private law means (name, signature, image, civil status) and public law means (identification code, registration, citizenship) (Volkova 2008, 5).

Considering that the right to use a name is an active opportunity for self-identification, it is justifiably based on free will. An individual independently decides whether to reveal their name. For example, when purchasing goods with restricted circulation, if a seller asks for identification, a person may refuse and not participate in the legal relationship. However, a person can be compelled to use their name when identification is mandatory, such as during a document check by law enforcement. In this case, the public interest compels the individual to exercise their right to use their name, regardless of their free will.

Therefore, in some cases, a person chooses to use a name of their own free will, while in others, its use is mandatory. For instance, when submitting documents for marriage registration, an individual will not be able to exercise certain rights without using their name.

As N. V. Volkova summarizes, the right to use a name serves three purposes: (1) formal individualization, to distinguish and personify a person; (2) social individualization, both in interpersonal communication and for legal purposes—such as refuting defamatory information; and (3) legal personality individualization, to determine if a person can be a participant in certain legal relations (Volkova 2008).

The issue of the right to use a famous person's name post mortem is problematic. It is normatively determined that the use of an individual's name in literary and other works (except documentary ones) as a character is allowed only with their consent, and after their death, with the consent of their children, spouse, and if none, parents or siblings (*Tsyvil'nyi kodeks Ukrainy* [Civil Code of Ukraine] 2003, art. 296).

For example, if a community decides to install a memorial plaque to a famous person, these relatives must give consent. However, the free will of the famous person themself is no longer taken into account. In practice, relatives act as bearers of the person's free will. But even if the person publicly declared their unwillingness to have their name used after death, relatives still have the right to use it. This is because there is no legal mechanism to appeal such a decision, and the will of the specified relatives will prevail. A conflict also arises when a spouse and children have different views. The law does not establish a clear hierarchy. Therefore, applying the analogy of law, particularly using rules on the order of inheritance, would be logical.

This situation is similar to the right to donate a deceased person's organs, where legal representatives make the decision. L. Maydanyk proposes a legislative ban on registering as trademarks designations that reproduce the names of famous people without their consent (or that of their relatives after death) to ensure proper protection of the right to a name and prevent circumvention of the law (Maydanyk 2013, 79).

The right to use a name implies using only one's officially registered name, surname, and patronymic. However, in reality, identifying a person only by these can create conflicts, as an unlimited number of people can have the same data. This is especially relevant given the ability to change one's name to any other. For example, it is possible to duplicate the name of a famous person and misuse it. Sometimes "lesser-known" people with the same surname impersonate relatives of "more famous" ones to obtain benefits (Stefanchuk 2005a, 92).

The right to use a name is closely related to the author's right to use a pseudonym. In this case, a person, of their own free will, decides to use a fictitious name in their creative activities. All the nuances outlined will apply to the pseudonym, taking into account intellectual property law. A person's name (or pseudonym) can be an object of intellectual property law if it is commercialised. It can be defined as a set of powers regarding the right to own the name, the exclusive right of the right-holder to use it, and the right to prohibit its illegal use (Moroz 2014, 245). Here, it is necessary to distinguish between cases where a name is used within the framework of personal non-property rights and intellectual property rights. However, in both cases, free will is at the core.

Concluding the study of the role of free will in the right to use a name, the following theoretical conclusions can be formulated:

1. Manifestation of Autonomy: The right to use a name is a direct manifestation of free will. It is the individual who independently decides the specific manner and extent to which their name is used in social and legal interactions.

2. Legislative Obligations: Free will in this context is not absolute. In specific cases established by law (such as official identification or legal proceedings), an individual is obligated to use their legal name, regardless of their personal preference or free will.
3. Third-Party Respect: The exercise of free will by the right-holder imposes a duty on others. Third parties are required to use an individual's name only in the manner prescribed or desired by that individual, provided it aligns with legal standards.

This framework ensures that while the name remains a primary tool of self-identification and a projection of the self, it also functions as a stable anchor for legal certainty and public order..

Some attention should be paid to the personal non-property right to respect for a deceased person. It should be noted that the legislator has distinguished this from the right to life by enshrining them in different chapters of the Civil Code. The right to life is a personal non-property right that ensures the natural existence of an individual, while the right to respect for a deceased person ensures their social existence. From this, we can conclude that the right to life is an internal right, without which a person's existence is threatened, whereas the right to respect for a deceased person has social significance.

The right to respect for a deceased person serves a regulatory function by restricting the free will of others, establishing obligations to treat the body and burial place with respect. In the event of desecration, family members and close relatives have the right to compensation for damages (*Tsyvil'nyi kodeks Ukrainy* [Civil Code of Ukraine] 2003, art. 298). Based on this, we understand that this right is more of an obligation for others and involves restricting their free will if it is aimed at violating this norm. In case of a violation, we are protecting the rights and interests of third parties, not the deceased.

The holder of this right cannot protect it themself. This is an exceptional situation where the right-holder is no longer a subject of legal relations. To exercise this right, a person must lose the ability to be a subject of legal relations. Such a situation appears paradoxical from a doctrinal perspective. Today, this issue receives no attention in scientific research, and even in commentaries on civil legislation, this norm is often omitted.

The right to respect for a deceased person can be linked to their free will only if there is a will or an inheritance agreement. In this case, the right-holder can exercise their free will by stipulating conditions and requirements concerning posthumous actions regarding their body and burial place. It is in this context that we should understand the connection.

The right to respect for a deceased person is problematic to implement. For example, when relatives fail to maintain a burial place, only other interested parties can protect this right. However, the legislation does not specify who is responsible for maintaining it. Therefore, a lawsuit by a husband against his deceased wife's parents for violating this norm seems hopeless.

There are ideas about the need for more detailed regulation of thanatological rights, with the connotation that the right to dignified treatment of the body after death is part of the right to life and dignity. However, such a decision would be purely declaratory and would not lead to a real change in legal structures. The only necessary solution is the normative delineation of the circle of persons who must ensure respectful treatment of the body and burial place, and to define their duties and responsibilities. Here we should agree with R.O. Stefanchuk that respect for a person is determined through the system of rights granted to them (Stefanchuk 2008, 32). In this context, it becomes clear that the right to respect for a deceased person is realised through restrictions on the free will of others and the possibility of expressing one's own will in a will or inheritance agreement.

A direct extension of the concept of introducing free will into personal non-property human rights is the right to individuality.

The personal non-property right to individuality is a development at the sectoral level of the constitutional provision guaranteeing every person the right to the free development of their personality, provided that the rights and freedoms of others are not violated.

The Civil Code of Ukraine clarifies this right with the norm that an individual has the right to preserve their national, cultural, religious, and linguistic identity, as well as the right to freely choose the forms and methods of expressing their individuality, if they are not prohibited by law and do not contradict moral principles (*Tsyvil'nyi kodeks Ukrainy* [Civil Code of Ukraine] 2003, art. 300).

The specified right embodies the very idea of free will, as all its elements are a manifestation of it. Even the right to preserve one's identity is connected with the person's will to maintain it or not. Thus, belonging to a national, cultural, religious, and linguistic identity occurs from birth, without taking into account the person's free will. However, later, the person independently determines, of their own free will, whether to adhere to these elements. Moreover, the opportunity to freely choose one's identity is primarily protected by the Constitution and norms prohibiting discrimination. From birth, a child is assigned to certain elements of identity at the parents' free will, who act in the child's best interests. However, at any moment, through their own development, the child can independently choose another culture or language.

Individuality (*individuitas*) is a set of peculiar features of a person that characterise their uniqueness, manifested in character traits and interests that distinguish one person from another. Individuality is determined by the spiritual and practical reality it creates, which is the cumulative result of self-reflection, conscience, and faith, giving rise to a spiritual person (Chepa 2001).

The right to individuality is a legally enshrined measure of possible behavior that provides a guaranteed opportunity to freely determine one's conduct in the private sphere, namely: to create, possess, change, and use one's individuality and demand protection in case of any violation.

The right to individuality is a set of qualities that allow one person to be distinguished from another, to realise their own views, ideas, and, as a result, their free will.

An individual realizes the right to individuality through the free choice of religion, appearance, language, voice, and manner of behavior. Certain personal non-property rights exist as a manifestation of the right to individuality, such as the right to change one's name. A particular manifestation of individuality begins at birth, but even its manifestations laid down at this moment can be changed.

According to the Civil Code of Ukraine, personal non-property rights belong to every individual from birth or by law (*Tsyvil'nyi kodeks Ukrainy* [Civil Code of Ukraine] 2003, art. 269). The right to a name as an element of individuality arises at birth. The free will of the right-holder is not taken into account, as the right is realised by the parents in the child's interest. In this case, the manifestation of individuality is associated with the emergence of a right from birth. However, a person can later change their name. This would be the exercise of a personal non-property right by law.

In some cases, specific actions become a manifestation of the right to individuality only when exercised in conjunction with another right. For example, there is no legally enshrined right to gender or its definition. But when exercising the right to change (correct) one's gender identity, we can speak of a manifestation of free will aimed at exercising the right to individuality. In this case, the exercise of this right will have both a medical and a civil law character. The medical component will be related to the medical-biological indications for changing gender identity—the mental and behavioral disorder of "transsexualism" according to the ICD-10. The civil law component will be related to the exercise of the right to individuality and health protection. But in both cases, the main reason for changing gender will be the patient's free will.

This is also confirmed by the Universal Declaration on the Human Genome and Human Rights, which states that a person's identity cannot be reduced to their genetic characteristics and requires respect for their uniqueness and diversity (UNESCO 1997, art. 2).

Therefore, in international law, the right to individuality is defined in the context of uniqueness, both at the biological level and at higher levels of human existence (Shalyhanova 2011, 978).

It can be agreed that individuality as a feature is related not just to a person, but to a person who has already undergone socialisation (Hontar 2017, 95). However, it should be added that the right to individuality arises at birth and is realised through the free will of legal representatives. Over time, as a person develops and the scope of their free will expands, so do the opportunities provided by the right to individuality.

The right to individuality encompasses self-identification, self-awareness, and self-expression through the manifestation of free will. One should also agree with B. Garasymiv that a person is individual in their essence and way of existence. At the same time, the concept of individuality does not coincide with that of personality. If the latter characterises a person from the position of their social conditioning, the former reveals the characteristic features of the personality, the form, and the way of its being (Harasymiv 2017, 77).

The following personal non-property rights can be conditionally grouped as "informational." All of them are related to information about a person, other persons, phenomena, facts, and events. In this context, it is necessary to consider the connection of free will with the following rights:

1. Dignity and Honor: The right to respect for dignity and honor.
2. Business Reputation: The right to the inviolability of business reputation.
3. Privacy: The right to a private life and its secrecy.
4. Information Access: The right to information.
5. Personal Papers: The right to personal papers and their disposal, as well as the right to access personal papers transferred to libraries or archives.
6. Communication: The right to secrecy of correspondence.
7. Visual Integrity: The right to the protection of interests when conducting photo, film, television, and video recordings, and the protection of the interests of a person depicted in photographs and other works of art.

The next personal non-property right based on free will is the right to respect for dignity and honor. The dignity and honor of a natural person are inviolable. A natural person has the right to apply to the court for the protection of their dignity and honor (*Tsyvil'nyi kodeks Ukrainy* [Civil Code of Ukraine] 2003, art. 297).

First, let's define these terms. Honor is a concept of moral consciousness and a category of ethics, which includes an individual's awareness of their social significance and the recognition of this significance by society. Honor is a special moral attitude of a person toward themself, manifested in the awareness of their social status, type of activity, and moral merits (and the corresponding attitude from society) (Serohin and Sorokina, 2016, 59).

Honor is a set of higher moral principles by which a person is guided in their public and personal behavior (*Slovnyk ukrains'koi movy...* [Dictionary of the Ukrainian Language...] 1980).

Dignity is a concept of moral consciousness that expresses the idea of the value of every person as a moral individual. It is a category of ethics that signifies a special moral attitude of a person toward themself and the attitude toward them from society, in which the value of the individual is recognized. Dignity is a set of features that characterise positive moral qualities and a person's awareness of their social weight and duty (*Slovnyk ukrainskoi movy: v 11 t.,* 1971). It is a category that characterises a person's self-respect and moral equality with others, determining their unconditional self-worth (Saveliev, 2009).

Dignity is a special moral attitude of a person toward himself, which is manifested in his awareness of his self-worth and moral equality with other people, the attitude of other people toward a person, in which his unconditional value is recognized (Toftul 2014, 94).

The categories of honor and dignity are often used interchangeably, but they are not identical. Honor is an external attitude toward a person, while dignity is internal self-esteem.

Honor and dignity are based on free will, although its manifestation in these cases differs. In a broader interpretation, honor is understood as a social assessment of a personality, formed in the process of social life and based on objective indicators such as actions and views (Kryvenko 2022, 145). At first glance, honor is the external perception of a person by others. However, it is based on the actions of the person themself and therefore stems from their free will.

We must proceed from the fact that respect for honor consists in the right of a person to claim a correct moral assessment of their personality or activity, as well as the right to demand that others refrain from violating this right (Romovska 2003, 14). Theoretically, this suggests the following relationship: a person, of their own free will, enters into legal relations, performs actions, and earns a reputation, and as a result, can demand to be treated accordingly.

In support of this, K. A. Appiah argues that: (1) honor is something you can lose if you violate the codes that define it; (2) the loss of honor leads to shame, a feeling that arises from one's own disgraceful behavior, while the adequate reaction of others is to cease respecting you and then actively treat you with contempt; (3) respect and contempt can also result from the actions of others because your honor is always the honor of a person with a certain social identity (Appiah 2015, 105).

Therefore, honor arises as a result of a causal link between actions based on free will and society's response to them. If a person's actions comply with legal and moral norms, they have the right to respect for the honor formed by these actions. One could say that even the presumption of innocence in criminal law exists to protect a person's honor. The law presumes that a person has honor (lives according to legal norms) until the contrary is proven in court.

A person of honor wishes to act in a way that deserves respect according to a code of honor, but they do not adhere to the code merely to gain respect (Ibid., 106). It should be added that a code of honor must be based on established legal norms, as it is they that normatively outline the boundaries of correct behavior. This thesis is fundamental because each person's "internal code of honor" may differ from established norms.

A somewhat different situation arises with dignity. Since dignity is understood as a person's self-assessment of their social qualities, it is what gives rise to honor. That is, a person participates in civil legal relations guided by their own dignity, of their own free will, as a result of which honor is formed.

The protection of respect for dignity is enshrined in international and national legislation. Article 7 of the International Covenant on Civil and Political Rights (1966) prohibits actions that degrade human dignity, and all persons deprived of liberty have the right to humane treatment and respect for their dignity. Article 3 of the European Convention for the Prevention of Torture and Inhuman or Degrading Treatment or Punishment (2002) guarantees the right to human dignity.

In Article 3 of the *Konstytutsiia Ukrainy* [Constitution of Ukraine] (1996), art. 3), dignity is recognized as the highest social value. Article 21 states that all people are equal and free in their dignity and rights (art. 21). The Constitutional Court of Ukraine emphasizes that human dignity must be interpreted as a right guaranteed by Article 28 of the Constitution and as a constitutional value that gives meaning to human existence and is the foundation for all other constitutional rights (*Rishennia Velykoi palaty Konstytutsiinoho Sudu Ukrainy* [Decision of the Grand Chamber of the Constitutional Court of Ukraine] 2018).

Therefore, regulated personal rights guarantee respect for human dignity and protect a person from improper treatment. The personal non-property right to respect for dignity is a person's awareness of their value and significance as an individual playing a social role (Svitlov 2015, 392).

The right to respect for dignity implies a fair assessment by a person of their own actions and a prohibition on others negatively influencing a person's self-esteem through unlawful actions. The latter includes the prohibition of torture, cruel, inhuman, or degrading treatment, and the prohibition of medical or scientific experiments on a person without their free consent (Shliakhtun 2005, 84-85).

Today, the issue of protecting dignity is receiving increasing attention, and its regulation is being detailed in current legislation. As some scholars rightly point out, this indicates a humanistic trend in the development of the institution of human rights and the growth of its intrinsic value (Rabinovych and Khavroniuk 2004, 9).

The protection of the right to respect for honor and dignity depends on the level of its violation. The use of torture by state bodies will have a significant negative impact on human dignity and will be a direct basis for an appeal to the ECtHR. In more private cases, an apology may be sufficient. O. V. Sobolev summarises that civil law protection is carried out through general methods (compensation for damages) and special methods (a response, refutation of inaccurate information, prohibition of dissemination of information) (Soboliev 2018, 127).

An apology can be considered a special method of protection if the court establishes that it corresponds to the manner of violation and its consequences (Ibid.). Several court cases serve as examples.

The first case involved a woman being called a "prostitute." The plaintiff filed a lawsuit for the protection of honor and dignity. The defendant filed a counterclaim, admitting to using obscene words but denying the dissemination of false information. The court ruled that such words are an insult, not false information, and therefore are not subject to refutation (Kiriushyn 2020).

Another case involved a person suing for the protection of honor, dignity, and business reputation after being insulted by an employee of a postal service in front of others. In motivating its decision, the court referred to Articles 297 and 299 of the Civil Code of Ukraine, which guarantee the right to respect for dignity and honor and the inviolability of business reputation (*Naukovo-praktychnyi komentar...* [Scientific and Practical Commentary...] 2020).

It should be borne in mind that cases concerning the protection of honor and dignity are often subjective. In cases where insults are evaluative judgments and cannot be proven or disproven, the court cannot satisfy the claim due to a lack of objective evidence. For example, if a person is called a "fool," the court has no basis to verify this judgment. On the other hand, if a person who has proven through their dignity and reputation that they do not fit this description (e.g., a university professor) is called this, then one can speak of the dissemination of false information and the protection of their business reputation. If a person believes that evaluative judgments disseminated in the mass media degrade their dignity or honor, they have the right to a reply and their own interpretation of the case in the same mass medium (Ibid.).

In the context of the right to respect for honor and dignity, it is necessary to understand what information can cause harm. Unreliable information is that which is not true, contains false data, or distorts facts. Negative information spread about a person is considered unreliable unless the person who spread it proves otherwise (Manzhosova 2019, 82).

The right to dignity arises from a person's own attitude toward themself, as they make decisions based on free will that shape their self-image. Honor arises from dignity and the actions that a person commits of their own free will, which creates an impression of them in the eyes of others. In turn, respect for honor and dignity performs a regulatory function by limiting the free will of others, establishing an obligation to treat another person objectively, in accordance with their behavior and reputation.

As N. V. Marushchak confirms, the peculiarity of the right to respect for honor and dignity is that these categories, as objects of legal protection, are inseparable from the personality of their holder. However, dignity as an object of legal protection exists in the consciousness of the right-holder and is related not only to their personality and perception of their social assessment but also to the evaluations given by others (Marushchak 2016, 330).

A simple illustrative example of the combination of the right to respect for honor and dignity with free will is as follows: a person identifies with a subculture, of their own free will wears appropriate clothing, and considers themself a supporter of a certain trend (dignity), which obliges others to respect this and treat them accordingly (honor). At the same time, this results in a restriction of the free will of others who are critical of this person's appearance. The same scheme is relevant for sexual and national minorities, adherents of a particular religion, etc., and is therefore closely related to the prohibition of discrimination. Other personal non-property rights also arise from these rights, including the right to individuality, private life, freedom of creativity, and choice of occupation.

The right to respect for honor and dignity is most closely related to the right to the inviolability of business reputation, which is guaranteed to every person (*Tsyvil'nyi kodeks Ukrainy* [Civil Code of Ukraine] 2003, art. 298).

Business reputation is understood as a good that indicates, on the one hand, a person's objective significance to society, determined by their professional activity, business and moral qualities, and level of qualification; and on the other hand, a subjective good that indicates the significance of a person's activity as a representative of the professional or business sphere based on their own consciousness and priorities (Zhydkova 2008, 5). Along with "business reputation," one can find the term "renown"—a public opinion attached to someone.

The law provides for the right to the inviolability of the business reputation of both individuals and legal entities. This is one of its fundamental differences from honor and dignity, which are understood only as personal non-property rights of an individual. Based on this, several normative definitions of business reputation should be given.

In the Law of Ukraine "On Financial Services and Financial Companies," business reputation is a set of documented information collected by the Regulator about a person, which allows for a conclusion about the compliance of their activities with the law, business practice, and professional ethics, as well as information about their professional and managerial abilities (*Pro finansovi posluhy ta finansovi kompanii* [On Financial Services and Financial Companies] 2021, art. 1).

In the Law of Ukraine "On Banks and Banking Activities," business reputation is defined as information collected by the National Bank of Ukraine on the compliance of a person's activities with the requirements of the law, business practice, and professional ethics, as well as information on their integrity and professional abilities (*Pro banky i bankivs'ku diial'nist'* [On Banks and Banking Activities] 2000, art. 2).

The Resolution of the Plenum of the Supreme Court of Ukraine of 27.02.2009 No. 1 defines the business reputation of an individual as the public assessment of their business and professional qualities acquired in the performance of their duties. The business reputation of a legal entity is understood as the assessment of their business, public, or professional activities (*Pro sudovu praktyku u spravakh...* [On Judicial Practice in Cases...] 2009).

Regarding the business reputation of legal entities, it is separately outlined that it consists of the prestige of its corporate name, trademarks, and other intangible assets among consumers (*Pro deiaki pytannia praktyky...* [On Certain Issues of the Practice...] 2007).

As can be summarised, business reputation is closely related to honor and dignity but pertains purely to professional qualities. Of their own volition, guided by free will, a person forms their business reputation, which is protected from unfair encroachment. Such encroachment is the unlawful use of information related to a person's professional activities that may cause harm.

Before the repeal of the Commercial Code of Ukraine, the legal framework provided a specific classification for the unlawful use of a business reputation. According to Article 33 (*Hospodars'kyi kodeks Ukrainy* [Commercial Code of Ukraine] 2003, art. 33), such actions included:

1. Misappropriation of Designations: The unlawful use of another's designations, advertising materials, or packaging, as well as the copying of the appearance of another's product or the use of comparative advertising that violates competition law.
2. Unauthorized Use of Identity: The use of another's name, trademark, or advertising materials without permission, specifically when such actions could lead to public confusion.
3. Misleading Use of Personal Names: While the use of a citizen's own name in a commercial name was considered lawful, it required the addition of a distinctive element to avoid confusion with existing entities.
4. Reverse Passing Off: Introducing another manufacturer's product under one's own designation.
5. Deceptive Copying: Copying the appearance of another's product without clearly and unmistakably indicating the actual manufacturer of the copy.

All these measures were aimed at preventing unfair competition and ensuring that the free will of consumers was not compromised by deceptive marketing practices.

A business reputation reflects the external attitude toward a person, which is formed by their own professional activities, guided by their free will. Considering that the free will of a legal entity is a cumulative manifestation of the free will of its employees, its business reputation arises as a result of the collaboration and synergy of all employees.

Understanding free will as free decision-making, business reputation becomes its direct result in professional activity. The consequence of this is the value of an individual as a specialist or entrepreneur.

For a legal entity, this directly affects goodwill—an intangible asset, the value of which is determined as the difference between the market price and the book value of the enterprise's assets, arising from superior management, a dominant market position, or new technologies (*Podatkovyi kodeks Ukrainy* [Tax Code of Ukraine] 2010, subpara. 14.1.40).

The free will that forms a business reputation directly impacts a person's income. For example, a person with a high level of business reputation can set a higher price for their services than a competitor. Thus, for legal entities, a brand arises, and for an individual, a "personal brand" is created.

Today, the issue of personal branding is receiving increasing attention, and, in general, it is a direct result of business reputation. T. Peters defines a personal brand as what other people think of us, encompassing the ideas and associations we evoke through our appearance and behavior (Peters 1977).

A personal brand is our image in the minds of others, how we are perceived, an image that generates additional value and creates benefits for us (Palamarchuk and Prystaiko 2010, 6).

Today, business reputation is inextricably linked with a personal brand. This thesis is confirmed by O. M. Pomaz, O. O. Tovkaylo, and O. I. Stetsenko, who write that the formation of a personal brand is of paramount importance for successful activity in any professional field (Pomaz, Tovkailo, and Stetsenko 2015, 203).

The right to the inviolability of business reputation serves a preventive purpose, aiming to prevent both property and non-property damage. For more effective regulation of this issue, Yu. Ya. Petrenko and E. O. Ryabokon propose regulating the conceptual apparatus, explicitly defining the concepts of "business reputation" and "non-property damage," and introducing methods of protection (refutation, right of reply) at the legislative level (Petrenko and Riabokon 2017, 56).

In summary, the current legislation does not contain definitions of dignity, honor, or business reputation, as they are moral-ethical categories and, at the same time, personal non-property rights to which the law gives the status of independent objects of judicial protection (*Postanova Plenumu Verkhovnoho Sudu Ukrainy* [Resolution of the Plenum of the Supreme Court of Ukraine] 2009, para. 4).

The personal non-property right to respect for dignity and honor, and to the inviolability of business reputation, are directly related to free will, because they arise from it. The very constructs of the "right to respect" and the "right to inviolability" create restrictions on the free will of other persons by imposing specific obligations.

The next personal non-property right enshrined in the Civil Code of Ukraine is the right to a personal life and its secrecy. This right also has two aspects in its relationship with free will: the manifestation of one's own will and the restriction of the free will of others.

One's own free will is manifested through the implementation of Article 301, paragraph 3 of the Civil Code of Ukraine (*Tsyvil'nyi kodeks Ukrainy* [Civil Code of Ukraine] 2003, art. 301, para. 3), which stipulates the right of an individual to independently determine their personal life and the possibility of others becoming acquainted with it. The restriction of the free will of others follows from the right to keep the circumstances of one's personal life secret, which imposes obligations on others.

At the same time, it can be observed that certain regulatory acts use the terms "private life," "family life," and "personal life." This raises the question of their correlation. Primarily, this right is guaranteed by the Constitution, which prohibits interference in personal and family life, except in cases provided for by *the Konstytutsiia Ukrainy* [Constitution of Ukraine] (1996, art. 32).

A similar norm is found in international law: (1) no one shall be subjected to arbitrary interference with his privacy, family, or home (United Nations General Assembly 1948); (2) everyone has the right to respect for his private and family life (Council of Europe 1950).

The implementation of these norms in national legislation ensures that the personal sphere remains protected from both state intrusion and the actions of other private individuals, thereby upholding the principle of free will in personal decision-making.

The doctrine offers various understandings of these terms. O. Andrievska considers the concept of "private life" to be broader (Andriievska 2012, 5).

"Personal life" is generally understood as the intimate sphere of human relations without the creation of a family, while "private life" encompasses this sphere as well as relations connected with the expression of personal tastes and life planning (Yemchuk 2015, 9).

Since distinguishing these concepts is not the purpose of this study, we support the position of K. Rezvorovych that "private life" and "personal life" are mainly used as synonyms, as they refer to the same social value—a personal non-property good (Rezvorovych 2020, 99). Therefore, it is logical to use these terms interchangeably, as they have the same connection with free will.

In addition to the above, the legislator uses the concept of "family life." The Constitutional Court of Ukraine provides an exhaustive definition: family life consists of the personal property and non-property relations between spouses and other family members, based on the principles defined in the *Simeinyi kodeks Ukrainy* [Family Code of Ukraine] (2002).

According to the Court, this concept includes: (1) the right to respect for one's family life; (2) protection from interference, except in cases established by the Constitution; and (3) regulation that takes into account the right to privacy and personal freedom

(*Rishennia Konstytutsiinoho Sudu Ukrainy* [Decision of the Constitutional Court of Ukraine] 2012).

Therefore, family life should be understood as a combination of the personal lives of spouses and other family members.

Having clarified the terminology, it is worth noting that the Civil Code of Ukraine regulates both the right to a personal life and the right to its secrecy separately. Each of these rights has a different connection with free will.

In itself, the right to a personal life arises from the individual's free will to have one or not. At the same time, the right to its secrecy gives rise to the right, of one's own free will, not to disclose information about one's personal life and creates restrictions on the free will of others—specifically, a prohibition on disclosure.

The dualism of these two rights is normatively explained in the *Tsyvil'nyi kodeks Ukrainy* [Civil Code of Ukraine] (2003, art. 301), where the legislator clearly states that an individual determines their own personal life and the possibility of others becoming acquainted with it. Thus, the proposed construction of the connection between free will and these rights is normatively confirmed.

The content of the right to a personal life consists of the following powers: to have a personal life; to determine one's personal life and the mode of access to information about it; and to demand that others refrain from interfering in this sphere (Bobryk 2004, 9).

Free will is the basis for realising this right—to have a personal life or not. On the one hand, no person can be forced into a personal life. On the other, it is impossible to imagine a situation in which a person is deprived of a personal life. It is necessary to agree with V. I. Bobryk that personal life (in the legal aspect) is a special part of the private sphere of human activity, consisting of various relationships and events that do not have public significance and are regulated by the person themself, guaranteed and protected by law from unlawful interference (Ibid., 14).

Even when a person's free will is limited—in places of confinement, for example—they still have a personal life. It can be assumed that the ability to have a personal life cannot be restricted at all; it can only be unlawfully interfered with. Therefore, of their own free will, a person can determine their personal life (its boundaries and content) and the mode of access to information about it. From this follows the right to keep the circumstances of one's personal life secret. The only grounds for disclosing such circumstances are the person's own wish, a court decision, or the public interest (in the case of public figures).

A court decision to disclose information from private life is possible only if the circumstances contain signs of an offense. This issue was studied in detail by Yu. O. Helych, who identified exceptional grounds for disclosing the secret of a person's personal life (the person's unambiguous consent; the informational need of a law enforcement agency or a court in connection with a case; the performance of lawful activities by a state authority; the establishment of employment or membership relations; the incapacity of a person, if disclosure is for their protection) and exceptional grounds for disseminating it (the person's unambiguous consent; the search for a criminal; the presence of signs of an offense confirmed by a court decision; public disclosure by the person themself) (Helych 2010, 5).

In fact, all information about a person can be attributed to their personal life. This is confirmed by the definition of a person's personal life as information about them, as well as events and phenomena in their life, which they wish to keep unknown and the disclosure of which harms their interests (Ibid.).

The secret of a person's personal life can take different forms, but all are based on free will and arise at the wish of the right-holder, creating an obligation of "non-disclosure" for others. N.V. Ustymenko distinguishes the following types of secrets: (1) lawyer-client privilege; (2) banking secrecy; (3) medical secrecy; (4) notarial secrecy; (5) secrecy of correspondence; (6) secrecy of adoption (Ustymenko 2001, 10–12).

However, this classification is related to special participants in legal relations and is not exhaustive. It is worth noting that even if personal information does not fall under these types, it is still protected by law.

Free will serves as a measure for understanding the boundary between personal information that a person wants to make public and that which they want to keep secret. For example, when a person publishes their photos on social networks, we must recognize that they are sharing a specific manifestation of their personal life within specific limits. This does not mean that the person has granted others the right to further use or publish this photograph. Similarly, we cannot say that if someone has made their personal life public, this creates a right for others to also publicise it. It is thanks to free will that a person independently determines which manifestation of their personal life to make public and which to keep secret.

Separately, it should be noted that there are restrictions on the free will of "public figures" in matters of the right to a personal life and its secrecy.

Public figures are those who are in the public eye, and thus some of their private lives become public, although this does not apply to all details (Borysova, 2011).

The US Supreme Court has defined in detail the range of persons who should be considered "public":

1. Limited-purpose public figures: Persons who have placed themselves at the center of a particular public discussion to influence its resolution.
2. All-purpose public figures: Persons who have achieved such fame and influence that they are considered public figures for all purposes.
3. Involuntary public figures: Persons who have become public involuntarily through participation in a high-profile event (*Gertz v. Robert Welch, Inc. 1974*).

In Ukrainian legislation, the concept of a "public person" is utilized in a Resolution of the Plenum of the Supreme Court and serves as a reflection of the definition stipulated in the Resolution on the Inviolability of Private Life.

Concurrently, official sources employ related terms that, while conceptually linked, possess distinct legal nuances:

1. "Official" (*Pro derzhavnu reiestratsiiu…* [On State Registration…] 2003, art. 2);
2. "Statesman" (*Kryminal'nyi kodeks Ukrainy* [Criminal Code of Ukraine] 2001, art. 344);

3. "Official person" (*Postanova Plenumu Verkhovnoho Sudu Ukrainy* [Resolution of the Plenum of the Supreme Court of Ukraine] 1995).

While these concepts are conceptually similar to that of a "public person," they are not legally identical, which underscores the necessity of developing a precise normative interpretation of this term.

Today, we must assume that information about the private life of a public figure can be disseminated without their consent only when the public interest in this information outweighs the person's private right. In these cases, the free will of the right-holder will be limited by public necessity. As O. O. Kulich correctly notes, a person's interest in feeling their autonomy, protected by the right to privacy, sometimes stands in dialectical contradiction with the interests of others and society, particularly in ensuring security and fighting crime. This contradiction cannot be resolved by giving preference to one interest over another; it requires an assessment and harmonisation of interests (Kulinich 2008, 35).

This right is closely related to another personal non-property right: the right to information. Article 302 of the Civil Code of Ukraine enshrines that an individual has the right to freely collect, store, use, and disseminate information. Here, we see a right that is also based on free will. At the same time, the right to information also provides for certain restrictions on the free will of others. This is confirmed by the norm that the collection, storage, use, and dissemination of information about an individual's personal life without their consent are not allowed, except in cases defined by law and only in the interests of national security, economic well-being, and human rights (*Tsyvil'nyi kodeks Ukrainy* [Civil Code of Ukraine] 2003, art. 302, para. 1).

B. M. Gogol defines the exercise of the right to information as the performance by an authorised person of specific actions regarding the collection, storage, processing, and dissemination of information to satisfy their information needs and interests (Hohol 2010, 7).

From this, it follows that a person's free will allows them to exercise the right to information only in the specified forms. A person performs these actions of their own free will, to the extent that they do not violate another person's right to privacy and information. The limits of free will in the right to information are outlined by legal guarantees.

Gogol reasonably includes among them: (1) the possibility of restricting the right only in cases provided for by the Constitution; (2) the prohibition of unjustified secrecy; (3) the accessibility of official information; (4) freedom of the media; (5) freedom of creative activity; (6) the existence of legal liability for violations (Ibid., 11).

The right to a personal life and its secrecy is the ability to disseminate and limit information about oneself of one's own free will. The right to information is the ability to receive information about other people, phenomena, and events of one's own free will. That is, in the first case, free will is directed internally (toward oneself), and in the right to information, externally (toward others).

In the first case, only the free will of others regarding the secret of private life is limited. One can disclose any information about oneself, and free will is not restricted. In the second case, it is clear that the right to information is based on restricting free will regarding the procedure, form, and methods of obtaining information. This conclusion is fully justified by the norm that an individual who disseminates information is obliged to verify its reliability (*Tsyvil'nyi kodeks Ukrainy* [Civil Code of Ukraine] 2003, art. 302, para. 2).

This means we already have conditions for collecting, storing, using, and distributing information. This right is not absolute.

The next informational personal non-property rights are the right to personal papers, the right to dispose of them, and the right to access personal papers transferred to libraries or archives.

S. V. Iasechko argues for considering personal papers as objects of civil law in several manifestations: as a personal non-property good, while the content of such papers is the object of personal non-property legal relations (documents, diaries, records), and also as an object that can be a commodity and the subject of transactions, namely an object of property rights (Iasechko 2013)

This position is logical, but personal papers should be understood in the context of personal non-property law. This is because it is through such a lens that we can fully see how free will determines the very possibility of their existence.

Personal papers are understood as a material form of recording information about a person's private life, aimed at satisfying spiritual, physiological, or material needs, the circumstances of which a person wishes to keep secret or with limited access (Klimovskyi 2013, 157).

Civil legislation refers to personal papers as documents, photographs, diaries, other records, and personal archival materials that are a person's property (*Tsyvil'nyi kodeks Ukrainy* [Civil Code of Ukraine] 2003, art. 303, para. 1).

Therefore, personal papers are an expression of a person's private life on a material/electronic medium. We are not talking purely about "papers," but about any material that reveals information about a person's private life.

Free will in the right to personal papers implies the dominance of the owner's free will, as familiarisation with them and their use (e.g., by publication) is permitted only with the consent of the individual to whom they belong (Ibid., art. 303, para. 2). By their own decision, an individual creates and uses personal papers, participates in their production and distribution, and determines their content and use. An individual, of their own free will, disposes of personal papers, including in the event of their death belong (Ibid., art. 304).

The granting of consent to the use of personal papers is recognized as a legal act. That is, by giving voluntary consent, the owner transfers a clearly defined object for a specific application. If a photograph is transferred for publication in a magazine, this does not confer the right to publish it in other sources or to use other photographs without consent. This confirms that the transfer of the right to personal papers is a legal act, not merely a factual one, as the latter are lawful actions with which the law associates legal consequences regardless of the subject's intent (Iasechko 2013).

If personal papers belong to several persons, their use is permissible only with the consent of all owners. For example, to publish the correspondence of several people, the consent of all participants is required. If the personal papers of one individual concern the private life of another, their use requires the consent of that other person (*Tsyvil'nyi kodeks Ukrainy* [Civil Code of Ukraine] 2003, art. 303, para. 3).

The use of personal papers without additional consent is possible if provided for by separate agreements or if we are discussing the papers of public figures. This was discussed above. Also, in the event of an individual's death, their personal papers may be used only with the consent of their children, spouse, and if none, their parents or siblings (Ibid., art. 303, para. 4).

The issue of the use of personal papers by persons who participate in their creation is relevant. In this case, the norms of copyright and service contracts apply. For example, a customer, of their own free will, commissions a photographer, who, of their own free will, creates personal papers (photographs).

The Law of Ukraine "On Copyright and Related Rights" recognizes photographic works as objects of copyright (*Pro avtors'ke pravo i sumizhni prava* [On Copyright and Related Rights] 2022, art.8).

The primary subject of copyright is the author of the work (the photographer). In the absence of evidence to the contrary, the person indicated as the author on the work is considered the author (presumption of authorship) (Ibid., art. 11).

Copyright arises from the fact of creation and does not require registration (Savchenko 2019, 85). As a general rule, the photographer will be the author of the personal paper, but the model will also acquire rights to the papers.

This situation is close to co-authorship. Copyright to a work created in co-authorship belongs to the co-authors jointly, regardless of whether the work is indivisible or consists of parts that can have independent significance (*Tsyvil'nyi kodeks Ukrainy* [Civil Code of Ukraine] 2003, art. 436).

Thus, the co-authors of a photograph can be the photographer, model, florists, decorators, and designers. However, practice shows that in most cases, a photograph is not a work characterised by co-authorship.

Free will is also exercised by giving consent to photo, film, television, and video recordings, which require permission. In the case of filming openly on the street, at meetings, conferences, and other public events, the consent of the person being filmed is not required, and their free will can be exercised only by tacit consent or an express prohibition. In such a case, the free will of the person being filmed will prevail over the presumption of automatic consent.

An individual who has agreed to be filmed may demand the termination of their public display in the part that concerns their private life. The costs associated with this shall be reimbursed by this individual (*Tsyvil'nyi kodeks Ukrainy* [Civil Code of Ukraine] 2003, art. 307, para. 2).

Filming an individual, including secretly, without their consent, may be carried out only in cases established by law (Ibid., art. 307, para. 3). However, even if a dispute arises, judicial practice is mostly in favor of photographers. Claims for the protection of honor and dignity in this area are generally not supported in court.

A continuation of this issue is the personal non-property right to the protection of the interests of an individual depicted in photographs and other works of art. A photograph or other work of art depicting an individual may be publicly displayed, reproduced, and distributed only with that person's consent, and in the event of their death, with the consent of others (Ibid., art. 308, para. 1).

Here, two cases should be considered: when a photograph is created on commission and when an individual posed for the author for a fee. In the first case, commercial use is possible only with the customer's consent. Non-commercial use is permissible without consent, within the author's moral rights. In practice, photographers conclude service agreements that stipulate permission for commercial and non-commercial use. In the case where an individual posed for a fee, the work may be publicly displayed, reproduced, or distributed without their consent. In such a situation, only the author's free will regarding the use of the work is important.

The model's free will is not taken into account, as their permission is not required. It should be considered that by agreeing to participate in the creation of the work under such conditions, the model has expressed their own will and consented to its further use without their approval. It should also be taken into account that a photograph may be distributed without the consent of the person depicted if this is necessary to protect their interests or the interests of others (Ibid., art. 308, para. 3).

From the analysis, it becomes clear that personal papers arise and are used with or without a person's free will, in cases specified by law. In cases of public filming, a presumption of consent applies. In most other cases, it is necessary to obtain consent for the creation and use of personal papers, including to protect a person's free will. The above applies by analogy to the personal non-property right to the secrecy of correspondence.

The right to freedom of literary, artistic, scientific, and technical creativity is also a personal non-property right and a direct embodiment of free will, without which it cannot exist. This right is based on two aspects: the manifestation of free will to exercise the right and the restriction of the free will of others. In the first case, we refer to the Civil Code of Ukraine, which establishes that an individual has the right to freedom of creative activity (Ibid., art. 309, para. 1).

We consider this a normative confirmation of the inviolability of free will for creative activity. It should be emphasised that without free will, creative activity cannot exist at all. Even if someone creates an object of creative activity on commission, through compilation, or in violation of plagiarism requirements, there will still necessarily be a manifestation of free will. In addition, an individual has the right to the free choice of spheres, content, and forms of creativity (Ibid., art. 309, para. 2).

This further reinforces the aforementioned points, as free choice consistently serves as the embodiment of free will. This perspective is validated by the conceptual understanding of creative activity, as summarized by N. A. Karpenko, who identifies five distinct categories of definitions for creativity:

1. Novelty-based: Definitions centered on novelty as the primary criterion;
2. Anti-conformist: Definitions that oppose creativity to conformity;
3. Process-oriented: Definitions that encompass the concept of the creative process;
4. Cognitive: An approach from the perspective of mental abilities;
5. Hierarchical: An approach based on defining distinct levels of creativity (Karpenko 2016, 8).

Of most significant interest is the understanding of creativity as a direct opposition to conformism—the tendency to behave or think like everyone else ("*Conformism*" 2023). Through this lens, it becomes evident that the personal non-property right to creative activity represents a confrontation between individual free will and external influence.

This is further confirmed by T. M. Milova, who proposes a specialized definition of the "constitutional right to freedom of scientific creativity." She describes it as a state-guaranteed opportunity for every individual to: (1) freely engage in intellectual creative activity aimed at obtaining and utilizing new scientific knowledge; (2) independently choose the directions and forms of such activity in accordance with their personal interests and capabilities (Milova 2008, 5).

The entire creative process is divided into three stages: motivational, search, and completion. Each of these stages is associated with a person's ability to make decisions freely and, therefore, with free will.

This perspective is validated by N. M. Opolska, who characterizes the stages of the creative process as follows:

1. Motivational Stage: Manifested in the deliberate will to exercise the right to the freedom of creativity.
2. Search Stage: Commences with a keen desire to realize an idea; it encompasses the search for necessary means, the

cognitive functions of both the consciousness and subconsciousness, and culminates in a decision regarding specific implementation methods.

3. Completion (Heuristic) Stage: Consists of the actual implementation of creative ideas, the verification of results, their critical evaluation, and subsequent publication (Opolska 2019, 235).

As we can see, the right to creativity is the ability to manifest free will as an element of mental activity aimed at self-expression, the discovery of new knowledge, and self-realisation. Thus, by exercising the right to freedom of creativity, a person expresses their own free will and realizes a whole set of other personal non-property rights: the right to use a name (authorship), the right to respect for dignity and honor, and the right to individuality.

In addition to the above, the right to freedom of creativity includes the prohibition of censorship of the creative process and its results. This creates restrictions on the free will of other persons who would like to apply such censorship. The Law of Ukraine "On Information" enshrines the prohibition of censorship—any requirement to coordinate information before its dissemination or to impose a ban on it (*Pro informatsiiu* [On Information], 1992, art. 24).

There is an opinion that censorship should be understood as government control over the content and dissemination of information (Volkova and Okhota 2017, 105). But censorship applies not only to mass media. When we speak of the prohibition of censorship of the creative process, we mean the protection of free will from the influence of another person or institution. The issue is so resonant that some scholars even propose prohibiting research aimed at developing methods for manipulating a person's volitional sphere and programming their behavior (Punda and Kolobova 2011, 84).

At the same time, the practice of the ECtHR confirms cases where restrictions on the right to freedom of creativity are recognized as lawful.

The main criteria for the lawfulness of such restrictions are: (1) legitimacy (the restriction must be provided for by law); (2) purpose (it must be justified and proportionate); (3) content (the restriction cannot be interpreted broadly and must correspond to the main content of the freedom) (Opolska, 2019, p. 191).

These criteria have been repeatedly used by the ECtHR in its decisions, for example, in the cases of *Muller and Others v. Switzerland, Handyside v. United Kingdom,* and *Otto Preminger Institut v. Austria.*

In summary, the right to freedom of literary, artistic, scientific, and technical creativity is a direct manifestation of free will and creates both opportunities for its realisation and restrictions for other persons through the prohibition of censorship.

Free will is also the basis for exercising the right to a place of residence, the inviolability of housing, and freedom of movement. These personal non-property rights are closely interconnected, which necessitates their study in totality. All these rights provide for personal choice, which justifies the mandatory application of free will for their exercise.

Citizens of Ukraine, as well as foreigners and stateless persons legally in Ukraine, are guaranteed freedom of movement and free choice of place of residence, except for restrictions established by law (*Pro svobodu peresuvannia...* [On Freedom of Movement...] 2003, art. 2).

These rights provide for the ability of a person to freely, independently, and without coercion make decisions regarding their choice of residence, movement, and the protection of their home's inviolability.

The definition of these rights is regulated by law: (1) freedom of movement is the right to move freely and without hindrance throughout the territory of Ukraine; (2) free choice of place of residence or stay is the right to choose the administrative-territorial unit where one wants to live; (3) place of residence is housing at a specific address where a person lives, or a social service institution (Ibid., art. 3).

From these concepts, the main principles should be distinguished: freedom, absence of obstacles, and the presence of one's own will. This all confirms the connection of these rights with free will.

However, these rights are not absolute and can be limited, often in relation to a person's age. For example, the place of residence of children under 14 and incapacitated persons is directly linked to the place of residence of their parents or guardians. One of the main types of punishment is deprivation of liberty, which consists of the forced isolation of a convicted person (Pikiner 2002, 98).

In specific legal contexts, an individual's free will is constrained, and the right to free choice is suspended. Ukrainian law establishes a definitive list of grounds for restricting the freedom of movement and the choice of residence. These primarily involve geographic restrictions in border zones, military territories, and restricted access areas.

Furthermore, restrictions may be imposed on specific categories of persons, including:

1. Criminal Justice and Supervision: Individuals under preventive measures related to deprivation of liberty; those serving a prison sentence; persons on probation; and those under administrative supervision.
2. Health and Safety: Persons subject to compulsory hospitalization and treatment.
3. Migration Status: Asylum seekers and foreigners lacking legal grounds for staying in Ukraine.
4. Military Obligations: Persons conscripted for military service and foreign military personnel.

These limitations represent a legally sanctioned boundary where public interest or state security overrides individual free will (*Pro svobodu peresuvannia…* [On Freedom of Movement…] 2003, arts. 12–13).

This list is not exhaustive, but it illustrates how free will can be limited in the exercise of certain personal non-property rights.

It should be noted separately that the right to freedom of movement also has its own specifics and imposes certain restrictions. On the one hand, an individual can freely move around Ukraine and cross its border.

However, a person under fourteen may travel within Ukraine only with the consent and accompaniment of their parents or guardians (*Tsyvil'nyi kodeks Ukrainy* [Civil Code of Ukraine] 2003, art. 313, para. 2).

From the age of sixteen, a person has the right to freely travel abroad independently (Ibid., art. 313, para. 3). Other specific grounds for restriction may arise, such as the travel restrictions imposed during the COVID-19 pandemic.

These restrictions do not apply to the exercise of the right to the inviolability of housing. As N.O. Horobets notes, the basis for the emergence of this right is a legal fact that does not require the individual to acquire a special status (Horobets 2010, 44).

That is, the mere fact of having a right to housing is sufficient, which can arise from a purchase and sale agreement, for example. It should be borne in mind that this is not a matter of ownership, as the right of lawful possession and use is enough. Thus, when we rent an apartment or stay in a hotel, the right to the inviolability of housing arises automatically. There is no doubt that the use and possession of housing can only occur with free will. After all, the emergence of a right based on a contract presupposes a conscious, free expression of will. This is a principle of contract law and will be discussed in detail in the next chapter. Even when a person exercises the right to housing through inheritance or a gift agreement, their free will is still necessarily present, as property rights arise only after the free acceptance of the inheritance or gift.

The right to the inviolability of the home provides for the prohibition of arbitrary entry, inspection, search, alienation, or appropriation. In urgent cases related to saving lives and property or the direct prosecution of suspects, the law may establish a different procedure for entry (*Tsyvil'nyi kodeks Ukrainy* [Civil Code of Ukraine] 2003, art. 311, para. 3). Eviction or other forced deprivation of housing is also permitted only in cases established by law.

To protect the right to the inviolability of the home, the legislation provides for special sanctions. In particular, theft or robbery with entry into a home is punishable by imprisonment from three to six and from four to eight years, respectively (*Kryminal'nyi kodeks Ukrainy* [Criminal Code] 2001, art. 185, para. 3; art. 186, para. 3).

The above confirms that personal non-property rights to a place of residence, inviolability of housing, and freedom of movement cannot exist without free will, except where restrictions are established. For example, a person moves and chooses a place of residence of their own free will, but when serving a sentence in a place of confinement, they are transported and housed without regard to their will.

The study of the relationship between free will and personal non-property rights should be continued through an analysis of the right to choose an occupation. This right is of fundamental importance for understanding free will, as it fully reflects a person's ability to choose their occupation, their path of development, and, as a result, to form their circle of interests and lifestyle by their own decision.

The studies of M. Törnroos, M. Jokela, and H. Hakulinen demonstrate that people choose their professions and occupations based on their personality (Törnroos, Jokela, and Hakulinen 2019). This means that a person exercises the right to choose an occupation based on their own characteristics, motives, and psychotype, through the manifestation of free will.

The Civil Code of Ukraine enshrines the right of an individual to choose and change their occupation (*Tsyvil'nyi kodeks Ukrainy* [Civil Code of Ukraine] 2003, art. 312, para. 1).

This right normatively enshrines the existence of free will, which allows one to choose and change professional activities, provide services, and hold positions at one's own discretion. The rights to private life, individuality, honor, and dignity primarily concern a person's private life. The right to choose an occupation is more related to professional activity aimed at satisfying a person's material and personal needs through socially beneficial actions. In general, this is the right to choose a job. Today, the issue of finding "one's place," self-actualisation, and career is receiving increasing attention. Even people with successful careers change jobs or start their own businesses.

This is logical, as a professional career influences a person's life path, self-realisation, and is important for their self-image and overall life satisfaction (Proskurka 2009, 31).

Guided by their own free will, a person independently chooses an occupation and can change it at any time. The ban on forced labour confirms this. That is, any work must be voluntary and conscious. This idea can be seen not only as an element of personal non-property law but also as a norm of labour legislation- Sometimes a person's consent to a specific activity is not required.

In particular, military or alternative service, work performed under a court sentence, or work during a state of martial law or emergency is not considered forced labour (*Tsyvil'nyi kodeks Ukrainy* [Civil Code of Ukraine] 2003, art. 312, para. 2).

In certain instances, the law establishes specific prerequisites for engaging in professional activities. These requirements serve as regulatory boundaries to an individual's free will in their choice of occupation, ensuring that specialized roles are filled by qualified personnel:

1. Healthcare and Pharmacy: Medical and pharmaceutical activities mandate specialized education *(Osnovy zakonodavstva... [Fundamentals of the Legislation...] 1992, art.* 74).
2. Academic Leadership: Heads of higher education institutions must possess an academic title, a scientific degree, and relevant work experience (*Tsyvil'nyi kodeks Ukrainy* [Civil Code of Ukraine] 2003, art. 287, para. 1).
3. Judiciary: Judges are subject to strict criteria regarding age, education, and professional experience (*Pro poriadok posvidchennia zapovitiv…* [On the Procedure for Certifying Wills…], art. 69, para. 1).
4. Legal Practice: To be admitted to the bar, lawyers must hold a higher legal education, possess work experience, and successfully pass a qualifying examination (*Pro advokaturu ta advokats'ku diial'nist'* [On the Bar and Practice of Law] 2012, art. 6, para. 1).

There are also special requirements for notarial, pharmaceutical, veterinary, and other activities. But here, it is appropriate to speak not of restrictions on free will, but of establishing requirements for the public interest and safety. By adhering to them, a person can choose and change their occupation of their own free will, based on the principle of equality and non-discrimination.

At the same time, the law provides for the possibility of prohibiting a person from a specific type of activity. This occurs as a sanction for an offense or within the framework of lustration requirements (*Pro ochyshchennia vlady* [On Lustration] 2014, art. 2).

This issue is primarily regulated by the Criminal Code of Ukraine: deprivation of the right to hold certain positions or engage in certain activities may be imposed as a main or additional punishment (*Kryminal'nyi kodeks Ukrainy* [Criminal Code of Ukraine] 2001, art. 55].

There is an active scientific discussion on this. If we recognize this as a restriction of labour rights, then it can be assumed that any punishment restricts human rights. This is one of the ideas of legal responsibility. For example, licensing restricts the right to freedom of enterprise, and competitive admission to higher education restricts the constitutional right to education. However, it is difficult to agree with this view. It is more appropriate to say that the rules should be equal, democratic, and transparent, in observance of the rule of law. Then all restrictions should be considered as protection of the public interest, which is higher than the private one. In this case, the manifestation of free will is possible only with the observance of regulatory requirements.

It is necessary to agree with I.V. Yeremenko that the essence of this punishment is to prohibit the convicted person from holding certain positions or engaging in certain activities to prevent them from committing a crime again. This goal can be achieved only with strict adherence to the law (Yeromenko 2015, 122).

Finally, it is worth noting that the right to choose and change occupations stems from free will, but many factors can influence the decision. N. Nicolaou and S. Shane demonstrated the influence of genetics on occupational choice. They applied quantitative genetic methods to a sample of twins and found that the heritability hypothesis is supported for the tendency to be self-employed, as well as for other professions, such as teaching, management, or sales (Nicolaou and Shane 2010).

Academic discourse highlights a complex interplay between external circumstances and individual autonomy in professional self-determination. While the right to choose an occupation is a manifestation of free will, it is frequently shaped by various socio-economic and psychological factors:

1. Career Orientation Types: M. Gerber, A. Wittekind, G. Grote, and B. Staffelbach demonstrate that diverse factors influence career orientation, suggesting that individuals categorize their professional paths based on specific latent classes of motivation (Gerber et al. 2009).
2. Professional Motivation: International comparative studies, such as those utilizing the FIT-Choice scale, prove that motivations for entering specific professions (e.g., teaching) are driven by a mix of intrinsic values, social utility, and personal ability perceptions (Watt et al. 2012).

From these studies, it can be concluded that while the choice or change of occupation may be influenced by external circumstances or systemic motives, the final decision remains an act of individual autonomy. The person acts as the ultimate arbiter, guided by their own free will within the framework of available opportunities.

The above proves that the personal non-property right to choose and change one's occupation is entirely based on the individual's free will; however, in some cases, the exercise of this right is associated with compliance with special legislative requirements and may be limited in the form of a sanction.

The last group of personal non-property rights whose undeniable connection with free will is proposed to be considered is the right to freedom of association and the right to peaceful assembly.

Individuals have the right to freedom of association in political parties and public organizations. Such association occurs at their own will; moreover, affiliation or non-affiliation with a political party or public organization is not a basis for restricting their rights or granting them privileges (*Tsyvil'nyi kodeks Ukrainy* [Civil Code of Ukraine] 2003, art. 314). This means that we must again speak of the mandatory presence of free will for the exercise of this right.

The right to association is primarily regulated by two foundational laws: the Law "On Political Parties in Ukraine" and the Law "On Public Associations." These statutes provide the following legal definitions, which delineate the scope of collective free will:

1. Political Party: A registered voluntary association of citizens who support a specific national program of social development. Its primary objectives are to facilitate the formation and expression of the political will of citizens and to participate in elections (*Pro politychni partii v Ukraini* [On Political Parties in Ukraine] 2001, art. 2).
2. Public Association: A voluntary association of individuals and/or legal entities established for the exercise and protection of rights and freedoms, as well as the satisfaction of various public interests (*Pro hromads'ki ob'iednannia* [On Public Associations] 2012, art. 1).

From these definitions, we can distinguish the main feature—the voluntariness of the association. We also see that such an association is contingent upon adherence to the program and ideas of the association. Therefore, the right to freedom of association is realised only through free will, when a person supports the principles and ideas of a particular association and wishes to act to achieve its goals.

The procedure for joining, suspending, and terminating membership in a political party is determined by its charter (*Pro politychni partii v Ukraini* [On Political Parties in Ukraine] 2001, art. 6).

An analysis of party charters reveals a significant discrepancy between the theoretical requirements for membership and the practical exercise of individual autonomy. While it is expected that a member should be familiar with a party's program and objectives, this often remains a purely theoretical construct.

The manifestation of free will in this context varies significantly across the political spectrum:

1. Some organizations explicitly provide for the termination of membership if an individual's actions are deemed incompatible with the party's charter or program (*Statut politychnoi partii "Ievropeis'ka Solidarnist'"* [Charter of the "European Solidarity" Political Party]. 2024).
2. In other instances, support for the national program is not considered mandatory, and its violation does not constitute grounds for exclusion from the party (*Statut politychnoi partii "Sluha Narodu"* [Charter of the "Sluha Narodu" Political Party] 2021.)

As evidenced by these examples, while it is normatively enshrined that individuals unite within political parties based on shared views, practice often diverges from this ideal. In such cases, free will acquires an absolute manifestation: an individual may join a party of their own volition and subsequently, of that same volition, choose not to support its core ideology.

Regarding civil associations, support for their principles is not mandatory at all. Here, the principle of voluntariness comes to the fore, which provides for the right of a person to freely participate or not participate in a public association, including in its formation, joining, or leaving it (*Pro hromads'ki ob'iednannia* [On Public Associations] 2012, art. 3, para. 2).

The content of the right to freedom of association has been subject to two doctrinal approaches. Supporters of the first emphasise a triad: (1) the right to voluntarily create associations; (2) the right to join or refrain from joining existing associations; (3) the right to freely leave an association.

This position is supported by A. A. Dodina (2001,27), A. M. Kolodii (1998), and P. M. Rabinovich (Rabinovich 2001, 79), among others. Another group of scholars identifies four components, with O. M. Vashchuk (2004) and N. G. Shuklina (2005, 263) adding the opportunity to participate in the activities of associations. However, in any case, the right to create, join, leave, and participate is voluntary and therefore based on free will.

It should be noted separately that persons aged 6 to 18 can also exercise the right to association through a children's public organization (*Pro osnovni zasady molodizhnoi polityky* [On the Basic Principles of Youth Policy] 2021, art. 1).

And although the normative definition does not establish the principle of voluntariness, this principle is provided for by the concept of a children's public association. This gives grounds to assert that, using the analogy of the law, persons aged 6 to 18 exercise the right to association through free joint activity.

Similar to the above and transitional to the right to peaceful assembly is association in trade unions. A trade union is a voluntary non-profit public organization that unites citizens connected by common interests in their professional activity (*Pro profesiini spilky...* [On Trade Unions...] 1999, art. 1).

The right to participate in trade unions has its specifics, as it is primarily exercised in the sphere of labour, combining labour and socio-economic rights and interests, as confirmed by Article 36 of the Constitution. Such associations are created voluntarily, through free will, to meet common needs. One of their activities is organising and participating in strikes, as a manifestation of the right to peaceful assembly.

Individuals have the right to freely assemble for peaceful gatherings, conferences, meetings, and festivals. A court may establish restrictions on the exercise of this right in accordance with the law (*Tsyvil'nyi kodeks Ukrainy* [Civil Code of Ukraine] 2003, art. 315).

Peaceful public assemblies allow citizens to express their beliefs collectively. They are a means of conveying their position to a significant number of people, thereby attracting public and governmental attention and influencing public opinion (Nikolska and Kirina 2013, 33).

Free will is manifested in the right to peaceful assembly in two ways. First, in organising and participating in them at one's own will. Second, the peaceful assembly itself is a way to convey and publicly express one's own free will.

The issue of exercising the right to peaceful assembly is highly relevant today. O. M. Kurakin and M. Yu. Romanov developed recommendations for a special law, aimed at solving existing problems, including: (1) developing specific terminology; (2) resolving the trend of authorities banning such assemblies, ensuring that "notification" does not become "permission"; (3) clarifying the concept of "timeliness" for applications; (4) a specific list of prohibitions regarding who can participate and where events can be held (Kurakin and Romanov 2016, 42).

However, it would be wrong to reduce peaceful assemblies only to strikes, demonstrations, and rallies. Primarily, they include conferences, meetings, and festivals. Thus, free will serves as a measure of the voluntariness of participation in such assemblies and, at the same time, finds its public expression. In some cases, to prevent riots or crimes, protect public health, or safeguard the rights of others, a court may prohibit such assemblies. In some states, this became widespread during the COVID-19 pandemic.

This in-depth analysis confirms that free will manifests in all personal non-property rights of an individual. In some cases, the exercise of a right is impossible without the application of free will. In others, the implementation of free will is associated with compliance with regulatory requirements that may limit it due to the primacy of public interests over private ones.

The right to a name arises at birth and initially does not depend on the child's free will, but an individual can later exercise their free will by changing it. The right to use a name is an active form that generates the ability to use it independently and creates obligations for others. In some cases, a person decides to use a name of their own free will, while in others, its use is mandatory. Free will serves a regulatory function in the context of the right to respect for a deceased person, through restrictions on the free will of others and the possibility of expressing this right in a will. Free will acquires special significance in the context of the right to honor and dignity.

The right to dignity arises from a person's own attitude toward themself, who, by their own free will, makes decisions that shape their self-image. Honor arises from dignity and the actions a person commits of their own free will. By their own actions, a person forms their business reputation, which is protected from unfair encroachment. The issue of the personal non-property rights of a legal entity is also based on the legal concept of free will, which in this case is the collective manifestation of the free will of its employees. An individual's free will allows them to determine their personal life independently, establish the possibility of others becoming acquainted with it, and keep its circumstances secret. Free will serves as a measure for understanding the boundary between information a person wants to make public and that which they want to keep secret. The right to creativity is the ability to exercise free will as an element of mental activity aimed at self-expression and the discovery of new knowledge.

The personal non-property rights to a place of residence, inviolability of housing, and freedom of movement cannot exist without free will, except where restrictions are established. The personal non-property right to choose and change one's occupation is entirely based on a person's free will, but in some cases, its exercise is associated with compliance with special legislative requirements and may be limited by a sanction.

The above provides reason to assume that free will serves as the basis for other sub-branches of civil law, in particular, for property rights and real rights to the property of others. This makes it appropriate to study this issue in detail in the next chapter of the dissertation.

Conclusions

Based on the study of the role of free will in personal non-property rights, conducted through an analysis of international legal acts, the current legislation, scholarly doctrine, and legal practice, the following conclusions have been drawn:

1. Free will manifests in all personal non-property rights of an individual. In some cases, exercising a right is impossible without the application of free will. In others, the implementation of free will is contingent upon compliance with regulatory requirements that may limit it due to the primacy of public interests over private ones.

2. An individual's free will is a component of their mental faculties. It can be exercised internally through the process of thought (the internal form of free will) or externally through the expression of will (the external form, which gives rise to rights and obligations). Free will arises at the moment of birth, and its scope changes throughout life. An increase in civil capacity is characterised by an expansion of free will, and vice versa. In the absence of civil capacity, free will is exercised through its internal form, in the context of the right to freedom of thought. If an individual loses the ability to think, they completely lose their free will. The scope of free will can increase with intellectual development, a change in civil capacity, or a change in legal status, and can decrease when capacity is restricted, legal status changes, or a person is declared incapacitated.
3. Free will can manifest in the personal non-property right to life through three main aspects:
   a. No one can be arbitrarily deprived of life. In such a case, free will is unlawfully negated, and the possibility of its application is lost.
   b. The state has a duty to protect human life. Without a guaranteed right to life, the ability to exercise free will is called into question. The protective duty of the state can limit free will, for example, when a person cannot refuse emergency medical assistance because the public interest in saving a life outweighs the desire to refuse care. The free will of state representatives performing this duty must be directed toward its fulfillment, as by protecting the right to life, they protect the ability to exercise free will;
   c. Everyone has the right to protect their life and health, and the life and health of others, from unlawful encroachments. For this purpose, the law provides the possibility to choose forms of protection (jurisdictional and non-jurisdictional) at one's own discretion. An individual independently decides how to protect their rights. Until the public interest outweighs the private, free will in choosing the form of protection for the right to life will be limited only by the regulatory framework.

4. The use of the death penalty completely contradicts the principle of free will, as such punishment is applied forcibly, without the consent of the convicted person, and leads to the irreversible termination of their free will. The prohibition of the death penalty is also based on the fact that it constitutes a complete restriction of a person's will, leaving no opportunity to reform one's behavior or influence one's own destiny through actions and the manifestation of will.
5. Regarding the issue of abortion, free will is understood to be present only in the mother. The embryo and foetus do not possess free will in the civil law sense. Although a foetus may have a specific legal personality in the context of acquiring rights after birth (for example, in inheritance relations), it cannot express its will, and the presence of its own will (thought) has not been proven. In the context of abortion, free will is exercised through the pregnant woman's right to medical care and her right to life.
6. When considering a patient's rights to medical care, such as an abortion, free will manifests as the patient's informed consent to the medical intervention. This construct is characteristic of all types of medical care and services, in which free will is of key importance as a prerequisite for giving informed consent or refusal.
7. The personal non-property right to life may be superior to free will. This is confirmed by the fact that even if a person attempts suicide or refuses emergency medical care of their own free will, the public interest in saving their life will prevail over a "right to die." In countries where euthanasia, assisted suicide, or the right to refuse emergency medical care is recognized, free will is not considered subordinate to the right to life in the same way.
8. The state's duty to protect human life is recognized as dominant over and limiting of free will. By protecting a person's life, the state protects their ability to exercise their free will.
9. To protect life and health from unlawful encroachments, the law provides the possibility to choose any form of protection (jurisdictional and non-jurisdictional) at one's own discretion. Based on the specific situation, a person independently decides

how to protect their rights. Until the public interest outweighs the private, free will in choosing a method of protection will be limited only by regulatory frameworks.

10. The right to health care is based on the principle of voluntariness, which requires the mandatory manifestation of free will in giving informed consent, refusing medical care, and in the grounds for restricting that will. Free will is realised when exercising the right to choose a doctor, treatment methods, and diagnostics. The only exceptions are cases of compulsory treatment.
11. Medical intervention occurs based on the free will of the individual who decides to become a patient, gives consent, and chooses treatment methods. Such consent and refusal are characterised by mandatory requirements: completeness and comprehensibility of information, and voluntariness (absence of physical or mental coercion). Free will is a necessary criterion for determining whether a given consent or refusal complies with these requirements. If they are met, we can state that the patient has exercised their free will.
12. The free will of a minor patient is limited by the free will of their legal representatives, as their wills must be coordinated. In most cases, a doctor must obtain the consent of the legal representatives. The free will of a younger minor is not taken into account at all, and the exercise of their right to health care depends on the free will of their legal representatives. In cases of conflict between the will of a minor patient and that of their legal representatives, the final decision on providing medical care is made by the doctor, based on the patient's best interests.
13. The grounds for conducting medical intervention without a patient's consent can be divided into two categories: (1) when the patient's condition limits their free will; (2) when the public interest prevails over the patient's free will.
14. Free will determines the personal non-property right to donation. The legal nature of its manifestation varies depending on whether the donation of anatomical materials is from a living or deceased person. In the first case, free will is manifested as informed consent to the transfer of anatomical material. In the second, it takes the form of an officially recorded prior consent

or refusal given during one's lifetime. Here, free will manifests as the intention to be or not to be a donor after death, realising the right to donate for the future.

15. The function of free will in exercising the right to confidentiality of health information is to determine the content and form of medical information, as well as the circle of persons to whom it may be provided. In particular, the patient independently designates a person (next of kin) to whom information about their health may be communicated.
16. The right to freedom as a personal non-property right entails two types of prohibitions: (1) a prohibition on the deprivation or restriction of physical liberty, except in cases provided for by law; (2) a prohibition on coercion and pressure to influence an individual's decisions. This right serves a protective function for free will. Unlawful deprivation of liberty occurs without consent and leads to the restriction of free will, for example, by making it impossible to participate in new legal relations. The use of coercion to influence decision-making interferes with free will and is grounds for recognising vitiating factors (defects of will) in contractual relations.
17. The exercise of the right to a family occurs only through free will, either by entering into marriage or by cohabiting with the intention of being a family. The right of children to a family arises at birth and does not depend on their free will.
18. A person's free will has limited significance when guardianship and custody are established over them, due to the prevalence of the public interest. However, there are exceptions: (1) a ward may initiate the dismissal of a guardian or custodian; (2) the wishes of a child who has reached the age of ten are taken into account when appointing a guardian; (3) a custodian for a capable adult who needs assistance may be appointed only at their request.
19. The right to a name arises at birth and initially does not depend on the child's free will, as the name is chosen by their legal representatives. An individual can exercise their free will later by deciding to change their name.
20. The right to use a name is an active form of the right to a name, which provides for the ability to use it independently through

one's own free will and also limits the free will of others by creating corresponding obligations.

21. In some cases, a person decides to use a name of their own free will; in others, its use is mandatory. For instance, when submitting documents for marriage registration, an individual cannot exercise certain rights without using a name.
22. The right to use a name is a direct manifestation of free will, as the person independently decides how and to what extent to use it.
23. In cases established by law, a natural person is obliged to use a name, regardless of their free will. The free will of other persons is limited by the obligation to use a person's name only as the right-holder wishes.
24. The right to respect for a deceased person performs a regulatory function by limiting the free will of others, establishing an obligation to treat the body and burial place with respect. This right can be directly linked to the deceased's free will only if a will or inheritance agreement specifies conditions regarding posthumous actions.
25. The right to individuality is a set of qualities that allow one person to be distinguished from another and to realise their own views, ideas, and, as a result, their free will.
26. The right to dignity arises from a person's self-perception, as they make decisions based on free will that shape their self-image. Honor arises from dignity and the actions a person commits of their own free will, which creates an impression of them in the eyes of others. In turn, respect for honor and dignity limits the free will of others by establishing an obligation to treat a person objectively, in accordance with their behavior and reputation.
27. Guided by free will, a person forms their business reputation through their own actions, which is protected from unfair encroachment. Such encroachment includes the unlawful use of information related to a person's professional activities that may cause them harm.
28. The free will of a legal entity is a cumulative manifestation of the free will of its employees; therefore, its business reputation arises from the collaboration and synergy of all its employees.

29. The personal non-property rights to respect for dignity, honor, and the inviolability of business reputation are directly related to free will, as they arise from it. The very constructs of the "right to respect" and "right to inviolability" create restrictions on the free will of others.
30. Information about the private life of a public figure may be disseminated without their consent only if the public interest in this information outweighs the individual's right to privacy. In such cases, the right-holder's free will is limited by public necessity.
31. The right to a private life and its secrecy is the ability to provide and limit information about oneself at one's own discretion. The right to information is the ability to receive information about others and events at one's own discretion, within the limits prescribed by law and taking into account the right to privacy of others.
32. Free will in the right to personal papers presupposes the dominance of the owner's free will, as access to and use of them (e.g., by publication) is permitted only with the consent of the individual to whom they belong.
33. Free will is exercised by granting consent to photo, film, and video recordings. In the case of filming openly in public spaces, the consent of the person being filmed is not required, and their free will can be exercised only by tacit consent or an express prohibition of filming.
34. Free will is exercised when creating and using personal papers, and the need for consent for their creation and use is intended to prevent interference with the free will of a person who might not wish for such actions to be taken.
35. Free will is exercised through the right to creativity as an element of intellectual activity aimed at self-expression, the discovery of new knowledge, and self-realisation. By exercising this right, a person expresses their free will and realizes a whole set of other personal non-property rights, such as the right to a name (authorship), dignity, and honor.
36. The personal non-property right to choose and change one's occupation is exercised through the application of free will, but in some cases, its exercise is associated with compliance with special legislative requirements and may be limited by sanctions.

3. Free Will in the Law of Property and in *Jura in Re Aliena* (Property Rights in the Property of Others)

3.1. Acquisition and Termination of Property Rights as a Way of Exercising Free Will

The right to property is one of the fundamental human rights, serving as the basis for other institutions and principles of civil law. In the first chapter, we noted that the principle of the inadmissibility of deprivation of property rights is a foundational idea for protecting civil legal relations based on the possession, use, and disposal of property. The right to property cannot exist without free will, a fact that follows directly from its definition.

This is consistent with the arguments of R. A. Maydanyk, who states that a person's dominion over a thing as a property object is a defining feature of property law conditioned by the autonomy of will. However, modern property law is characterised by a trend of transitioning from the concept of a formally defined autonomy of will to the concept of "regulated property rights." This new concept is based on an essential (functional) understanding of property law as the right of the most complete dominion over a thing, rather than one formally defined by statute (Maydanyk 2019b, 10).

Although there is a liberalisation of property rights today, with increasing attention given to the principle of *numerus clausus* and "hidden" property rights, free will continues to play a key role. It not only affects the principle of the inadmissibility of deprivation of property rights but is also necessary for the dynamics of this right. The principle of inadmissibility is a passive construct that becomes active only when violated. In contrast, the right to property facilitates the dynamics of legal relations through its acquisition and termination. Having recognized that free will is of fundamental importance for the principles of civil law, it should be assumed that it has a similar impact on the right to property.

There is some debate about whether the right to property is natural or artificial. This debate is based on the historical fact that property rights emerged only after the abolition of collective property in primitive societies.

Arguments in favor of this position are presented by L. Murphy and T. Nagel, who argue that the right to private property is entirely artificial, constituted by legal norms and agreements (Murphy and Nagel 2002, 74). Initially, the right to property did not exist and only gained legal force after its normative consolidation. However, this argument is controversial, as all rights were once not normatively recognized. Even the natural right to life was selective, not extending to enslaved people. We support the position that the right to property holds an essential place alongside natural rights, a view confirmed by its constitutional status.

A concise definition of property rights was proposed by P. Eleftheriadis, who defined it as a right to things, where the right of private property establishes an exclusive relationship between a thing and one person. In a private property regime, the owner is the exclusive holder of the right to a thing (Eleftheriadis 2008). However, this definition does not fully correspond to the legal understanding of property rights, as rights to a thing also arise in licensed use, leases, rentals, and other legal relations. The thesis of an exclusive relationship between a thing and one person is also questionable, as private property can be held jointly by more than one owner.

We believe that Eleftheriadis's main idea was that the right to property determines an exclusive legal relationship between a thing and its owner, who is individualised and endowed with the exclusive right to determine the thing's legal fate. This understanding is close to defining ownership as a rule according to which, for each object, the individual whose name is associated with it must determine how and by whom it will be used (Waldron, 1991). This is not limited to transferring the right of use but also involves how the owner will use the thing themself.

The concept of property rights depends on the specific theory applied. L. M. Mandryka distinguishes the following theories: theological, labour, contractual (exchange), psychological, materialistic, and socio-axiological (Mandryka 2009).

Modern civil legal relations are changing due to many factors (particularly the development of information technologies), which influence the grounds for the emergence of private property rights (Nekit 2020, 101).

Today, the theological theory is difficult to recognize as relevant, as it continues the ideas of determinism and the recognition of God as the ultimate cause of everything, including property. In the labour theory, property rights are not reduced to things or a sum of material goods; they are understood as an integrity that combines a person's life, will, and property. If someone interferes with another's property, that person has the full right to protect themself and their property (i.e., both freedom and property) (Locke 2023, 13).

The more a person works, the more property they have. In the contract theory, property rights establish that free will must first give itself a tangible existence, and the first material for this is things, i.e., external objects. This type of freedom is what we define as property (Patten 1995).

The contract is understood as a form of ownership. According to the psychological theory, the attribute of "mine" is determined not by external conditions but by a psychic moment of "appropriation"—an internal establishment of a boundary (Azimov, Sybilov, and Borysova 2000, 197). The materialist theory is based on the thesis that a person's attitude toward a thing as their own is possible only if others treat that thing as belonging to someone else. Actual possession can be exercised only by excluding others from such dominion (Ibid., 193). According to the socio-axiological theory, property is a social phenomenon in the profound sense that the concept logically implies a certain social connection, without which property cannot be conceived (Ibid., 360).

If we generalize these theories, we can see that the right to property is directly related to free will, which is necessary to create a legal relationship between the owner and the thing. For the will theory, the value of property is related to the value and status of freedom, where freedom is not an absolute value (Eleftheriadis 2008).

T. Nagel concluded that some system of property rights plays an indispensable role in defining the protected sphere of personal liberty (Nagel 1995). This is the relationship between free will and the right to property.

Free will is necessary for the exercise of property rights and for determining the legal fate of a thing. Through free will, we acquire and terminate property rights. At the same time, the right to property is another way of expressing free will.

The connection between property rights and free will is also emphasised in Article 316 of the Civil Code of Ukraine, which defines the right to property as the right of a person to a thing (property), which they exercise in accordance with the law at their own will, regardless of the will of others (*Tsyvil'nyi kodeks Ukrainy* [Civil Code of Ukraine] 2003, art. 316). The content of this right is based on the classical triad of powers: possession, use, and disposal.

Possession is defined as the owner's ability to hold an object that legally belongs to them; it represents the actual power exercised over the thing (*Bürgerliches Gesetzbuch* [Civil Code] 1896, § 854).

Good faith possession arises as a distinct manifestation of free will. In this context, an individual consciously enters into civil legal relations with a will directed toward the lawful acquisition of rights. They are unaware—and could not reasonably be expected to be aware—that they are acquiring the object from a non-owner.

Even in instances of unlawful possession, if it is held in good faith, a manifestation of free will remains present:

1. Lack of Legal Grounds: Such possession may arise without formal legal grounds if the person is not obliged to know of the illegality.
2. Intent vs. Validity: For example, when a person acquires a stolen item without knowledge of the other party's lack of right to alienate it, both parties manifest the free will to enter a civil legal relationship.
3. Divergent Motivations: While the improper alienator uses their free will to violate the law for unlawful gain, the buyer

manifests their free will without realizing the invalidity of the relationship.

A different legal situation arises with bad faith possession. Unlike good faith scenarios, bad faith possession is categorized by the possessor's knowledge of the lack of right, and it can occur both with and without the exercise of free will.

Let's consider two situations. The first is when a person does not intend to become a bad faith possessor. For example, finding someone else's property among one's belongings or accidentally taking someone else's item. By law, such possession is in bad faith, but the person had no such intention. In this case, one must do everything possible to return the item to its rightful owner. Here, a manifestation of free will will determine whether the possessor consciously violates the law or not. If a person purchases an item from a bad faith possessor, free will manifests differently. Acquiring an item is a manifestation of free will with the intention of entering into a purchase-sale relationship and becoming the owner. In this case, the transaction will be considered unlawful for two reasons. First, the right of disposal belongs only to the rightful owner. Second, the buyer expressed a will to enter into a lawful transaction. This situation could be qualified as a transaction with vitiating factors (a defect of will) due to mistake, as the seller did not disclose their lack of the right to alienate.

The other situation occurs when a person becomes a bad faith possessor knowingly and intentionally. In this case, free will is not violated. If we knowingly acquire a stolen item, we begin illegal and bad faith possession through an exercise of free will, with all the legal consequences that follow.

Use is the extraction of a thing's useful properties (e.g., harvesting crops, consuming food, wearing clothes) (Kopeichykov 2003, 158). Here, free will will have the same manifestation as in good and bad faith possession, depending on whether the use is lawful. Use can also occur without the influence of free will, such as when a person is unaware of their actions or uses property accidentally.

A. M. Honoré identified three ways of exercising the right of use: (1) the personal right to use and consume a thing; (2) the right to decide how and by whom the thing will be used; (3) the right to receive the fruits, rent, profit, and other income it generates (Honoré 1961, 372). The first and third methods are aimed at the owner and involve the use of their free will to satisfy their own interests. The second method is intended to grant another person the opportunity to extract the useful properties of a thing. This method of use is relevant for *jura in re aliena* (property rights in the property of others), which will be examined separately.

The personal right to use and consume a thing implies the owner's ability to decide for themself what to do with the property. This includes not only the ability to use or not use the thing but also the right to choose how to do so. However, the right of use may be limited.

In this regard, O. V. Rozgon substantiates the following conclusions: (1) the limits of the right of use are determined by regulations that restrain the owner's will, power, and interests—not to violate the rights of others or society, and to act within a specific regime (e.g., adhering to construction rules, sanitary conditions); (2) these limits are established by law and take into account the property's intended purpose (for example, owners of a residential building are obliged to ensure its safety, carry out repairs at their own expense, maintain the adjacent territory, and participate in management costs and taxes) (Rozhon 2005, 33).

The right of use not only allows the exercise of free will but also imposes obligations on the owner. A violation of this dualism may result in the termination of a contract. For example, a donor has the right to demand the termination of a gift agreement if, due to the donee's negligent attitude, a culturally valuable item is at risk of being destroyed or significantly damaged (*Tsyvil'nyi kodeks Ukrainy* [Civil Code of Ukraine] 2003, art. 727, para. 3). Similarly, a donation contract may be terminated if the donation is used for an unintended purpose (Ibid., art. 730, para. 3).

Restrictions on free will in the right of use can also be found in international acts. S. Burdeniuk writes about Ukraine's acceptance of obligations to comply with convention guarantees on human rights, the essence of which is that a violation is met with a reaction based on a common will and common values (Burdeniuk 2016, 22).

The Protocol to the Convention for the Protection of Human Rights and Fundamental Freedoms proclaims the right to the peaceful enjoyment of one's property, which prohibits being deprived of the ability to use it (Council of Europe 1952, art. 1). Although the rest of this article primarily concerns restrictions on state interference in private property, the above establishes the right to use one's property only in a way that does not harm the rights of others.

It should also be added that the use of property may occur without being a manifestation of free will when it is done unconsciously. Even the use of one's own property while intoxicated will be lawful if it does not violate the rights of others.

Disposal is the ability of the owner to determine the actual and legal fate of a thing. Lawful disposal occurs as a manifestation of free will because only the owner has the right to decide what to do with the thing. The disposal must be conscious and voluntary. Exceptions include cases of forced alienation as a sanction for a criminal offense or under special circumstances.

While the rights of possession and use correlate with the emergence of the right to property, the right of disposal is the basis for its termination.

Disposing of a thing is an active manifestation of the owner's free will, with the aim of transferring rights to it through donation, sale, succession, or by its destruction or abandonment.

The right of disposal correlates with the right of use, particularly in the context of deciding how and by whom a thing will be used. The right of disposal does not necessarily lead to the transfer of ownership, which is preserved when a thing is leased, for example. Free will cannot be complete in property rights without the right of disposal.

This is confirmed by the thesis of J. Waldron that this right is an integral part of respecting a person as a free moral subject (Waldron 1991). It is noted that freedom of disposal allows people to come to agreements with others on their own terms to satisfy needs they cannot meet alone (Ibid.).

The importance of the right of disposal is enshrined at the international level and is a crucial condition for legal relations, as is evident in the requirements of the North American Free Trade Agreement and the Energy Charter Treaty. In *Continental Casualty Co. v. Argentina* (2008), the International Center for Settlement of Investment Disputes held that state interference with one or more key characteristics of property, such as the power of disposal, would be tantamount to expropriation.

With certain exceptions, the rights of possession, use, and disposal cannot exist without the free will that is necessary for their exercise. The abolition or unlawful restriction of one of the elements of the right to property renders it ineffective and affects free will, leading to a systematic violation of other rights.

Having clarified the influence of free will on the content of property rights, we can determine its significance for their acquisition and termination.

The acquisition of property rights is divided into lawful and unlawful. The lawfulness of acquisition is related to the concept of bona fide possession, which is based on the principle of justice.

The connection between justice and property rights was detailed by R. Nozick, who noted that a person is entitled to a holding if and only if they acquired it through a history consisting exclusively of two kinds of events: (1) initial acquisition, especially of unowned things; and (2) transfer, by gift, sale, or other voluntary agreement, but not by theft (i.e., by force or fraud) (Coleman, Frankel, and Phillips 1976).

Nozick's theory boils down to the fact that the redistribution of holdings without the owner's consent is theft. Therefore, the owner's desire—their will—to transfer property is the only legitimate condition for the lawful acquisition of ownership by another person. The only exceptions are inheritance by law and forced alienation of property, which are regulated by legal norms.

The principle of justice is expressed through the principle of good faith with the formula that the acquisition of property rights is in good faith if a person's behavior in civil legal relations complies with the law and is, therefore, lawful (Kharchenko 2012, 52).

This is confirmed in Article 328 of the Civil Code of Ukraine, which stipulates that the right of ownership is considered to be acquired lawfully unless it directly follows otherwise from the law, or unless the illegality of the acquisition is established by a court (*Tsyvil'nyi kodeks Ukrainy* [Civil Code of Ukraine] 2003, art. 328)

The lawful acquisition of property rights is possible only with compliance with legislation. On the one hand, free will is a mandatory condition confirming a person's desire to transfer or acquire property. On the other, it demonstrates the parties' willingness to enter into a civil legal relationship, confirmed by their conduct.

In this, we see confirmation of the mandatory combination of will and the expression of will. A person's will is expressed as a desire to acquire property rights, while the expression of will serves as the external manifestation of that will in the form of specific actions.

Good faith assumes that a person was entitled to acquire ownership of a specific thing. When acquiring ownership by a unilateral act (e.g., creating a thing, finding something), only the free will of one person is taken into account. If a person creates a new object of civil rights, the will of others is not considered, and ownership is acquired from the fact of its creation. This correlates with personal non-property rights (e.g., the right to individuality and creativity) and intellectual property rights, particularly copyright.

Free will has a different meaning in the acquisition of property rights resulting from a bilateral expression of will. In this case, free will illustrates the good faith of both the acquirer and the alienator. Let us consider four models of such legal relations: (1) both participants act in good faith; (2) the acquirer acts in bad faith; (3) the alienator acts in bad faith; (4) all participants act in bad faith.

When both participants act in good faith, each, guided by their free will and within their rights and obligations, enters into the legal relationship in accordance with the law. For example, an owner with full legal capacity concludes a sale agreement for their property, and the buyer voluntarily accepts the agreement, having the right to do so.

An acquirer in bad faith is a person who purchased property under a contract from a person who did not have the right to alienate it, a fact they knew or should have known. But this definition refers to a situation where all participants are acting in bad faith, for example, when the buyer knew they were purchasing a stolen item. Such a situation leads to the invalidity of the transaction and is grounds for legal liability. It can be assumed that an acquirer can be in bad faith only in relation to another person.

Let us consider the case of acquiring ownership by a person who does not have the right to purchase the item. This is particularly relevant for objects with restricted circulation. For example, the sale of alcoholic beverages to persons under 18 is prohibited (*Pro derzhavne rehuliuvannia vyrobnytstva i obihu…* [On State Regulation of the Production and Circulation…] 1995, art. 71, para. 1).

The seller checks for age compliance, but when a minor buys beer, they are aware that they are violating regulatory requirements and cannot acquire ownership. It can be assumed that in this case, the buyer becomes an acquirer in bad faith. However, this conclusion is incorrect. The acquisition of ownership did not occur because the contract was concluded in violation of legal requirements, making the transaction void. The minor exercised their free will to acquire ownership but became a bad faith possessor of the item. Such a legal relationship does not align with the parties' interests or the subject of a retail sale agreement. The consequence will be restitution and legal liability.

Close to the above is the case where both parties act in bad faith. This applies to instances where none of the participants have the right to acquire or transfer ownership. This can occur due to non-compliance with capacity requirements, violation of legislation, or dealing with objects excluded from civil circulation. Let us consider two cases that demonstrate the significance of free will differently.

The first situation is when the seller knows the buyer is under eighteen but sells them an alcoholic beverage, and the buyer knows they do not have the right to purchase it. In this case, the parties' free will is aimed at concluding a void transaction. From a civil law perspective, the sale occurs under a sale agreement. From the participants' perspective, their interest aligns with the subject of the sale. But the main difference lies in the misaligned application of free will. The free will of the parties to a sale agreement should be aimed at transferring ownership. In the example above, the parties' free will is aimed at establishing only the right of possession. This is a key factor for qualifying the bona fide acquisition of ownership.

The last model is associated with the bad faith of the alienator. In such cases, it is common to speak of the alienation of property to which the person had no right of ownership. However, other cases exist, related to restrictions on certain types of economic activity. For example, if a non-bank financial institution concludes a loan agreement in a foreign currency, it would be an alienator in bad faith, as it does not have the right to dispose of foreign currency. This is confirmed by the decision of the Zdolbuniv District Court of Rivne Region No. 562/482/20, which ruled that a factoring agreement was invalid because the defendants did not have the required currency license (*Rishennia Zdolbunivs'koho raionnoho sudu…*[Decision of the Zdolbuniv District Court…]2020).

If property is alienated by a person who had no right to do so, a bona fide acquirer acquires ownership of it if, in accordance with Article 388 of the Civil Code of Ukraine, the property cannot be claimed from them. A crucial point here is confirming the acquirer's bona fide intention. Only if the acquirer did not know and could not have known that the counterparty had no right to alienate can we speak of a desire for lawful acquisition. Otherwise, we are referring to a case where all participants are in bad faith, meaning their will was aimed at creating a void transaction.

As we can see, the qualification of the lawfulness of acquiring property rights depends on the free will of the participants. It is free will that determines the desire and interest of the participants to acquire and transfer ownership, rather than to conclude a void transaction.

The exercise of free will in acquiring ownership depends on the thing's previous legal history and on succession. Three models can be distinguished: (1) a thing without a previous owner (a newly created thing); (2) a thing whose owner is unknown (an ownerless thing, a find, a treasure); (3) a thing that has an owner (a gift, a sale).

The primary right of ownership to a thing arises at the moment of its creation. The exception is natural resources. In all other cases, primary property rights arise in relation to a newly created thing. In other words, every thing is initially newly created, as primary ownership rights arise from that moment. Before creation, a thing is not an object of civil rights. The emergence of a thing and, accordingly, the primary emergence of rights to it is a manifestation of the free will of the person who creates it, if this happens consciously. However, a thing can be created outside a person's will, for example, by a person with a mental disorder or in a state of intoxication.

In some cases, the free will of the person for whom the thing is created is also important. Guided by their own will, a person creates a thing but automatically becomes its owner only if two conditions are met: (1) they use their own materials; (2) there is no contract or law providing for the emergence of ownership in another person.

Ownership of a movable thing arises from the moment of its creation. However, a contract or law may provide for the emergence of rights in another person, for example, when an object is created on commission. But if a person creates a thing from their own materials based on a contract, they automatically become its owner (*Tsyvil'nyi kodeks Ukrainy* [Civil Code of Ukraine] 2003, art. 331, para. 1).

This applies to both manufacturing for one's own needs and economic activity. If an item is made by an employee within their employment, the employer is considered the manufacturer. This is confirmed by the correlation of wills: the employer's will is aimed at production for economic purposes, while the employee's will is aimed at fulfillling labour duties. Thus, only the producer's will is aimed at the emergence of property rights.

For the emergence of ownership of newly created real estate, the will to create the object is not enough. The content of Article 331 of the Civil Code of Ukraine requires the person to direct their will toward fulfillling additional requirements: commissioning and state registration. Until this point, the person is considered the owner of the materials and equipment used in the construction.

As in previous cases, the public interest prevails over individual free will. A person's desire to create a real estate object is insufficient. The need for commissioning protects the public interest, ensuring compliance with building codes and standards and preventing the operation of potentially dangerous objects (Pohrebniak 2020, 72).

This is confirmed by a resolution of the Cassation Economic Court, which states that ownership of a newly created real estate object does not arise before its commissioning and state registration (*Postanova Kasatsiinoho hospodars'koho sudu…* [Resolution of the Cassation Economic Court…]. 2019).

Free will is essential not only for commissioning real estate. The issue arises in the case of unauthorised construction, i.e., creating property in violation of regulatory requirements. In this case, free will is aimed either at the emergence of possession, not ownership, or at the subsequent acquisition of ownership after the violation. G.G. Novosyolova and A.O. Pedorenko recognize two ways of acquiring ownership of illegally constructed property: by providing the land plot to the person for the already built real estate and by filing a lawsuit to transfer the developer's rights (Novosolova and Pedorenko 2021, 103).

It is necessary to agree with the authors that one must consider whether the unauthorised construction was deliberate or if the person built it due to insufficient awareness without violating the interests of others (Ibid.). This will serve as the basis for qualifying the participant's free will.

A different procedure for applying free will is used for things that had a previous owner. The primary importance here is defining the person's will as directed toward either a bona fide or mala fide acquisition of ownership.

In the case of acquiring ownership of a processed thing, it is essential to establish: (1) whether the processing was unauthorised; (2) who owned the material; (3) whether the cost of processing and the new thing created significantly exceeds the cost of the material.

The answers to these questions make it possible to establish the aim of the person's free will. If a person wanted to acquire ownership through lawful processing, they will acquire the corresponding rights. If not, the actions can be qualified as a household contract or provision of services.

Special attention is paid to acquiring ownership of an ownerless thing. This case should be distinguished from a find and a movable thing that the owner has abandoned. An ownerless thing is a thing that has no owner or whose owner is unknown (*Tsyvil'nyi kodeks Ukrainy* [Civil Code of Ukraine] 2003, art. 335, para. 1).

After the acquisitive prescription period, a person may acquire ownership. In the case of a find, the person who found the lost item must immediately notify the owner and return it (Ibid., art. 337, para. 1).

The actual difference is that in the second case, we assume an owner exists. However, a person who wants to acquire ownership may not know this. Only by their own free will does a person choose how to qualify such an item and in what order to acquire ownership. A priori, having found an item, a person must find its owner. However, if the item is not being sought and is movable, it can easily be qualified as ownerless. The Ministry of Justice (2011) confirms that the concepts of "has no owner" and "owner unknown" are united by the absence of a person who could dispute ownership.

In the case where the owner has abandoned a movable thing, the person who takes possession of it acquires ownership from that moment (*Tsyvil'nyi kodeks Ukrainy* [Civil Code of Ukraine] 2003, art. 336).

The main criterion here is establishing the fact of abandonment, which can be done by a declaration or by other actions. In this case, guided by their own free will, the person seeking to acquire ownership must independently determine if it is lost or abandoned. In some cases, this is obvious, based on customary norms. For example, items left in a rubbish bin are considered abandoned. However, customs may vary. In the UK, people leave items outside their houses for others to take, a tradition not widespread in Ukraine.

Disputable situations may arise, for example, when a person mistakenly throws something away or leaves items near their house without intending to abandon them. From this, it should be concluded that it is the person who wants to acquire ownership who must, of their own free will, ascertain whether the item has an owner and whether they can acquire rights to it. The situation is similar for abandoned domestic animals and treasure.

The methods of terminating property rights are generally classified by the criterion of will. However, D. Biletskyi also identifies other classification methods: by the type of legal fact (actions and events), by place in the system (general, special), by legal regime (movable and immovable), and by lawfulness (Biletskyi 2018, 10).

The division of termination methods into voluntary, involuntary, and compulsory serves as the most effective framework for illustrating the manifestation of free will within Ukrainian legislation. Building upon this tripartite division, we propose to categorize the grounds for the termination of property rights into three groups based on their inherent connection to the owner's volition:

1. Direct Connection (Voluntary Termination): This category encompasses actions where the owner's free will is the primary driver of the legal outcome.
   a. Alienation of property by the owner (e.g., sale, gift);
   b. Renunciation of ownership (the owner's explicit refusal to hold the right).
2. Variable Connection (Contingent Termination): In these instances, the termination depends on circumstances that may or may not align with the owner's immediate intent, or where free will is mediated by external events.
   a. Destruction of property;
   b. Redemption of cultural heritage monuments;
   c. Termination of a legal entity or the death of the owner.
3. No Connection (Compulsory Termination): These grounds represent the absence or overriding of the owner's free will by the state or legal necessity.
   a. Termination of ownership of property that cannot legally belong to a person;
   b. Forced alienation for reasons of public necessity;
   c. Seizure of property for the fulfilllment of obligations;
   d. Requisition, confiscation, and sanctions;

e. Nationalization;
f. Civil forfeiture (recognition of assets as unfounded).

In grounds for termination that have a direct connection with free will, the owner exercises their rights at their own discretion, without coercion, and in their own interests. The owner's renunciation of property rights was examined above, so let us focus on the alienation of property by the owner.

Alienation by the owner refers to cases where the owner, at their own will and discretion, exercises their powers and transfers the thing into the ownership of another person (Misiats 2011, 281).

Such alienation occurs through sale, exchange, and donation and corresponds to the right to acquire, which means an individual or legal entity can acquire ownership without unjustified interference from the state or third parties (Sprankling 2014).

In addition to compliance with the requirements of the law of obligations, which will be examined separately, the alienation requires the alignment of free will with three features of this mechanism: (1) desynchronisation of legal and factual actions; (2) presumption of synchronisation of the will of joint owners; (3) exercise of preferential rights of third parties (Kostruba 2021).

The first feature pertains to the coordination between a person's will to alienate and their actual actions. This norm stems from the principle of *venire contra factum proprium*, which means that a person's conduct creates rights and obligations they cannot later waive. This is where the duty of parties to act in good faith when fulfillling their obligations under a contract originates (Valihura 2020a, 15).

The introduction of the principle of good faith is a measure aimed at strengthening the moral foundations of civil law regulation (Valihura 2020b, 120). This concept is continued in the principle of *protestatio facto contraria non valet*, which states that an expressed reservation is invalid if it contradicts the person's actual behavior (Flume 1979, 76).

H. Brox and W.-D. Walker explain this as the irrelevance of a reservation that contradicts the interpretation of a person's conduct (Brox and Walker 2022). Regarding the termination of property rights, this should be understood as a prohibition on inconsistency in the will of the person alienating the property. A desynchronisation of intent and factual actions leads to the non-termination of property rights. For example, a seller concludes a sale agreement but does not transfer the goods.

The second feature relates to the alienation of property held in joint ownership. While this involves the individual expression of will of a participant, the alienation of joint property requires a joint expression of will. In this case, the free will of one co-owner needs to be correlated with that of the other co-owners.

The third feature of property rights alienation necessitates strict adherence to the interests of third parties who possess a preferential (pre-emptive) right to acquire ownership. In such instances, the manifestation of the owner's free will cannot occur in isolation; it must be coordinated with the will of the entitled party.

A preferential right of purchase is applicable in several critical legal scenarios, including:

1. Agricultural Land: Regarding the sale of a land share by a tenant (Ministry of Justice of Ukraine 2022);
2. Corporate Law: In the case of an additional issuance of shares (*Pro aktsionerni tovarystva* [On Joint-Stock Companies] 2022, art. 31);
3. Housing Law: During the sale of leased housing (*Tsyvil'nyi kodeks Ukrainy* [Civil Code of Ukraine] 2003, art. 822, para. 2).

In these circumstances, the owner's free will (the intent to terminate ownership) must align with the free will of the counterparty (the intent to acquire it). However, it is important to note that these requirements do not extend to gift agreements, where a preferential right to acquire ownership remains legally inapplicable.

The alienation of property by an owner through a contract will be examined in more detail in the next chapter.

In the grounds for termination of ownership that have a variable connection with free will, the owner exercises their rights either at their own discretion or through the intervention of other persons. Variability implies the possibility of termination both at the owner's will and at the will of others.

The right to destroy one's property comes from *jus abutendi*. When destroying one's property, a person's will is aimed either at consuming the thing's useful properties or at directly destroying it. In the first case, the person exercises the right of use, as a result of which the thing is destroyed. The will is not aimed at destruction but at consumption or transformation. Termination of ownership here is a consequence, not a goal. A different situation arises when the owner intentionally destroys the thing, and their will is aimed at terminating ownership.

The rationality of such a right raises doubts for E. J. McCaffery, as it allows an owner to destroy valuable resources without justification, which is a moral offense in a world affected by poverty (McCaffery 2000, 81).

This position aligns with established international norms that prohibit the destruction of cultural heritage (*UNESCO 2003; Hague Convention 1954*), literary and artistic works (*Berne Convention 1886*, art. 2.1), and natural resources (*Stockholm Declaration 1972*).

However, the validity of this restrictive approach is questioned by J. G. Sprankling, who emphasizes that the "right to destroy" is an integral component of property law (Sprankling 2014). From this perspective, the right to property would be fundamentally incomplete without the right to destroy, as it represents a crucial method of exercising individual free will over one's assets.

In the above options for termination of property rights, the owner's free will gives them the right to destroy the thing, regardless of their intent. However, the termination of ownership upon destruction may not depend on the owner's free will. This applies to cases where property is destroyed accidentally or intentionally by another person. In the case of accidental destruction, we must consider the presence of intent. The cause of destruction should not be linked to a desire for such an outcome. If another person intentionally destroys the property, their free will is aimed at causing such consequences, and the owner's will is not taken into account.

In some cases, when property is destroyed, there is neither free will nor a subject who destroyed it. This applies to cases of force majeure and natural disasters. However, this only applies when there is no person who destroyed the property. If the destruction occurred due to military actions, the case should be classified as intentional or negligent destruction.

In summary, the destruction of property involves a variable connection with the owner's free will. In cases of destroying one's own property, the owner's free will is present only when termination was not the goal. If the owner intentionally destroys their property, there is a direct connection. In cases of destruction of another's property, the owner's free will is not considered.

Variability is also provided for the termination of ownership of cultural heritage monuments. If, as a result of the owner's actions or inaction, a monument is threatened with damage or destruction, the relevant protection authority issues a warning (*Tsyvil'nyi kodeks Ukrainy* [Civil Code of Ukraine] 2003, art. 352, para. 1).

This warning creates an opportunity for the owner to preserve their property rights by complying, or to lose them. Free will is manifested in the owner's decision. However, in cases of urgent necessity, a claim for its redemption may be filed without a warning (Ibid., art. 352, para. 3). In this case, the owner's free will is irrelevant, and the redemption price will be set by the court.

The last variable ground for termination is the liquidation of a legal entity or the death of the owner. Free will has a direct connection in the case of voluntary liquidation or the owner's suicide. There is no connection with the owner's free will in cases of forced liquidation or when the owner's death occurs by the will of others or without any influence of free will. In this context, the transfer of property by inheritance by law is of particular interest, where the testator's will is absent, and the transfer occurs by the public will of the state, consistent with the will of the heir. This will be discussed in detail in Chapter Six.

The process of the forced liquidation of a legal entity is executed exclusively via a court decision. Historically, the specific grounds for such actions were detailed in Article 38 of the Law "On

State Registration of Legal Entities..." (*Pro derzhavnu reiestratsiiu iurydychnykh osib...* [On State Registration of Legal Entities...] 2003, art. 38). However, since 2015, these legal norms have been modified to become more generalized.

These legislative amendments align with the academic perspectives of P. O. Povar (Povar 2009, 65) and V. S. Shcherbyna (Shcherbyna 2006, 142). Furthermore, the proposal by V. O. Khomenko to establish specific grounds for liquidation within specialized legislation is considered highly expedient (Khomenko 2017, 26).

Currently, while Ukrainian law lacks a single, consolidated list of such grounds, they generally encompass the following categories:

1. Insolvency: Bankruptcy proceedings;
2. Registration Defects: Declaration of the state registration as invalid;
3. Legal Non-compliance: Systematic or gross violations of the law;
4. Operational Absence: The confirmed absence of the legal entity at its officially registered address.

Forced liquidation occurs without the consent of the founder(s), so their free will does not affect the termination of property rights. A similar situation occurs when the death of the property owner is caused by others (intentional murder) or occurs without the influence of free will (accident, manslaughter, illness). The main factor in qualifying such cases is determining whether a participant's will was directed at causing death.

The last group of grounds for termination of ownership assumes no connection with the owner's free will. On these grounds, termination occurs without the owner's consent, due to external circumstances, or at the will of others.

The termination of ownership regarding property that cannot legally belong to a person occurs through either voluntary or compulsory mechanisms. While the initial stage may involve a manifestation of free will, the underlying driver is regulatory coercion.

Voluntary Phase: The law often provides a grace period for the transfer of ownership. For instance, the Land Code of Ukraine obliges foreigners who inherit agricultural land to alienate it within one year (*Zemel'nyi kodeks Ukrainy* [Land Code of Ukraine] 2001, art. 81, para. 4). During this period, the owner's free will is manifested in their ability to select the method of alienation and the counterparty. However, the causal link demonstrates that the primary reason for termination is legal necessity, not the owner's autonomous desire to divest.

Compulsory Phase: If the property is not alienated within the specified timeframe, a forced sale procedure is initiated. Initially, the owner may still exercise their will regarding the price and counterparty during the auction process. If the property remains unsold, it is transferred to the state via a court decision at a price determined by the court. In this final stage, the owner's free will has no legal effect on the termination of ownership

As we can see, the termination of ownership of property that cannot legally belong to a person occurs under regulatory coercion. In some cases, the owner's will allows them to influence the procedure, but not the necessity of the alienation itself.

A similar situation arises in the case of the forced alienation of private land plots and other real estate for public necessity. This method of termination is correlated with the right to the inviolability of private property under Article 41 of the Constitution. Forced alienation may be applied only as an exception for public necessity, based on and in the manner established by law, and with prior and full compensation. Forced alienation with subsequent compensation is permitted only under conditions of martial law or a state of emergency (*Konstytutsiia Ukrainy* [Constitution of Ukraine] 1996, art. 41).

The public interest provides for the termination of ownership without the owner's consent. Their free will can only affect the amount of compensation and consent to receive equivalent property, not the termination of ownership.

The situation with requisition is almost identical. The difference lies in the expansion of grounds for forced termination and their application to movable property. In the event of a natural disaster, accident, epidemic, or other extraordinary circumstances, property may be forcibly alienated for public necessity with prior and full compensation (*Tsyvil'nyi kodeks Ukrainy* [Civil Code of Ukraine] 2003, art. 353, para. 1).

The same is permissible under martial law or a state of emergency, with the difference that compensation is subsequent, not prior (Ibid., art. 353, para. 2).

The seizure of property to satisfy an owner's outstanding obligations constitutes a distinct legal ground for the termination of ownership regardless of the individual's will. According to Ukrainian law, this process involves a sequence of enforcement actions, including:

1. Attachment (Arrest): The initial legal restriction on the right to dispose of the property.
2. Seizure: The actual removal or taking control of the asset by enforcement officers.
3. Forced Sale: The realization of the property through public auctions to satisfy creditor claims (*Pro vykonavche provadzhennia* [On Enforcement Proceedings] 2016, art. 48, para. 1).

These enforcement mechanisms represent the state's proportional response to an owner's failure to fulfilll their legal or contractual obligations. In such instances, the public interest—specifically the principle of the certainty of contracts and the protection of creditors' rights—overrides the individual's free will.

Arrest and seizure do not constitute termination of ownership but may lead to it. At these stages, the owner's free will still has an impact, as they can fulfill their obligations, which will lead to the end of enforcement proceedings and the preservation of ownership (Ibid., art. 39, para. 1; art. 61, para. 6). However, if the property is forcibly sold, ownership will terminate without the owner's will.

A different situation arises in the case of confiscation, as the owner's free will has no effect on the termination of their ownership. Confiscation is carried out by court decision as a sanction for grave mercenary crimes, as well as crimes against national and public security (*Kryminal'nyi kodeks Ukrainy* [Criminal Code of Ukraine] 2001, Art. 59, para. 2).

Without the owner's consent, confiscated property is transferred to the state budget or to a requesting party to compensate victims (*Kryminal'nyi protsesual'nyi kodeks Ukrainy* [Criminal Procedure Code of Ukraine], art. 586).

Similar to confiscation are sanctions and nationalisation as grounds for terminating property rights. They differ in procedure and grounds, but they also have no connection with the free will of the property owner. Sanctions are applied by a decision of the National Security and Defense Council and introduced by a presidential decree. They are used for actions of a foreign state, entity, or individual that create threats to Ukraine's national interests, security, and sovereignty. The procedure for applying sanctions differs from other grounds for termination and involves approval by the Supreme Anti-Corruption Court.

Nationalisation involves the forced seizure of property belonging to the Russian Federation and its residents in Ukraine. This is a specific method of terminating property rights without considering the owner's will, applied to specific subjects. This procedure provides for the forced seizure of property for reasons of public necessity (including military necessity) in favor of the state of Ukraine (*Pro osnovni zasady prymusovoho vyluchennia…* [On the Basic Principles of the Forcible Seizure..], art. 1).

It is noteworthy that Article 346 of the Civil Code of Ukraine currently lacks explicit provisions for sanctions and nationalization as grounds for the termination of property rights. Consequently, these mechanisms are currently categorized under the broader umbrella of "other cases... established by law."

Given the heightened relevance of these legal institutions in the context of ongoing military operations and state security, a legislative update is required to ensure legal certainty. We propose to explicitly enshrine the definitions and substantive content of sanctions and nationalization within Article 346 of the Civil Code of Ukraine.

This amendment would achieve several key objectives:

1. Aligning the general civil legislation with specialized wartime and national security statutes.
2. Creating a comprehensive list of grounds for the termination of property rights within the primary civil law instrument.
3. Explicitly delineating these as compulsory mechanisms where the manifestation of the owner's free will is lawfully superseded by the public interest of national defense.

Although the Civil Code of Ukraine allows for the expansion of grounds for the termination of property rights, the final ground explicitly enshrined in Article 346 is the recognition of assets as unfounded and their subsequent recovery by the state. This legal institution, established in 2019, represents a significant shift in property law.

The termination of ownership on this ground is entirely independent of the owner's free will. It is applied under specific conditions outlined in the Civil Procedure Code of Ukraine (*Tsyvil'nyi protsesual'nyi kodeks Ukrainy* [Civil Procedure Code of Ukraine] 2004, art. 290, para. 2).

The substantive requirements for this mechanism include:

1. Assets are deemed unfounded if the discrepancy between their value and the legal income of a public official exceeds the subsistence minimum by five hundred times or more.
2. A landmark ruling by the Supreme Court (*Postanova Velykoi Palaty Verkhovnoho Sudu Ukrainy* [Resolution of the Grand Chamber of the Supreme Court of Ukraine] 2018) confirms the dominance of state and public interests over individual autonomy in such cases.

This judicial position allows for the transfer of ownership to the state without the owner's consent, effectively superseding individual free will in the interest of anti-corruption and legal accountability.

The above proves that the right to property is directly related to free will, which is necessary to create a legal relationship between the owner and the thing. In the right of use, free will has the same manifestation as in good and bad faith possession, depending on whether the use is lawful. The right of disposal occurs as a manifestation of free will, as only the owner has the right to decide what to do with the thing, with exceptions for forced alienation. Disposal is an active manifestation of the owner's free will to transfer rights to the thing through gift, sale, succession, or its destruction. In general, apart from certain exceptions, the rights of possession, use, and disposal cannot exist without the free will necessary for their exercise.

3.2. The Manifestation of Free Will in the Possession and Use of Another's Property

Jura in re aliena (property rights in the property of others) are a set of rights to property owned by another person, granting the ability to use it to satisfy specific needs, including personal or economic ones (Yanovytska and Kuchera 2014, 353).

In a broad sense, these rights include the right to possess and use another's property with the owner's consent or by a court decision. Initially, the emergence of such rights is based on the free will of the owner, who voluntarily transfers these rights to another person. In some cases, if the owner refuses, their free will can be negated by state coercion. Based on this, it is advisable to establish how and when the owner's free will affects the emergence of property rights for another person in their property, how this correlates with the will of the acquirer, and in which cases the owner's free will is not taken into account.

The primary feature of jura in re aliena [rights in another's property] is their derivation from the owner's right, which is not itself transferred but rather burdened.

Researchers generally distinguish the following seven core features of these limited property rights:

1. Right of Following (*Droit de Suite*): The right persists regardless of changes in the ownership of the underlying asset.

2. Encumbrance: They encumber the property, imposing a legal obligation on the owner not to obstruct the right-holder's exercise of their authority.
3. Inviolability and Continuity: These rights are legally protected against interference and transfer automatically from one owner to another upon the alienation of the property.
4. Utility: They serve specifically to satisfy the economic or personal needs of the right-holder.
5. Legal Exclusivity (*Numerus Clausus*): Such rights can only be established and defined by law, not by private contract alone.
6. Temporal and Financial Flexibility: Their use may be for a fixed term or indefinite, and they can be either paid or free of charge.
7. Statutory Grounds: They arise strictly on the specific grounds prescribed by legislation (Ianovyts'ka and Kuchera 2011, 172).

Today, four main types of *jura in re aliena* can be distinguished in Ukrainian law: (1) the right of possession; (2) the right of use (easement/servitude); (3) the right to use a land plot for agricultural purposes (emphyteusis); and (4) the right to develop a land plot (superficies).

We have previously studied the right of possession in the context of ownership. However, in the context of rights in another's property, the right of possession is a manifestation of the free will of both the owner and the authorised person and implies temporal characteristics.

Actual possession does not automatically create a right of possession, as it may be unlawful. If the owner's will was not directed at the transfer of rights, actual possession can be qualified as unlawful. In the case of theft or robbery, the owner's will is not aimed at transferring rights, which creates grounds for criminal liability and does not give rise to a right in another's property. In the case of a find or treasure, the owner's will is also not directed at transferring rights, which gives rise to civil obligations for the actual possessor, who may become the owner if they comply with the law. If these requirements are met, possession will be considered lawful and can be a basis for the emergence of ownership.

This thesis is supported by V. M. Kossak, who writes about the possibility of possession emerging upon the discovery of a treasure (Kossak 2008, 332).

D. Kasilova objects to this. To substantiate her position, she cites Article 343 of the Civil Code of Ukraine, which does not specify any terms for acquiring ownership, and the inadmissibility of applying the terms of acquisitive prescription is directly indicated (Kasilova 2012, 302). Therefore, Kasilova concludes that the right of ownership to a treasure arises immediately upon its discovery, and the person who discovered it becomes its owner, not its possessor (Ibid.).

The relationship between possession and ownership is particularly nuanced in the context of treasure discovery (*skarb*). We believe the position that ownership arises immediately is not sufficiently substantiated, as in these cases, the right of possession (*volodinnia*) necessarily precedes the right of ownership (*vlasnist*). Possession begins from the moment of the actual physical seizure of the property, while ownership arises only upon the fulfilllment of specific regulatory requirements.

For instance, if a person discovers a treasure while excavating without the consent of the property owner, it is the property owner who acquires the right of ownership. In this specific scenario, only a right of possession arises for the finder, not ownership. Consequently, their free will must be legally directed toward transferring the property to the rightful owner.

To illustrate this distinction, the Civil Code of Ukraine establishes several scenarios regarding the manifestation of free will and the acquisition of rights.

Table 1: Legal Consequences of Treasure Discovery Based on the Manifestation of Will

Scenario	Legal Outcome	Manifestation of Will
Discovery without owner's consent	Ownership for the property owner; right of possession only for the finder (*Tsyvil'nyi kodeks Ukrainy* [Civil Code of Ukraine] 2003, art. 343, para. 3).	The finder's will must be directed solely toward transferring the property to the owner.
Discovery of cultural heritage	State ownership; the finder acquires only temporary possession (Ibid.).	The finder is legally obligated to transfer the treasure to state authorities.
Discovery in another's property (with consent)	Joint partial ownership in equal shares for the finder and the owner (Ibid.).	The finder's will must be directed toward locating the owner and coordinating the transfer.

Source: Compiled by the author.

It is critical to note that discovering a treasure does not automatically confer ownership. The "right to destroy" or "right to keep" is contingent upon following statutory procedures. If the finder fails to comply with the duty to notify or transfer, their actions may be reclassified from lawful discovery to theft and unlawful possession.

Ultimately, even when ownership is successfully established, the new owner then holds the right of possession as a constituent element of their comprehensive ownership rights. In this hierarchy, the initial act of physical possession serves as the prerequisite for the legal recognition of the owner's free will.

Beyond statutory discovery, the right of possession frequently arises as a direct manifestation of the owner's free will through the conclusion of a contract.

Historically, the 1996 Draft Civil Code of Ukraine sought to codify this more explicitly. Article 400 of the draft stipulated that possession arises from either the actual seizure of property (a unilateral act) or the transfer of property by the previous possessor (*Proekt Tsyvil'noho kodeksu Ukrainy* [Draft Civil Code of Ukraine] 1996, art. 400).

While this clear distinction was conceptually sound, its implementation in the current Civil Code has been more fragmented. Rather than providing a direct generalization of all grounds for the emergence of possession, the current Code incorporates these principles implicitly across various specific norms. This "non-specific" approach requires legal scholars to synthesize the grounds from disparate articles rather than relying on a centralized statutory definition.

As R. A. Maydanyk notes, a full-fledged, independent institution of possession involves holding a thing under one's control as "if for oneself." In this case, the essence is determined by the volitional element (*animus possessionis*) or a combination of the objective/factual element (*corpus possessionis*) and the volitional element (Maydanyk 2019a, 54).

The right to possess another's property is based on the mutual will of the owner and the possessor. The owner agrees to transfer the property (volitional element), and the other person agrees to possess it (factual possession).

In the case of actual, *bona fide* possession without the owner's consent (e.g., a find), the possessor is obliged to obtain permission from the owner. Otherwise, the owner retains the right to reclaim the property. Exceptions include cases where the owner is unknown or the period of acquisitive prescription has expired. This typically involves bona fide, open, and continuous possession of real estate for ten years or movable property for five years (*Tsyvil'nyi kodeks Ukrainy* [Civil Code of Ukraine] 2003, art. 344, para. 1).

The paramount principle here is good faith (*bona fides*), which can be the basis for the possessor acquiring ownership at the time of transfer in some cases, or the right to acquisitive possession with the possibility of later acquiring ownership in others (Guivan 2021, 8).

In some cases, even unlawful possession can give rise to a property right. C. Kim argues that when the statute of limitations expires before the owner files a lawsuit, title can be transferred from the owner to the possessor, who acquires ownership through adverse possession (Kim 2004). That is, adverse possession becomes a means of acquiring property by using it for a long time without timely objections from the original owner (Ibid.). In this case, the free will of the owner and possessor is not taken into account. We must proceed from the facts that the owner did not file a lawsuit within the limitation period and the adverse possessor actually possessed the property. The owner's desire to retain ownership and the possessor's intent (or lack thereof) are not considered.

The principle of good faith is also relevant in the context of illegal possession. For example, if a person purchases an item from a non-owner, not knowing the seller lacks the appropriate title. P. D. Guivan explains the need for legal regulation of such possession by the fact that although the property continues to belong to the owner, the owner is practically deprived of the ability to exercise their rights, while the actual possessor, despite having no immediate prospect of acquiring ownership, exercises the functions inherent in that right (Guivan 2019, 44).

In turn, O. O. Mykhailenko considers it inappropriate that current legislation only protects possession that arises on a legal basis, creating the problem of unprotected illegal bona fide possession (Mykhailenko 2003, 13).

The need to coordinate the right of possession with the owner indicates the need for the holder of another's property to have broader powers than mere actual possession. O. A. Pidopryhora emphasizes that the right of possession of another's property, as set out in the Civil Code, does not achieve its goal because it protects a right of possession that is already protected, but fails to protect actual possession, which should have such protection (Pidopryhora 2003, 150).

However, the Civil Code also inadequately regulates the issue of coordinating the free will of multiple possessors of another's property.

Lawful possession of another's property often creates a scenario involving multiple possessors, where the rights of each party are inherently limited by the rights of others. As U. M. Pliatsko notes, possession can be viewed as a functional element of ownership, wherein the owner remains a possessor while others hold rights to the "other's thing" (*jura in re aliena*) (Pliatsko 2015, 11).

When several non-owner possessors exist simultaneously, a complex legal necessity arises: the coordination of the free will of all possessors with the overarching will of the owner. Given the current lack of explicit statutory regulation regarding joint possession in Ukrainian law, we propose the application of the analogy of law (*analogia legis*).

The Supreme Court of Ukraine has affirmed that the analogy of law is permissible only in instances of substantive similarity between unregulated relations and existing legal frameworks (*Postanova Verkhovnoho Sudu Ukrainy* [Resolution of the Supreme Court of Ukraine] 2015). Based on the principles of Article 358 of the Civil Code of Ukraine (joint ownership), we propose the following framework for joint possession:

1. Consensual Exercise: The right of joint possession should be exercised by all possessors based on their mutual consent and in strict coordination with the property owner.
2. Contractual Procedure: The specific procedure for exercising possession can be established via a mutual agreement between all possessors and the owner.
3. Right to Partition or Compensation: Each possessor should have the right to a part of the property in kind that corresponds to their specific share or, alternatively, the right to demand appropriate material compensation.

We propose to enshrine these regulatory mechanisms within Chapter 31 of the Civil Code of Ukraine. This update should focus on developing comprehensive norms for the maintenance of such property, as well as establishing the legal correlation of rights among various possessors and their relationship with the owner.

In instances where a specific analogy of law (*analogia legis*) is absent, legal practitioners should proceed from the general principles of legislation, often referred to as the analogy of right (*analogia iuris*). This approach is supported by judicial guidance, which emphasizes that the spirit of the law and general principles of justice must prevail when specific statutory gaps exist (*Postanova Plenumu Verkhovnoho Sudu Ukrainy* [Resolution of the Plenary of the Supreme Court of Ukraine] 2009).

The method of analogy demonstrates that free will is of fundamental importance for the possession of another's property, manifesting in the owner's granting of use, the coordination of possessors' rights, and serving as a condition for recognising the lawfulness of possession.

Free will manifests itself distinctly in the termination of possession, depending on whether the possession is actual (*de facto*) or titular (*de jure*). Article 399 of the Civil Code of Ukraine (*Tsyvil'nyi kodeks Ukrainy* [Civil Code of Ukraine] 2003) establishes the following grounds for termination:

1. Renunciation: Refusal by the possessor to possess the property;
2. Reclamation: Recovery of the property by the owner or another authorized person;
3. Destruction: Physical loss or destruction of the property;
4. Statutory Grounds: Other cases established by law.

We contend that this statutory list is theoretically imprecise, as it fails to distinguish between the nature of actual and titular possession. This distinction is crucial for understanding the legal effects of an individual's free will:

1. Actual Possession: A possessor's unilateral refusal to hold a thing effectively terminates actual possession.
2. Titular Possession: In contrast, a simple refusal does not automatically terminate the legal relations arising from a contract (e.g., a lease or bailment). Since titular possession is rooted in a bilateral legal act, its termination typically requires the coordinated will of both parties or specific legal procedures to dissolve the underlying obligation.

Consequently, while the manifestation of free will can unilaterally end the physical holding of an object, the "title" to that possession remains legally binding until the contractual or statutory requirements for its dissolution are met.

The recovery of property from a possessor by the owner occurs either through the owner's unilateral will or via a mutual agreement between the parties. The specific legal mechanism depends primarily on the underlying basis of the right to possess.

If the right to possess arises from a contract (e.g., a pledge or pawn), the owner's will alone is insufficient for recovery. For instance, in a pledge agreement, recovery requires mutual consent; the possessor may legally refuse to return the property if the owner has failed to fulfilll their contractual obligations.

If the property was obtained through other means (e.g., finding lost property), recovery is generally based on the owner's will. However, such recovery often triggers compensatory relations.

According to the Civil Code of Ukraine, a person who detains a lost domestic animal is entitled to the reimbursement of maintenance expenses and may also have a right to a reward (*Tsyvil'nyi kodeks Ukrainy* [Civil Code of Ukraine] 2003, art. 342). Importantly, the right to a reward does not restrict the owner's freedom to reclaim the property, as these compensatory obligations arise only after the physical return of the animal (Ibid.).

The interaction between the owner and the possessor typically unfolds across five distinct legal scenarios:

1. Successful Reclamation: The owner claims and successfully receives the property.
2. Unlawful Retention: The owner reclaims the property, but the possessor refuses to return it (triggering rules on unlawful possession and *vindicatio*).
3. Voluntary Return: The possessor returns the property without a prior claim. If the owner refuses to accept it, the object may be classified as ownerless.
4. Satisfied Compensation: The owner compensates the possessor for maintenance costs and provides a reward.
5. Disputed Compensation: The owner refuses to compensate the possessor. While this provides grounds for judicial protection of the possessor's financial interests, it does not grant the possessor a legal right to retain the object.

In these dynamics, the owner's free will governs the procedures of reclamation, acceptance, and the decision to compensate.

Conversely, the possessor's free will is manifested in the voluntariness of the return, the initiation of compensation demands, and the acceptance of the awarded funds.

The procedure for reclaiming property is associated with defining possession as illegal or reclaiming it from a bona fide acquirer. The claim of a non-possessing owner against an illegal possessor for the recovery of property is made by filing a vindicatory action (Kharytonov, Kharytonova, and Nekit 2018, 20).

N. Golubeva writes that the party to a vindicatory action can be not only the owner but also a lawful possessor (Holubieva 2008c, 96).

However, we believe that a lawful possessor of another's property can only reclaim it through self-defense; for judicial protection, they must apply to the owner, which follows from the nature of vindication.

This is confirmed by R. O. Stefanchuk, who defines the parties in a vindicatory action as the owner deprived of the ability to use and dispose of the thing, and the illegal actual possessor. The content of the action is the recovery of a specific thing that has left the owner's legal possession (Stefanchuk 2005b, 160). In this case, the illegal possessor must return the item to the owner, not to the person who merely has the right to possess it. When an owner reclaims property, their free will is aimed at terminating the possession by another person. When a lawful possessor reclaims property from an unlawful one, their free will is aimed at restoring their own right of possession.

A pertinent illustration of these principles is found in the Decision of the Tlumach District Court of Ivano-Frankivsk Oblast. In this case, the plaintiff sued to reclaim a horse from illegal possession. The plaintiff, a long-term horse breeder, had lost an animal in 2011 after it went missing from an open grazing field. Two years later, he identified the horse on the defendant's farm.

The defendant admitted to finding the animal unattended in a field and taking it into his care but refused to return it upon the plaintiff's demand. Crucially, the defendant had failed to report the find to the authorities. Consequently, the court concluded that the defendant was in unlawful possession of the property and could not be classified as a bona fide acquirer. The claim was satisfied (*Rishennia Tlumats'koho raionnoho sudu* [Decision of the Tlumach District Court] 2014).

This case underscores that a successful court decision for property recovery hinges on two fundamental components:

1. The Manifestation of Will: This includes the plaintiff's decision to file a lawsuit and the possessor's explicit refusal to return the property.
2. The Evidentiary Basis: The plaintiff provided substantial evidence of ownership, including original police reports and a detailed physiological description of the animal.

The defendant's bad faith was established by his failure to comply with statutory conditions for acquiring ownership of a lost animal. Although he exercised his free will by admitting he found the animal, his subsequent failure to notify the owner or local authorities constituted a legal violation.

In contrast, the Cherkasy Court of Appeal reached a different conclusion in a separate matter, dismissing a similar reclamation claim due to a lack of sufficient evidence regarding the plaintiff's ownership (*Postanova Cherkas'koho apeliatsiinoho sudu* [Resolution of the Cherkasy Court of Appeal] 2020).

As evidenced by these cases, the recovery of property by an owner is fundamentally anchored in two principles: the free will of the parties and the burden of proof regarding ownership and the lawfulness of possession. These principles are of foundational importance for the entirety of civil procedural law.

In specific legal scenarios, the owner may exercise the right to reclaim property even from a bona fide acquirer (a person who purchased the property in good faith without knowing the seller lacked the authority to alienate it). According to the Civil Code of Ukraine, this is permissible under the following five conditions:

1. Valuable Acquisition from a Non-Owner: The property was acquired for value from a person who had no right to alienate it, provided the acquirer was unaware and could not have been aware of this fact.

2. Loss of Possession: The property was lost by the original owner.
3. Theft: The property was stolen from the owner or an authorized possessor.
4. Involuntary Deprivation: The property left the owner's possession against their will in any other manner.
5. Gratuitous Acquisition: The property was acquired without payment (gratuitously) from a person who had no legal right to alienate it (*Tsyvil'nyi kodeks Ukrainy* [Civil Code of Ukraine] 2003, art. 388).

Under these specific circumstances, the legal weight is shifted entirely toward the original owner. The owner's will to reclaim the property serves as a sufficient legal basis for the court to satisfy the claim (*vindicatio*). Crucially, the free will or the "good faith" intent of the bona fide acquirer is not taken into account when the property was lost, stolen, or otherwise removed from the owner's control involuntarily. This hierarchy of interests ensures that the protection of the rightful owner's autonomy prevails over the stability of commercial transactions in cases of involuntary loss.

The manifestation of free will in the destruction of property as a basis for terminating possession coincides with its manifestation in the termination of ownership under similar circumstances, as detailed above. However, it should be added that in the context of possession, destruction terminates both titular and actual possession. Titular possession, which arose from a contract, is terminated due to the impossibility of its performance for a reason for which neither party is responsible (Ibid., Art. 607).

That is, if the free will of the parties was not directed at the destruction (accidental destruction), then possession is terminated without legal consequences. If destruction occurred as a manifestation of the possessor's will, they are obliged to compensate for damages. If destruction occurred at the owner's will, this creates an obligation for the owner to compensate the possessor (for lost profits, etc.).

Other cases of termination of the right of possession include the loss of actual control over the thing (Ibid., art. 397, para. 1), failure to file a claim for recovery from a bad faith possessor within the statute of limitations (Ibid., art. 400), and the unification of the possessor and owner in one person.

The actual loss of control may depend on the possessor's will (intentional abandonment), the will of another person (destruction, theft), or occur without the influence of free will (loss, accident).

Failure to file a claim for recovery within the statute of limitations depends only on the owner's free will, as filing a claim is always an active expression of a person's will.

In the case of the unification of the possessor and owner in one person, there will be a manifestation of free will, as the grounds for this are concluding a contract, accepting an inheritance, or possessing for the period of acquisitive prescription. All these cases are related to the possessor's free will and exclude coercion.

Having determined the manifestation of free will in the possession of another's property, it is necessary to examine its manifestation in easements, emphyteusis, and superficies to comprehensively understand its connection with property rights.

It is normatively determined that an easement may be established in relation to a land plot or other immovable property to satisfy the needs of other persons that cannot be met in any other way (Ibid., art. 401, para. 1).

Civil law doctrine contains an ongoing discussion regarding the appropriate range of objects within easement (servitude) relations. This debate centers on whether such rights should be restricted to real estate or extended to movable assets.

Several scholars argue for a wider application of easements.

O. A. Pidopryhora notes that the object of an easement can encompass both immovable and movable property (*Tsyvil'nyi kodeks Ukrainy: Naukovo-praktychnyi komentar* [Civil Code of Ukraine: Scientific and Practical Commentary] 2004).

This position is shared by Ch. Azimov (Azimov 2000) and T. V. Predchuk (Predchuk 2016, 61).

V. Sloma characterizes the easement as a property right to use another's property in a specific respect, which does not obligate the owner to perform positive actions, notably without linking the concept to the property's physical characteristics (Sloma 2016).

Conversely, other researchers advocate for a narrower scope.

D. P. Tsvihun disagrees with the broad interpretation, defining an easement strictly as a property right of use established in relation to a specific land plot or other immovable property (Tsvihun 2021, 82).

Despite these doctrinal variations, the current Civil Code of Ukraine (Article 401) establishes that easements are restricted exclusively to immovable property. While certain contractual obligations (such as leases or rentals) may share a similar functional nature, they belong to entirely different legal institutions.

This legislative stance is reinforced by the arguments of O. V. Dzera, N. S. Kuznietsova, and V. V. Luts. They emphasize that the provisions of Chapter 32 of the Civil Code of Ukraine cannot be applied to the legal regime of using another's property if those rights arose from either general property relations or obligatory (contractual) relations (Dzera, Kuznietsova, and Luts 2019, on art. 401).

The main difference between easements and other grounds for using another's property lies in the interest and free will of the parties. While a lease transfers property for the extraction of its useful properties, an easement provides for the use of another's property to satisfy needs that cannot be met otherwise. That is, the will of the parties is aimed at granting a right of use only for a specific purpose not related to extracting useful properties. This condition allows for the compulsory establishment of an easement by a court, without regard to the owner's free will.

Based on a court decision, an easement is established if the landowner does not consent, and there is no other way to ensure the rights of the person applying for the easement (Trydub and Osipov 2020).

In the context of a compulsory easement, the will of the dominant party (the servitude holder) prevails over the will of the servient owner. This legal construction functions similarly to a prohibitory injunction (*nehatornyi pozov*), where the plaintiff demands the removal of existing obstacles to the exercise of their property rights

(*Postanova Velykoi Palaty Verkhovnoho Sudu Ukrainy* [Resolution of the Grand Chamber of the Supreme Court of Ukraine] 2018).

The core essence of a compulsory easement is to provide a right of use in circumstances where, without such access, an individual would be effectively barred from exercising their own property rights. In these instances, the law prioritizes the functional necessity of the dominant estate over the absolute autonomy of the servient owner.

The forced establishment of an easement involves a clash between the free will of the property owner and the servitude holder. We have previously noted that restricting a person's free will is justified by public interest. However, in this case, we have two persons with equal legal status. Giving preference to the servitude holder's free will limits the owner's rights, and vice versa. This conflict should be interpreted based on the level of restriction of rights.

Thus, not granting an easement will make it impossible for the servitude holder to exercise their rights, while granting it will only limit the owner's rights. This proportionality is based on two conditions: (1) the need to prove the impossibility of exercising one's rights without an easement; and (2) the compliance of the easement's purpose with one of its legally prescribed types.

The primary legal requirement for establishing a compulsory easement is designed to protect the owner's rights from unreasonable interference. In practice, the difficulty of proving the absolute necessity of such an encumbrance remains the leading cause for the dismissal of claims.

An analysis of judicial practice indicates that most claims fail because the plaintiff cannot satisfy three critical criteria:

1. Precise Formulation: Clearly defining the scope and nature of the requirements.
2. Absolute Necessity: Proving that the property cannot be used without the easement.
3. Least Burdensome Option: Demonstrating that the proposed easement is the least restrictive for the owner.

A notable example is the Decision of the Truskavets City Court of Lviv Oblast, where a claim was dismissed because the plaintiff failed to meet the evidentiary threshold. Specifically, the court found that the plaintiff did not: (1) prove the physical or legal impossibility of using her property without encumbering the defendant's land; (2) provide the necessary technical documentation defining the specific boundaries of the proposed easement (*Rishennia Truskavets'koho mis'koho sudu L'vivs'koi oblasti* [Decision of the Truskavets City Court of Lviv Oblast] 2021).

As demonstrated, the owner's free will is afforded legal priority. It may be curtailed only in cases of extreme necessity. While a servitude holder's needs can dominate the owner's autonomy, this occurs strictly as a last resort—only when the impossibility of exercising a right significantly outweighs the level of restriction imposed on the owner.

The second essential condition for the compulsory establishment of an easement pertains to its specific purpose. It is significant that Ukrainian legislation explicitly details the types of predial (land) easements that may be established. According to the Land Code of Ukraine, owners or land users are entitled to demand the following easements:

1. Access and Transit: The right of passage and the right of way for vehicles.
2. Infrastructure and Utilities: The right to lay water pipelines, place infrastructure for irrigation systems, and install or run utility networks (including those for industrial parks).
3. Water Usage: The right to drain water, draw water from natural reservoirs, and water livestock.
4. Agricultural and Maintenance Needs: The right of way for livestock and the right to install scaffolding for building maintenance.
5. Structures: The right to place temporary structures.
6. Residual Category: Other land easements as prescribed by law (*Zemel'nyi kodeks Ukrainy* [Land Code of Ukraine] 2001, art. 99).

It is specifically these categories of easements that may be established with a formal restriction on the owner's free will. This regulatory approach is reflected in local administrative practices, such as the Procedure for Concluding Easement Agreements in Zaporizhzhia, which provides a framework for balancing public utility with private property restrictions (*Pro zatverdzhennia Poriadku...* [On Approval of the Procedure...] 2012).

Sometimes, the will of the parties is insufficient due to the requirement of state registration of the land easement, which is possible only if there is information about its boundaries in the State Land Cadastre. The will of the parties serves only as a basis for making changes to the cadastre and for subsequent state registration.

A somewhat different manifestation of free will occurs in personal easements. The subject of such an easement is buildings, structures, and other immovable property; they are not obligatory in nature and can belong to a person for life. A classic example is the right of family members of a homeowner who live with them to use the dwelling (*Tsyvil'nyi kodeks Ukrainy* [Civil Code of Ukraine] 2003, art. 405).

Such an easement arises automatically if the parties live together and are family members. The will of the parties is coordinated by defining the living space. If the servitude holder does not wish to use the property, it is sufficient for them not to exercise their right for more than one year (Ibid., art. 405, para. 2).

Thus, a personal easement can arise from a fact, by agreement, or through judicial coercion. The law does not prohibit establishing personal easements for non-family members, but the provisions of Article 405 of the Civil Code of Ukraine cannot be applied in that case. The list of persons who can automatically or by court decision receive an easement to use a family member's housing is limited to the spouse, children, and parents. We note that the housing legislation defines the right of a wife living with her husband, but does not regulate the right of a husband living with his wife. It can be assumed that this construction is erroneous and needs to be corrected to protect spousal equality.

Also, the content of this norm does not apply to persons in de facto marital or same-sex relationships. Given European integration processes, this normative position needs to be harmonised with European law.

Other ways of using another's property are *emphyteusis* and *superficies*. The legal regulation of these relations shares similar ideas and normative content. Their main difference is the purpose of use. *Emphyteusis* is the right to use another's land for agricultural purposes, while *superficies* is for construction. The specificity of this mechanism involves the acquisition by the *emphyteuta* and *superficiary* (land users) of a wide range of rights not inherent in a lease. This right of use can be sold or bequeathed; the land user has many of the rights of an owner but must also pay for the use of the land, as in a lease (Bagnall 2012).

The legal nature of *superficies* and *emphyteusis* remains a subject of significant scholarly debate, primarily concerning the recognition of mixed legal relations where property law (*in rem*) and contractual elements converge. While Ukrainian law maintains these as distinct institutions, Western European jurisdictions often utilize hybrid models or strict restrictive lists.

In the Hybrid Model used in France and the Netherlands, the distinction between a lease and a property right is bridged by specific statutory constructs.

Specifically, the Civil Code (*Burgerlijk Wetboek*) in the Netherlands explicitly categorizes emphyteusis as Erfpacht, defined as a property right (*zakelijk recht*) that grants the use of another's land (*Burgerlijk Wetboek* 1992, Book 5, art. 5:85). This status distinguishes it from a standard lease (*huur*), despite the requirement for a periodic payment known as a "canon," while *superficies* is recognized as *Recht van opstal*, regulated under a separate title of the same code (Ibid., art. 5:101).

Similarly, France utilizes the "emphyteutic lease" (*bail emphythéotique*), governed by the Rural and Maritime Fishing Code, which grants the lessee a temporary property right (*Code rural et de la pêche maritime* 2026, art. L451-1).

In contrast, Swiss civil law adheres to the principle of *numerus clausus* (a closed list of property rights), prohibiting the creation of rights not explicitly provided by the code. Because *emphyteusis* is not included in this exhaustive list, it cannot be registered as an independent property right (*Schweizerisches Zivilgesetzbuch* [Swiss Civil Code] art. 641). Instead, Swiss law relies on the institute of *Baurecht* (the right of building) to address similar functional needs (Ibid., art. 675, 779–779l).

Free will affects the emergence and termination of *emphyteusis* and *superficies*, as well as the procedure for using the land. Civil and land legislation provides for only two grounds for their emergence: a contract and a will. In both cases, key importance is given to the will of the owner, who voluntarily transfers the land for use. Unlike an easement, influencing the owner's free will through judicial coercion does not apply. The other party also acquires the status of a land user only of their own free will, by concluding a contract or accepting an inheritance. Therefore, the parties' free will has equal force in establishing the right of use. The emergence of use through inheritance occurs at the owner's initiative, but such relations will not arise without the heir's consent.

Emphyteusis and *superficies* grant the land user a significant number of rights regarding possession and use. They can use the plot at their own discretion, with restrictions being its intended purpose and the need to obtain the owner's consent to transfer the rights. The land user also acquires rights analogous to those under a lease. In particular, the land user has a pre-emptive right to purchase the land, but the owner also has a pre-emptive right to redeem the *emphyteusis* or *superficies* (Hespanha, 2015). Given that land use cannot be terminated unilaterally, the redemption by the owner is a way to terminate such relations.

In general, *emphyteusis* and *superficies* are terminated based on a specific set of statutory grounds: (1) the unification of the owner and land user in one person; (2) the expiration of the established term; (3) the alienation of the land for public needs; (4) a decision by an authorized body to utilize state or municipal land for public needs; (5) the non-utilization of the land for construction for a period of three years, applicable specifically to *superficies*; (6) the termination of a contract within a public-private partnership framework; and (7) by mutual agreement of the parties (*Zemel'nyi kodeks Ukrainy* [Land Code of Ukraine] 2001, art. 102-1, para. 9).

These grounds for termination are designed to facilitate either the alignment of the free wills of both parties or the application of state coercion, while notably excluding the possibility of unilateral termination. This legal structure confirms the equality of the scope of free will among participants, as it ensures that neither the owner nor the land user can arbitrarily dissolve the relationship without mutual consent or a clear statutory mandate. Such a configuration serves as a safeguard for the stability of property relations and the protection of the interests of the right-holder against the owner's potential interference.

It should be noted that the subject of the right to possess and use another's property is not only land plots but also other objects of property rights, but such relations arise as a result of obligations, in particular when concluding lease and rental agreements.

In the context of *jura in re aliena*, the right of possession is a manifestation of the free will of both the owner and the authorised person and provides for temporal characteristics. The method of analogy shows that free will is of fundamental importance for the possession of another's property, manifesting in the granting of use by the owner, the coordination of possessors' rights, and serving as a condition for recognising the lawfulness of possession. Free will is manifested differently in the termination of possession, depending on whether it was actual or titular.

Conclusions

1. The right of ownership and limited property rights (*jura in re aliena*) are fundamentally tethered to free will, which serves as the catalyst for establishing the legal bond between a right-holder and an object. Free will is the prerequisite for exercising the powers of possession, use, and disposal. While free will is not a structural element of real rights per se, its exercise necessitates an "expression of will" – the external manifestation of an internal state. Thus, the presence of free will is the *sine qua non* for the conscious and lawful exercise of property rights.
2. Good faith possession emerges as a deliberate manifestation of free will where an individual enters a legal relationship with the intent of lawful acquisition, unaware of any defects in the alienator's title. Even unlawful possession may constitute a manifestation of free will if it is exercised in good faith. Conversely, possession may occasionally arise independently of the possessor's will, such as in cases of accidental acquisition.
3. In the right of use, free will mirrors the dynamics found in possession, fluctuating based on the lawfulness of the act. Usage can occur without the intervention of free will only in exceptional cases, such as when a person acts without awareness or uses property by pure accident.
4. The right of disposal stands as the ultimate manifestation of free will, reserved exclusively for the owner. The only deviations from this principle are instances of state-mandated forced alienation, typically serving as a sanction for criminal offenses or responding to extraordinary public circumstances.
5. Disposing of a thing requires an explicit external expression of the owner's free will to transfer rights – whether through sale, donation, or succession – or to terminate the right altogether via destruction or abandonment.
6. The interdependence of property powers means that, with few exceptions, possession, use, and disposal cannot function without the free will required for their exercise. Any unlawful restriction of these powers effectively nullifies the right of ownership, rendering it an "empty shell" and infringing upon the individual's autonomy.

7. A change of ownership is primarily a voluntary act. However, the owner's free will is bypassed in specific statutory regimes, such as inheritance by law, the finding of lost property, or forced alienation for public necessity.
8. Acquisition of property rights involves two stages: the internal desire to gain the right (will) and the external manifestation of that desire through specific legal actions (expression of will).
9. Bilateral expressions of will serve as a litmus test for the good faith of both the acquirer and the alienator. When both parties act in accordance with legal norms and their own free will, the resulting legal relationship is stable. Free will protects the good-faith acquirer even when the alienator lacks authority, provided the acquirer remained reasonably unaware of the unauthorized nature of the transaction.
10. The legal qualification of acquisition depends heavily on free will. It is this internal intent that distinguishes a valid transfer of property rights from a void or sham transaction.
11. The exercise of free will is never occurring in a vacuum; it is historically and legally constrained by the object's prior legal history and the established rules of succession.
12. Newly created movable property requires only the free will of the producer for ownership to emerge. In contrast, immovable property is subject to the primacy of public interest, requiring additional state-mandated steps such as commissioning and state registration to finalize the right of ownership.
13. Acquisition from a previous owner shifts the focus to the quality of the acquirer's will—specifically, whether it was directed toward acquisition in good faith (*bona fide*) or bad faith (*mala fide*).
14. Processing (*specificatio*) requires a three-fold inquiry to determine the aim of the free will involved: the authorization of the processing, the ownership of the materials, and the comparative value of the labor versus the material. If the processor intended to acquire ownership through lawful labor, the law recognizes their right; otherwise, the act may be reclassified as a service contract.

15. The termination of property rights can be categorized by its connection to free will: direct connection (voluntary alienation), variable connection (destruction of property or death), and no connection (confiscation or nationalization).
16. Voluntary termination involves the owner acting in their own interest, whereas involuntary termination occurs under the influence of external circumstances or the will of the state, regardless of the owner's consent.
17. Destruction of property possesses a variable link to will. A direct connection exists only if the owner intentionally destroys the object; if destruction is accidental, the termination of ownership is a consequence rather than a goal.
18. The cessation of a legal entity or the death of a natural person marks the limit of individual free will. Notably, intestate succession (inheritance by law) illustrates a "public will" of the state acting in concert with the heir's will to ensure the continuity of property relations when the testator's specific will is absent.
19. In limited property rights (*jura in re aliena*), the right of possession is a temporal manifestation of the coordinated free wills of both the owner and the right-holder.
20. Actual possession is a conscious act of physical holding. However, it does not automatically equate to a *legal* right of possession, especially if it lacks a legal basis or contradicts the owner's will.
21. The analogy of law demonstrates that free will is the foundation of possessing another's property. It manifests in the owner's grant of use and the necessary coordination of rights among multiple possessors.
22. Termination of possession differs between actual and titular forms. A possessor's unilateral refusal terminates actual possession, but terminating titular possession (based on a contract) requires the coordinated will of both parties.
23. The loss of control over a thing can result from intentional abandonment (the possessor's will), theft or destruction (another's will), or accidental loss (no will).

24. Compulsory servitudes represent a unique hierarchy where the servitude holder's will may prevail over the owner's autonomy, but only as a "last resort" based on extreme necessity.
25. *Emphyteusis* and *superficies* are governed by an equal scope of free will between the participants, affecting everything from the emergence and usage procedures to the eventual termination of the relationship.

4. Free Will in the Law of Obligations

4.1. Free Will in Contractual Obligations

4.1.1. Free Will in the Principles of Contract Law

The law of obligations is a sub-branch of civil law that regulates civil turnover—that is, the transfer of material and intangible goods from one person to another, which takes the form of a civil obligation based on a contract or other grounds specified in law (Holubieva 2013, 5).

The conclusion of a contract stands as one of the most common grounds for the emergence of civil obligations and represents what we consider to be the most objective manifestation of free will within the civil law framework. The principles forming the foundation of contract law reflect the fundamental ideas that underpin civil legal relations, serving to provide general guidance, facilitate the interpretation of norms, and fill legal gaps when necessary (Report to the President 2016). Given that these principles mirror the core ideas of the field, studying their correlation with free will is highly relevant for understanding the autonomy of parties.

In his study of the fundamental components of contractual principles, M. A. Eisenberg identified four basic tenets of contract law that illustrate this connection. First, the primary purpose of contract law should be to effectuate the objectives of the parties, provided they adhere to moral and policy constraints such as freedom from duress and fraud, as well as limitations concerning capacity and legality. Second, any constraints on achieving these objectives, and the methods by which they are established, should consist of rules that account for all applicable meritorious policy, moral, and empirical considerations. Third, in instances where the parties have not directly or indirectly addressed a specific issue, the relationship should be governed by a default rule provided by law. Finally, other administrative rules of contract law—such as those governing specific performance, remedies for breach, and excuses for non-performance—should be determined through the same evaluative process (Eisenberg 2018, 21). These principles collectively ensure that while the manifestation of free will is the driving force of the contract, it operates within a balanced framework of legal certainty and social policy.

The comparative legislative manifestation of these principles reveals a sophisticated evolution across various legal systems, particularly within the civil law tradition. In France, the 2016 reform of the law of obligations explicitly codified these foundational ideas, embedding them into the freedom of contract (Code civil [Civil Code] 2026, art. 1102), the binding force of contracts (Ibid., art. 1103), and the requirement of good faith (Ibid., art. 1104). This statutory recognition ensures that the autonomy of the parties' will remains the central pillar of the contractual bond, while simultaneously imposing a duty of loyalty and cooperation throughout the lifecycle of the agreement.

In a broader comparative context, O. O. Merezhko synthesized the contractual principles of Great Britain, France, the Netherlands, Germany, the USA, and other jurisdictions to propose a multidimensional framework for private law. This vision encompasses the principles of freedom of contract, justice, good faith, reasonableness, the binding force of the agreement, trust, the non-abuse of rights, cooperation, and the equality of the parties (Merezhko 2003, 52–93). While this synthesis provides a robust doctrinal foundation, it also invites a critical observation: several of these principles—such as good faith, reasonableness, and equality—are not strictly unique to the contractual sphere. Instead, they often duplicate the general principles of civil law, suggesting that contract law is not a legal silo but rather a specific field where general civil values are intensified through the direct expression of the parties' free will.

The first Ukrainian scholar to study the principles of contract law in detail was N. S. Kuznetsova, who identified freedom of contract, freedom of entrepreneurial activity, judicial protection of civil rights, justice, good faith, and reasonableness as principles of primary importance for the law of obligations (Kuznietsova 2003). This position has received broad scholarly support, notably from T. Bodnar (Bodnar 2005, 110–122).

Given the absence of a single normative or doctrinal approach to classifying the principles of contract law, and as this study does not aim to develop a new classification, we will focus on the relationship between free will and those principles where its manifestation is greatest. In this subsection, we will concentrate on the principles of freedom of contract, proper performance of contractual obligations, and the binding force of a contract. These principles reflect the specific application of the general civil law principles of justice, good faith, reasonableness, non-abuse of rights, and morality.

The principle of freedom of contract defines the entire legal specificity of contractual relationships. It is this principle that lays the foundation for other tenets of contract law and creates a paradigm for the development of civil law. The principle is of such great importance that it serves as the basis not only for the national law of Ukraine but also for international contract law, as reflected in the UNIDROIT Principles of International Commercial Contracts. The global nature of the principle of freedom of contract is confirmed by its wide application in common law, as established in the case of Printing and Numerical Registering Co v Sampson.

The principle of freedom of contract can be viewed in two aspects: (1) as a constitutional symbol of laissez-faire, which prohibits or limits state intervention in entrepreneurial activity; and (2) as a banner for the theory of contract law and private law in general, which emphasizes the free will of individuals and the role of law in supporting their freedom to conclude any contracts they wish (Shapiro and Sweet 2002, 296). It is in this latter context that we will analyse in detail the relationship between the principle of freedom of contract and free will.

According to the principle of freedom of contract, parties can independently agree on the content and terms of the contract, as well as its subject matter. In effect, this principle allows parties to regulate their contractual relations independently within the limits set by law. This confirms that free will is the basis of the principle of freedom of contract and, therefore, of other principles of contract law.

At the same time, freedom of contract is not unlimited. Legal norms establish essential terms, mandatory forms, and other requirements. For example, parties may agree on the form of a contract at their own discretion, but only if the law does not provide otherwise. A contract for the sale of an apartment must be in writing. In this case, the parties can choose between a simple written form or a notarial certification, even if the law otherwise allows for an oral form for other types of contracts. The same applies to determining the price. A contract for the provision of services is presumed to be for a fee, but the parties, of their own free will, can determine its gratuitous nature (Tsyvil'nyi kodeks Ukrainy [Civil Code of Ukraine] 2003, art. 901).

The independent determination of the amount and procedure for payment stands as a primary manifestation of free will within the overarching principle of freedom of contract. However, as S. Rowan emphasizes, this freedom is not absolute and is increasingly constrained by statutory requirements in modern legal systems. Specifically, Rowan identifies three critical areas where law overrides party autonomy: (1) mandatory obligations, such as the requirement for motorists to purchase insurance; (2) regulatory constraints, exemplified by the prohibition of discrimination in an employer's selection of employees; and (3) content limitations, particularly within public contracts where mandatory rules impose non-negotiable obligations on the parties (Rowan 2012, 32). These restrictions illustrate that while free will serves as the engine of contractual relations, it must operate within a framework of social policy and public interest to remain legally effective.

The principle of freedom of contract underscores the significant legal importance of personal will, as it is the free will of the parties that governs contractual relations alongside the law. But since legal norms are also a manifestation of the free will of individuals (the legislator), one could argue for the absolute nature of free will in the law of obligations.

This position is supported by I. Tedoradze, who proposes considering freedom of contract in two aspects: (1) as an economic principle on which all market economies should be based; and (2) as a moral principle according to which the justification of contractual obligations is linked to the will of the parties (Tedoradze 2017, 63). This vision is expressed in continental Europe by the concept of "contractual autonomy" or "autonomy of the will" and has clear roots in the philosophy of Rousseau and Kant, which can be described as a "voluntarist" view of freedom of contract (Ibid.).

The principle of dispositivity (dyzpozytyvnist) is often distinguished from the principle of freedom of contract, though their conceptual boundaries are frequently debated. A. L. Sviatoshniuk posits that the capacity to freely select a counterparty and determine contractual terms is a direct manifestation of dispositivity (Sviatoshniuk 2019, 76). However, we contend that these specific capacities are manifestations of freedom of contract, which serves as a specialized legal expression of the broader dispositivity principle.

While the two are intrinsically linked, they operate on different levels: the principle of freedom of contract is confined to contractual relations (Maydanyk 2012), whereas dispositivity functions as a foundational civil law principle. This broader principle underpins several core provisions of the Civil Code of Ukraine, including the freedom to exercise civil rights at one's own discretion (art. 12, para. 1), the right of parties to regulate their relations autonomously (art. 6, para. 3), and the protection against being forced to perform non-obligatory actions (art. 14, para. 2).

As N. F. Chubokha observes, the principle of dispositivity illuminates the application of "one's own discretion" in law—a concept understood as the independent, volitional activity of a subject in making legal decisions and selecting the means to achieve their objectives. In this context, forming a legal decision requires the application of the subject's internal will, developed independently of any external coercion (Chubokha 2013, 301).

A. L. Sviatoshniuk further investigates the correlation between the principle of freedom of contract, the autonomy of the parties' will, and their freedom of discretion. The author posits that while each party possesses autonomy of will, the principle of freedom of contract necessitates the consideration of the counterparty's interests; consequently, Sviatoshniuk argues it is difficult to agree with scholars who suggest that freedom of discretion "absorbs" the principle of freedom of contract (Sviatoshniuk 2019, 78).

We consider this specific argumentation to be theoretically imprecise, as the term "absorption" does not accurately reflect the nature of this legal construction. Instead, it is more appropriate to analyze the correlation and hierarchy between free will and the principle of freedom of contract. In our view, the principle of freedom of contract acts as a mechanism requiring the coordination of the parties' wills, serving as a manifestation of both dispositivity and equality. While free will allows parties to internally determine the potential terms of an agreement, the principle of freedom of contract provides the external legal framework to establish and apply these terms. Effectively, the principle of freedom of contract is the practical embodiment of free will in civil commerce.

Furthermore, Sviatoshniuk proposes supplementing the Civil Code of Ukraine by explicitly enshrining the principle of freedom of contract, the principle of dispositivity of the parties, and the principle of autonomy of will as three distinct pillars of contract law (Sviatoshniuk 2019, 78). This proposal remains highly controversial, as these principles are profoundly interrelated and emerge from the same philosophical and legal foundations. We contend that the principle of freedom of contract is inherently a manifestation of the principle of dispositivity, fundamentally anchored in the autonomy of the parties' wills, rather than a separate or competing entity.

The functioning of contract law is impossible without the principle of proper performance of contractual obligations, which embodies the principles of good faith and justice. This principle is based on the idea that parties, having concluded a contract of their own free will, desire the intended legal consequences and, therefore, must fulfill the rights and obligations arising from the transaction.

The principle of proper performance may be violated in the event of procedural or substantive unconscionability. A. Leff defined procedural unconscionability as bargaining naughtiness and substantive unconscionability as unfairness in the resulting terms, even if not accompanied by procedural issues (Leff 1967). The result of either will be an unwillingness to properly perform contractual obligations, which completely contradicts the purpose of a contractual relationship. If a party concludes a contract that does not meet its interests, it will try to sabotage its obligations. In this case, it is necessary to determine the party's interest. If, at the time of concluding the contract, the party knew in advance that it would not or could not perform the obligations properly, then there is a free will aimed at concluding a sham transaction. If, however, improper performance was not planned but occurred due to new circumstances, then the person's will should be directed at fulfillling their obligations.

Improper performance should be distinguished from non-performance, as it involves performance in violation of the conditions specified in the obligation (Tsyvil'nyi kodeks Ukrainy [Civil Code of Ukraine] 2003, art. 610, para. 1). That is, the principle of proper performance involves the use of the parties' free will to prevent delays and non-compliance with quality, quantity, or assortment requirements. By the agreed will of the parties, the consequences of improper performance may include: termination of the obligation, a change in its terms, payment of a penalty, and compensation for losses and moral damage (Ibid., art. 611, para. 1).

Free will is of key importance for liability for breach of an obligation, as liability typically arises only in the presence of fault (intent or negligence), unless otherwise established by contract or law. A person is considered not at fault if they prove that they took all dependent measures for the proper performance of the obligation (Ibid., art. 614, para. 1).

The connection between free will and the principle of proper performance is indisputable. This is confirmed by the thesis that this principle is largely based on the predicate that private actors are the best judges of their own utility (Eisenberg 2018, 69). If parties have concluded a contract, they must be aware of the obligation to perform its terms properly and, in the event of unforeseen circumstances, make every possible effort to fulfill their duties. Given that this principle is mandatory, it can be stated that the free will of the counterparties is, a priori, aimed at the proper performance of the contract.

The principle of freedom of contract is further expanded through the binding force of a contract (pacta sunt servanda), a concept that grants parties a unique norm-creating power. This power is implemented as parties formulate mandatory rules of conduct for themselves, effectively embodying their collective free will within the contractual content. A classic expression of this construction is found in the Franch Civil Code, which confirms the self-legislating nature of private will through the famous formula: "Agreements legally formed take the place of law for those who have made them" (Code civil [Civil Code] 2026, art. 1103).

The normative condition of the binding force of a contract is firmly established in the legislation of Ukraine (Tsyvil'nyi kodeks Ukrainy [Civil Code of Ukraine] 2003, art. 629) and is mirrored in the Principles of European Contract Law (PECL). According to the PECL, a party remains strictly obligated to fulfilll its duties even if the performance has become significantly more burdensome, emphasizing that the initial manifestation of free will creates a persistent legal necessity (Principles of European Contract Law 2017, art. 6:111).

The principle of the binding force of a contract is sometimes referred to as the principle of stability, which is logical, since contractual relations can be stable only when the parties intend to fulfill their commitments. At the heart of this principle is the formula pacta sunt servanda, which gives rise to the obligation to fulfill assumed commitments. This is not only seen as promoting legal certainty but is also a key justification for the central role of specific performance as a remedy for breach of contract (Rowan 2012, 49–50).

Free will is manifested throughout the entire lifecycle of contractual relations, fundamentally driving the progression through four critical stages. At the initial stages—when the parties determine the terms and subsequently conclude the contract—their individual wills are systematically aligned. The acceptance of an offer serves as the definitive legal confirmation of this shared intention to perform future obligations.

At the third stage, during the performance of the contract, the free will of the counterparties remains active but shifts its focus toward compliance and the prevention of a breach. Finally, at the termination stage, free will manifests either as a coordinated collective will in the case of dissolution by mutual agreement, or as a decisive unilateral will when the law or the contract permits one party to withdraw independently. Throughout this process, the continuity of free will ensures that the contractual bond remains a product of party autonomy rather than mere external imposition.

If a party fails to fulfilll its obligations due to circumstances beyond its control, it may be granted an exemption from civil liability. However, when a violation arises from the counterparty's deliberate free will, it establishes a foundation for compensatory relations. A pertinent illustration is found in the Decision of the Ternivka City Court of Dnipropetrovsk Oblast. In this case, the plaintiff and defendant entered into a contract for the manufacture and installation of a structure, but the defendant failed to fulfilll the obligations within the agreed timeframe. Because the defendant could not prove an absence of fault, the court satisfied the plaintiff's claims for both contract termination and compensation (Rishennia Ternivs'koho mis'koho sudu [Decision of the Ternivka City Court] 2021).

The qualification of this case through the lens of free will reveals a dynamic shift in the parties' legal intentions. Initially, the parties established mutual free will by defining the contractual terms, a commitment the customer subsequently reinforced by making an advance payment. The contractor, however, exercised their free will by failing to perform on time. Even as the customer signaled a continued will to see the contract performed by sending a formal claim, the contractor's will was manifested in a lack of response. Consequently, the customer's free will transformed from an interest in performance to a desire to terminate the contract via judicial intervention. Ultimately, the contractor's will was legally characterized as being aimed at violating the fundamental principle of the binding force of the contract.

This principle is generally applicable only in ordinary cases, where there is a real right of choice, competition, and an absence of coercion. That is, the circumstances of the contract's conclusion must correspond to ordinary practice. The free will of the parties must reflect the principles of justice, good faith, and reasonableness. Only under these circumstances is the behavior of the counterparties regulated by this principle. This is because the principle is not absolute, and in some cases, non-performance is permitted.

M. A. Eisenberg explores the intricacies of contractual free will through the hypothetical case of "The Desperate Traveler." In this scenario, a musician (A) is stranded in the desert without water and faces death until a geologist (B) arrives. B agrees to rescue A only on the condition that A promises to pay two-thirds of her fortune, or $100,000, whichever is greater. Although A agrees, she later refuses to pay, prompting B to sue.

On the one hand, a contract appears to have been concluded as A voluntarily accepted B's offer. In traditional legal doctrine, the qualification of duress requires a specific causal link: the promisor's predicament must be caused by a wrongful act or threat from the promisee (Supreme Court of New Hampshire 1978). If B had caused A's distress through a wrongful act, the contract would be void; however, Eisenberg emphasizes that B did not cause A's distress, and B's threat to withhold help is not inherently "wrongful" in a legal sense. This is because tort and criminal law generally do not impose a duty on strangers to rescue those in peril (Eisenberg 2018). Ukrainian legislation similarly limits the right to demand the elimination of danger primarily to the person who created it (Tsyvil'nyi kodeks Ukrainy [Civil Code of Ukraine] 2003, art. 1163) or to individuals who had a specific duty of care (Kryminal'nyi kodeks Ukrainy [Criminal Code of Ukraine] 2001, art. 135).

From this perspective, the parties' free will was technically aligned: B was not legally obliged to rescue A and thus exercised his right to set the conditions for his assistance. Nevertheless, Eisenberg concludes that the contract is unconscionable. He argues that a potential rescuer has a moral—and in some frameworks, a legal—duty to assist when the cost and risk are insignificant. The bargain represents an unfair exploitation of distress, characterized by two key factors: (1) the agreement was not formed within a competitive market, and (2) B's behavior violates generally accepted moral norms (Eisenberg 2018). This case highlights the tension between the formal expression of free will and the substantive justice required to maintain the integrity of the legal system.

As we can see, the principle of the binding force of a contract can have a complex relationship with free will, and the qualification of that will determines whether its terms must be complied with. Free will becomes important when declaring transactions invalid, a topic that will be discussed in more detail later.

The analysis confirms the fundamental importance of the legal idea of free will for the principles of contract law. The principle of freedom of contract demonstrates the legal significance of personal will, proving that it is the will of the parties, alongside the law, that regulates contractual relations. The principle of freedom of contract requires the coordination of the parties' wills as a manifestation of dispositivity and equality. The connection between free will and the principle of proper performance is evident in the fact that when concluding a contract, parties must be aware of the obligation to perform its terms properly. This is expanded by the principle of the binding force of a contract, which grants the parties norm-creating power, with their free will reflected in the contract's content. However, normative regulation prevails over contractual regulation, which confirms the dominance of public free will (the will of the state and society) over individual will.

The principles of contract law reflect the specific application of the general principles of civil law, for which free will serves as the basis, and they determine the legal nature and content of specific types of civil law contracts.

4.1.2. Free Will in Specific Types of Civil Law Contracts

A civil law contract serves as one of the primary mechanisms for establishing legal relations, acting as the formal consolidation of the counterparties' free will. It is specifically aimed at establishing, changing, or terminating civil rights and obligations, functioning as the external embodiment of free will as it transitions from an internal, passive state to an active, legally significant one. The conclusion and performance of an agreement are the principal ways through which free will is transformed into a definitive expression of volition. This transition is normatively confirmed by statutory definitions across major legal systems. In the French Civil Code, a contract is explicitly recognized as an "agreement of wills" (*Code civil* [Civil Code] 2026, art. 1101), while the Civil Code of Ukraine defines it as an "agreement" (*Tsyvil'nyi kodeks Ukrainy* [Civil Code of Ukraine] 2003, art. 627), a terminology mirrored in the German Civil Code (*Bürgerliches Gesetzbuch* 1896, § 311).

In effect, the contract is an agreement of wills, rendering it the most vital legal instrument in systems predicated on the principle of private autonomy. This perspective aligns with the theoretical framework of Charles Fried, who views the contract as a moral invention. According to Fried, contracts allow individuals to bind themselves, thereby enabling free persons to expand their capabilities and agency by engaging in reliable, structured cooperation with others (Fried 2014). By committing to a shared manifestation of will, parties move beyond mere individual intent into a realm of reciprocal legal certainty.

Based on the principles of freedom of contract and binding performance, a contract is a means of transforming the parties' free will into a rule of conduct. Through a contract, free will acquires a legal force akin to that of a legal norm. This is confirmed by M. M. Sibilov's thesis on the existence of two basic models of regulating contractual relations: internal regulation (self-regulation) and external (imperative, state regulation) (Sibilov 2014, 58).

I. R. Kalaur agrees that the law determines the rights and obligations of the parties only in cases where they have not determined the terms of the agreement at their own discretion (Kalaur 2016, 116). In our opinion, this statement is not entirely accurate. On the contrary, parties determine the terms of a contract "within the framework" of the law and choose how to implement legal norms into their agreement. A contract cannot cancel or alter a legislative norm. The normative regulation of relations prevails over contractual regulation, which confirms the dominance of public free will (the will of the state and society) over individual will.

As has been demonstrated, free will is of key importance for the principles of contract law. This suggests that it affects all types of civil law contracts. At the same time, each type of contract has its own characteristics, which necessitates the study of free will within specific contractual forms.

The classification of civil law contracts involves a complex system based on various scholarly perspectives. A simple classification can be carried out in two ways: (1) by dividing objects of study into an unlimited number of groups based on necessary characteristics, which forms a simple system without structural links; or (2) by dividing contracts according to the principle of dichotomy, where one group has a certain characteristic and the other does not.

L. K. Veretelnyk developed a two-level typological system where the first level reflects the contract's general characteristics, and the second is based on its legal nature, purpose, and place in the system of contract law (Veretelnyk 2007, 6).

In general, the systematization of contracts is carried out according to the following criteria: (1) their objective or purpose; (2) the distribution of obligations between the parties; (3) the moment of conclusion; (4) the presence of counter-consideration; (5) the beneficiary of performance; and (6) the sequence of achieving the parties' goals (Yanovytska and Kuchera 2011, 246).

To determine the role of free will in specific types of contracts, we utilize a classification based on their objective, as this criterion most effectively demonstrates the direction of the counterparties' will and their underlying interests. According to this classification, the following categories of contracts are distinguished:

1. Contracts for the transfer of property into ownership, such as sale, gift, or annuity agreements, where the parties' will is directed at the permanent alienation of an asset.
2. Contracts for the transfer of property for use, including lease and loan-for-use agreements, where the manifestation of free will concerns temporary possession and utility without the transfer of title.
3. Contracts for the performance of work, exemplified by works contracts and R&D agreements, where the parties' wills focus on achieving a specific material result.

4. Contracts for the provision of services, such as mandate, commission, insurance, and storage agreements, where free will is centered on the process of activity or the management of risks.
5. Contracts in the financial sector, including loan, credit, and bank deposit agreements, where the alignment of wills concerns the movement of capital and interest.
6. Contracts in the field of intellectual activity, such as copyright and licensing agreements, where free will is exercised over intangible assets and the scope of their exploitation.
7. Joint activity agreements, where the parties' wills are not opposing but rather unified toward a common legal and economic goal (Yanovytska and Kuchera 2011, 246).

Contracts for the transfer of property into ownership are aimed at the emergence and termination of property rights, and in this context, the role of free will correlates with its significance for property rights in general. When concluding such contracts, free will has a dispositive nature, as the legal link between the property and the owner is severed. While an owner retains property rights under a lease agreement, under a sale and purchase agreement, the owner's will is aimed at the irrevocable termination of those rights. The alienator cannot reclaim or use the property.

D. L. Carey Miller emphasizes that concluding a contract for the transfer of property rights implies two mandatory conditions: (1) the transferor has the capacity and right to transfer it; and (2) the requirement for a legal act of transfer, which implies an intention to transfer ownership (*animus transferendi dominii*) on the part of the transferor, and an intention to acquire it (*animus accipiendi dominii*) on the part of the acquirer (Brox and Walker 2022, 727).

To these conditions, it should be added that the person acquiring the property right must possess both the legal capacity and the authority to do so. The acquirer must be consciously aware of their ability to fulfilll their obligations—such as ensuring they have the necessary funds for payment—as well as their compliance with specific legal requirements, including sufficient legal capacity.

This awareness reflects the critical importance of free will in contracts for the transfer of property. First, when concluding the contract, both parties must possess a coordinated will to transfer or acquire the property, which is comprised of a mutually agreed intention and the objective ability to fulfilll their respective obligations. Second, the parties must genuinely intend for the transfer of ownership to occur and be prepared to execute their specific duties. In this context, the parties' free will is realized and manifested through their simultaneous declaration of capacity and intent.

This construction can be supplemented by the observations of K. S. Reid, who suggests that in the context of a change of ownership, a single decisive action or event is identified as the driving factor. In the vast majority of cases involving derivative acquisition, Reid argues that the transfer of ownership, when it occurs, is invariably instantaneous (Reid, Gretton, and Duncan 1996, 603). This assertion assumes that the parties' free will is directed specifically toward the immediate fulfilllment of obligations. However, such a conceptualization appears inconsistent with the established legal practice of dividing contracts into real (those requiring the delivery of the thing) and consensual (those based on the mere agreement of wills). In consensual contracts, the manifestation of free will precedes the actual transfer, creating a temporal gap that challenges the notion of an instantaneous "event" as the sole driver of the transition.

In contracts for the transfer of property for use, the parties' free will is directed toward the temporary possession and utility of an asset rather than its permanent alienation. Within the framework of regulatory norms, the parties independently negotiate the contract's content, frequently utilizing model contracts as a structural foundation. These model agreements are typically recommendatory in nature; rather than restricting party autonomy, they are designed to assist the parties in articulating their will in a manner that remains compliant with complex legal requirements.

For example, model lease agreements for state property do not diminish the principle of freedom of contract; instead, they define the specific parameters required for transactions involving special objects of property. These instruments are developed to reflect both foundational legal principles and current state policy. A prime illustration is the typical contract between a lessor and an electronic platform operator, which must be approved by the central executive body responsible for implementing state policy in the field of asset sales (*Pro orendu derzhavnoho ta komunalnoho maina* [On the Lease of State and Municipal Property] 2019, art. 13, para. 6). Thus, model contracts serve as a bridge between individual free will and the overarching requirements of public order.

The free will of the parties allows them to define a contract as consensual or real, and as for-value or gratuitous. Legislation should be perceived not as a way of restricting the parties' free will, but as a set of official means for participants to exercise it. This statement requires explanation.

For example, consider a scenario where parties intend to conclude an agreement for the gratuitous use of property. While the principle of freedom of contract suggests they could negotiate the issue of payment, a lease agreement is intrinsically defined as a for-value relationship under Article 759 of the Civil Code of Ukraine and related legislation (*Podatkovyi kodeks Ukrainy* [Tax Code of Ukraine] 2010, art. 170; *Pro zatverdzhennia Metodyky…* [On the Approval of the Methodology…] 2010).

Crucially, this does not represent a normative restriction on free will; rather, the legislator provides distinct contractual structures to best meet the parties' specific interests. For the transfer of property for gratuitous use, a loan-for-use agreement (*pozyka*) should be utilized, as it is specifically designed for gratuitous relations. Thus, the parties' free will is aligned with regulatory requirements through their independent selection of the appropriate legal mechanism. The normative definition of a specific contract's features is not an encumbrance on autonomy but a procedural framework for its implementation, which the parties choose themselves.

This perspective is confirmed by a Resolution of the Zakarpattia District Administrative Court in case No. 807/1504/15. In this instance, a plaintiff was granted temporary gratuitous use of premises under a loan-for-use agreement. The tax authority attempted to reclassify the arrangement as a lease and taxed it as the "free receipt of rental services." The court found the tax authority's actions unlawful, ruling that a loan-for-use agreement does not share the legal characteristics of a lease and subsequently satisfied the claim (*Postanova Zakarpats'koho okruzhnoho administratyvnoho sudu* [Resolution of the Zakarpattia District Administrative Court] 2015).

Therefore, parties independently select the type of agreement that fulfillls their objectives. Consequently, it is theoretically incorrect to assert that the legal impossibility of concluding a "gratuitous lease agreement" constitutes a restriction on free will, as the parties remain free to achieve the same economic result through the correct legal instrument.

Choosing the type of contract that aligns with one's interests is a clear example of the manifestation of freedom in civil law. This becomes particularly important in the context of contracts for the performance of work and the provision of services.

The central issue for these two types of contracts is the basis for their distinction. The legal characteristics of these contracts allow the parties to independently choose the process for achieving their mutual goal. The distinction has been studied in detail and comes down to differences in purpose, the form of the result, and whether a result is guaranteed.

The purpose of a works contract is not the process itself but its tangible result, whereas the purpose of a service contract is the process of its provision. Depending on their interests, the parties independently choose the relevant type of contract. This can be demonstrated with an example from medical relations. If the goal is the manufacture or repair of a medical item with the transfer of its result to the customer, a works contract is concluded (Savchenko 2014, 46). If the goal is the process of treatment, diagnostics, or consultation, a service contract is concluded.

The parties' free will is realised by choosing the form of the result—material or immaterial. If their interest lies in obtaining a material result (a newly created object, a repair), they enter into a works contract. In the case of a service contract, the parties' will is aimed at an intangible result, which may lead to material changes, but these changes are inseparable from the activity itself. G. Yu. Sharkova confirms that in some cases this result is tangible (e.g., loading cargo), while in others it is not (Sharkova 2014, 123).

The parties' free will allows them to influence whether a result is guaranteed. A service contract is characterised by the impossibility of guaranteeing a result, as it is process-oriented. Therefore, the issue of proper performance and quality is limited to compliance with requirements regarding the process itself (Batozhska 2010, 29). In contrast, a works contract guarantees a specific result.

V. V. Rieznikova supplements these grounds for distinction with the following features of services: (1) a useful effect; (2) inseparability from the source (the service is consumed as it is provided); (3) invisibility and intangibility; (4) immateriality; (5) variable quality (a lack of a final result does not necessarily indicate poor quality); (6) exclusivity (the service is closely tied to a specific provider); (7) non-storability; and (8) inexhaustibility (Rieznikova, 2010). Although this classification has some overlaps, it shows that contracts for services and works are distinct ways of exercising free will.

Depending on their specific objectives, parties exercise their free will through various legal mechanisms, which necessitates compliance with the rules inherent to their chosen contract type. A particularly sophisticated manifestation of this autonomy is the creation of hybrid contracts (*zmishani dohovory*), which combine the distinctive features of multiple agreements into a single legal instrument.

Such constructions are increasingly common in the IT sector, where a single agreement frequently encompasses both software development (the performance of work) and subsequent technical maintenance (the provision of services). These hybrid models allow for a precise legal distinction between the specific grounds for liability in the event of a breach. This differentiation is supported by judicial practice; for instance, a Decision of the Yenakiieve City Court of Donetsk Oblast confirmed a clear distinction between claims for compensation regarding a low-quality dental prosthesis (classified as a "work" or *robota*) without extending that liability to the quality of the prosthetic services themselves (*Rishennia Yenakiivs'koho mis'koho sudu* [Decision of the Yenakiieve City Court] 2013). By utilizing hybrid structures, parties can tailor the distribution of risks and responsibilities to align with the multifaceted nature of modern commercial transactions.

Free will acts as a guarantor of the fiduciary nature of contracts in the financial sphere (also known as credit agreements or financial service agreements). In common law, fiduciary duties include the duties of loyalty and care. In civil law, they include a duty of care (*Sorgfaltspflicht*), a duty of fidelity (*Treupflicht*), and a duty of diligence and advice (*devoir de diligence et conseil*) (Fleischer et al. 2016).

There are many approaches to classifying such contracts. N.V. Drozdova, for instance, suggests dividing them based on their nature into: (1) obligations to provide legal services (e.g., factoring); (2) obligations to provide factual services (e.g., storage of financial assets); (3) obligations to provide both (e.g., trust management); and (4) obligations to provide financial and monetary services (Drozdova 2005, 9).

The specific manifestation of free will in such contracts is associated with the coordination of an individual's will with the will of a special entity (a business), which expresses a collective will through an authorised person. The peculiarity is that one of the parties is always a bank or another financial institution (Trishch and Kuz 2011, 210). This specificity is characteristic of all legal relations where a business entity is a party.

Let us consider this using the example of a credit agreement. The parties' free will is directed toward concluding the agreement, but the decision to do so depends on the will of the person making the decision on behalf of the institution. That is, their individual will conveys the collective will of the financial institution. In effect, the conclusion of the agreement depends on which specific person represents the lender. Although, *de jure*, the employer's will prevails over the employee's (as the business entity is the party to the contract), *de facto*, the conclusion of the deal depends on the individual will of the institution's representative.

A person authorised to conclude a contract on behalf of a business must act in its interests, realising its will. However, in practice, an authorised person may act in their own interests, for example, by approving a loan due to corrupt motivation.

Individual free will has limited significance when participating in financial legal relations with state bodies. A good example is provided by O. V. Makukh:

> When a person wishes to purchase state securities (an expression of will), the state then establishes the procedure for their circulation. Therefore, dispositivity in such relations ends at the stage where the subject expresses the desire to purchase the securities; from that point on, imperativeness takes over as the state issues mandatory regulations. (Makukh 2016, 74)

Agreements on joint activity are also a manifestation of collective free will, reflecting the agreed-upon or unified will of all or some of the participants. As O. E. Blazhivska notes, a joint activity agreement is always characterised by a single-vector orientation of the participants' will toward achieving a single, mutually desired goal (Blazhivska 2007, 21).

Free will in joint activity agreements is clearly manifested in their main features. V. V. Rieznikova identifies the following: (1) the presence of a common goal and motivation for all participants; (2) the division of the activity process into functionally related components distributed among the participants; (3) the combination and coordinated implementation of the individual efforts of the subjects; (4) the presence of management; (5) the achievement of common final results; and 6) the unified spatio-temporal functioning of all participants (Rieznikova 2013, 272).

These features prove that the essence of a joint activity lies in coordinating the participants' wills to achieve an identical goal. Although the parties have equal rights and obligations, they independently determine the distribution of profits, functions, and so on.

The combination of several participants for a joint activity stems from the potential insufficiency of one person's resources to achieve a goal and, consequently, the need to combine efforts and/or property to maximise the probability of success (Hutsuliak 2022, 91). Because of this, the joint activity agreement is a clear example of the coordinated free will of the parties, which is equal and not subject to external influence or coercion.

Contracts in the field of intellectual activity require a separate, detailed study. The specificity of these contracts is associated with the correlation between property and personal non-property rights of intellectual property, and the manifestation of free will depends on the object and subject of these rights. Contracts in this field form a complex system and are divided into copyright agreements, patent-licensing agreements, know-how transfer agreements, and commercial concession agreements, among others. These contracts are a way for participants to manifest their free will in the sphere of the creation, use, and protection of intellectual property. As intellectual property law is a separate sub-branch of civil law, the manifestation of free will within it will be examined in detail in a subsequent chapter.

As we can see, defining the role of free will in specific types of contracts is primarily reflected in their classification by objective, as this criterion best demonstrates the direction of the counterparties' will, their interests, and their purpose. Contracts for the transfer of property into ownership are aimed at the emergence and termination of property rights, and in this context, the role of free will correlates with its significance for property rights as a whole.

When concluding such a contract, both the alienator and the acquirer must have the will to transfer/acquire the property, which consists of a mutually agreed will and the real ability to fulfill their obligations. In contracts for the transfer of property for use, the parties' free will is aimed at the transfer and acquisition of property for temporary use and possession. The parties' free will allows them to define the contract as consensual or real, for-value or gratuitous. Legislation should be perceived not as a way to restrict the parties' free will, but as a set of officially recognized ways for them to exercise it. Choosing the type of contract that aligns with one's interests is a clear example of the manifestation of freedom in civil law. Depending on the goal, the parties exercise their free will through various mechanisms, which involves adhering to the rules inherent in the chosen contract.

4.2. Free Will in Non-Contractual Obligations

The legal nature of non-contractual obligations involves the emergence of rights and duties from unilateral actions. They are characterised by the absence of a coordinated (unified) will among the participants and their inability to alter the scope of these rights and duties at their own discretion. Unlike contractual commitments, obligations from unilateral actions arise from facts directly defined in legislation (such as a public promise of a reward or rescuing a person's life or property), and the individual will of the parties plays a much smaller role.

Free will can be expressed through constructs other than the traditional model of offer and acceptance, which allows for an analysis of obligatory legal relations from a broader perspective (Lerner 2004, 49). This makes it appropriate to define the legal relationship between free will and non-contractual obligations.

Non-contractual obligations are characterized by several distinct features: they invariably constitute a new legal obligation, arise from the violation of absolute rights, are governed primarily by imperative norms, and possess an ongoing nature. In such obligations, the manifestation of free will is generally less significant than in contractual relations, which are predicated entirely on the principles of freedom of contract and dispositivity. Nevertheless, the principle of freedom of contract remains relevant, particularly for obligations arising from unilateral actions, due to the inherent dynamics of non-contractual obligations as they progress through three stages: emergence, existence, and termination.

While the emergence of a non-contractual obligation is anchored to a legal fact that cannot arise from a contract—such as a tort—the parties may exercise their free will during the subsequent existence and termination stages. At these points, participants are permitted to conclude a contract to regulate the performance of the obligation. For instance, it is legally permissible to enter into agreements regarding the securing of performance, the assignment of a creditor's claim, or the transfer of a debtor's debt (Uzhva and Kruhlova 2021, 65).

Critically, the conclusion of such a subsequent contract does not transform the underlying obligation into a contractual one, as the original legal basis for the rights and duties remains the governing factor. Thus, while non-contractual obligations often arise from facts unrelated to free will (such as unintentional harm), the participants can later apply their free will to establish a contractual procedure for performance, guided by the principle of freedom of contract to settle their legal relations.

The above makes it possible to define non-contractual obligations. Currently, there is no established concept on this issue. The library of European law contains many works on contract law, tort law, and restitution (Schlechtriem 2000; Beatson and Schrage 2003), but there is no exhaustive account of the concept and principles of non-contractual obligations. The same applies to national legal systems (Jansen 2010, 16).

V. M. Parasyuk, M. V. Parasyuk, and N. M. Grabar define non-contractual obligations as those arising on a basis other than a contract, in which one party (the debtor) is obliged to perform a certain action for the benefit of the other party (the creditor) (Parasiuk et al. 2014, 537). However, this definition is tautological, as it essentially states that non-contractual obligations are those that do not arise from a contract, without revealing their essence.

A more thorough definition is offered by N. Jansen, who argues that non-contractual obligations should be understood as instruments that protect a citizen's interests from unwanted violations of their legally protected status quo, including bodily integrity, personality, and property rights, rather than being based on voluntary agreements (Jansen 2010, 16). This perspective closely aligns with the underlying framework of Regulation (EC) No 864/2007, commonly known as the Rome II Regulation, which governs the law applicable to non-contractual obligations across the European Union. Although the Regulation applies the concept in a general sense to specific categories—such as torts, unjust enrichment, *negotiorum gestio*, and *culpa in contrahendo*—it does not provide a formal definition of the concept itself, relying instead on the established functional boundaries of civil law protections and the historical development of the law of obligations (*Regulation (EC) No 864/2007 2007*).

M. D. Tedoradze posits that the grounds for the emergence of non-contractual obligations can be categorized into two primary groups. The first group encompasses obligations arising from a unilateral expression of will, such as a public promise of a reward or acting in the property interests of another without explicit authorization. The second group comprises obligations triggered by legal facts prescribed by law, fundamentally rooted in the duty to protect health, life, and property; this includes obligations arising from the creation of a threat, the causing of harm, or unjust enrichment (Tedoradze 2014). Notably, Article 1163 of the Civil Code of Ukraine reinforces this by stipulating that an individual whose life, health, or property is threatened maintains the right to demand the elimination of that threat from the responsible party.

Expanding on this framework, V. M. Ignatenko synthesizes these categories under the umbrella of "regulatory obligations." These are designed to govern standard relations between civil law subjects that arise from legitimate, non-contractual grounds, including public promises of reward, management of affairs without instruction (*negotiorum gestio*), and obligations arising from rescuing life or property or from testamentary dispositions (Ihnatenko 2012).

Furthermore, I. O. Kharitonov and O. I. Kharitonova refine this classification by proposing that actions taken without authority specifically to prevent harm to another person should be distinguished as a separate, specialized category (Kharytonov and Kharytonova 2021, 7). This distinction highlights the nuanced role of will in interventions intended to preserve the status quo of another's rights in the absence of a prior agreement.

The division of non-contractual obligations into the following has also become widespread: (1) obligations arising from lawful actions (e.g., public promise of a reward, acting in another's interest); and (2) obligations arising from unlawful actions (e.g., creating a threat, causing harm, unjust enrichment) (Kharytonov 2015, 32).

To understand the role of free will in non-contractual obligations, it is necessary to examine its relationship with specific types of such obligations.

First, it should be noted that the manifestation of free will in the acquisition and preservation of property without a sufficient legal basis (unjust enrichment) was considered in detail in the third chapter. Therefore, to avoid duplication, it is inappropriate to reconsider this issue.

There are two main concepts for understanding a public promise of a reward. The first considers it an offer to enter into a contractual relationship, a position supported in American law. An example is the case of *Carlill v Carbolic Smoke Ball Co.* The defendant advertised its product, offering a reward to anyone who used it and still contracted influenza. The plaintiff did so but was denied the reward. The court recognized the advertisement as an offer for a unilateral contract, which the plaintiff had accepted by performing the conditions (*Carlill v. Carbolic Smoke Ball Co.* 1893). The judicial position is justified by the fact that common law bases contracts on a promise, not necessarily a formal agreement (Samuel 1991, 42).

In contrast, the Civil Code of Ukraine explicitly classifies a public promise of a reward as a non-contractual obligation. As noted by V. V. Yakovenko and N. V. Filyk, a public promise of a reward is a unilateral transaction in which the promisor undertakes to pay a reward to whoever achieves the stipulated result (Yakovenko and Filyk 2017, 139). The authors conclude that it is a legal fact for which the expression of will of only one person is sufficient (Ibid.).

We believe this proposal requires clarification. On the one hand, a public promise of a reward is a manifestation of the free will of the one who offered it. On the other, such a legal relationship cannot exist without the will of the reward's recipient. If no person is willing or able to fulfill the conditions, the promisor cannot achieve their goal. This construction is similar to a public offer, which also does not give rise to legal relations if no one accepts it. Therefore, defining a reward as a purely unilateral promise relates to the broader question of the place of unilateral will as a source of obligations (Moccia 1994, 819).

The promise of a reward does not in itself create a legal relationship and requires a combination of two legal facts: (1) a public announcement of the reward; and (2) the achievement of the result specified in the announcement (Dzera, Kuznietsova, and Maydanyk 2017, 956).

A public promise of a reward is based on the free will of both participants in the obligation: the will of one person to give a reward for the performance of a task, and the will of another who seeks to perform the task for the reward.

The announcement of a reward merely indicates the person's interest in a particular result and the obligation to pay upon its achievement (Chaban 2022, 449). The party that announced the reward exercises its free will when determining the content of the task, its deadline, and the terms of the promise.

The performer of the task exercises their free will by accepting the announced conditions, choosing the method of performance, and exercising the right to receive the reward.

The parties must be aware of the aleatory (contingent) nature of such a transaction. Its defining feature is that the performance is conditioned by an uncertain outcome (Maydanyk 2007, 218). For the party who announced the reward, there is a risk that their requirements will not be met. However, for the claimant, the aleatory nature is more significant, as they may begin the task but not receive the reward in case of non-performance, improper performance, or losing a competition. The claimant can only demand compensation for damages in specific cases, such as when the task is changed after they have already begun (*Tsyvil'nyi kodeks Ukrainy* [Civil Code of Ukraine] 2003, art. 1147, para. 2), or if a change in conditions makes performance impossible or uninteresting for them (Ibid., art. 1147, para. 3; art. 1152, para. 2).

The promise of a reward does not mean that someone will necessarily complete the task and receive it. It is merely an invitation to a legal relationship, a manifestation of the free will of the person announcing the reward. This free will is primary to that of the performer, who merely accedes to the offer. A change of parties is impossible in this relationship, unlike in contractual obligations.

Acting in the property interests of another person without their authorisation (*negotiorum gestio*) is closely related to the legal categories of "free will" and "interest."

D. M. Pestruev proves that *negotiorum gestio* arises from such actions, where one participant (the *gestor*) voluntarily undertakes to act to protect the property interests of another (the principal or *dominus*), while the principal has the right to proper management and is obliged to reimburse the expenses incurred if they were justified (Piestruiev 2020, 10). These obligations may arise when a person's property interests are threatened, and another person has the right to act without instruction to prevent, eliminate, or reduce potential negative consequences (*Tsyvil'nyi kodeks Ukrainy* [Civil Code of Ukraine] 2003, art. 1158, para. 1).

Therefore, for this legal relationship to arise, only the free will of one party, the *gestor*, is sufficient. It is they who decide to create the legal relationship by actually taking action in the interest of the other person. This position is supported by I. O. Michurin, who concluded that acting in another's interest without their authorisation cannot give rise to a non-contractual obligation if there is no personal initiative from the *gestor* (Michurin 2018, 347).

The legal nature of *negotiorum gestio* (management of affairs without mandate) is defined by its focus on protecting property interests, a concept rooted in the broader interpretation of legally protected interests. I. V. Venediktova defines a legally protected interest as a subject's conscious claim to obtain a specific material or non-material benefit, or to alter a legal status. This claim motivates the subject to act or refrain from acting, remains within the established legal field, and receives state support (Venediktova 2013, 9).

In turn, a property interest specifically involves the preservation or improvement of the volume or quality of an individual's assets (*Pro zatverdzhennia Metodychnykh rekomendatsii…* [On the Approval of Methodological Recommendations…] 2019). In the context of *negotiorum gestio*, this interest provides the justification for an intervenor to act on behalf of another without prior authorization, provided their actions are directed toward maintaining the principal's "legally protected status quo" and are consistent with their presumed will.

Acting in the property interests of another without their authorisation is a unilateral manifestation of the *gestor's* free will to preserve or increase the *dominus's* property.

The free will of the *dominus* is effectively suspended within the context of *negotiorum gestio* until they explicitly refuse the *gestor's* actions, at which point their autonomy becomes the dominant legal factor. This dynamic correlates with French judicial practice, which requires the *gestor's* intervention to be objectively appropriate and, crucially, not contrary to the known wishes of the *dominus* (*Cour de cassation* [Cass.] 1986; *Cour de cassation* [Cass.] 1942).

This framework establishes a unique requirement for the coordination of wills: while the *gestor* does not need to obtain prior permission in the absence of a direct refusal, any expressed opposition by the *dominus* grants their free will immediate precedence. If no such refusal is voiced, the *dominus* is legally obliged to accept a formal report on the actions taken (*Tsyvil'nyi kodeks Ukrainy* [Civil Code of Ukraine] 2003, art. 1159) and to reimburse any incurred expenses (Ibid., art. 1160). This structure represents a fundamental departure from agency relationships, where the principal initiates the legal bond of their own free will and remains the active driver of the relationship from its inception.

The *gestor's* free will must also meet other special conditions. The intervention must be useful to the *dominus* (Kortmann 2005), which is possible only if the actions are successful (Terré, Lequette, and Simler 2002, 1041). That is, for these obligations to arise, in addition to the *gestor's* will, a positive result is required.

The *gestor's* intervention must also be expedient. As reflected in a decision of the French Court of Cassation, for an intervention to be expedient, it must at least appear to the *gestor* that the *dominus* cannot protect their own interests (*Cour de cassation* [Cass.] 1999). It should also be noted that the intervention must be voluntary and spontaneous (*Code civil* [Civil Code] n.d., art. 1372).

Although the requirements of voluntariness, spontaneity, expediency, and utility are not directly enshrined in Ukrainian civil legislation, they correspond to the principles of civil law and the essence of negotiorum gestio. This makes it advisable to enshrine these principles in Chapter 79 of the Civil Code of Ukraine for a better understanding of the nature of these obligation.

This position is continued in the institution of rescuing the health and life of an individual or the property of a person or legal entity. In fact, this institution embodies the same conditions as *negotiorum gestio*. The key difference is that the interest is not purely proprietary but is related to health, life, and property. Another difference lies in the subject of compensation for damage caused by the rescue. The person in whose interest the actions were taken compensates for the damage personally only if the damage was to the property of the rescuer (*Tsyvil'nyi kodeks Ukrainy* [Civil Code of Ukraine] 2003, art. 1162, para. 2). In all other cases, the damage is compensated by the state (Ibid., art. 1161; art. 1162, para. 1).

Importantly, the rescuer's will must be directly aimed at saving the life, health, or property. If the rescue was merely an incidental result of the person's activity, the specified obligations do not arise (Kharytonov 2011, 7). This does not apply to persons who perform rescue as part of their professional duties. For example, a doctor cannot be a *gestor* if they are employed by a state or municipal body for which preventing harm is a goal of its activity, or if such actions are part of their job description (Buletsa 2012, 92).

From the above, it also follows that the *dominus* cannot refuse actions taken to save their life and health. Here, one can apply an analogy regarding the impossibility of refusing emergency medical care. This position is based on the proclamation of human life and health as the highest social value (*Konstytutsiia Ukrainy* [Constitution of Ukraine] 1996, art. 3). This is due to the supremacy of the will and interests of the state over an individual's free will, with exceptions where the latter can challenge a public will that is not imperative.

Unlike negotiorum gestio, a successful outcome is not a condition for these legal relations. As I. O. Kharitonov emphasises, a positive result ("rescue") is not a condition for the emergence of obligations. This follows from the fact that Article 1161 of the Civil Code of Ukraine states that the person "was rescuing," not "rescued," the life and health of an individual (Buletsa 2012, 92). That is, for these obligations to arise, the *gestor's* will alone is sufficient without the need for a positive result; the focus is on the process, not the outcome.

The above allows us to conclude that in obligations arising from rescuing a person's life, health, or property, the free will of the *dominus* plays a lesser role due to the priority of the *gestor's* free will, which must be directly aimed at the rescue.

A logical continuation is the obligation that arises when a threat is created to the life, health, or property of a person or legal entity. In this case, the free will of the participants has the opposite meaning compared to the non-contractual obligations discussed above.

The initiator of such legal relations is the person who is threatened. Unlike in previous cases, it is their free will that should be directed toward the creation of rights and duties.

These relations should be distinguished from the creation of a threat due to the non-performance of a contract. As Yu. O. Zaika notes, if a housing maintenance organization fails to carry out timely repairs, and residents face a cold winter, their claims will be based not on Chapter 81 of the Civil Code of Ukraine, but on their service contract (Zaika 2014, 24). Thus, obligations arising from the creation of a threat stem from non-contractual legal facts that express the free will of both the person threatened and the person whose actions or inaction create the threat.

The free will of the person threatened is expressed in demanding the threat's elimination from the one who creates it. This involves an active, external manifestation of free will. Such legal relations cannot arise without a direct demand from the person to eliminate the danger. Of their own will, a person independently chooses the method of protecting their right within the limits specified in Article 16 of the Civil Code of Ukraine.

The free will of the person threatened manifests in three forms: (1) initiating legal relations to eliminate the danger; (2) choosing a method of protection; and (3) agreeing on the legal consequences (e.g., demanding compensation for damages).

The person whose actions or inaction create the threat manifests free will in creating and then eliminating or not eliminating the threat. Importantly, the presence of intent in creating the threat is of secondary importance. It does not matter whether the actions were aimed at creating a threat; only the fact of its occurrence and the causal link are considered. It is also irrelevant whether the person was aware that their actions could create a threat.

The key factor is the free will of this person after receiving the demand to eliminate the threat. If they eliminate it voluntarily, the legal relationship is terminated, as the harm was only potential. But if the threat is not eliminated, the interested person may, of their own free will and without coordination with the other party, demand: (1) urgent measures to eliminate the threat; (2) compensation for damages; or (3) prohibition of the activity that creates the threat.

In the first case, self-defense will take place, the method of which the person chooses of their own free will, among those not prohibited by law and in accordance with the nature of the right being violated (*Tsyvil'nyi kodeks Ukrainy* [Civil Code of Ukraine] 2003, art. 19).

In the case of demanding the prohibition of the activity, it is necessary to coordinate the will of this person with the will of the body authorised to make such decisions.

The requirement for compensation is relevant only if harm has already been caused and is not applied as a preventive measure when only a threat exists.

Compensation for damages is a separate type of non-contractual obligation with a special connection to free will. It will be examined in detail in the next subsection in the context of the significance of free will in the breach of obligations, as obligations to compensate for damages arise as a consequence of violating the duty not to cause harm.

From the analysis above, it is evident that the legal nature of non-contractual obligations involves the emergence of rights and duties from unilateral actions, typically characterized by the absence of a coordinated will and the inability of participants to alter the scope of their legal relations at their own discretion. Unlike contractual commitments, these obligations arise from facts explicitly defined by statute, where individual will plays a significantly more constrained role.

A public promise of a reward, for instance, is a primary manifestation of the promisor's free will; however, such legal relations cannot reach fruition without the subsequent will of the recipient who performs the required action. Similarly, acting in the property interests of another (*negotiorum gestio*) constitutes a unilateral manifestation of the *gestor's* free will. In this dynamic, the *dominus's* free will is effectively suspended until they explicitly refuse the intervention, at which point their autonomy becomes the dominant legal factor. For the *gestor's* actions to be legally recognized, their free will must satisfy the conditions of voluntariness, spontaneity, expediency, and utility.

This conceptual framework extends to the institution of rescuing a person's life, health, or property, where the rescuer's will must be directed specifically toward the act of rescue. In these obligations, the *dominus's* free will is afforded less weight due to the legal priority granted to the rescuer's altruistic manifestation of will. Conversely, in obligations arising from the creation of a threat, the free will of the participants takes on an opposing significance compared to other non-contractual categories, as the law focuses on the preemptive suppression of a harmful will to protect the "legally protected status quo" of the potential victim.

4.3. The Importance of Free Will in Breach of Obligations

The emergence of an obligation can be directly related to free will (e.g., the conclusion of a contract) or have an indirect connection (e.g., in torts). Contractual obligations arise from the agreement of the parties' wills, in accordance with the principles of contract law, and are based on a voluntary expression of will. Non-contractual obligations arise from the normative enshrinement of human rights and duties. Failure to comply with such obligations creates a duty to compensate for any resulting harm. In general, the breach of both contractual and non-contractual obligations leads to the imposition of civil liability. This thesis is confirmed by O. V. Batozhska, who emphasizes that a legal wrong as a basis for civil liability always causes negative consequences for the creditor (Batozhska 2012, 323).

The manifestation of free will has a different structure in contractual and non-contractual obligations. In the former, free will affects the conclusion of the contract and its performance, improper performance, or non-performance. While the emergence of a contractual relationship is based on the parties' free will, a breach can occur regardless of their will (e.g., due to *force majeure*). Non-contractual obligations exist independently of the will of the participants. For example, the obligation not to harm another person's health arises from constitutional law and does not depend on the free will of individuals. At the same time, the non-contractual obligation to compensate for harm caused to health may arise either as a result of a manifestation of free will (intent) or not (negligence).

To determine the role of free will in a breach of obligations, it is necessary to understand the reasons why participants fail to fulfill their duties.

Legal obligations can be considered through the concept of a "promise." A breach of contractual obligations is a failure to fulfill the promises stipulated in the agreement, whereas a breach of non-contractual obligations is a failure to fulfill the "promises" imposed on a person by legal norms. Charles Fried, a proponent of the moralist theory of contract, posits a general obligation to keep promises, of which contractual obligations are a special case where certain promises have acquired both legal and moral force (Atiyah and Fried 1981).

Fried's theory centers on the necessity of fulfillling promises, which constitute the content and idea of contracts. A participant in a legal relationship exercises free will by concluding a contract and, therefore, must fulfill the resulting obligations. Fried supports this by noting that an individual is morally obliged to keep their promises because they have invoked a convention whose function is to give others grounds to expect performance (Ibid. 1981).

An analysis of the moralist theory suggests that a breach of contract is the result of a moral decision. That is, a party to the agreement, of its own free will, decides not to perform its contractual obligations properly. We believe this statement is not entirely accurate, as a breach may be beyond the party's control or may not involve a moral component. This position is supported by Joseph Raz, who makes an important objection to the moralist theory, which lies not in its consequences for remedies, but in its very basis as an application of legal moralism to contract law (Raz 1982).

In the instrumental theory of contract, promise-keeping is viewed from a more practical perspective. L. Murphy argues that while a deviation from a remedy may not cause harm, a publicly accepted justification for a legal regime in which breach is often socially desirable would tend to undermine the practice of promising and contract (Murphy 2014). In other words, if a party were given the right to breach contractual obligations, the contract would lose its meaning as a civil law mechanism for regulating relations.

In contrast, Seana Shiffrin raises concerns about the consequences of contract law's divergence from the morality of promising and moral free will (Shiffrin 2007). The scholar suggests that the inability to renounce obligations limits the parties' free will. In our opinion, the parties' free will is realised at the moment of agreeing to the terms, concluding, and performing the contract. By accepting contractual obligations, a party consciously and of its own free will expresses a desire to fulfill the terms and gives the promise legal force. At the same time, a party retains the right not to fulfill its obligations in cases provided for by law, or by choosing to accept civil liability instead of performance.

In conclusion, a breach of contractual obligations is a manifestation of free will when the party acts consciously. In this case, there is intent, which reflects an interest in breaching the obligations. Confirmation of this thesis can be found in the work of David Owens, who argues that people can do things intentionally only if they see some point in them, and they can see a point in them only if it seems worthwhile to them (Owens 2012).

In the case of a breach of non-contractual obligations, free will plays a different role. Here, the existence of a contractual promise is irrelevant. We proceed from the assumption that any person within a jurisdiction implicitly promises to comply with established legal rules and not to harm others. A breach of this "promise" creates a new obligation in the form of compensation for damages.

A breach of obligations leads to either contractual or non-contractual civil liability, or to an exemption from it.

Contractual liability arises in the form of compensation for damages, payment of a penalty, or loss of a deposit for the non-fulfillment or improper fulfillment of an obligation arising from a contract. The basis for such liability is a breach of contractual obligations.

An important issue in determining the role of free will in a breach of contract is establishing its presence or absence. If a contract is a manifestation of the parties' free will, a breach of its terms may occur independently of it, which makes it appropriate to analyse such cases.

A breach of contractual obligations is the non-performance or improper performance of the essential terms of the contract, which reflect the parties' free will and their interests. As I. V. Venediktova notes, the contractual form is an ideal means of realising legally protected interests, harmoniously combined with the dispositive method of regulating private relations. The protected interests of the parties are safeguarded by granting them the status of essential terms or by enshrining them in the contract (Venediktova 2013, 29). The contract is the optimal legal expression of free will, as it allows parties to independently determine its content and create legal relations at their own discretion.

A party breaches its obligations for several reasons: (1) concluding an invalid transaction; (2) impossibility of performance; (3) a change in circumstances; or (4) the fault of the other party.

The conclusion of a transaction is related to its purpose and motive. The purpose is the primary impetus for a person to enter into a transaction and depends directly on their will, while the motive is the psychological stimulus that prompts them to do so (Skydanov 2015b, 33). If a party does not intend to fulfill the terms of a contract but concludes it anyway, this indicates a violation of the principles of contract law and creates a dissonance between the declared and actual intention. Such a transaction will be considered invalid and, depending on the content of the parties' will, is classified as either sham or fictitious. It should be agreed that a common feature of sham and fictitious transactions is that the discrepancy between the will and its external manifestation results from the intentional actions of the participants, aimed at obtaining a benefit. In both cases, the expression of will does not correspond to the actual will of the parties (Skydanov 2015a, 99).

If a party enters into a transaction where its will is not aimed at creating the corresponding legal consequences, the transaction is considered fictitious (*Tsyvil'nyi kodeks Ukrainy* [Civil Code of Ukraine] 2003, art. 234). If the parties' will is aimed at concluding a transaction to conceal another one, it is considered a sham (Ibid., art. 235). The peculiarity of such transactions is that while they formally comply with the law, the actual will of the parties does not correspond to their expression of will (Skydanov 2013, 2). That is, at the moment of concluding the contract, the party already knew it would breach its obligations. In this case, free will is directly aimed at non-performance. As K. V. Skydanov notes, will and the expression of will in a transaction must be "balanced," as a discrepancy can cause the transaction to lose legal force, violating the rights of counterparties (Ibid., 10).

This allows us to distinguish such contracts from transactions with vitiating factors (defects of will), which include: (1) transactions made by a capable person who, at the time, was unaware of the significance of their actions; (2) transactions made under the influence of mistake; (3) transactions made under the influence of fraud; (4) transactions made under the influence of duress; (5) transactions made under the influence of dire circumstances (Zaborovskyi and Popovych 2015, 19).

The presence of vitiating factors violates the very idea of a civil law contract and the principle of free expression of will, deforming the parties' free will. This is confirmed by the definition formulated by R. V. Aleksii, who states that a defect of will is a deformation of a participant's will due to circumstances that prevent a person from correctly formulating their inner will when entering into a transaction (Aleksii 2020, 4). However, defects of will can arise not only from an incorrect formulation of the inner will but also from an influence on its external expression. In some voidable transactions, the inner will and its expression coincide, even though the inner will itself was formed incorrectly (e.g., transactions made under the influence of mistake).

O. L. Zaitsev divides transactions with defects of will into two types: (1) those without an internal will to conclude the transaction; and (2) those with an incorrectly formed internal will (Zaitsev 2007, 365).

R. V. Aleksii distinguishes two criteria for classification: (1) by the influence of external and internal factors on the person; and (2) by the presence of intent in the actions of the participants or third parties (Aleksii, 2018, p. 21).

These positions can be revised to divide transactions with vitiating factors into those that arise from an influence on the internal will and those that involve an influence on its external form (the expression of will).

The grounds for challenging transactions due to vitiating factors are characterized by their distinct impacts on the mechanics of free will, categorized primarily by whether they distort the internal intent or the external expression.

First, a mistake specifically affects the formation of the internal will, which nonetheless remains consistent with the subsequent expression of will. In this context, an error in the external expression is generally not legally significant if the underlying internal will was correctly formed; for instance, mistakenly concluding one type of contract instead of another may be qualified as negligence or an ignorance of the law rather than a defect in the manifestation of will itself.

Second, in transactions executed under the influence of fraud, the internal will coincides with its expression and is directed toward achieving the transaction's objective. However, the formation of that will was corrupted by external distortions that masked the subject's true intent. Legal doctrine emphasizes that fraud impacts only the internal will, as a direct impact on the expression of will itself would likely be reclassified as criminal fraud.

Third, dire circumstances (extreme necessity) similarly impair the formation of the internal will, forcing a choice that the subject would not otherwise make under normal conditions.

Finally, transactions concluded under the influence of duress (violence or threats) are uniquely characterized by an impact on the expression of will, creating a fundamental inconsistency between the internal intent and the external act. Duress stands as the only ground for challenging a transaction that involves a direct, coercive influence on the external manifestation of free will, effectively bypassing the subject's internal autonomy.

Table 2. The Relationship Between Vitiating Factors and Free Will

Vitiating Factors	**Form of Free Will**		**Correspondence Between Inner Will and its Expression**
	Inner Will	External Will	
The Impact of Deception	+ Affected	- (If affected, may constitute grounds for criminal fraud)	+ Will corresponds to the inner intention, though formed under deception.
The Impact of Mistake	+ Affected	- (If affected, it is considered a mistake resulting from one's own negligence and has no separate legal significance)	+ The expression of will corresponds to the inner will, but the latter was formed under the influence of the mistake.
The Impact of a Dire Circumstance	+ Affected	- Not affected	+ The expression of will corresponds to the inner will, but the latter was formed under the influence of the dire circumstance.
The Impact of Duress	- Not affected	+ Affected	- The expression of will does not correspond to the inner will.

Source: Compiled by the author.

The findings discussed above necessitate a formal proposal to amend Part 3 of Article 203 of the Civil Code of Ukraine, which currently stipulates that "the expression of a party's will must be free and correspond to their inner will" (*Tsyvil'nyi kodeks Ukrainy* [Civil Code of Ukraine] 2003, art. 203, para. 3). As our analysis has demonstrated, in transactions concluded under the influence of fraud, mistake, or dire circumstances, the external expression of will actually does correspond to the internal will, as the subject intentionally performs the act based on a distorted perception of reality. This formal alignment creates a doctrinal paradox that could theoretically negate the possibility of challenging such transactions under the current wording.

To resolve this inconsistency, it is appropriate to rephrase the provision to account for the integrity of the will-formation process. The proposed amendment would read as follows:

> The expression of the will of a party to a transaction must be free and correspond to their inner will, provided that such inner will was not formed under the influence of fraud, mistake, or dire circumstances.

This modification ensures that the law protects not only the correspondence between intent and action but also the autonomy and correctness of the internal psychological process that precedes the legal act.

When legal relations arise due to influence on the free will of the parties (coercion, deception), or if a participant is not aware of their obligations (e.g., due to intoxication or mental disorders), or their will is directed in advance toward a breach (sham and fictitious transactions), grounds arise for declaring the transaction invalid and for the imposition of civil liability.

A party may also breach its obligations when it did not plan to do so in advance. Examples include the impossibility of performance and a change in circumstances. It is essential to note that this does not refer to an impossibility that the party was aware of at the time of concluding the contract (e.g., a lack of funds or legal title). The lack of initial intent is crucial. That is, at the contracting stage, the party did not intend to breach, but the situation later changed. For example, a person may lose property received under a rental agreement and be unable to return it, giving rise to compensatory relations. Or a person pays a deposit for real estate but loses interest in concluding the sale. This is particularly relevant for preliminary contracts.

The final reason for a breach of contractual obligations is the fault of the other party, where the breach occurred through no fault of one's own. For example, if a breach occurred due to the creditor's fault, the court will reduce the amount of damages and penalties recovered from the debtor (Ibid., art. 616, para. 1). Similarly, a contractor has the right to suspend work if the customer fails to provide the necessary materials, making performance impossible (Ibid., art. 851). In these cases, the breach occurred not through the debtor's will, but through the creditor's actions or inaction.

In this context, the issue of fault acquires special significance. A. L. Tkachuk concludes that fault is an optional element of contractual liability and serves as a legal means of optimising the interests of the creditor and debtor by distributing the risk of breach between them (Tkachuk, 2002, p. 5). The author suggests understanding fault in contractual liability as the offender's failure to take measures aimed at proper performance with the degree of care and prudence required by the customs of commerce (Ibid.). Fault exists when there is a causal link between the unlawful conduct and the negative consequences. When fault takes the form of intent, the guilty party's free will is directed at the conscious non-performance of obligations. In the case of negligence, the party's fault remains, but their free will is not directed at the breach.

In the event of a breach, legal consequences established by the contract or law arise, including: (1) termination of the obligation; (2) a change in its terms; (3) payment of a penalty; (4) compensation for losses and moral damage (*Tsyvil'nyi kodeks Ukrainy* [Civil Code of Ukraine] 2003, art. 611, para. 1).

The choice of one of these consequences occurs at the creditor's discretion, taking into account the terms of the contract. For example, the parties may agree to change the terms, but the final decision on the legal consequences rests with the party whose rights were violated. The parties may also agree to terminate the obligations by mutual will through novation, debt forgiveness, or other means (Senin 2013, 6).

In general, the parties' free will is of direct importance for the imposition of contractual liability, as they themselves agree on its scope and conditions. In this case, the free will of the party whose rights were violated takes priority; if their claims are not satisfied by the guilty party, they can go to court, which will effectively negate the counterparty's free will.

Free will is of fundamental importance in the breach of non-contractual obligations, which arise from the commission of unlawful acts by one person against another in the absence of a contract between them. A breach of non-contractual obligations gives rise to the duty to compensate for damages.

The obligation to compensate for damages is a legal institution that gives rise to non-contractual legal relations. Based on the imperative norms of civil law, the creditor (the victim) has the right to demand full compensation from the debtor (the tortfeasor) for the harm caused (Kivalova 2008, 6).

In this case, free will is characterised by the absence of prior agreements between the participants. New obligations arise as a result of the harm caused, due to the violation of the normatively established duty not to infringe upon the rights of another person. This is confirmed by N. P. Baadzhi, who argues that an unlawful act corresponds to a legal duty to refrain from encroaching on prohibitions established by law and on the subjective rights of others (Baadzhy 2008, 187).

We support the position that non-contractual and tort liability cannot be equated, as their legal foundations and scopes of application differ significantly. Tort liability arises exclusively in the event of direct harm to a person or property—grounded specifically in a civil tort—whereas non-contractual liability encompasses a broader range of legal anomalies. For instance, the liability of a party who enters into an invalid transaction in bad faith is considered non-contractual, yet it is not based on a tortious act (Tserkovna and Ellarian 2014, 244).

In this context, non-contractual and tort liability are related as a whole to a part. Broadly defined, non-contractual obligations include those arising from tort, unjust enrichment, *negotiorum gestio* (management of affairs without a mandate), or *culpa in contrahendo* (fault in conclusion of a contract). This categorization is consistent with the judicial interpretation provided by the Court of Justice of the European Union, which clarifies that the concept of non-contractual obligations must be understood autonomously, covering all actions that seek to establish the liability of a defendant which are not related to a "contract" in the strict sense (*Ergo Insurance SE* 2016).

Unlike non-contractual obligations based on lawful acts (e.g., a public promise of a reward), the obligation to compensate for damages is based only on unlawful acts (Bubina 2008, 180). That is, regardless of the person's will, their actions must violate the rights of others, be unlawful, and meet the general conditions for the emergence of such an obligation.

The general conditions for the emergence of an obligation to compensate for damages include: (1) harm; (2) the unlawfulness of the perpetrator's conduct; (3) a causal link between the unlawful conduct and the harm; and (4) the fault of the perpetrator (Baadzhy 2008, 186). Each of these conditions is associated with free will.

Harm, in a general theoretical sense, is the reduction or destruction of the victim's property, non-property, or other sphere (Shemshuchenko 2004). In effect, harm is the depreciation of a legally protected good. It is divided into property and moral harm, and its compensation constitutes forms of civil liability.

Material harm refers to the loss that a person has already suffered or must inevitably suffer to restore their original state. Moral harm consists of physical pain and suffering due to injury; mental anguish due to unlawful conduct toward oneself or family members; mental suffering due to the destruction of property; or the humiliation of one's honor, dignity, or business reputation (*Tsyvil'nyi kodeks Ukrainy* [Civil Code of Ukraine] 2003, art. 23, para. 2).

The victim's free will is manifested primarily at the stage of formulating and substantiating claims for damages. This autonomy is particularly significant in the context of compensation for moral harm, as the requested amount is determined independently by the claimant and is limited only by their own will. Unlike material harm, which must be strictly substantiated by empirical evidence, moral harm remains an entirely subjective experience.

This subjective nature is frequently confirmed by judicial practice, where the amount awarded for moral damages may significantly exceed that of material damages, often in cases where specific evidence of suffering is not formally attached. A pertinent example is found in a Decision of the Inhulets District Court of

Kryvyi Rih (2021). In this instance, the court partially satisfied a claim for 60,000 UAH in moral damages, acknowledging that the plaintiff's quality of life had fundamentally changed due to the onset of occupational diseases (*Rishennia Inhulets'koho raionnoho sudu* [Decision of the Inhulets District Court] 2021). In such cases, the victim's free will serves as the primary gauge for the "valuation" of their internal suffering within the legal process.

Thus, the free will of the injured person is applied when making claims for damages and determining their amount. The tortfeasor's free will is realised when they accept and agree to the victim's claims. At the same time, the participants choose the method of resolving the conflict of their own free will. The guilty party can accept the victim's terms or offer their own. However, the will of the person whose rights have been violated will be dominant, as they make the final decision on applying jurisdictional or non-jurisdictional methods of protection.

The unlawfulness of the perpetrator's conduct is also a condition for the emergence of an obligation to compensate for harm. Unlawful conduct is anti-normative; it violates a prohibitive or mandatory norm of law, is socially harmful, and entails undesirable consequences for the subject, primarily legal liability (Tymoshenko 2011, 60). It is behavior that violates the law in its objective sense and the subjective right of the victim (Baadzhy 2008, 187).

Free will manifests in unlawful conduct in the context of determining motivation. Three groups of motives are distinguished: those partially or fully conscious; those usually unconscious but which can become conscious; and those completely repressed into the unconscious (Tymoshenko 2011, 65). In the first two types, free will has direct significance as a condition for the actions or decisions that led to the breach. In the third case, free will is absent, as the harm occurred without awareness of one's own behavior.

The issue of motive should not be equated with intent. Even when a tortfeasor is fully aware of their motives, their free will may not be directed at causing harm. For example, if a person knowingly exceeds the speed limit, gets into an accident, and injures another person, their goal may not have been to cause harm. In this case, free will was directed at violating traffic rules, but the intent to cause harm was absent.

The existence of a causal link between the unlawful conduct and the harm should not directly stem from free will, as it is sufficient that the cause precedes and generates the effect. It does not matter whether the tortfeasor's will was directly aimed at causing harm. This is important for determining intent, but not for causation. As A. A. Herz notes, the causal link should not be probable or hypothetical; it should exist in objective reality and not change its character depending on imagination (Herts 2019, 41).

Any action or inaction is a cause that generates consequences. However, in the context of a breach of obligations, legal actions must have a negative impact on the rights of another person. This construction should be supplemented by the statement of S. D. Hrynko that a cause generates a consequence if it is direct, immediate, and has legal significance for the person who caused the harm (Hrynko 2010, 77).

Therefore, free will is not directly relevant for determining a causal link; it is only necessary to establish its existence, regardless of the tortfeasor's intent. However, if the harm is caused through the fault of the injured person, this will be grounds for releasing the tortfeasor from liability. For example, if the victim intentionally threw themself under a car, the causal link will show that the harm occurred by the victim's will.

The final condition for an obligation to compensate for damages is the fault of the perpetrator. Fault is traditionally considered a person's mental attitude toward their unlawful conduct and its consequences (Tserkovna 2018, 132).

However, this position raises reasonable doubts. Defining fault as a mental attitude would make liability dependent on whether the violator themself considers their conduct reprehensible (Karnaukh 2014, 31). In that case, we would have to assert the absolute nature of free will when qualifying fault. Such implicit subjectivity cannot be applicable in civil law, as the absence of self-condemnation would negate fault. We believe that the significance of free will for determining fault must be considered in the context of its forms – intent and negligence (*Tsyvil'nyi kodeks Ukrainy* [Civil Code of Ukraine] 2003, art. 614, para. 1).

While the concept of intent is not explicitly enshrined in civil legislation, a robust definition can be derived through an analogy with Article 24 of the Criminal Code. In the civil law context, intent signifies a deliberate violation of obligations wherein an individual is aware of the unlawful nature of their actions, foresees the subsequent consequences, and either desires or consciously permits them to occur. Guilt in this form is invariably predicated on a manifestation of free will that is specifically directed toward the breach of a legal duty.

The internal structure of intent consists of a precise combination of intellectual and volitional characteristics: awareness, foresight, and desire. When all three elements are present, the law recognizes direct intent. Conversely, if a subject possesses awareness and foresight but lacks a specific desire for the outcome – yet consciously allows the breach to happen – the intent is classified as indirect (eventual). Furthermore, if an individual is entirely unaware of the unlawful nature of their act, this may indicate either a personality defect that excludes liability or the presence of negligence, where the volitional aim was not directed at the harm itself (Veresha 2010, 74).

The foundational concept of negligence rests on the requirement that individuals must exercise reasonable care in their conduct, specifically accounting for potential harm that is reasonably foreseeable (Feinman 2018). While the specific parameters of liability vary by jurisdiction, negligence is generally established through four core elements: (1) a duty of care owed by the defendant to the plaintiff; (2) a breach of that duty; (3) harm or injury suffered by the plaintiff; and (4) causation, where the harm is a direct consequence of the defendant's breach (Boehm 2003).

The structural interpretation of these elements varies globally; some jurisdictions consolidate the analysis into three elements (duty, breach, and harm), while others utilize a more granular five-element framework – duty, breach, actual cause, proximate cause, and harm (Owen 2007).

This variation reflects different legal traditions' approaches to the manifestation of will: while intent focuses on a deliberate aim, negligence focuses on a volitional failure to meet the objective standard of a reasonable person, thereby linking the actor's free will to the societal expectation of cautious behavior. Negligence is based on the concept of the duty of care (Quill 2014, 19).

Each person must, of their own free will, respect the rights of others and not cause them harm. If, in the case of intent, the tortfeasor's will is directly aimed at violating obligations, then in the case of negligence, the will is aimed at behavior that may violate the rights of others. Unlike in indirect intent, in negligence, the tortfeasor is unaware of, does not foresee, and does not desire the breach. However, the specific feature of negligence is that a person is obliged to foresee the negative consequences of their behavior, and free will should be directed at this when committing any legal actions.

In most cases, the absence of fault is a basis for exemption from civil liability. Such grounds include *casus* (an accident), necessary defense, extreme necessity, *force majeure*, and the victim's intent (Tserkovna 2008, 5).

Casus is a basis for exemption from liability if the harm caused is beyond the control of the debtor or third parties. The tortfeasor must independently prove their absence of fault, justifying that their actions or inaction could not have been the cause of the breach (Matveev 1955, 94).

The subjective approach is based on the position that the incident occurred because a person was unaware or did not foresee the illegality of their actions (Bratel 2003, 9). We could agree with S. D. Hrynko, who emphasizes that an accident cannot be foreseeable, because if a person foresees its occurrence, they also envisage the creation of a threat of harm (Hrynko 2012, 176).

Casus is a basis for exemption from liability precisely because free will is in no way connected to the failure to fulfill obligations; the breach occurred due to an event whose consequences could not have been foreseen. Unlike in negligence, where the tortfeasor should have foreseen the negative consequences, an accident excludes this possibility. Therefore, unpredictability negates free will and serves as a basis for exemption from liability.

Force majeure also makes it impossible to exercise free will. Usually, such circumstances include: (1) war, civil unrest, or piracy; (2) natural disasters such as hurricanes, earthquakes, or floods; (3) explosions or fires; (4) strikes, lockouts, or other work stoppages; (5) acts of government (Kryvenko 2022, 639).

Free will loses its meaning in circumstances of *force majeure*, as they are extraordinary, unavoidable, and atypical events that make performance impossible. The only exception is harm caused by injury or death, which is subject to compensation even in the case of force majeure (*Tsyvil'nyi kodeks Ukrainy* [Civil Code of Ukraine] 2003, art. 1166, para. 3).

This thesis correlates with the obligation to resist the negative impact of *force majeure* by all possible means. Therefore, the occurrence of force majeure is a basis for exemption from liability but simultaneously creates an obligation to direct one's free will to take all possible measures to fulfill one's duties or to prevent or reduce the negative outcome.

In summary, *force majeure* is an objective phenomenon, an event that does not depend on a person's will or consciousness and could not have been prevented.

Necessary defense and extreme necessity are based on the direction of the tortfeasor's free will. In these cases, two components must be taken into account: (1) the free will is aimed at protecting rights, not at causing harm; (2) the harm is caused under the influence of external circumstances.

Necessary defense consists of self-defense or the protection of another person or public interests from a socially dangerous encroachment by inflicting harm on the aggressor that is necessary and sufficient to immediately prevent or terminate the encroachment, provided the limits of such defense were not exceeded (*Kryminal'nyi kodeks Ukrainy [Criminal Code of Ukraine]* 2001, art. 36).

Extreme necessity is characterised by taking actions aimed at eliminating a danger that threatened civil rights or interests, if this danger could not be eliminated by other means under the given conditions.

In both cases, there is an external influence of circumstances on a person's free will, which is aimed at protecting rights and interests, not at causing harm. The key factor is the impossibility of fulfillling obligations combined with a lack of interest in doing so.

Failure to fulfill obligations due to the victim's intent was discussed above. However, it should be noted that in this case, there is a normative condition that the debtor is not considered in default if the obligation cannot be fulfillled due to the creditor's delay. Under such circumstances, the victim's intent will be recognized as their mental attitude toward their unlawful actions and their consequences, manifested in the anticipation of negative outcomes and the desire or conscious allowance of their occurrence (Tserkovna 2008, 11).

Finally, it is worth noting that in some cases, the absence of fault is not a prerequisite for liability. Liability without fault is associated with the public interest in sanctioning unlawful conduct by applying state coercion. The presence of fault and the manifestation of free will are not required when the public interest prevails over the private. Examples include the liability of parents for damage caused by a minor child and that of an employer for the actions of an employee.

This study confirms that a breach of contractual obligations is a manifestation of free will when the party acts consciously. In this case, there is an intent that reflects an interest in breaching the obligations. In the case of a breach of non-contractual obligations, free will plays a different role. Here, the presence of a contractual promise is irrelevant, as the duty to comply with regulatory rules prevails. A crucial aspect in determining the role of free will in a breach of contract is establishing its presence or absence. If the contract is a manifestation of the parties' free will, then a breach of its terms may occur independently of it.

Conclusions

1. The principle of freedom of contract requires the coordination of the parties' wills as a manifestation of their dispositivity and equality. Freedom of contract and free will relate to each other as a whole to a part, where the former acts as the practical embodiment of the legal idea of the latter. Through this principle, the internal will of the participants takes an external form, reflected in the contractual terms.
2. The connection between free will and the principle of proper performance is anchored in the parties' awareness of their obligation to comply. Their will should, *a priori*, be directed toward fulfilllment; thus, a breach or the occurrence of force majeure is seen as an exception to the normal development of legal relations. This necessitates a shift toward alternative dispute resolution (ADR), such as mediation, which is mandated in jurisdictions like the Netherlands and Germany to honor the voluntary nature of the original agreement.
3. Based on the binding force of a contract, parties exercise norm-creating powers, establishing mandatory rules of conduct for themselves. This allows for the independent regulation of areas where legislation is insufficient, such as the Internet of Things, e-commerce, and data privacy.
4. Free will manifests at all stages of the contractual lifecycle: (1) determination of terms, (2) conclusion, (3) performance, and (4) termination. While the first two stages require an alignment of wills, the performance stage focuses on preventing a breach, and termination may involve either a coordinated or a unilateral manifestation of will.
5. Normative regulation generally prevails over contractual regulation, confirming the dominance of public free will (state and society) over individual will, except where the latter may challenge non-imperative public norms.
6. In contracts for the transfer of property into ownership, free will is dispositive, as it seeks the irrevocable termination of the alienator's rights. This distinction is fundamental in cases of property reclamation, challenges to transactions, and restitution.

7. A valid transfer requires the transferor and acquirer to declare both capacity and intention. This includes a mutually agreed-upon will and the real ability to fulfilll obligations (e.g., making payment). A violation of this constant provides grounds for declaring a transaction invalid, particularly when a party claims a misunderstanding of terms.
8. The public announcement of capacity and intention is reflected in the general conditions for a transaction's validity, ensuring the external expression corresponds to the inner will.
9. In contracts for use, free will is directed at temporary possession. Parties often utilize model contracts, which serve as recommendatory tools to help them express their will in compliance with legal requirements rather than as restrictions on their autonomy.
10. Choosing a contract type that aligns with specific interests—such as a works contract for a material result or a service contract for an intangible activity—is a primary manifestation of freedom. Recognizing these as independent ways of realizing will is essential for the practice of hybrid (mixed) contracts.
11. In dealings with legal entities or representatives, free will involves the coordination of the principal's will and the special subject's expression. One must determine if the authorized person acted in the interests of the represented party to properly qualify the relationship.
12. Joint activity agreements reflect a collective or unified free will. Participants coordinate their wills to achieve a common goal, independently determining the distribution of profits and functions.
13. Non-contractual obligations arise from unilateral actions or facts defined by law, characterized by the absence of a coordinated will. In these cases, such as a public promise of reward or the rescue of property, individual will plays a secondary role compared to contractual relations.
14. A public promise of a reward requires the will of the promisor (the offer) and the recipient (the performance). Judicial practice must treat a refusal to pay as a breach of obligation to protect the creditor's rights.

15. *Negotiorum gestio* (acting in the interest of another) is a unilateral manifestation of the *gestor's* will to preserve the *dominus's* property. The *dominus's* will is negated until they explicitly refuse the intervention.
16. The *dominus* cannot legally refuse actions taken to save their life or health, as the state's interest in preserving life is presumed to take priority over individual free will.
17. In rescue obligations, the *gestor's* will is prioritized, provided it is directly aimed at the act of rescue.
18. In obligations arising from the creation of a threat, the person threatened initiates the legal relationship. Their free will is directed toward creating the rights and duties necessary for the threat's elimination.
19. This manifestation of will is active and external; a person independently chooses the method of protecting their rights within legislative limits.
20. The will of the threatened person takes three forms: (1) initiating the relationship, (2) choosing the protection method, and (3) agreeing on legal consequences (e.g., compensation).
21. The person creating the threat exercises will in both its creation and its potential elimination, though the intent behind the threat's creation is of secondary legal importance.
22. Free will is the benchmark for determining the nature of a breach, establishing intent, fault, and causation, and applying exemptions from liability.
23. While contractual will affects conclusion and performance, non-contractual obligations can exist independently of will, though they may arise from either intent or negligence..
24. A breach of contract is a manifestation of will when the party acts consciously, reflecting an interest in non-performance.
25. Vitiating factors (defects of will), such as coercion or fraud, deform the parties' free will and provide grounds for invalidating transactions and imposing liability.
26. A breach caused by the creditor's fault is characterized by a unilateral will that should preclude holding the debtor liable.

27. Intent involves the conscious non-performance of duties, while negligence implies a breach where the will was not directed at the harm. We propose that parties in cases of negligence should have the right to voluntarily fulfilll the obligation without additional penalties.
28. In a dispute, the injured party's will takes priority. If the party at fault fails to satisfy demands, the court's intervention ultimately negates the counterparty's will.
29. Non-contractual obligations from unlawful acts arise from the violation of the duty not to harm others, irrespective of prior agreements.
30. The victim's will is expressed in the substantiation of claims, while the tortfeasor's will is realized through the acceptance of those claims.
31. Causation does not require the harm to stem directly from free will; it is sufficient that the conduct preceded the effect, regardless of whether the tortfeasor aimed to cause harm.
32. Liability practice requires determining fault. Intent is based on a will directed at the breach, while negligence is based on the failure of the duty of care.
33. *Casus* (an accident) exempts a party from liability because the event occurred outside their will and foresight.
34. Force majeure renders free will irrelevant due to its extraordinary and unavoidable nature, except in cases of injury or death, which remain compensable.
35. Necessary defense and extreme necessity involve a will directed at protecting rights rather than causing harm. In these cases, the external influence on free will justifies the actions taken in defense of a protected interest.

5. Free Will in Intellectual Property Law

5.1. Free Will in Copyright and Related Rights

Copyright and related rights serve as a fundamental mechanism for exercising the right to freedom of literary, artistic, scientific, and technical creativity. As previously established, these personal non-property rights are a direct embodiment of free will, a necessary condition for their existence. This suggests that free will acts as the bedrock for all intellectual property law, particularly when determining the specific content, objects, and the legal grounds for the emergence and exercise of copyright and related rights.

This theoretical framework is especially relevant in jurisdictions within the continental legal system, which is predicated on the postulate of the author as the primary creator. In this tradition, intellectual property is viewed not merely as a commercial asset but as the most personal and indisputable of all types of property, representing the externalization of the author's unique persona and volition (Ennan 2021, 36).

The current landscape of intellectual property law is increasingly viewed as being in a state of transition, if not crisis. As noted by Giovanni Dosi and Joseph Stiglitz, the urgency of reforming intellectual property regimes cannot be overstated; poorly designed systems frequently fail to enhance aggregate welfare and can, ironically, stifle the very innovation and societal development they were intended to foster (Dosi and Stiglitz 2014).

To date, the legal community has lacked comprehensive research into the fundamental relationship between free will and intellectual property law. This absence of a foundational link suggests that current frameworks may be building on shifting sands. Addressing this theoretical gap is not merely an academic necessity but a prerequisite for developing a new paradigm for this subbranch of civil law. Such a paradigm must reconcile the autonomous manifestation of the creator's will with the broader socio-economic requirements of the digital age, ensuring that the legal expression of creativity serves as a catalyst for progress rather than a barrier to entry.

As P. P. Cherevko notes, copyright as a part of civil law is designed to ensure the interests of authors in the process of creating and using their works as the results of intellectual activity (Cherevko 2022, 336). This statement should be supplemented, as copyright is primarily aimed at protecting the free will that is realised in the process of intellectual and creative activity.

The justification for copyright encompasses a spectrum ranging from natural rights-based ownership of intellectual products to utilitarian expectations. The latter posits that granting authors property rights incentivizes the creation of works for the ultimate benefit of society (Dreyfuss and Pila 2017). Within this framework, the public interest presupposes the development of copyright as a primary engine for innovation in cultural, scientific, and technological spheres. This implies that the public will should be strategically directed toward stimulating creative activity and, by extension, encouraging the exercise of individual free will.

However, as D. Kennedy, J. Stiglitz, and others emphasize, intellectual property rights are subject to inherent limitations and are never absolute (Kennedy and Stiglitz 2013). In the context of intellectual property, restrictions arise from two primary concerns: (1) the prevention of abuse of rights, such as using property claims to unreasonably restrict competition; and (2) the necessity of public use, where instruments like compulsory licenses play an essential role in ensuring access to knowledge deemed vital to the public interest (Dosi and Stiglitz 2014). Consequently, legal doctrine must acknowledge the persistent conflict between the public interest in stimulating creativity and the implementation of regulatory restrictions designed to safeguard the common good.

Copyright represents one of the most accessible legal protections to secure, as the right to a work arises automatically from the mere fact of its creation (*Pro avtors'ke pravo i sumizhni prava* [On Copyright and Related Rights] 2022, art. 9, para. 1). The uniqueness of this regime lies in the principle that a simple manifestation of free will is generally sufficient for the right to vest, though, as will be explored, these rights can occasionally emerge even in the absence of conscious application.

Currently, global standards do not impose rigorous requirements regarding the objective quality or aesthetic level of a work, which imbues copyright with a profoundly subjective character. In the European Union, the threshold for protection is satisfied if a work constitutes the author's "own intellectual creation" (*Directive 2001/29/EC* 2001). In the United States, judicial doctrine requires that a work meet a "modicum" or "minimum degree of creativity" to warrant protection (*Feist Publications, Inc. v. Rural Telephone Service* 1991). Despite these definitions, the specific standard for "creative quality" remains a point of legal contention, as evidenced by cases such as *Burge v. Swarbrick,* which highlight the ongoing difficulty in distinguishing between purely functional designs and protectable artistic works (*Burge v Swarbrick* 2007).

The emergence of copyright does not require awareness or comprehension of the process of expressing will. When an artist paints a picture while intoxicated, their free will is suppressed, but copyright still arises. This is further confirmed by the fact that a minor also has free will and can hold copyright, even if they do not realise the significance of their own actions. Even a newborn child can exercise their free will through the prism of legal personality, acquiring rights and obligations without fully understanding their actions. For example, when a young child draws chaotic lines on a sheet of paper, they are exercising personal non-property rights associated with creative activity. In this case, they exercise the right to artistic creativity in the context of their legal personality, not their legal capacity (Savchenko 2022, 75).

Furthermore, the principle of voluntariness does not strictly apply to copyright. If an author creates a work under duress, as a result of deception, or out of extreme necessity, their free will is subject to external influence, but copyright still arises because the work is the result of a legal act, not a legal transaction.

When an author consciously creates an object of copyright, they exercise their own free will in the form of creative activity. The emergence and exercise of copyright do not require registration or any other special formalities. Even the use of the © symbol or the official registration of a work is the author's right, not an obligation, and is done at their discretion (*Pro avtors'ke pravo i sumizhni prava* [On Copyright and Related Rights] 2022, art. 9).

Similarly, by the author's free will, a work is given a specific objective form (written, material, digital, etc.), which is the sole condition for the emergence of copyright (Ibid., art. 9, para. 1). At this moment, free will transitions from an idea or thought (an internal form of will) into an objective form with an external manifestation. Without this transformation, free will remains an internal component of the personality, regulated by the right to freedom of thought. During the creation of a work, the right to freedom of thought is transformed into copyright. In the case of co-authorship, the free wills of all authors are coordinated to achieve a common goal, and the copyrighted work becomes the result of their collective will.

The legal status of objects created using computer programs, particularly Artificial Intelligence (AI), warrants specialized analysis. Under current legislation, if an object is generated solely as a result of a computer program's functioning—differing from existing works but created without the direct participation of a natural person—a special *sui generis* right arises, and the object is classified as "non-original" (Ibid., art. 33). Such objects are excluded from traditional copyright protection (Ibid., art. 8, para. 4), which is reserved strictly for the results of human creative activity.

Conversely, works created by individuals who utilize computer technologies as tools are not categorized as non-original computer-generated objects (Ibid., art. 33). This creates a nuanced conflict: for an object to merit copyright protection, its creation must be linked to the direct participation of a natural person, yet the law does not define the requisite degree of participation. This ambiguity suggests that even a minimal level of human interaction might prevent an object from falling into the *sui generis* category.

When a person employs a program like a text editor, their participation is indisputable. However, the generation of content via AI—such as poetry from ChatGPT or images from Midjourney—also involves human participation through the entry of technical prompts and commands. Because this participation is direct, the *sui generis* right to non-original objects may technically only apply when a program operates with zero human input, a scenario currently deemed improbable. This relationship is functionally analogous to a work created on commission, where a customer provides a technical task to a performer; by extension, the user sets the parameters for the program that executes the object.

Determining the required degree of direct participation is of fundamental importance, as this unresolved ambiguity complicates the practical application of Article 33 of the Law of Ukraine "On Copyright and Related Rights." The central legal tension lies in the threshold of originality: is a marginal intervention—such as editing an AI-generated text by adding a comma or splitting a sentence—sufficient to transform a *sui generis* object into a "work" protected by copyright?

Under the current framework, this lack of a defined "modicum of creativity" creates a significant loophole. If any human touch, however mechanical, were to qualify as "direct participation," the distinction between copyright-protected works and non-original computer-generated objects would effectively collapse. This necessitates a more robust legislative approach. It is advisable to supplement Article 33 with specific norms defining the requisite degree of human intellectual effort. Such criteria should distinguish between:

1. Human-Assisted Creation: Where the natural person makes creative, individualized choices regarding the structure, style, or specific elements of the output, thereby retaining copyright.
2. Purely Technical Generation: Where the person merely activates the software or provides basic prompts, resulting in a non-original object subject to *sui generis* protection.

This clarification would resolve the current legal vacuum, ensuring that only works reflecting the "personal touch" of a human author receive the 70-year term of protection, while purely technical outputs remain within the 25-year *sui generis* regime.

Free will possesses distinct significance depending on whether it is applied to the author's personal non-property (moral) rights or their economic rights. In the context of moral rights—often referred to as the "moral rights of the author" (Ennan 2021) —free will is manifested through their conscious and active exercise. These rights are deeply tied to the author's persona and include:

1. The right of attribution, which allows the author to demand formal recognition of their authorship.
2. The right to anonymity, enabling the author to prohibit the use of their name in connection with the work.
3. The right to a pseudonym, granting the freedom to choose an alternative creative identity.
4. The right of integrity, which empowers the author to preserve the work's original form and oppose any distortion or alteration made without their explicit consent.
5. The right to title, allowing the author to name the work or leave it untitled according to their artistic vision.
6. The right to dedication, which involves the voluntary act of dedicating the work to a specific person, event, or date (*Pro avtors'ke pravo i sumizhni prava* [On Copyright and Related Rights] 2022, art. 11).

Because these rights are inalienable and closely linked to the creator's internal volition, their exercise represents a pure manifestation of free will that remains independent of the work's commercial exploitation. All of these rights are specifically aimed at protecting the free will that was embodied in the creation of the copyrighted work. Each work is imbued with the unique spiritual and intellectual content that the author invested in it, making the work an extension of the author's personality.

The manifestation of free will in an author's moral rights frequently coincides with its manifestation in other personal non-property rights that ensure social existence. For example, the right of attribution and the right to use a pseudonym are intrinsically linked to the broader right to a name. Similarly, the right of integrity and the right to dedicate a work directly stem from the constitutional right to freedom of creative activity.

Therefore, we can conclude that one of the primary functions of this category of rights is to safeguard the free will expressed in a work of literature, art, or science. These rights exist in a complex relationship with volition: some cannot be exercised without an active expression of free will, some serve to limit it in certain social contexts, and others function as the definitive mode of its implementation in the legal sphere.

In the author's economic (property) rights, free will is of more fundamental importance, as it involves the conscious exercise of ownership over the work, which has a connection to free will analogous to that of other property rights. The copyright holder has the right to use the work in any way, as well as the exclusive right to permit or prohibit its use by others (Ibid., art. 12, para. 1), and to transfer (alienate) these rights in whole or in part (Ibid., art. 12, para. 2).

It is thanks to the free will of the copyright holder that the following actions occur: reproduction; inclusion in a collective work; distribution of copies; public performance and display; public communication; translation; adaptation; arrangement; and other similar alterations.

Copyright infringement involves interfering with the copyright holder's free will. In the absence of permission to distribute a work, the author's free will is aimed at restricting the use of the intellectual property object. Some of the most common examples of such violations are unauthorised copying of text or images, uploading a work to a web resource without permission, and digital reproduction (Logvynenko, Karikh, and Dykovets 2019, 23). When a copyrighted work is used without the author's consent, the inviolability of their free will—which was not directed at granting permission—is violated.

These situations must be distinguished from the free use of a work without the author's consent, a context in which a delicate balance is struck between public and private interests (Trotska 2016, 32). This dynamic presents a direct contrast between public and individual free will. The specific list of such "fair use" or "fair dealing" exceptions is codified in Articles 22–28 of the Law of Ukraine "On Copyright and Related Rights."

Judicial practice indicates that establishing the lawfulness of such use often hinges on an examination of the defendant's purpose—an inquiry that is difficult to resolve without resorting to general civil law principles such as good faith and reasonableness (Pryimenko 2021, 67). This trend further confirms the primacy of public interests over private ones in specific regulatory contexts. As R. E. Ennan notes, the trajectory of EU intellectual property law shows a shifting balance of interests from creators toward commercial users (Ennan 2010).

This developmental vector poses a significant threat to the autonomy of individual free will. We support the position of scholars who emphasize that even specialized international instruments recognize the imperative to find an equitable equilibrium between the rights of creators and society's access to cultural heritage (Yurynets, Bielkin, and Bielkin 2019, 63). The preservation of this balance is essential to ensure that the public will does not entirely eclipse the creative volition that serves as the foundation of intellectual property.

Special attention should be paid to copyright in a work created for hire or on commission. In this case, the exercise of the right to creative activity occurs under the influence of the customer or employer who initiates the process. On the one hand, the creation happens at the author's free will; on the other, it is the free will of the customer or employer that necessitates the work's creation. This construction results in a specific distribution of rights and obligations.

Ukrainian civil legislation explicitly proclaims the inviolability of the author's free will, realized through the inalienability of moral rights (*Pro avtors'ke pravo i sumizhni prava* [On Copyright and Related Rights] 2022, art. 11) and the statutory declaration that these rights in a work made for hire belong to the employee whose creative labor produced the work (Ibid., art. 14, para. 1). This framework preserves the essential link between the creator's internal volition and the external result of their labor, even within a commercial context.

Simultaneously, the legal system safeguards the rights of the customer or employer, whose will is recognized as the foundational catalyst for the work's creation. This protection is codified in the legal construction where economic rights to a work made for hire are transferred to the employer in full from the moment of creation, unless otherwise stipulated by law or the employment contract (Ibid., art. 14, para. 2). This norm acknowledges the employer's will as the driving force, which typically manifests in two distinct forms:

1. Direct Instruction: Where the employer commissions a specific object, such as a private photo shoot or a targeted technical report.
2. Performance of Duties: Where the creation occurs within the general scope of employment without a specific order—for instance, a scientist at a research institution selecting a topic and publishing a monograph.

In both scenarios, even in the absence of a direct assignment for a specific work, the author exercises their will at the employer's behest. This position rests on the rationale that the employer hired the employee precisely to generate intellectual property; therefore, any creative output produced in the course of their duties is effectively executed by the employer's overarching will and commission.

For related rights, free will carries a significance analogous to its role in copyright, though the subject matter and legal objects are distinct. The subjects of related rights include:

1. Performers (e.g., actors, singers, musicians);
2. Phonogram producers and videogram producers;
3. Broadcasting organizations;
4. Heirs and successors of these entities (*Pro avtors'ke pravo i sumizhni prava* [On Copyright and Related Rights] 2022, art. 35, para. 2).

In instances where a single individual holds both copyright and related rights, the manifestation of free will is unified and requires no external coordination. However, when these rights are distributed among different participants, a coordination of wills becomes necessary. In this dynamic, the author's free will traditionally remains dominant, as related rights are often derived from the underlying copyrighted work. This hierarchy is justified by the chronological and creative sequence of production; for instance, the performance of a song is necessarily preceded by its composition.

This conceptual framework has long dominated legal science, though related rights have only recently undergone comprehensive harmonization, catalyzed first by international treaties and subsequently by EU legislators (Nordemann, Vinck, and Hertin 1990, 127). C. Sganga further argues that contemporary national laws and EU directives signal an intention to utilize related rights as a functional, practical tool designed to address specific market needs within the broader architecture of copyright law (Sganga 2021).

The change in the legal understanding of related rights is connected to the fact that, in some cases, they arise without a connection to a copyrighted work and do not depend on the author's free will. An example is an improvisation without a pre-prepared work. In this case, free will is aimed at creating related rights, and copyright may not arise at all. An example of this is a lecturer's speech without prior preparation, which is not fixed in any material form.

The presence of free will is not a mandatory condition for the emergence and exercise of related rights, which is confirmed by the absence of any formal requirements (*Pro avtors'ke pravo i sumizhni prava* [On Copyright and Related Rights] 2022, art. 36, para. 3). Regardless of their awareness, a participant in a legal relationship becomes the holder of related rights from the fact of each performance, production of a phonogram/videogram, or first broadcast (Ibid., art. 36, para. 1).

However, such cases require a clear qualification of their lawfulness. If a phonogram producer acts without the consent of the rightsholder, their actions are recognized as piracy—a type of use of objects without prior permission (Shtefan 2023, 24). In this case, the free will of the rightsholder, who did not consent to the use of their object, is affected.

The infringement of related rights has gained significant prominence in the digital era, particularly regarding the unauthorized dissemination of digital content. If an individual posts a digital copy of a musical work on a social media platform, this act may constitute a violation of related rights. However, such digital sharing is conceptually compared to traditional behaviors, such as recording a song onto a storage device for playback in a vehicle or lending a physical book to another person.

These scenarios spark intense debate, particularly regarding the Digital Millennium Copyright Act (DMCA). Critics argue that the DMCA—a primary tool utilized by platforms like Google to enforce intellectual property—is frequently directed against ordinary users rather than large-scale infringers (*Unintended Consequences* 2010). This creates a direct opposition between the user's free will and the rightsholder's interests.

Nevertheless, even when a work is used for personal purposes, the user's free will cannot be recognized as dominant over the author's. By distributing copies, the rightsholder grants permission for use only within the strict boundaries established by law. In Ukrainian legislation, this principle is reinforced by the statutory declaration that related rights and the right of ownership over the material object in which they are embodied are independent of one another (*Pro avtors'ke pravo i sumizhni prava* [On Copyright and Related Rights] 2022, art. 36, para. 2). This legal separation ensures that possessing a physical or digital copy does not grant the user the volitional authority to redistribute the underlying intellectual property.

Therefore, related rights arise as a manifestation of free will when their objects are created consciously, as well as during performance, production, distribution, and the transfer of rights. It is important to note that the transfer of economic rights to copyrighted and related objects occurs as a result of the rightsholder's free will when based on a contract, but may not take into account their will in the case of inheritance by law.

Summarizing the significance of free will within the realms of copyright and related rights, it is evident that copyright possesses a unique legal character: while a manifestation of free will is sufficient for a right to a work to arise, such rights can emerge even in its absence. This is due to the lack of a regulatory requirement for a conscious, formalized expression of will, meaning the principle of voluntariness does not strictly apply to the *inception* of the right.

If an author creates a work under duress, their free will is undeniably compromised by external influence; nonetheless, copyright still arises. This occurs because the creation of a work is classified as a legal act (an objective fact of creation) rather than a legal transaction, which would require a defect-free will. Conversely, when an author creates a work consciously, they exercise their free will through the medium of creative activity. In scenarios involving co-authorship, the wills of all participants must be coordinated, resulting in an object that serves as the embodiment of a collective free will.

Within the sphere of the author's moral rights, free will is manifested through their conscious exercise, specifically aimed at safeguarding the creative intent invested in the work. In contrast, free will takes on a more fundamental, proprietary importance regarding economic rights. Here, it involves the conscious exercise of ownership, establishing a connection to volition similar to that found in traditional property rights.

When a work is created for hire or on commission, the creative activity is exercised under the influence—and typically the specific instruction—of the customer or employer. For related rights, free will carries a similar weight; however, its presence is not a prerequisite for their emergence, a fact confirmed by the absence of formal requirements for the legal birth of these rights.

5.2. Free Will in Industrial Property Law and Legal Means of Individualising Participants in Civil Turnover

The primary feature of industrial property law is its connection to economic activity. Unlike copyright and related rights, industrial property law is directly related to satisfying the interests of a business entity, is professional in nature, and the manifestation of free will within it is more complex.

According to the continental tradition, patent law is part of industrial property law (*propriété industrielle* or *gewerblicher Rechtsschutz*). However, the increasingly popular Anglo-American nomenclature is somewhat broader, encompassing industrial property law, copyright, and related rights within the general field of intellectual property law (Menell 2019).

The Paris Convention for the Protection of Industrial Property serves as the cornerstone regulatory act in this field; however, it notably fails to provide a formal definition of "industrial property rights" (Paris Convention 1883). Ukrainian legislation similarly lacks a unified definition. Historically, the statutory framework primarily offered a taxonomy of intellectual property objects utilized in business operations, which included:

1. Inventions and utility models;
2. Industrial designs;
3. Plant varieties and animal breeds;
4. Trademarks;
5. Commercial names;
6. Geographical indications;
7. Trade secrets;
8. Computer programs (*Hospodars'kyi kodeks Ukrainy* [Commercial Code of Ukraine] 2003, art. 155, para. 1).

This categorization aligns with the structure of the Paris Convention, which divides industrial property into two broad functional groups: first, the results of scientific and technical activity (inventions, utility models, and industrial designs); and second, the means of individualizing participants in civil circulation (trade names, trademarks, and indications of origin) (Yakubivskyi 2021, 107). Beyond these traditional categories, legal doctrine distinguishes non-traditional objects of intellectual property, encompassing discoveries, rationalization proposals, integrated circuit layouts, trade secrets, and plant varieties (Buletsa and Chepys 2019).

Thus, the main components of industrial property law are patent law and the means of individualising participants in civil turnover, goods, and services. It can be assumed that the primary specific of the relationship between these intellectual property objects and free will lies in their purpose: application in the business sphere to improve results, achieve economic goals more effectively, and provide identification to distinguish from other participants in economic relations.

Industrial property is understood as the social (production and economic) relations that arise from a producer's monopoly use of legally protected intellectual solutions and market identifiers in the process of organising and carrying out its economic activity (Koval 2013, 18).

K. V. Overkovsky proposes to define industrial property rights as a set of economic (exclusive) rights to objects of industrial property (Koval 2013, 69). The emphasis on economic rights is justified by the author on the grounds that, given the intangible nature of intellectual creations, they must be expressed and fixed in the form of an absolute right—namely, the economic rights to the corresponding results—to be introduced into market circulation (Ibid., 65).

In this context, we see a certain similarity in the role of free will in these rights and in copyright and related rights. Free will becomes the basis for creating an object of industrial property, but for rights to arise over it, that free will must acquire an external, material form.

R. L. Okediji, M. A. Bagley, and other prominent scholars maintain a clear distinction between the broader field of industrial property law and the specific domain of patent law (Okediji and Bagley 2014). A fundamental divergence exists in how these legal regimes interact with human volition: while copyright protects the individual free will expressed as creative activity, industrial property law specifically protects the form of the realization of that will.

Consequently, industrial property objects are subject to a more rigorous mechanism for the emergence of rights. Unlike the automatic vesting of copyright, free will in the industrial context must undergo state recognition—typically in the form of a patent—to be legally operative. This requirement is normatively anchored in Part 1 of Article 459 of the Civil Code of Ukraine, which stipulates that an invention is eligible for protection only if it is fundamentally new, involves a distinct inventive step, and remains industrially applicable.

The criteria for this state validation vary across legal systems. In the United States, for instance, there is an additional utility requirement that demands a demonstration of specific, substantial, and credible utility (*Conditions of Patentability* 2010). This indicates that for industrial property, the creator's free will is not sufficient in isolation; it must be channeled through objective, socially beneficial criteria to merit a state-sanctioned monopoly.

The legal landscape of industrial property necessitates a precise reconciliation between the individual will of the creator—such as an inventor—and the will of the state. This interaction is not a limitation of creative freedom; rather, it is a process of verification. The state must formally recognize the novelty, inventive step, and industrial applicability of the creator's ideas before granting exclusive proprietary rights. If an application for industrial property rights is denied, the expression of free will is not extinguished; it simply shifts into the sphere of copyright, which is predicated solely on the objective fact of creation rather than formal registration.

Consequently, to acquire the enhanced protections offered by patent law, the material form of the subject's manifestation of free will must satisfy specific regulatory criteria. The embodiment of this will, particularly through an invention or utility model, can manifest as a product (such as a device or substance) or a process (a specific method) (*Pro okhoronu prav na vynakhody i korysni modeli* [On the Protection of Rights to Inventions and Utility Models] 1993, art. 6, para. 2).

In essence, at the moment an intellectual property object emerges, free will first attains an external form protected by copyright. This "base" form can then be transformed into an object of industrial property law, provided it aligns with the state's requirements for technical innovation and social utility.

In particular, an invention must satisfy the criterion of novelty, meaning the essence of the technical solution must not have formed part of the state of the art prior to the application filing date. During this evaluation, the state of the art encompasses the content of any prior patent applications filed within Ukraine. The fundamental importance of this criterion lies in the protection of the rights of third parties and the prevention of plagiarism.

As L. Walter and F. C. Schnittker observe, because a patentable invention constitutes a form of legal monopoly, a rigorous qualitative analysis is indispensable to ensure that such monopolies are granted only for genuinely innovative achievements (Walter and

Schnittker 2016). Any failure to strictly enforce this rule would infringe upon the free will of existing rightsholders or unfairly restrict the rights of future innovators.

The legal definition of "novelty" is thus a cornerstone of judicial practice, directly impacting the validity of a patent. This is exemplified by a resolution of the Cassation Economic Court within the Supreme Court, which overturned lower court decisions and remanded a case involving the invalidation of a utility model patent for a "Pharmaceutical composition based on chondroitin sulfate and glucosamine sulfate." The core of the dispute rested on a lack of confidence in the expert's conclusion regarding the fulfilllment of the novelty criterion (*Postanova Kasatsiinoho hospodars'koho sudu u skladi Verkhovnoho Sudu* [Resolution of the Cassation Economic Court within the Supreme Court] 2020).

The next criterion for patentability is industrial applicability. This means that the solution must be capable of being implemented in practice. A classic example of a solution that fails this criterion is a perpetual motion machine, which contradicts fundamental physical laws. The primary purpose of testing for industrial applicability is to establish whether the invention can achieve the declared result in any field of social production. This requirement includes the "utility" criterion characteristic of the Anglo-American patent system. If an invention cannot be industrially applied, it cannot be used or scaled and will not bring social benefit. While a copyrighted work may have no utility, this is unacceptable for a patented object. This implies the need to adjust the free will of the right-holder, which should be aimed at the mandatory use of the patented object.

The final criterion for patentability is the inventive step. This criterion can be subjective, as it depends on the discretion of the specialist who assesses it. Consequently, compliance with the "inventive step" condition is the most debatable (Tomachynski 2022, 112).

An invention is deemed to involve an inventive step if, for a person skilled in the art, it is not obvious from the existing state of the art (*Pro zatverdzhennia Pravyl skladannia…* [On Approval of the Rules for Drafting…]. 2024, para. 2.4). This "person skilled in the art" is defined as an individual possessing standard knowledge and average skills in the relevant technical field, based on information that was publicly accessible prior to the application filing date (Ibid.).

To accurately evaluate the inventive step, the state of the art is comprehensively considered, including the technical content of any previously filed patent applications (Ibid.). This requirement ensures that the state recognizes the creator's free will only when the result surpasses a routine or predictable application of existing knowledge, thereby maintaining the balance between individual reward and the public domain.

Beyond the core criteria of novelty and utility, legal systems often impose additional patentability requirements that reflect the specific nature of the intellectual property. For instance, an industrial design must possess an individual character, ensuring that the overall impression it produces on an informed user differs from any previously available design (*Tsyvil'nyi kodeks Ukrainy* [Civil Code of Ukraine] 2003, art. 461, para. 1).

Furthermore, the manifestation of a creator's free will through industrial property is subject to ethical boundaries. Both national and international frameworks, such as the European Patent Convention (EPC), exclude from patentability inventions that are contrary to morality or public order (*Convention on the Grant of European Patents* 1973, art. 53(a)). This ensures that while the state recognizes individual innovation, it maintains the authority to negate the legal recognition of will if the resulting object violates fundamental societal values.

In summary, the criteria for patentability are not designed to restrict free will but to establish the necessary conditions that its external, material embodiment must satisfy to attain the status of an industrial property object. This transition from a subjective idea to a state-sanctioned monopoly ensures that individual innovation aligns with broader objective standards.

Furthermore, the legislator determines the parameters of use for such objects to ensure they serve the public interest. This regulatory oversight mandates that an object must be utilized in a manner consistent with ethical standards; specifically, the patent must either presuppose a moral application or explicitly delineate a restricted mode of use that conforms to societal norms (Rogers 2007). This confirms that while the creator's volition is the primary catalyst for industrial property, its legal recognition is contingent upon its alignment with the collective will and public order.

The manifestation of free will in industrial property law depends on the subject of the rights. O. V. Rozgon emphasizes that a key problem requiring research is the regulation of relations in which a creator (author, inventor) working in a science park or as an employee can commercialise and protect their intellectual rights (Rozhon 2020, 177).

The free will of the inventor and the creator of an industrial design is realized primarily through the process of creating the intellectual property object, as well as through the subsequent exercise of their personal non-property and economic rights—contingent upon these rights not being legally assigned to another entity, such as an employer. In this context, the invention serves as the tangible embodiment of free will within the sphere of intellectual and mental activity.

A second distinct category of subjects in industrial property law encompasses any natural or legal persons who did not independently create the intellectual product but hold personal non-property and/or economic rights by virtue of law or agreement (Kovalchuk 2014, 153). The free will of these subjects is manifested through the strategic exercise of their economic rights, which include:

1. The right to use the invention, utility model, or industrial design in commercial or industrial processes;
2. The exclusive right to authorize its use by others through the issuance of licenses;
3. The exclusive right to prevent and prohibit unlawful use by third parties;
4. Other economic rights specifically established by statutory law (*Tsyvil'nyi kodeks Ukrainy* [Civil Code of Ukraine] 2003, art. 464, para. 1).

This structure ensures that the volitional intent of the rightsholder—whether the original creator or a successor—remains the central mechanism for the exploitation and protection of industrial innovations.

In the context of industrial property objects created on commission or within the scope of employment, the employer's (or customer's) free will is recognized as primary. Individual labor relations involve a reciprocal framework where the employee performs a specific labor function, and the employer provides the necessary resources and remuneration (Sychov 2009, 7). Consequently, the creation of an object is viewed as the fulfilllment of labor or contractual obligations, meaning the right to obtain a patent or certificate vests with the employer or customer.

This construction is codified in the laws On the Protection of Rights to Industrial Designs (1993, art. 8) and On the Protection of Rights to Inventions and Utility Models (1993, art. 9). However, a nuanced approach is found in Article 429, paragraph 2 of the Civil Code of Ukraine, which stipulates that economic intellectual property rights to objects created in connection with official duties belong to the employee and employer jointly, unless otherwise stipulated by contract. T. V. Yaroshevska argues that this provision fundamentally altered the regulation of works made for hire (Yaroshevska 2017, 93).

We contend that there is no conflict between the Civil Code and specialized laws; the latter simply provide the procedural mechanisms for exercising these rights. The employer's will remains prioritized: only if they fail to exercise their will to obtain a patent can the creator do so. For example, regarding a service invention, an employer has four months after notification to file an application, transfer the right, or classify the invention as confidential, while simultaneously concluding a remuneration agreement (*Pro okhoronu prav na vynakhody i korysni modeli* [On the Protection of Rights to Inventions and Utility Models] 1993, art. 9, para. 3). If the employer remains inactive during this period, the registration right passes to the inventor, though the employer retains a preferential right to acquire a license (Ibid., art. 9, para. 4).

In addition to the will of primary and secondary subjects, it is necessary to consider the will of intellectual property representatives (patent attorneys) and the national intellectual property authority.

The status of patent attorneys is regulated at the legislative level in many countries, including Germany, France, and Poland, which indicates the importance of these legal relations (Ohneviuk 2010, 228). Representatives in intellectual property cases are referred to by various titles, such as Patent Attorneys, Patent Agents, or Benrishi.

The legal status of patent attorneys in Ukraine is governed by Order of the Ministry of Economy of Ukraine No. 20599 and the Law of Ukraine "On Copyright and Related Rights." The primary task of these professionals is the representation of interests within the sphere of intellectual property. This mandate includes the authority to sign applications, modify invention descriptions, withdraw filings, and represent right-holders before both state and judicial bodies (*Pro zatverdzhennia Polozhennia…* [On Approval of the Regulation…] 2023).

Of particular importance in the context of free will is the capacity of patent attorneys to prepare documentation, submit filings to the Ukrainian National Office for Intellectual Property and Innovations (UKRNOIVI), and amend invention descriptions. These actions constitute a direct manifestation of the patent attorney's professional will, the consequences of which fundamentally affect the rights of industrial property subjects. For example, if an attorney's modification to an application leads UKRNOIVI to refuse the issuance of a patent, a causal link is established between the attorney's actions and the negative result. Effectively, this reveals a specific legal construction: (1) the subject of industrial property rights exercises free will by creating an object and deciding to seek registration; and (2) the IP representative exercises their own will in the procedural preparation, which may lead to the non-realization of the subject's original intent to obtain state protection.

The realization of free will for the emergence of industrial property rights necessitates a coordination of wills: the individual will of the creator and the public will of the state, represented by

UKRNOIVI. The creator's individual will is not sufficient in isolation; the acquisition of rights to an invention, utility model, or industrial design must be certified by a formal patent or certificate (*Tsyvil'nyi kodeks Ukrainy* [Civil Code of Ukraine] 2003, art. 462, para. 1).

If UKRNOIVI refuses to issue a patent, this does not nullify the fact of the invention's creation, but it does preclude the acquisition of industrial property rights. In such cases, the creator's expressed free will is restricted to the form of a copyrighted object, which arises by the mere fact of creation without the need for state recognition.

Thus, the acquisition of industrial property rights requires the reconciliation of the creator's free will with the public will of the state.

Special attention should be paid to the manifestation of free will in the intellectual property rights to a commercial name, a trademark, and a geographical indication.

The primary purpose of these objects is the individualization of goods and participants in economic circulation. Therefore, at the heart of these rights is a free will aimed at distinguishing oneself from other subjects and objects. These IP objects are characterised by a special semantic content in the relationship between consumers and businesses, allowing them to perform discourse functions in the cultural space of a consumer society and, ultimately, to be recognisable, dynamic, and unique (Zhukova 2021, 132).

O. P. Svitlychnyi defines a commercial name as a necessary means of individualising legal entities, which allows one firm to be distinguished from another (Svitlichnyi 2016, 21).

However, this position contains a fundamental error, as a commercial name can be held by more than just a legal entity. This approach is enshrined in the Civil Code of Ukraine, where the subject of a commercial name is recognized as a "person," without emphasis on its legal form. It is determined that legal protection is granted to a commercial name if it makes it possible to distinguish one person from others and does not mislead consumers about their true activities (*Tsyvil'nyi kodeks Ukrainy* [Civil Code of Ukraine] 2003, art. 489, para. 1).

There are other requirements. O. O. Pidopryhora adds that the name should correspond to the nature of the activity, a concept known in foreign legislation as the "principle of the truthfulness of the firm" (Pidopryhora 2003, 39). Therefore, the expression of free will in a commercial name is variable but not absolute; it is determined by the name's purpose, the need to distinguish business entities, and the prevention of consumer deception.

For intellectual property rights to a commercial name to arise, only a manifestation of the business entity's free will is sufficient. Such rights are valid from the moment of the name's first use and are protected without mandatory application or registration, regardless of whether the commercial name is part of a trademark (*Tsyvil'nyi kodeks Ukrainy* [Civil Code of Ukraine] 2003, art. 489, para. 2).

A commercial name is the embodiment of free will, as it is a manifestation of the intellectual and creative activity of a business entity. When the right-holder is a legal entity, it represents the collective free will of its founders and the individuals who develop the name. If the name is developed by another person on commission, the free will of the customer and the executor is coordinated.

In effect, a commercial name is a means of self-identification for a business entity, which may not be directly derived from its legal name. For example, a legal entity named "South LLC" may give its restaurant the name "West." From the moment this name is first used, rights to the commercial name arise.

The ability of a sole proprietor to exercise their will in choosing a commercial name is more debatable. M. O. Stefanchuk and L. L. Davyd draw attention to Article 159 of the Commercial Code, which stated that a citizen-entrepreneur has the right to declare their surname or given name as a commercial name (Stefanchuk and Davyd 2014, 53). As the scholars note, the use of the conjunction "or" in this norm complicates the situation, as a literal interpretation suggests that a sole proprietor cannot use their surname and given name simultaneously (Ibid., p. 53). This raises the question of the legal status of the name an entrepreneur gives to their business. It can be assumed that when an entrepreneur names their restaurant "West," this name is protected only by copyright, not by industrial property law. We recognize this situation as an unjustified restriction on an individual's free will, which requires regulatory clarification.

The manifestation of free will in trademark rights is almost the same as in a commercial name. The main difference is that the acquisition of intellectual property rights in a trademark is certified by a certificate (*Tsyvil'nyi kodeks Ukrainy* [Civil Code of Ukraine] 2003, art. 494, para. 1).

A trademark and a commercial name are different objects of intellectual property, but words can be both (Stefanchuk 2005a, 238). In terms of their content, these objects can be identical. In effect, a trademark is a commercial name that has undergone state registration.

This creates the need to reconcile the free will of the subject with the will of the state. In this, we see a similarity between the significance of free will in trademarks and in patent law.

Therefore, trademarks are the embodiment of a business entity's free will in the form of a sign suitable for distinguishing its goods or services from those of others, and this requires coordination with the will of the state through registration.

The final means of individualization is a geographical indication. The relevance of this issue is confirmed by the fact that as of 2020, over 3,000 geographical indications were protected in Ukraine, most registered under the Association Agreement (Kodynets and Sidorenko 2020, 25).

A geographical indication is defined as the name of a place identifying a product that originates from that location and possesses a specific quality, reputation, or other characteristic essentially attributable to that origin, provided at least one stage of production is carried out in that territory (*Pro pravovu okhoronu heohrafychnykh zaznachen* [On the Legal Protection of Geographical Indications] 1999, art. 1, para. 3).

This concept underscores the limited nature of the free will of right-holders, as they cannot independently determine or invent the place of origin. An individual can only exercise their volition when selecting the geographical location of a production stage, which is subsequently reflected in the registration of rights. This correlates with the conclusion that a geographical indication is one of the few objects that does not result from creative activity but is nevertheless protected by intellectual property law (Kodynets 2007).

O. O. Karashchuk notes that although the creative element is absent, the intellectual (informational) element remains, as the geographical indication provides information about the product's place of origin and its associated qualities or reputation (Karashchuk 2019, 92). This legal status significantly limits the subject's free will, as a geographical indication is not a manifestation of creative activity, and the intellectual activity is embodied only as information reflecting the actual place of production, not the will of the subject. In fact, a geographical indication is a type of information that belongs to the results of human intellectual activity but does not contain signs of creativity (Kokhanovska 2006, 214).

As with some other industrial property objects, the emergence of rights to a geographical indication requires the coordination of the will of the producer with the will of the state, as the right arises from the date of state registration (*Tsyvil'nyi kodeks Ukrainy* [Civil Code of Ukraine] 2003, art. 501, para. 1). The business entity's free will is reflected in submitting the application, and the state's will is reflected in its approval or rejection.

The business entity's free will is manifested when it chooses the form of the geographical indication. For example, a product may be labelled as made in Kharkiv, in Ukraine, or in Europe. Products made in EU member states often bear the inscription "Made in EU." Another example is indicating that a product is manufactured in one country but designed in another ("Designed in California. Assembled in China") or indicating only the country of design ("French design").

At the same time, free will is manifested in the abuse of geographical indications, particularly when a finished product is brought to another country, undergoes minor modifications (painting, assembly, packaging), and that country is indicated as the place of origin.

Additionally, the importance of free will for non-traditional intellectual property objects, such as discoveries, rationalisation proposals, integrated circuit layouts, trade secrets, plant varieties, and animal breeds, warrants special attention. However, due to their specificity, such an analysis will be conducted separately, outside the scope of this study.

As we can see, free will becomes the basis for creating an object of industrial property, but for rights to arise, it must acquire an external, material form. Patent law requires the coordination of the creator's individual will with the will of the state, which must recognize the object's novelty, inventive step, and industrial applicability.

At the moment of its creation, the object first acquires copyright protection, which can then be transformed into an object of industrial property law if it meets the regulatory requirements. The criteria for patentability are not aimed at restricting free will but at creating the conditions that its external embodiment must meet to obtain legal status.

Conclusions

1. Free will possesses profound theoretical and practical significance within intellectual property (IP) law, serving as the catalyst for determining the content, objects, and grounds for the accrual and exercise of copyright and related rights. The public interest necessitates the development of copyright as a primary mechanism to foster innovation across cultural, scientific, and technical domains. Consequently, the public will should be oriented toward stimulating creative activity by encouraging individual manifestation of will. However, the regulatory framework of IP law reveals an inherent tension between the public interest in fostering creativity and the imposition of normative restrictions.
2. A defining characteristic of copyright is that the mere manifestation of free will is sufficient for the accrual of rights to a work. Notably, these rights may emerge even in the absence of a con-

scious or comprehended expression of will, as the act of creation does not strictly require a formal volitional intent. Conversely, in instances involving objects generated by computer programs without the direct intervention of a natural person, a special right (*sui generis*) is applied to govern the legal status of the output.

3. The principle of voluntariness, as conceptualized in contract law, does not directly apply to the initial accrual of copyright. Even if an author creates a work under duress, deception, or extreme necessity—situations where free will is compromised by external pressure—copyright still arises. This is because the creation of a work is classified as a legal act rather than a legal transaction. When an author consciously produces a work, they realize their free will through the exercise of the right to freedom of creative expression.
4. Through the author's free will, a work is endowed with a specific objective form (written, material, digital, etc.), which remains the fundamental condition for the emergence of copyright. At this juncture, free will transitions from a subjective idea or internal thought to an objective, external manifestation. Without this transformation, the creative impulse remains an internal component of the personality, protected only under the right to freedom of thought. Thus, the creative process serves as the mechanism through which the freedom of thought is legally transformed into copyright.
5. In scenarios of co-authorship, the individual free wills of all contributors are coordinated to achieve a common objective, rendering the work an embodiment of their collective will. This collective nature must be considered when determining the scope of rights and the distribution of economic benefits. In the absence of a specific agreement defining shares, it is presumed that the co-authors' shares are equal, reflecting an equal realization of their respective free wills. Judicial practice should adhere to this principle of equality, rather than proportionality, regardless of the work's specific content.
6. In the sphere of moral rights, free will is manifested through their conscious exercise by the author. In economic rights, however, free will takes on a more foundational role, involving the

conscious exercise of ownership analogous to property rights. The copyright holder's will dictates acts of reproduction, distribution, public performance, translation, and adaptation. Any copyright infringement constitutes an unlawful interference with this will.

7. When a work is created on commission or for hire, the author's creative will is exercised under the influence of the customer or employer. This creates a dual volitional structure: the work is produced by the author's creative effort, yet it is the employer's will that necessitates and directs its creation. This construction results in a specific statutory distribution of rights among the participants, often prioritizing the economic interests of the entity that initiated the creative process.
8. For related rights, free will serves a role similar to that in copyright, though they differ regarding their subject and object. The presence of a conscious manifestation of will is not a mandatory prerequisite for the accrual of related rights, as evidenced by the lack of formal requirements. This necessitates the normative consolidation of the principle that related rights are directly linked to protected creative activity.
9. Related rights manifest as free will when objects—such as performances or broadcasts—are created consciously. However, these rights may also arise unconsciously. While the transfer of economic rights based on a contract is a direct result of the rightsholder's free will, other forms of transfer, such as inheritance by law, may occur independently of the subject's contemporary intent.
10. Patent law requires the individual will of the inventor to be reconciled with the will of the state, which must formally recognize the criteria of novelty, inventive step, and industrial applicability. This requirement does not restrict individual freedom; rather, a refusal of state registration merely shifts the expression of the author's will into the domain of copyright, which is secured by the fact of creation alone.
11. At the moment of creation, an intellectual property object first assumes an external form within the framework of copyright. This status may subsequently be transformed into an object of industrial property law (such as a patent or industrial design)

provided the object satisfies the specific regulatory requirements of the state.

12. The criteria for patentability are not designed to inhibit free will but to establish the objective conditions that its material embodiment must satisfy to attain the legal status of industrial property.
13. The free will of an inventor or the creator of an industrial design is realized both during the creative process and through the subsequent exercise of personal non-property and economic rights. The resulting invention stands as the tangible embodiment of free will realized through intellectual and mental activity.
14. In cases where an industrial property object is created as a work for hire, the free will of the employer or customer is primary. The creator's actions are viewed as the fulfilllment of a labor or contractual obligation, which determines the initial allocation of rights to the resulting object.
15. For commercial names, a manifestation of the business entity's free will through first use is sufficient for protection to accrue. Unlike trademarks, commercial names do not require mandatory registration and are viewed as the embodiment of the entity's creative and commercial will. Conversely, the acquisition of trademark rights requires the coordination of the subject's will with the will of the state, certified by a formal certificate.
16. Trademarks represent the embodiment of a business entity's free will expressed through a sign capable of distinguishing its goods or services. The legal recognition of this intent is contingent upon state registration, which harmonizes the private interest with public order.
17. In the context of geographical indications, the exercise of free will is inherently limited. Right-holders cannot independently determine or invent the product's place of origin, as this is dictated by objective geographical and historical factors. The subject's will is restricted to the choice of the geographical location for a specific production stage.

18. The emergence of rights to a geographical indication necessitates the coordination of the applicant's will with the state's will. The right accrues from the date of state registration, ensuring that the use of the indication conforms to established public standards of origin and quality.

6. Free Will in Inheritance Law

6.1. Free Will in Testate Succession and in an Inheritance Agreement

Most scholars associate inheritance law with the event of a testator's death, suggesting that its subject of regulation is the legal relations that arise thereafter with the participation of heirs (Sus 2022, 491). The primary scholarly debate centers on the formulation of the definition of inheritance law. Some researchers associate it with the transfer of the property rights and obligations of a deceased citizen (Zaika 2007, 19), while others define it through the transfer of rights and duties that belonged to the testator at the moment of death (Kravchyk 2018, 103).

We contend that the existing proposals differ primarily in their level of complexity, leading to various interpretations. The most concise and transparent concept is enshrined in Article 1216 of the Civil Code of Ukraine: inheritance is the transfer of rights and obligations (the estate) from a deceased individual (the decedent or testator) to other persons (the heirs). Generally, inheritance law is aimed at determining the post-mortem fate of property (Stefanchuk 2008, 547). It must be noted that this refers to the future status of property, rather than post-mortem legal relations that can arise prior to the owner's death—such as an inheritance agreement or a will—which function as instruments of the owner's expressed will while they are still living.

Most scholars associate inheritance law with the event of a testator's death, suggesting that its subject of regulation comprises the legal relations that arise thereafter with the participation of heirs (Sus 2022, 491). The primary scholarly debate focuses on the precise definition of inheritance law: some researchers associate it with the transfer of the property rights and obligations of a deceased citizen (Zaika 2007, 19), while others define it through the transfer of rights and duties that belonged to the testator at the moment of death (Kravchyk 2018, 103).

We contend that the existing definitions differ primarily in their level of complexity, leading to various interpretations. The most concise and transparent concept is enshrined in Article 1216 of the Civil Code of Ukraine: inheritance is the transfer of rights and obligations (the estate) from a deceased individual (the decedent or testator) to other persons (the heirs). Generally, inheritance law is aimed at determining the post-mortem fate of property (Stefanchuk 2008, 547). This refers to the future status of the property rather than post-mortem legal relations that can arise prior to the owner's death—such as an inheritance agreement or a will—which function as instruments of the owner's expressed will during their lifetime.

In this sub-branch of civil law, the manifestation of free will is contingent upon the method of transferring rights. A will and an inheritance agreement are predicated on the free will of the property owner, serving as the tangible embodiment of their wishes through a conscious and voluntary expression of intent. Conversely, in the case of inheritance by law (intestate succession), the free will of the decedent is legally irrelevant; in this context, only the desire and consent of the heir to accept the inheritance are considered. This underscores the critical yet heterogeneous role of free will within the various institutions of inheritance law.

A will is a personal disposition of an individual in the event of their death regarding their property, including property rights and obligations (Nestertsova-Sobakar 2017, 49). A will reflects the testator's internal will and a presumption of its superiority over inheritance by law, a presumption that can only be denied by a direct indication of the law.

The testator independently determines what property, in what amount, and to whom they want to transfer it and can disinherit a person from among the legal heirs. In this case, that person will not receive the right to inherit (*Tsyvil'nyi kodeks Ukrainy* [Civil Code of Ukraine] 2003, art. 1235, para. 2).

In this matter, the testator's individual free will prevails over the public will of the state as expressed in the mechanism of intestate succession. However, a will is not absolute, as it cannot deprive persons who are entitled to a compulsory share of the inheritance (Ibid., art. 1235, para. 3). For example, the exclusion from a will of minor, adult disabled children, a disabled spouse, or disabled parents does not negate their right to inherit.

Recognising a will as a legal transaction, we must state the mandatory compliance with regulatory requirements for the emergence and termination of obligations, the connection of which with free will was considered in previous chapters. A will is an agreement made on behalf of one person as a disposition of a purely authoritative nature. Therefore, it cannot be executed through a representative and is a gratuitous, causal, and formal transaction (Zhylinkova 2000, 14).

Ya. Kovalchuk notes that by granting an individual permission to make a will, the national legislator imposed an obligation to comply with the provisions of current law, thereby somewhat limiting their will in resolving issues related to establishing the circle of persons who may accept their property (Kovalchuk 2016, 32). At first glance, the accuracy of this thesis is doubtful, as the author writes about limiting the circle of potential heirs.

However, the Civil Code of Ukraine states that the testator may appoint one or more individuals as their heirs, regardless of any family relationship, as well as other participants in civil relations (*Tsyvil'nyi kodeks Ukrainy* [Civil Code of Ukraine] 2003, art. 1235, para. 1). Although this norm provides broad opportunities for the exercise of free will, the limitations lie in the impossibility of excluding certain persons (those entitled to a compulsory share) from the list of heirs, as noted above.

Making a will is necessary to clarify or, within permissible limits, to alter the post-mortem distribution of the testator's property as established by law. According to official statistics, inheritance by will is significantly less common in Ukraine than intestate succession.

Various theories have been proposed to explain this trend. M. M. Chanieva and N. A. Filipova attribute the Ukrainian practice to a decrease in citizens' income, leading to insufficient funds for state notarization fees, alongside a general distrust of the institution of wills (Chanieva and Filipova 2021, 181). In France, Germany, and Latin American countries, the majority of inheritance also occurs by operation of law, though this is primarily due to high public satisfaction with the default statutory rules (Dutoit 2003; Schmidt 2015; Zimmermann 2015).

Conversely, in Australia and New Zealand, individuals actively prefer to execute wills, believing that the rules of intestate succession do not align with their specific needs or because a will provides a clearer mechanism for establishing the guardianship of their children (Reid, Waal, and Zimmermann 2015).

Generalizing these approaches, it can be concluded that making a will is the preferred instrument when individuals seek to directly express a free will that is not adequately represented by the default rules of intestate succession.

The expression of will through a will is permitted only for a legally defined circle of individuals. T. V. Fedina argues that persons who have not reached the age of eighteen, even those possessing full civil capacity, face limitations in their right to execute a testament, which constitutes a specific restriction of their rights (Fedina 2015, 64). However, this assertion does not align with the provisions of the Civil Code of Ukraine, which explicitly grants the right to make a will to any individual with full civil capacity (*Tsyvil'nyi kodeks Ukrainy* [Civil Code of Ukraine] 2003, art. 1234, para. 1).

Under the emancipation procedure, a minor acquires full civil capacity and the corresponding right to execute a will. Currently, the category of persons excluded from making a will encompasses only legal entities and individuals with incomplete, partial, or limited legal capacity, without specifying further age conditions. This approach has sparked significant scholarly debate. In particular, I. V. Zhylinkova observes that minors with incomplete civil capacity already possess the right to dispose of their earnings and other income; consequently, the transfer of such assets via a will should be statutorily provided (Zhylinkova 2000, 23).

The execution of a will relies on the conditions of voluntariness and awareness, requiring formal certification. The official certifying the document (such as a notary) may remain unaware of its content—as is the case with a secret will—which confirms the dispositive nature of the testament's form. We consider it necessary to normatively consolidate the right of persons with incomplete civil capacity to execute a will. During the certification process, the relevant official verifies the compliance of the testator's expression of will with specific legal requirements, rendering the existing restriction unfounded and an unnecessary barrier to their expression of will.

To draw up a will, the testator's free will alone is insufficient; it must be formally validated through notarial certification (*Pro notariat* [On the Notariate] 1993, art. 34, para. 1) and subsequent entry into the Unified State Register (*Pro zatverdzhennia Polozhennia pro Spadkovyi reiestr* [On Approval of the Regulation on the Inheritance Register] 2011).

In circumstances where a notary is unavailable, certification may be performed by other designated officials (*Pro poriadok posvidchennia zapovitiv…* [On the Procedure for Certifying Wills…] 1994, cl. 1). While this alternative procedure introduces specific complications—such as the mandatory presence of witnesses—it serves as a vital secondary mechanism for the expression of individual volition.

The state actively protects the manifestation of free will in post-mortem relations through a flexible yet structured regulatory framework. For example, if a testator is unable to sign a document due to physical disability, a proxy may sign on their behalf in the presence of the testator and two witnesses. Furthermore, a will need not be handwritten; a notary may transcribe it from the testator's oral instructions, after which it must be read aloud to ensure total correspondence with the testator's intent (*Tsyvil'nyi kodeks Ukrainy* [Civil Code of Ukraine] 2003, art. 1248, para. 2).

In these specific instances, the involvement of witnesses becomes a crucial safeguard. Without their presence, the conformity of the written document with the testator's inner will remains legally unverifiable. This principle was upheld by the Kharkiv Court of Appeal, which declared a will invalid in a case involving an illiterate testator. In that instance, a village council secretary had drafted the document from the testator's words and read it back without witnesses present (*Postanova Kharkivs'koho apelyatsiynoho sudu* [Resolution of the Kharkiv Court of Appeal] 2019). The court determined that because the testator was unaware of the document's precise contents, the expression of will was neither free nor representative of their actual intent.

The public interest in creating a procedure for expressing will through a will is confirmed by the introduction of new implementation mechanisms. In particular, a Resolution of the Cabinet of Ministers in 2022 introduced changes allowing wills certified by authorised persons under martial law to undergo state registration in the Inheritance Register.

At the same time, free will cannot be enshrined in a will in oral form or with other violations of the law. In our opinion, such requirements serve to protect the rights of the testator and potential heirs, ensuring a full and legitimate expression of will, rather than complicating the procedure and restricting free will.

Judicial practice confirms that the primary purpose of a will is to reflect the testator's will, and therefore, certain formal violations can be disregarded. A Resolution of the Supreme Court of Ukraine overturned a cassation decision, leaving the first instance court's decision unchanged, indicating that the absence of an age-appropriate photo in the testator's passport—a mandatory requirement—does not constitute grounds for declaring the will invalid.

The awareness of one's own actions and the specific content of a testament is a fundamental condition for its validity. This legal requirement frequently results in a significant volume of litigation, where wills are challenged based on the testator's physical or mental condition at the time of execution. For instance, judicial practice includes decisions declaring a will invalid due to the presence of severe illness and the cognitive side effects of medications that impaired the testator's ability to comprehend the consequences of their actions (*Rishennia Frunzens'koho raionnoho sudu m. Kharkova* [Decision of the Frunzenskyi District Court of Kharkiv] 2013).

At the same time, the issue of recognising a will where the testator's wishes are expressed in violation of regulatory requirements in cases of extreme necessity remains unresolved. For example, when a person makes a "will" on a phone or a napkin during a plane crash. Due to significant procedural violations, this manner of expressing a will would not be recognized as valid.

The legislation of EU member states regulates this issue through the use of holographic (handwritten) and emergency wills. A holographic will is one written entirely by the testator in their own hand. Such wills can only be made by adults and must be signed and dated (Loviak and Perepichai 2014, 19).

Emergency wills provide for the possibility of making a will if there is a fear of imminent death or if exceptional circumstances make compliance with the ordinary form impossible. In this case, the testator has the right to express their last will orally in the presence of at least three witnesses (Ievinia 2014, 16). The introduction of these forms into Ukraine's legislation would create new opportunities for reflecting free will in post-mortem legal relations, which is especially relevant in conditions of military operations. The possibility of implementing these institutions requires a detailed analysis, the results of which will be covered in separate studies.

An additional method of reflecting free will within inheritance relations is the will with a condition. The testator may render the right to inherit contingent upon a specific condition, regardless of whether it pertains to the heir's behavior (e.g., the birth of a child or obtaining an education (*Tsyvil'nyi kodeks Ukrainy* [Civil Code of Ukraine] 2003, art. 1242, para. 1). In this framework, the testator designates the specific circumstances under which the heir may receive the estate.

However, such conditions are strictly limited by several legal requirements: (1) they cannot contradict the law or moral principles (Ibid., art. 1242, para. 2); (2) at the moment the inheritance opens, the theoretical possibility of the condition occurring must persist (Zaika 2009, 110); and (3) the conditions must exist at the time of the opening of the inheritance (Kharytonov, Chervonyi, and Bilousov 2003, 1009).

Consequently, events such as the birth of a child or the completion of an education occurring after the opening of the inheritance cannot serve as valid conditions upon which the right to inherit depends (Yarema et al. 2005, 810). Conversely, a condition requiring the completion of higher education by the time the inheritance opens is considered valid. In this context, N. V. Chernohor distinguishes between the specific condition of receiving a diploma and the mere status of being a student (Chernohor 2010, 220). This ensures that the testator's volition is exercised within a framework that respects both individual intent and objective legal certainty.

L. Shapoval highlights the problematic nature of such a situation with an example: a testator makes a will conditional on the heir receiving a higher education. The heir begins their education, but the testator dies before it is completed, making it impossible to fulfill the condition (Shapoval 2021, 56). It can be assumed that the testator's interest was in the heir receiving an education, and even if this condition is fulfillled after the testator's death, it would correspond to their will. But since the condition must exist at the time the inheritance opens, the heir cannot inherit in this case. We believe this is an artificial restriction on the free will of parties who wish to transfer/receive an inheritance under certain conditions but are unable to realise their interest due to circumstances beyond their control.

Additionally, the terms of a will cannot infringe upon the absolute, constitutional rights of the heir. Conditions requiring marriage to a specific person or forbidding a change of residence or occupation will be null and void.

Thus, a will with a condition is a way of contrasting the free will of the testator and the heir, where the latter must fully fulfill the conditions set by the testator, even if they contradict their own wishes. In effect, this is a legal way of influencing the free will of another person, since the conditional will is based on the principle of voluntariness, and the testator's interest creates a new interest for the heir. At the same time, we support the position that the current wording of the norm in the Civil Code indicates not an expansion of testamentary freedom, but, on the contrary, its artificial restriction.

The possibility of expressing free will through establishing conditions for inheritance is further detailed through the drafting of an inheritance agreement.

An inheritance agreement under Ukrainian law is not classified as a form of succession; however, in certain jurisdictions, such as Germany, it is recognized as an independent, third form of succession. In Ukraine, while an inheritance agreement is technically a type of obligatory legal relationship, it is situated within Book Six, "Inheritance Law," of the Civil Code of Ukraine. This placement stems from its inherent connection to inheritance law—specifically, the transfer of ownership under the agreement upon the opening of the inheritance (Dovhert 2000, 288).

Nonetheless, the expediency of classifying an inheritance agreement strictly under inheritance law remains a subject of scholarly skepticism (Bychkivskyi 2010, 136). Critics argue that its legal nature belongs more properly to the law of obligations. This view is reinforced by the Supreme Court of Ukraine, which emphasizes that such an agreement does not constitute a separate type of succession (*Pro sudovu praktyku u spravakh pro spadkuvannia* [On Judicial Practice in Inheritance Cases] 2008). Consequently, the relationship between an inheritance agreement and free will is determined to be analogous to other institutions within the law of obligations, where the exercise of volition is centered on contractual intent rather than testamentary disposition.

The definition of this contract as bilateral or unilateral causes some discussion. While the obligations of the acquirer are defined in the Civil Code (to perform certain actions), the obligations of the alienator are not normatively defined. Scholars who recognize the agreement as bilateral emphasise the alienator's obligation not to cancel or unilaterally change its terms (Skopychenko 2015).

This position is supported by V. Vasylchenko (2003), A. Verbansky and R. Karpenko (2019, 40), and A. Yevstihnieiev (2005, 38). In Germany, Latvia, Austria, and Switzerland, a succession agreement often serves as a third basis for succession, providing the heir with a choice (Chepys and Pysarieva 2021, 1545).

However, a succession agreement is a contract in the event of death, not a contract of succession, and the concept of the Civil Code of Ukraine does not allow it to be considered a type of succession alongside testate and intestate succession (Kukhariev 2021, 75).

Some scholars contend that the inheritance agreement is a unilateral contract, as obligations are primarily imposed upon the acquirer. In this view, the alienator is not strictly obliged to perform a transfer of property, as ownership transitions "automatically" upon their death, independent of any further manifestation of their will at that moment (Pechenyi 2012).

This perspective is supported by R. A. Maydanyk (Maydanyk 2007, 92) and Z. V. Romovska, who argue that while the inheritance agreement is a bilateral transaction (requiring two parties to sign), it remains a unilateral contract because the alienator bears no substantive obligations (Romovska 2003, 16). The Ministry of Justice of Ukraine also maintains this position. Defining the agreement as unilateral appears logically consistent, as it is predicated on the alienator's will, while for the acquirer, it often assumes the characteristics of a contract of adhesion.

However, an alternative view proposed by I. Samoilova suggests that the law does not explicitly prohibit the imposition of specific obligations upon the alienator within the agreement. Such provisions would transform the arrangement into a bilateral contract with mutual obligations (Samoilova 2021, 56). For example, the agreement might stipulate the acquirer's right to reside in a specific portion of the residential premises during the alienator's lifetime (Kukharev 2016, 142).

The main differences between an inheritance agreement and a will with conditions are the ability to provide for the performance of actions after the opening of the inheritance and the ability for both natural and legal persons to be the acquirer (*Tsyvil'nyi kodeks Ukrainy* [Civil Code of Ukraine] 2003, art. 1305, para. 1; art. 303, para. 2).

Thus, an inheritance agreement makes it possible to avoid the problems characteristic of a will with conditions, as listed above. Also, an inheritance agreement is for-value, which differs from a will, which is a gratuitous transaction (Khamula and Kuznetsova 2020, 120). In this case, the value lies in the necessity of performing certain actions.

As we can see, an inheritance agreement is a means of expressing the owner's will regarding the transfer of rights to property in the event of their death, provided that the acquirer fulfills the obligations specified in the contract. Such an agreement expands the possibilities for expressing will but requires its coordination with the will of the other party, who accepts the terms and assumes the obligations. This contract is somewhat similar to a life maintenance contract, with the difference that the latter is an alternative to a sale, property rights arise during the alienator's lifetime, and the acquirer's obligations are limited to providing maintenance and/or care for life.

The transfer of property rights through a will or an inheritance agreement creates ample opportunities for the property owner to exercise their free will; however, the will of the acquirer plays a secondary role. The opposite situation arises in cases of inheritance by law.

We emphasise that testate succession and inheritance agreements are based on the free will of the property owner, as they embody their desire and involve a conscious, voluntary expression of will. A will reflects the testator's inner will and the presumption of its superiority over intestate succession. The testator independently determines what property to transfer, in what amount, and to whom, and can disinherit a legal heir. The primary purpose of a will is to reflect the testator's intentions, and therefore, certain formal defects can be disregarded. An inheritance agreement is a means of expressing the owner's will regarding the transfer of rights to their property upon their death, provided the acquirer fulfills the specified obligations. Such an agreement expands the possibilities for expressing will but requires coordination with the will of the other party.

6.2. Free Will in Intestate Succession and the Exercise of the Right to Inheritance

Intestate succession (inheritance by law) occurs if an individual did not leave a will, if the will is invalid, if the conditions of a conditional will are not met, if the heirs under the will did not accept the inheritance, or if the individual disposed of only part of their property (Pavliuk and Solomeniuk 2021, 146). Therefore, intestate succession takes place when the testator's free will, as expressed in a will or inheritance agreement, was not a sufficient basis for the inheritance of their entire estate, or when the will of the designated heirs was not directed toward accepting the inheritance.

Intestate succession does not require the expression of the testator's free will. It stems from the public will of the state, which normatively establishes the order of succession and requires coordination with the will of the heirs who agree to accept the inheritance. Intestate succession occurs according to clear regulatory rules that determine the conditions, grounds, circle of heirs, and their order of priority. The testator's free will cannot influence these matters.

The primary objective of intestate succession is the efficient transfer of a deceased person's property. Consequently, a pivotal challenge for this legal institution is the precise determination of the order of succession. The principles that guide legislators in defining the circle of legal heirs remain among the most rigorously debated topics in civil law.

In the Civil Code of Ukraine, the order of succession is structured into five distinct classes:

1. The decedent's children (including those born posthumously), the surviving spouse, and the parents.
2. Full and half-siblings of the decedent, and their grandparents.
3. The decedent's aunts and uncles.
4. Individuals who resided with the decedent as a family unit for at least five years prior to the opening of the inheritance.
5. Other relatives up to the sixth degree of kinship (with closer relatives excluding those more distant), and the decedent's dependents who were not family members (*Tsyvil'nyi kodeks Ukrainy* [Civil Code of Ukraine] 2003, art. 1261–1265).

This statutory approach is questionable, as an attempt to interpret the unexpressed will of the testator may not accurately reflect their true interests. The legislator states, rather than assumes, that the testator would have wanted to leave the inheritance to their closest relatives as defined by the statutory order of succession, although this may not correspond to reality. Thus, the legislator decides on behalf of the testator. And while this approach is debatable, it remains the only way to transfer property when the testator's will is not expressly enshrined in a will.

In the matter of the order of succession, the free will of the heirs affects the possibility of moving to the next class of heirs. They can independently decide not to accept the inheritance, to refuse it, or to change the order and redistribute the property (*Tsyvil'nyi kodeks Ukrainy* [Civil Code of Ukraine] 2003, art. 1258, para. 2; art. 1259).

The transfer of the right of inheritance to the next class occurs at the heir's will when they renounce the inheritance, or automatically, without their will, if they do not accept it. In this case, renunciation is an active manifestation of the heir's free will, while non-acceptance is a passive one. Also, by a court decision, an individual from a lower class of legal heirs may be granted the right to inherit alongside heirs of a higher class, provided they cared for and materially supported the testator, who was in a helpless state (Ibid., art. 1259, para. 2). Such a case is based on the free will of the interested person, who must apply to the court. However, we can imagine a situation where a person files a lawsuit to change the order of succession but, after it is granted, refuses the inheritance.

N. M. Pavliuk and A. M. Solomeniuk identify a significant shortcoming in the legislative regulation of inheritance by dependents: the lack of clarity in determining the period during which material assistance was received (Pavliuk and Solomeniuk 2021, 231). They emphasise that, according to the content of Article 1265 of the Civil Code of Ukraine, any period in the dependent's life could be recognized as a basis for inheritance. For example, if a person received financial assistance from the testator for several years, but this relationship then ended, under the current article, if the fifth class of heirs is called to inherit, such a person (a former dependent) may still receive the right to inherit, as the Civil Code does not link the dependency to the time of the testator's death (Ibid., 231).

This example confirms that the normatively established order of succession may not correspond to the testator's wishes. However, we must state that, from a legal perspective, intestate succession does correspond to the testator's will. We proceed from the legal fiction that if a testator did not express their will through a will or an inheritance agreement, they are deemed to have consented to the statutory order of succession. Although this may not reflect the testator's true interests, the law must rely on such a constant. Otherwise, in the absence of a will, the legislator would have to interpret this as an inability to transfer property due to the uncertainty of the testator's will. Under such circumstances, the inheritance would be deemed escheat, and the property rights would pass to the local community (*Tsyvil'nyi kodeks Ukra*iny [Civil Code of Ukraine] 2003, art. 1277).

Special attention is due to the manifestation of free will in an agreement to change the order of succession. Yu. Orzikh highlights the problematic nature of this issue when there are several heirs of the same class—for example, two children of a deceased father, one of whom refuses to conclude such an agreement (Orzikh 2013, 100).

In this regard, notarial practice addresses this problem in two primary ways:

1. Unilateral Application: By drafting an application from one heir granting the right to inherit to an heir of another class. This is often viewed as a formal violation of Article 1259 of the Civil Code of Ukraine, which explicitly refers to an agreement (a bilateral or multilateral act) rather than a unilateral one.
2. Partial Agreement: By concluding an agreement involving only the heir of the higher class and the specific heir to whom the right to inherit is being granted. In this scenario, no formal violations are immediately apparent due to the abstract nature of the legislative construction, which allows for a broad interpretation of the phrase "interested heirs" and emphasizes the central legal category of interest (Ibid.).

Although these practices exist, we contend they contradict both the free will of the testator and the rights of the dissenting heir. First, as established previously, the statutory order of succession embodies the presumed will of the testator. For example, if a testator has two children and remains intestate, it is under the assumption that they will inherit the property equally. Altering the order of succession post-mortem effectively overrides this presumed intent. Second, an heir who does not consent to the change finds their own will nullified by an agreement executed without their participation, creating an inequitable distribution that ignores the collective will of the class.

The legal status of de facto spouses in inheritance relations remains a significantly complex issue. Under the Civil Code of Ukraine, the right to inherit in the first class is restricted to the surviving spouse, children, and parents (*Tsyvil'nyi kodeks Ukrainy* [Civil Code of Ukraine] 2003, art. 1261, para. 1).

These specific rights accrue only upon the formal state registration of a marriage (*Simeinyi kodeks Ukrainy* [Family Code of Ukraine] 2002, art. 21, para. 1).

Although a family is defined as a unit of persons who cohabit and share mutual rights and obligations (Ibid., art. 3, para. 2), this does not automatically confer spousal status. Cohabitation without formal marriage is not a legal basis for the emergence of spousal rights and duties (Ibid., art. 21, para. 2). Furthermore, recognizing such individuals as a family can be legally challenging, as the Family Code stipulates that a family is traditionally founded upon marriage, blood relationship, or adoption (Ibid., art. 3, para. 4).

Consequently, individuals in a de facto marriage who choose not to register their union, or those who lack the legal right to do so (such as same-sex couples), are deprived of the right to inherit by operation of law as spouses. For these subjects, the only mechanisms to exercise their free will and ensure post-mortem property transfer are the execution of a will or an inheritance agreement.

The primary exception applies to a man and a woman cohabiting as a family without marriage. In such cases, property acquired during cohabitation is considered joint common ownership, unless a written agreement stipulates otherwise (Ibid., art. 74, para. 1). However, the fact of cohabitation must be judicially established through a lawsuit, which requires proving a common budget, shared expenses, and other circumstances indicative of a genuine family relationship. Crucially, this procedure currently does not apply to same-sex couples, further limiting their ability to realize their will in inheritance matters.

In the context of European integration, Ukraine faces the significant task of harmonizing its domestic legislation, particularly concerning family and inheritance relations. The last decade has been characterized by profound social shifts regarding the public understanding of sexual orientation and gender identity (SOGI) and the fundamental rights of LGBT persons (Russell and Horn 2016, 5).

Notably, same-sex relationships have been legalized in numerous European jurisdictions, including Austria, Belgium, Spain, and France. Furthermore, the European Parliament, in a 2021 resolution, called for the guarantee of equal rights for same-sex couples across all EU member states. While current European legislation does not yet mandate the legalization of same-sex unions in every member state, the trend toward formal recognition is steadily increasing.

To address these evolving legal standards, a draft law "On the Institute of Registered Partnerships" was submitted to the Verkhovna Rada of Ukraine in 2023. This draft law proposes the creation of a new legal institution: the registered partnership. This institution is envisioned as a voluntary family union of two adults—regardless of sex—founded on mutual respect and support.

Upon state registration, partners would attain the status of close relatives of the first degree of kinship. Consequently, they would be granted the right to inherit within the first class of legal heirs. Such a reform would substantially expand the possibilities for exercising free will for participants in inheritance relations. Moreover, the adoption of gender-neutral laws is gaining increasing resonance as a necessary step toward legal modernization and social equity.

The distribution of rights based on gender, while relevant during the historical struggle for women's rights, now introduces complexities into the modern rule of law. This issue is particularly poignant given the growing recognition of a diverse spectrum of gender identities. C. O'Connor (2019) argues that while biological sex is frequently associated with gender identity, an individual can possess a sex and gender that do not align. In contemporary discourse, more than thirty-one distinct genders are recognized, reflecting a shift from binary models to a more fluid understanding of identity.

For the majority of human history, personality was assessed in isolation from the various intersectional components of identity, such as race, ethnicity, religion, and the multifaceted aspects of sex and sexuality (Brabender 2022). One of the most significant formal recognitions of gender diversity emerged during the scholarly debate over whether the norms for psychological instruments should remain gender-based or transition toward more inclusive models (Baker and Mason 2009).

While it is not the primary purpose of this monograph to provide an exhaustive examination of free will within gender studies, it can be reasonably assumed that gender identity does not inherently impact the scope or validity of a person's free will. As S. Mookerjee (2019) contends, the implementation of gender-neutral laws leads to a demonstrable increase in individual autonomy. Therefore, the adoption of relevant gender-neutral legislation within Ukrainian inheritance law would expand the mechanisms for exercising free will and abolish discriminatory norms. Such reforms would eliminate restrictions currently faced by individuals due to their choice of same-sex relationships, their preference for unregistered partnerships, or their self-identification outside the traditional male/female gender binary. Supporting this position is the principle of equality, which mandates that the state provide a legal framework for all persons in long-term relationships to formalize their partnerships and secure their mutual rights (Mendzhul 2020, 253).

The above proves that intestate succession is not directly influenced by the testator's free will; rather, the legislator is guided by the principle that, in the absence of a will, the testator expresses their consent for the post-mortem transfer of property in the manner prescribed by law. It is necessary to agree with M.B. Kravchyk that inheritance relations do not arise from the will of their subjects; their basis is an event (death), and the testator cannot always influence the content of the legal relations, especially given the compulsory share for certain heirs regardless of the will's content

(Kravchyk 2018, 104). At the same time, inheritance is directly related to the heir's free will, through their exercise of the right to inheritance.

The exercise of inheritance rights is the activity of active subjects – the heirs – aimed at achieving a particular result: the transfer of the inheritance to them or their refusal of it. It is a form of ensuring the person's interests (Shcherbyna 2015, 93). The testator's free will has different meanings for various forms of inheritance, but it is the heir's free will that ultimately determines the transfer of property rights. This is because even in the case of inheritance by will, which is a manifestation of the testator's free will, it is the heir who makes the final decision on accepting the inheritance.

The inheritance acceptance system is highly consistent with the principles of freedom of exercise of civil rights and the dispositivity of civil law regulation. It corresponds to the essence of the subjective right to inheritance, as the acquisition is based on the heir's clearly expressed will to become the legal successor to the testator's rights and obligations (Fedorych 2018, 62). But the heir does not have full autonomy regarding the disposal of the subjective right of inheritance, which originates from the testator's will.

However, by virtue of possessing this subjective right, the heir's expression of will determines the mechanism for increasing inheritance shares or the order of calling heirs to succession by law (Kozlovska 2014, 48). The registration of inheritance rights is intended not only to strengthen the position of the heirs but also to provide them with the opportunity, within the limits established by law, to be a continuation of the testator's legal essence (Fomichova 2008, 212).

An heir by will or by law has the right to accept the inheritance or not, but their will cannot be conditional or subject to reservations (*Tsyvil'nyi kodeks Ukrainy* [Civil Code of Ukraine] 2003, art. 1268). Acceptance of the inheritance is directly related to the heir's free will, as they must submit an application for acceptance to a notary (Ibid., art. 1269, para. 1). Such an application must be submitted in person, or through a legal representative if the heir is a minor or incapacitated (Ibid., art. 1269, para. 4). The legislation provides for the possibility of changing one's decision and withdrawing the application within the established period (Ibid., art. 1269, para. 5).

However, certain categories of persons acquire an inheritance without needing to exercise their will by filing an application. An heir who permanently resided with the testator at the time of the inheritance opening, as well as minors and incapacitated persons, are considered to have accepted the inheritance unless they have declared their renunciation of it within the established period (Ibid., art. 1268).

Time limits are of fundamental importance in exercising inheritance rights, as they serve as a limiting condition for the heir's exercise of free will. N. V. Chernogor suggests dividing such periods into general and special: (1) the general period for accepting the inheritance is six months from the day the inheritance opens; (2) the special period is established for heirs whose right to inherit depends on the non-acceptance or refusal of other heirs (Chernohor 2011, 12).

The general period is for the primary heir. The special period allows subsequent heirs to exercise their free will if the primary heir did not exercise theirs (e.g., by missing the deadline) or voluntarily renounced the inheritance. The only exceptions are cases where the other heirs or the court allow an heir who missed the deadline for a valid reason to submit an application (*Tsyvil'nyi kodeks Ukrainy* [Civil Code of Ukraine] 2003, art. 1272). In this case, their free will is coordinated with the will of other heirs or the public will of the state, as implemented by the court.

As mentioned earlier, a will may contain certain conditions for receiving an inheritance, which allows the testator to exercise their free will. At the same time, the heir may exercise their own will by accepting or rejecting a testamentary bequest.

Such obligations can be called non-contractual and regulatory. As a formal act, a testamentary bequest is a disposition of the testator within a will, which is essentially a transaction. Its legal effect is mediated by the existence of the testator's will and requires other legal facts (the testator's death, the existence of the will containing the bequest, the heir's acceptance of the inheritance, and the legatee's acceptance of the bequest), which together constitute a legal composite (Tsybulska 2012, 383). This position is supported by V. V. Vasylchenko, who emphasizes that the relations arising from a testamentary bequest are obligatory legal relations, the grounds and content of which are determined by the will (Vasylchenko 2004, 323).

The heir's free will is also exercised when renouncing an inheritance. Such a renunciation is carried out only by means of a unilateral transaction by the heir (the submission of an application) (Fedorych 2018, 4). Renunciation is a separate way of exercising free will, consisting in a direct expression of will, and differs from non-acquisition due to missing the application deadline. Renunciation also gives other potential heirs the right to exercise their free will.

N. V. Fomicheva emphasizes that persons whose right to inherit depends on the non-acceptance or renunciation of others are considered only potential heirs because an heir who has renounced can still withdraw their renunciation within the period established for acceptance (Fomichova 2014, 95).

The analysis demonstrates that intestate succession does not require the expression of the testator's free will but rather stems from the public will of the state, which normatively establishes the order of succession and requires coordination with the will of the heirs. In the case of intestate succession, the legislator states, and does not merely assume, that the testator would have wanted to leave the inheritance to their closest relatives, though this may not correspond to reality. In the matter of the order of succession, the heirs' free will affects the possibility of transferring the order to another class. From a legal point of view, intestate succession corresponds to the testator's will, which does not require direct expression; the legislator is guided by the principle that, in the absence of a will, the testator expresses their consent for the post-mortem transfer of property in the order determined by law. The testator's free will has different meanings for different forms of inheritance, but it is the heir's free will that determines the transfer of property rights. Acceptance of an inheritance is directly related to the heir's free will, as they must submit an application. Renunciation is a separate way of exercising free will, consisting in a direct expression of that will.

Conclusions

1. The significance of free will in inheritance relations is fundamentally contingent upon the selected method of property transfer. A will and an inheritance agreement serve as the primary embodiments of the owner's volition, involving a conscious and voluntary expression of intent. Conversely, in intestate succession (inheritance by law), the testator's free will remains legally irrelevant to the emergence of the right; the focus shifts entirely to the heir's desire and consent to accept the estate.
2. A testament reflects the inner will of the testator and carries a legal presumption of superiority over intestate rules—a presumption that can only be rebutted by direct statutory provision. The testator possesses the autonomy to determine the volume and destination of the assets and may explicitly disinherit legal heirs. In this context, individual free will prevails over the state's public will. However, this autonomy is not absolute, as it is restricted by the compulsory share (forced heirship), protecting vulnerable parties regardless of the testator's intent.
3. Executing a will is an essential mechanism for clarifying or altering the post-mortem distribution of property within permissible legal limits. It is particularly vital when a testator seeks to express a will that contradicts the default "socially average" expectations of intestate succession.
4. Current restrictions on the circle of persons eligible to make a will include only legal entities and individuals lacking full civil capacity. We argue for the normative recognition of the right of persons with incomplete civil capacity (minors) to execute a testament. Since the certification process involves a notary (or other official) who verifies the presence of voluntariness and awareness, the current blanket restriction is an unfounded barrier to the exercise of their free will.
5. The expression of a testator's will is insufficient in isolation; it requires formal notarial certification and registration in the Unified State Register of Inheritance Cases. This ensures that the internal creative will is transformed into a stable, legally

recognized external form, protecting it from post-mortem distortion.

6. The state's commitment to protecting the expression of free will is evidenced by the variability of the testamentary procedure. There is a clear public interest in ensuring that even individuals with physical disabilities can realize their intent through proxy signatures or oral dictation in the presence of witnesses.
7. Free will cannot be legally recognized in an oral form or through other substantial procedural violations. These formal requirements serve to protect the legitimacy of the expression rather than to restrict freedom. Nevertheless, it is appropriate to consider equating video-recorded expressions of will in extraordinary circumstances with the written form to better capture intent in crises.
8. Because the primary objective of a will is to reflect the testator's genuine intent, certain formal defects should be secondary to the condition of awareness. The high volume of litigation regarding the testator's mental or physical state underscores the need for a judicial approach that prioritizes the "spirit" of the free will over the "letter" of the formal document where awareness can be proven.
9. The legal system currently lacks a resolution for wills made in situations of extreme necessity that violate regulatory formalities. Implementing holographic (handwritten) and emergency wills—particularly relevant during military operations—would create vital new pathways for exercising free will when standard notarial services are inaccessible.
10. A will with a condition represents a unique intersection of the testator's and the heir's free wills. By setting conditions (e.g., obtaining an education), the testator legally influences the heir's future behavior. This creates a new interest for the heir, who must voluntarily decide whether to align their own will with the conditions set by the decedent.
11. The inclusion of a testamentary bequest (*legatum*) further demonstrates the testator's autonomy, allowing them to impose specific obligations on the heir. The heir, in turn, exercises their own volition by choosing to accept or reject the inheritance along with its accompanying burdens.

12. An inheritance agreement functions as a specific manifestation of the owner's will that links property transfer to the performance of an obligation by the acquirer. While it expands the scope of the owner's control, it necessitates a coordination of wills typical of the law of obligations, distinguishing it from the unilateral nature of a will.
13. Intestacy serves as a fallback mechanism when the testator's free will was either not expressed, was legally insufficient, or when the chosen heirs exercised their own will to reject the estate.
14. Intestacy originates from the public will of the state. It establishes a normative order of succession that assumes a "default" intent, which only becomes effective upon the active or passive consent of the heirs to accept the rights and obligations.
15. In defining the order of succession, the legislator decides on behalf of the testator based on a standardized model of family proximity. While this "legislative proxy" is debatable, it remains the only viable method for property transfer in the absence of an express testamentary declaration.
16. The free will of heirs significantly impacts the hierarchy of succession. Heirs can collectively decide to redistribute property or change the order of succession by agreement, provided such actions do not infringe upon the rights of non-participating "interested heirs."
17. The transition of rights to subsequent classes occurs either through an active manifestation of will (renunciation) or a passive one (non-acceptance). Both actions represent the heir's autonomy in deciding whether to enter the legal relationship.
18. Legally, intestate succession is framed as the testator's implicit consent. By not executing a will, the testator is presumed to agree to the post-mortem transfer of their property according to the statutory framework provided by the state.
19. The exclusion of de facto spouses from first-class inheritance remains a critical issue. Adopting gender-neutral legislation and recognizing registered partnerships would abolish discriminatory barriers. This would allow individuals in same-sex relationships or those choosing not to enter formal marriage to fully realize their free will in post-mortem relations.

20. Ultimately, the heir's free will is the final arbiter of property transfer. Even a perfectly executed will—a masterpiece of the testator's volition—is contingent upon the heir's final decision to accept the inheritance.
21. Acceptance is a dynamic exercise of will. An heir may submit an application to accept and subsequently exercise their right to withdraw that application, reflecting the continuous nature of volitional control during the inheritance process.
22. Renouncing an inheritance is a distinct, active manifestation of free will. It is fundamentally different from the mere failure to meet deadlines, as it explicitly directs the estate toward other potential heirs, thereby triggering new opportunities for the exercise of their own free will.

General Conclusions

As a result of the research conducted, based on an in-depth systemic and structural analysis of legislation and scholarly doctrine, and drawing upon scientific works from various branches of law as well as national and international legal acts, a number of conclusions have been formulated. These conclusions are aimed at identifying and resolving a complex of theoretical and practical problems related to understanding the significance of free will in civil law. The main conclusions are as follows:

1. **The evolutionary development of free will, from Antiquity to the present, has culminated in its crystallization as a foundational legal norm grounded in the doctrine of natural law.** While external factors—specifically legislative regulations—govern the outer manifestations of human conduct, they cannot infringe upon the internal component of free will, as the individual's own reason serves as its ultimate measure. In the sphere of legal relations, participants exercise their discretion to adhere to or deviate from legal norms, guided by internal moral imperatives. Consequently, law and free will exist in a state of dialectical interdependence, where each serves as a developmental vector for the other.
2. **The conceptual framework and systematic placement of the legal idea of free will within civil law are established through the following foundational theses:**
   a. **Ontological Nature and Limitations:** As a fundamental legal idea, free will expresses the autonomy of the person's will across various civil law institutions. However, this autonomy is not absolute; it is subject to limitations imposed by law, morality, and the public interest. Such restrictions are considered legitimate only when they are lawful, justified, and proportionate, ensuring that the exercise of one individual's free will does not infringe upon the rights and freedoms of others.

b. **Functional Hierarchy:** While intrinsically linked to the principles of civil law, free will serves as a broader meta-concept rather than a mere principle or institution. It acts as a primary idea that precedes and influences the formulation, implementation, and functioning of the entire legal system, providing the basis for the realization of all subjective rights.
c. **Ideological Reflection and Ideologemes:** Though often lacking explicit normative definition in regulatory acts, free will constitutes a vital component of civil law ideology. In the absence of direct enshrinement, it is manifested through ideologemes—normative constructs such as "voluntariness," "consent of the parties," "free expression of will," and the "prohibition of coercion." These ideologemes reflect the individual's capacity to consciously and independently implement decisions and bear legal responsibility for their actions or inactions within civil relations.

3. **Free will embodies the fundamental essence of civil legal relations, serving as the foundational element for principles of freedom, equality, and the autonomy of expression.** Its manifestation is systemic, permeateing the application of several core legal principles:
   a. **Inadmissibility of Arbitrary Interference:** This principle safeguards free will as an inherent component of a person's private life and subjective rights, protecting the individual from unauthorized external encroachment.
   b. **Inadmissibility of Deprivation of Property Rights:** The relationship here is defined by the prohibition of restrictive influences on an owner's powers, ensuring that the disposal of property remains a volitional act of the proprietor.
   c. **Freedom of Contract:** Free will is the primary determinant of a party's capacity to enter into contractual relations and is a mandatory condition for a contract's legality. Consequently, the vitiation of will through mistake, fraud, or duress constitutes categorical grounds for invalidity.
   d. **Freedom of Entrepreneurial Activity:** Free will dictates the ability of an individual to engage in private enterprise and manage business risks at their own discretion.

   e. **Judicial Protection and Good Faith:** Free will is realized through the autonomous decision of a person to seek legal recourse and in the conscious choice of honest behavior (good faith) within legal interactions.
   f. **Justice and Reasonableness:** Free will serves as the qualitative measure for understanding the legal nature of a participant's conduct. Given the subjective nature of reasonableness, free will allows for a more adequate and nuanced qualification of specific legal cases.
   g. **Legal Equality and Free Expression:** The principle of legal equality ensures an equal scope of free will for all participants of the same legal status. Furthermore, the free expression of will acts as its absolute manifestation, requiring that such expression be conscious, free, and genuine.
   h. **Property Independence:** The implementation of property independence is deemed legitimate only when it is rooted in the authentic free will of the legal subject.
4. **Free will is intrinsically manifested within the personal non-property rights of an individual, where its exercise serves as both a prerequisite for the realization of these rights and a measure of their legal scope.**
   a. **Dynamic Nature and Civil Capacity:** Free will emerges at the moment of birth, with its legal and practical scope evolving throughout the individual's lifecycle. It expands in correlation with intellectual development and the acquisition of full civil capacity, while inversely contracting in instances where such capacity is legally restricted.
   b. **Public vs. Private Interests:** While free will is central to personal rights, its manifestation is subject to regulatory frameworks that may impose limitations based on the primacy of public interests over private autonomy.
   c. **The Right to Life:** Within this context, free will is expressed through a tripartite structure: (1) the categorical prohibition against the arbitrary deprivation of life; (2) the state's positive obligation to protect human life; and (3) the individual's inherent right to the active defense of their own life and the lives of others.

d. **Health Care and Informed Consent:** The right to health care is fundamentally rooted in the principle of voluntariness. This requires a mandatory manifestation of free will through the mechanism of informed consent or refusal, ensuring that medical intervention remains a volitional act of the subject.
e. **The Right to Freedom:** This right provides two essential prohibitions that safeguard the volitional sphere: 1) the prohibition against the unlawful deprivation or restriction of physical liberty; and 2) the prohibition against coercion or undue pressure in the individual's decision-making process.
f. **Family Rights:** The right to a family is realized exclusively through the exercise of free will, materialized through marriage or cohabitation predicated on a clear volitional intent to establish a familial bond.

5. **Free will serves as the constitutive element for the exercise and protection of a broad spectrum of personal non-property rights, acting as both a catalyst for individual self-realization and a boundary for the conduct of others.**
   a. Identity and Individuality: While the right to a name originates at birth independently of the child's volition, its subsequent exercise—specifically the decision to change one's name—constitutes a deliberate application of free will. Furthermore, the right to individuality provides the essential qualities that enable a person to realize their specific views and ideas, thereby manifesting their free will in a social context.
   b. **Dignity, Honor, and Deceased Respect:** The right to dignity is rooted in an individual's self-perception, shaped by autonomous decisions. Conversely, the respect for honor and dignity imposes a legal obligation on third parties, limiting their free will to ensure objective treatment of the person. This restrictive function also extends to the right to respect for a deceased person, which operates primarily by curtailing the free will of others to protect the memory and sanctity of the departed.

c. **Collective and Corporate Will:** The free will of a legal entity is characterized as a collective manifestation of the volitional acts of its employees. Its business reputation is a direct outcome of this collaborative intellectual and professional engagement.
d. **Privacy and Intellectual Activity:** An individual's free will allows them to demarcate the boundaries of their personal life and maintain its secrecy. This autonomy is absolute in the right to personal papers, where the owner's free will dominates, as any use or disclosure requires their explicit consent. Similarly, free will is expressed through creativity as a fundamental component of intellectual and spiritual activity.
e. **Movement, Residence, and Occupation:** The rights to a place of residence, the inviolability of housing, and freedom of movement are inherently dependent on volitional choice; they cannot effectively exist without the application of free will, except where legally established restrictions apply. Similarly, the right to choose or change one's occupation is a manifestation of free will, though its exercise may be subject to specific regulatory requirements or professional sanctions.

6. **The right of ownership and limited property rights (*jura in re aliena*) are intrinsically linked to free will, which serves as the necessary catalyst for establishing the legal relationship between the right-holder and the object.**
   a. **Exercise vs. Structure:** Free will is not a structural element of real rights *per se;* however, their actualization presupposes an expression of will, which constitutes the essential external manifestation of the individual's internal autonomy. Consequently, the exercise of the triad of ownership powers—possession, use, and disposal—is a primary mode of manifesting free will in civil commerce.
   b. **Volitional Intent in Possession and Use:** Good faith possession emerges as a conscious manifestation of free will, where the participant's volitional intent is specifically directed toward the lawful acquisition of rights. Similarly,

the right of use is generally volitional, though it is distinguished by the fact that use may occasionally occur through fortuitous or accidental circumstances without the direct influence of free will.

c. **Disposal as the Supreme Manifestation:** The right of disposal represents the most definitive expression of the owner's free will, as it grants the proprietor the exclusive authority to determine the legal fate of the property. This power requires an explicit external manifestation of intent, with exceptions reserved only for instances of compulsory alienation.

d. **Proposed Classification of Termination:** This study proposes a novel classification of the grounds for the termination of property rights based on their nexus with the subject's free will:

   i. **Direct Connection:** Termination resulting from the owner's proactive volitional acts (e.g., voluntary alienation).

   ii. **Variable Connection:** Grounds where the link to free will depends on specific circumstances (e.g., the destruction of property, which may be intentional or accidental).

   iii. **Absent Connection:** Involuntary termination occurring independently of the owner's intent (e.g., confiscation or nationalization).

7. **Within the framework of limited property rights (*jura in re aliena*), free will acts as the mediating force that balances the interests of both the owner and the right-holder, defining the temporal and qualitative parameters of the legal relationship.**

   a. **Bilateral Nature of Possession:** The right of possession is a concurrent manifestation of the free will of both the owner and the holder of the limited right. Actual possession is intrinsically volitional, originating from the intentional holding of an object. While a possessor's unilateral decision to cease possession terminates actual possession, the termination of titular possession generally necessitates the coordinated will of both legal parties.

b. **Loss of Control and Volition:** The actual loss of control over an object is classified by its nexus to the possessor's will: it may be voluntary (intentional abandonment), result from the opposing will of another (theft), or occur independently of any volitional influence (fortuitous loss or accident).

c. **Servitudes and Extreme Necessity:** In the context of servitudes, the free will of the right-holder may, in exceptional circumstances, prevail over the owner's will. However, such a hierarchy is legally permissible only in cases of extreme necessity, ensuring a balance between private autonomy and urgent legal requirements.

d. **Emphyteusis and Superficies:** Free will is the decisive factor in the emergence and termination of emphyteusis (long-term land lease) and superficies (the right to use land for building). In these relations, the legal system recognizes an equal scope of free will for both participants, maintaining the parity of their respective volitional expressions.

8. **The principle of freedom of contract serves as the primary practical manifestation of private autonomy, establishing that the parties' free will, in conjunction with statutory law, functions as a fundamental source of regulation for contractual relations.**

   a. **Conceptual Relationship:** Free will and the freedom of contract exist in a part-to-whole relationship, where the principle acts as the objective legal embodiment of the abstract idea. Through this principle, the participants' internal volition transcends the subjective sphere to acquire an external, legally binding form.

   b. **Norm-Generative Capacity:** Under the principle of the binding force of a contract (*pacta sunt servanda*), parties are endowed with norm-creating powers. This allows them to translate their free will into the specific content of the contract, which subsequently governs their conduct with the same authority as legal norms.

c. **Hierarchy of Will:** While individual autonomy is expansive, normative regulation generally prevails over contractual stipulations. This hierarchy confirms the overarching dominance of public will over individual intent, ensuring that private agreements do not contravene the mandatory requirements of the state, except in instances governed by dispositive (non-imperative) norms.

9. **The legal nature of non-contractual obligations is defined by the emergence of rights and duties from unilateral acts, characterized by the absence of coordinated bilateral will.** While these obligations arise primarily from facts specified in legislation, the role of individual volition varies significantly across different legal constructs:
   a. **Unilateral Manifestations and Reciprocal Volition:** A public promise of a reward is a primary manifestation of the promisor's free will; however, the resulting legal relationship remains inchoate until the recipient's will is expressed through the performance of the specified act.
   b. **Negotiorum Gestio (Management of Affairs):** Acting in the property interests of another constitutes a unilateral manifestation of the gestor's free will directed toward the preservation of the dominus's property. In this context, the *dominus's* free will is legally negated or presumed to be in agreement until an explicit refusal of the intervention is communicated.
   c. **Priority of State Interests in Rescue:** In obligations arising from the rescue of life and health, the *dominus* is legally deprived of the right to refuse the *gestor's* actions. This restriction on personal autonomy is necessitated by the presumed priority of the state's interest in the preservation of human life over individual private discretion.
   d. **Causal Connections to Volition:** This study concludes that the emergence of obligations maintains a spectrum of connectivity to free will: ranging from a direct connection (contractual agreements) to an indirect or mediated connection (non-contractual obligations and torts).

10. **Free will serves as the conceptual basis for determining the legal nature and consequences of a breach of obligations, enabling the assessment of intent, fault, and the applicability of exemptions from liability.**
    a. **Breach and Volitional Intent:** A breach of contract is viewed as a manifestation of free will when a party acts with conscious intent. However, a breach may also occur independently of that will, particularly in cases of negligence or external interference. When a transaction is entered into without the genuine intention of producing legal consequences, it is classified as fictitious, while the presence of vitiating factors (defects of will) fundamentally violates the legal idea of the contract.
    b. **Contractual vs. Non-Contractual Liability:** In the sphere of contractual liability, the parties' free will is of primary importance, as they autonomously agree upon the scope and terms of responsibility. Conversely, in the breach of non-contractual obligations, the manifestation of free will is characterized by the absence of prior consensus, where the obligation arises from the act itself rather than a coordinated agreement.
    c. **Degrees of Fault:** Legal responsibility is inextricably linked to the quality of the subject's volition. Intent is always rooted in free will, as the party's desire is directed toward non-performance. In contrast, negligence is grounded in the violation of a duty of care. Furthermore, a breach occurring due to the creditor's fault is characterized by the unilateral will of the creditor, which may impede the debtor's performance.
    d. **Causation and Exemptions:** While a causal link does not necessarily stem directly from the subject's free will, the grounds for exemption from liability are often defined by the *absence* of volition. Casus (accident) serves as a basis for exemption precisely because the event occurred through an unforeseeable circumstance rather than the party's will. In instances of force majeure, free will loses its legal significance as the event transcends the individual's capacity for control or choice.

11. **Free will possesses profound theoretical and practical significance within intellectual property law, serving as the bridge between internal creative thought and external legal protection.**
    a. **The Doctrine of Creative Act vs. Legal Transaction:** A defining peculiarity of copyright is that the mere manifestation of free will is sufficient for the right to arise. However, because creation is categorized as a legal act rather than a legal transaction, the principle of voluntariness does not strictly apply. Consequently, copyright may emerge even if a work is created under duress, as the legal protection is triggered by the objective result of the effort rather than the intent behind it.
    b. **Objective Form and the Right to Creativity:** When an author consciously creates a work, they exercise their freedom of creativity, manifesting their free will by granting the work an objective form. This transition from internal thought to external expression is the fundamental condition for the emergence of copyright protection.
    c. **Moral vs. Economic Rights:** Within the author's moral rights, free will is manifested through the conscious exercise of personal non-property interests. However, free will gains even greater significance in the context of economic rights, as these involve the deliberate and strategic exercise of ownership and the commercial exploitation of the work.
    d. **Coordination in Co-authorship:** In instances of co-authorship, the individual free wills of all contributors must be coordinated, forming a collective volitional expression that governs the rights to the shared work.
    e. **Related Rights:** While the presence of free will is not a mandatory prerequisite for the emergence of related rights (neighboring rights), these rights do arise as a manifestation of volition when the underlying objects are created through conscious human activity.

12. **In patent law, the manifestation of free will requires a strategic coordination between the individual volition of the creator and the regulatory will of the state, which establishes the criteria for legal recognition.**
    a. **The Intersection of Copyright and Industrial Property:** At the moment of creation, free will achieves an external form protected by copyright; however, this same volitional expression can be transformed into an object of industrial property law only if it satisfies the specific statutory requirements of novelty, inventive step, and industrial applicability.
    b. **The Nature of Patentability Criteria:** The criteria for patentability are not intended as restrictions on free will but rather as standardized conditions that its external embodiment must fulfill to gain the status of a monopoly right. These requirements serve as the bridge between private creative intent and public industrial utility.
    c. **Hierarchies of Will in Commissioned Works:** When an object of industrial property is created for hire or on commission, the free will of the employer or customer is prioritized. In such legal relations, the creator's volitional activity is directed toward the fulfillment of a pre-existing contractual obligation, thereby subordinating the creator's autonomy regarding the ownership of the result to the primary will of the commissioning party.
13. **In the sphere of inheritance relations, the legal significance of free will is contingent upon the mechanism of property transfer, balancing the testator's testamentary freedom with the heir's right to accept or refuse the succession.**
    a. **Testamentary vs. Intestate Succession:** A will and an inheritance agreement serve as the definitive expressions of the owner's free will. Conversely, in intestate succession, the testator's volition is legally irrelevant; the focus shifts entirely to the heir's desire and consent to accept the inheritance. A will is specifically required when an individual seeks to override the default statutory rules of succession through a personalized volitional act.

b. **Proposed Reform for Minors:** This study identifies the current restriction on a minor's right to make a will as legally unfounded. It is proposed to normatively enshrine the right to testament for individuals with incomplete civil capacity, provided that a notary verifies the voluntariness and awareness of their expression of will.

c. **Formal Validity and Certification:** The testator's free will alone is insufficient for the legal validity of a will due to the mandatory requirement for notarial certification. Similarly, the prohibition of oral wills in various jurisdictions is necessitated by the state's interest in protecting the rights of both the testator and the heirs from potential fraud or misinterpretation.

d. **Emergency and Holographic Wills:** The legal status of wills made under extreme necessity remains a critical unresolved issue. The implementation of holographic and emergency wills is recommended to safeguard the testator's final wishes when formal certification is impossible.

e. **Wills with Conditions:** A will containing conditions represents a unique dynamic between the free will of the testator and that of the heir. In such instances, the heir's exercise of volition regarding the inheritance is predicated on the fulfillment of the testator's instructions, even when those conditions conflict with the heir's own interests.

14. **Intestate succession serves as the legal default when a testator's free will is either absent, incomplete, or the designated heirs fail to accept the inheritance, shifting the focus from actual to presumed volition.**

    a. **Doctrine of Presumed Will:** In the absence of a formal will or inheritance agreement, the legislator does not merely assume but actively asserts that the testator would have intended to leave their estate to their closest relatives. Intestate succession thus corresponds to the testator's presumed will, based on the legal principle that, by not creating a will, the individual tacitly consents to the post-mortem transfer of property in the manner prescribed by statutory law.

b. **The Heir's Final Autonomy:** Ultimately, the actual transfer of property rights remains contingent upon the heir's free will. Regardless of the testator's intent or the statutory order of succession, the heir retains the absolute right to make the final decision to accept or refuse the estate.
c. **Renunciation as a Volitional Act:** The act of renouncing an inheritance is recognized as a distinct and proactive method of exercising free will, allowing the heir to unilaterally terminate their potential legal relationship with the estate.
d. **Legal Reform and Gender-Neutrality:** This study identifies the current legal status of *de facto* spouses in inheritance relations as a critical issue. The adoption of gender-neutral legislation in Ukraine is recommended as a necessary step to abolish discriminatory norms and expand the mechanisms through which all participants can effectively exercise their free will within the familial and succession framework.

Bibliography

"Absoliutni prava" [Absolute Rights]. 2007. In *Praktyka zastosuvannia terminiv, sliv ta slovospoluchen' u yurysprudentsii* [Practice of Using Terms, Words, and Phrases in Jurisprudence], *Ligazakon.net*. https://ips.ligakon.net/document/TS000005.

"Absoliutni prava" [Absolute Rights]. 2019. In *Velyka ukrains'ka entsyklopediia* [Great Ukrainian Encyclopedia]. https://vue.gov.ua/Абсолютн і_права.

Acampora, Christa Davis. 2013. *Contesting Nietzsche*. Chicago: University of Chicago Press.

Adakhovs'ka, N. 2012. *Mainovi prava fizychnykh osib pry opitsi* [Property Rights of Individuals under Guardianship]. *Aktual'ni problemy derzhavy i prava* 62: 405–411.

Aleksashyna, Yu. 2012. *Realizatsiia pryntsypiv dobrosovisnosti, spravedlyvosti, rozumnosti pry dohovornomu rehuliuvanni tsyvil'nykh vidnosyn* [Implementation of the Principles of Good Faith, Justice, and Reasonableness in the Contractual Regulation of Civil Relations]. *Yurydychna Ukraina* 11: 88–92.

Aleksii, R. V. 2018. *Aktual'ni problemy klasyfikatsii pravochyniv iz vadamy voli* [Current Problems of Classification of Transactions with Vitiated Will]. *Pravovi novely* 6: 16–22.

Aleksii, R. V. 2019. *Zlovzhyvannia svobodoiu dohovoru v deiakykh pravochynakh z vadamy voli* [Abuse of Freedom of Contract in Certain Transactions with Vitiated Will]. *Yurydychnyi naukovyi elektronnyi zhurnal* 1: 55–58.

Aleksii, R. V. 2020. *Pravochyny z vadamy voli: problemy teorii ta praktyky* [Transactions with Vitiated Will: Problems of Theory and Practice]. Abstract of a PhD dissertation, Vasyl' Stefanyk Precarpathian National University.

Alpers, Ann, and Bernard Lo. 1997. "Does It Make Clinical Sense to Equate Terminally Ill Patients Who Require Life-Sustaining Interventions with Those Who Do Not?" *JAMA* 277 (21): 1705–1708.

Analitychnyi ohliad prava na svobodu ta osobystu nedotorkanist' v Ukraini [Analytical Review of the Right to Liberty and Personal Inviolability in Ukraine]. 2015. Ukrains'ka Hel'sins'ka spilka z prav liudyny. Accessed October 4, 2025. https://helsinki.org.ua/articles/analitychnyj-ohlyad-prava-na-svobodu-ta-osobystu-nedotorkanist-v-ukrajini/

Andrianov, M. 2005. *Zabezpechennia vykonannia dohovirnykh zobov'iazan' ta pryntsyp publichnosti yak element zabezpechennia vykonannia dohovirnykh zobov'iazan'* [Ensuring the Performance of Contractual Obligations and the Principle of Publicity as an Element of Ensuring Performance]. *Yurydychnyi zhurnal* 6: 69–75.

Andriievs'ka, *O. O.* 2012. *Okhorona ta zakhyst prav na pryvatne zhyttia osoby* [Protection and Defense of the Rights to a Person's Private Life]. *Chasopys Akademii advokatury Ukrainy* 14: 1–6.

Appiah, K. 2015. *Nalezhna povaha: chest u zhytti prava* [Due Respect: Honor in the Life of the Law]. *Filosofiia prava i zahal'na teoriia prava* 1–2: 102–119.

Aristotle. 2003. *Polityka* [Politics]. Translated by O. Kysliuk. Kyiv: Osnovy.

Atiyah, P. S., and Charles Fried. 1981. "Contract as Promise: A Theory of Contractual Obligation." *Harvard Law Review* 95 (2): 509. https://doi.org/10.2307/1340714.

Augustine. *On the Trinity*: Books 8-15. Edited by Gareth B. Matthews. Translated by Stephen McKenna. Cambridge: Cambridge University Press, 2002.

Azimov, Ch. N. 2000. *Servituty v tsyvil'nomu pravi Ukrainy* [Servitudes in the Civil Law of Ukraine]. *Visnyk Akademii pravovykh nauk Ukrainy* 20 (1): 107–114.

Azimov, Ch. N., M. M. Sybilov, and V. I. Borysova. 2000. *Tsyvil'ne pravo Ukrainy. Ch. 1* [Civil Law of Ukraine. Part 1]. Edited by Ch. N. Azimov, S. N. Prystup, and V. M. Ihnatenko. Kharkiv: Pravo.

Baadzhy, N. 2008. *Pidstavy ta umovy vynyknennia zobov'iazan' z vidshkoduvannia shkody* [Grounds and Conditions for the Emergence of Obligations for Damages]. *Aktual'ni problemy derzhavy i prava* 41: 184–190.

Babych, O. 2011. *Zghoda na medychne vtruchannia* [Consent to Medical Intervention]. SlideShare. Accessed October 4, 2025. https://www.slideshare.net/rmesvasyamba/ss-8770375.

Bagnall, Roger S. 2012. *The Encyclopedia of Ancient History*. Malden: Wiley-Blackwell.

Baker, N. L., and J. L. Mason. 2009. "Gender Issues in Psychological Testing of Personality and Abilities." In *Handbook of Gender Research in Psychology*, 63–88. New York: Springer.

Basai, *O.* 2014. *Zahal'ni zasady (pryntsypy) tsyvil'noho zakonodavstva Ukrainy* [General Principles of Civil Legislation of Ukraine]. Abstract of a Dr. of Laws dissertation, National University "Odesa Law Academy."

Basai, O. 2018. *Oznaky pryntsypiv tsyvil'noho prava* [Features of the Principles of Civil Law]. *Yurydychnyi chasopys Natsional'noi akademii vnutrishnikh sprav* 16 (2): 68–77.

Basai, O. V. 2013. *Neprypustymist' svavil'noho vtruchannia u sferu osobystoho zhyttia yak zahal'na zasada tsyvil'noho zakonodavstva Ukrainy* [Inadmissibility of Arbitrary Interference in the Sphere of Personal Life as a General Principle of Civil Legislation of Ukraine]. *Chasopys Natsional'noho universytetu "Ostroz'ka akademiia." Seriia "Pravo"* 2 (8).

Basai, O. V. 2018. *Spravedlyvist' yak fundamental'na katehoriia tsyvil'noho prava Ukrainy* [Justice as a Fundamental Category of Civil Law of Ukraine]. *Naukovyi visnyk Natsional'noi akademii vnutrishnikh sprav* 4 (109): 87–98.

Batozhs'ka, O. V. 2010. *Dohovir zberihannia avtotransportnykh zasobiv* [Contract for the Storage of Motor Vehicles]. PhD dissertation, Yaroslav Mudryi National Law University.

Batozhs'ka, O. V. 2012. *Porushennia zobov'iazannia yak pidstava tsyvil'nopravovoi vidpovidal'nosti* [Breach of Obligation as a Basis for Civil Liability]. *Visnyk KhNUVS* 56 (1): 320–325.

Beatson, Jack, and Eltjo J. H. Schrage, eds. 2003. *Cases, Materials and Texts on Unjustified Enrichment*. London: Bloomsbury Publishing.

Belo, L. 2019. *Mainova samostiinist' sub'iektiv tsyvil'nykh (pryvatnykh) vidnosyn yak odna iz zasad tsyvil'noho prava* [Property Independence of Subjects of Civil (Private) Relations as One of the Principles of Civil Law]. *Pravova pozytsiia* 23 (2): 90–95.

Berne Convention for the Protection of Literary and Artistic Works. 1886. September 9.

Biga, Lindsay M., ed. 2025. *Anatomy and Physiology*. 2nd ed. Oregon State Open Educational Resources. https://open.oregonstate.education/anatomy2e/

Bilets'kyi, D. 2018. *Sposoby prypynennia prava pryvatnoi vlasnosti za tsyvil'nym zakonodavstvom Ukrainy* [Methods of Terminating the Right of Private Property under the Civil Legislation of Ukraine]. PhD dissertation, National University "Odesa Law Academy."

Biriukov, I. A., and Yu. O. Zaika. 2006. *Tsyvil'ne pravo Ukrainy. Zahal'na chastyna* [Civil Law of Ukraine: General Part]. Kyiv: KNT.

Blazhivs'ka, O. 2007. *Dohovir pro spil'nu diial'nist'* [Joint Activity Agreement]. Abstract of a PhD dissertation, Taras Shevchenko National University of Kyiv.

Blikhar, V. 2015. *Filosofs'ko-pravova interpretatsiia svobody voli* [Philosophical and Legal Interpretation of Free Will]. *Naukovyi visnyk Uzhhorods'koho natsional'noho universytetu. Seriia "Pravo"* 3 (34): 149–152.

Blitz, Marc Jonathan, and Jan Christoph Bublitz, eds. 2021. *The Law and Ethics of Freedom of Thought, Volume 1: Neuroscience, Autonomy, and Individual Rights*. Cham: Springer Nature Switzerland AG.

Bobryk, V. 2004. *Tsyvil'no-pravova okhorona osobystoho zhyttia fizychnykh osib* [Civil Law Protection of the Personal Life of Individuals]. Abstract of a PhD dissertation, Yaroslav Mudryi National Law University.

Bodnar, T. 2005. *Vykonannia dohovirnykh zobov'iazan' u tsyvil'nomu pravi* [Performance of Contractual Obligations in Civil Law]. Kyiv: Yurinkom Inter.

Boehm, Theodore R. 2003. "A Tangled Webb – Reexamining the Role of Duty in Indiana Negligence Actions." *Indiana Law Review* 37 (1).

Boethius, A. 1999. *Consolation of Philosophy*. London: Penguin Classics.

Bondar, N. 2015. *Preventyvnyi zakhyst tsyvil'nykh prav* [Preventive Protection of Civil Rights]. Abstract of a PhD dissertation, Yaroslav Mudryi National Law University.

Borysova, L. 2011. *Publichni liudy: de zakinchuiet'sia "suspil'nyi interes" i pochynaiet'sia pryvatnist'?* [Public Figures: Where Does "Public Interest" End and Privacy Begin?]. *Informatsiino-analitychna hazeta "Kontrast."* Accessed October 4, 2025. http://www.kontrast.org.ua/news/1294.html.

Borysova, V. 2017. *Pryntsypy tsyvil'noho prava* [Principles of Civil Law]. *Pravo Ukrainy* 7: 67–75.

Borysova, V., L. Baranova, and I. Zhylinkova. 2007. *Tsyvil'ne pravo Ukrainy* [Civil Law of Ukraine]. Vol. 1. Edited by V. Borysova, I. Spasybo-Fatieieva, and V. Yarotskyi. Kyiv: Yurinkom Inter.

Boudon, Raymond. 2003. "Beyond Rational Choice Theory." *Annual Review of Sociology* 29 (1): 1–21.

Brabender, Virginia. 2022. "Gender, Gender Identity, and Sexual Orientation in Personality and Personality Assessment." In *The Oxford Handbook of Personality and Psychopathology Assessment*, 2nd ed. Oxford: Oxford University Press.

Bratel', O. 2003. *Tsyvil'no-pravovi naslidky nadzvychainykh sytuatsii* [Civil Law Consequences of Emergency Situations]. Abstract of a PhD dissertation, Yaroslav Mudryi National Law University.

Brooks, Thom. 2012. *Hegel's Philosophy of Right*. Oxford: Wiley.

Brovko, N. I. 2007. *Osobysta svoboda indyvida yak forma realizatsii idei svobody voli v filosofii prava H.V.F. Hehelia* [Personal Freedom of the Individual as a Form of Realisation of the Idea of Free Will in the Philosophy of Law of G.W.F. Hegel]. *Naukovyi visnyk Kyivs'koho natsional'noho universytetu vnutrishnikh sprav* 3: 43–51.

Brovko, N. I. 2010. *Zakhyst prava liudyny na osobystu svobodu v konteksti protydii torhivli liudmy: filosofs'ko-pravovi zasady* [Protection of the Human Right to Personal Liberty in the Context of Combating Human Trafficking: Philosophical and Legal Principles]. Abstract of a PhD dissertation, National Academy of Internal Affairs.

Brown, Chris, Terry Nardin, and Nicholas J. Rengger, eds. 2002. *International Relations in Political Thought.* Cambridge: Cambridge University Press.

Brox, Hans, and Wolf-Dietrich Walker. 2022. *Allgemeiner Teil des BGB* [General Part of the BGB]. Munich: Vahlen.

Bubina, A. 2008. *Deiaki problemy pravovoho rehuliuvannia vidshkoduvannia shkody, zavdanoi dzherelom pidvyshchenoi nebezpeky* [Some Problems of Legal Regulation of Compensation for Damage Caused by a Source of Increased Danger]. *Aktual'ni problemy derzhavy i prava* 43: 180–184.

Buletsa, S. 2012. *Vidshkoduvannia shkody pry riatuvanni zhyttia ta zdorovia fizychnoi osoby* [Compensation for Damage while Rescuing the Life and Health of an Individual]. *Visnyk Zaporiz'koho natsional'noho universytetu* 1 (2): 90–94.

Buletsa, S. B. 2004. *Pravo na zhyttia zarodku: tsyvil'no-pravove rehuliuvannia shtuchnoho pereryvannia vahitnosti (abortu)* [The Right to Life of the Fetus: Civil Law Regulation of Artificial Termination of Pregnancy (Abortion)]. *Aktual'ni problemy derzhavy i prava* 22: 584–590.

Buletsa, S. B. 2012. *Vidmova vid likuvannia yak odne z tsyvil'nykh prav patsienta* [Refusal of Treatment as One of the Civil Rights of a Patient]. *Aktual'ni problemy derzhavy i prava* 66: 504–512.

Buletsa, S. B., and O. I. Chepys, eds. 2019. *Pravo intelektual'noi vlasnosti* [Intellectual Property Law]. Uzhhorod: RIK-U.

Burdeniuk, S. 2016. *Harantii zakhystu prava vlasnosti vidpovidno do art. 1 Pershoho protokolu konventsii pro zakhyst prav liudyny i osnovopolozhnykh svobod* [Guarantees of Protection of Property Rights in Accordance with art. 1 of the First Protocol to the Convention for the Protection of Human Rights and Fundamental Freedoms]. *Pidpryiemnytstvo, hospodarstvo i pravo* 12: 19–23.

Bürgerliches Gesetzbuch [Civil Code]. 1896. Gesetze im Internet. https://www.gesetze-im-internet.de/bgb/.

Burgerlijk Wetboek (Dutch Civil Code), Book 5. 1992. (As amended). https://wetten.overheid.nl/BWBR0005288/.

Burge v Swarbrick. 2007. HCA 17; 232 CLR 336.

Bychkivs'kyi, O. 2010. *Spadkovyi dohovir: problemni pytannia zakonodavchoho vrehuliuvannia* [Inheritance Agreement: Problematic Issues of Legislative Regulation]. *Visnyk Zaporiz'koho natsional'noho universytetu* 2: 136–141.

Campbell, Tom D., and Jeremy Waldron. 1990. "The Right to Private Property." *Journal of Law and Society* 17 (2): 263. https://doi.org/10.2307/1410091.

Carey Miller, David L. 1996. "Transfer of Ownership." In *Southern Cross: Civil Law and Common Law in South Africa*, 726–758. Oxford: Oxford University Press.

Carlill v. Carbolic Smoke Ball Co. 1893. 1 QB 256 (CA).

Carter v. Canada (Attorney General). 2015. 1 S.C.R. 331.

Cour de cassation [Cass.] [supreme court for judicial matters] 1e civ., Feb. 11, 1986, J.C.P. 1986, IV, 110 (Fr.)

Cour de cassation [Cass.] [supreme court for judicial matters] civ., Oct. 28, 1942, D.C. 1943, 29 (Fr.).

Cour de cassation [Cass.] [supreme court for judicial matters] com., Jan. 12, 1999, J.C.P. 1999, II, 10070 (Fr.).

Chaban, O. M. 2022. *Zobov'iazannia z publichnoi obitsianky vynahorody bez oholoshennia konkursu* [Obligations from a Public Promise of a Reward without Announcing a Competition]. In *Suchasni napriamy rozvytku ekonomiky, pidpryiemnytstva, tekhnolohii ta yikh pravovoho zabezpechennia*, 449–452. Lviv: LEB.

Chan, B., and Margaret Somerville. 2016. "Converting the 'Right to Life' to the 'Right to Physician-Assisted Suicide and Euthanasia': An Analysis of *Carter v. Canada (Attorney General)*, Supreme Court of Canada." *Medical Law Review* 24 (2): 143–175.

Chanieva, M., and N. Filipova. 2021. *Spadkuvannia za zapovitom yak spetsial'nyi vyd spadkuvannia* [Inheritance by Will as a Special Type of Inheritance]. *LXXVI Mizhnarodna naukovo-praktychna internet-konferentsiia: "Naukovi pidsumky"*, 180–185.

Chepa, M.-L. 2001. *Shliakh vid narodzhennia do smerti: osmyslennia sutnisnykh rivniv liuds'koho rozvytku* [The Path from Birth to Death: Understanding the Essential Levels of Human Development]. *Problemy zahal'noi ta pedahohichnoi psykholohii* 3 (2): 31–40.

Chepys, I. V., and E. A. Pysarieva. 2021. *Osoblyvosti pravovoho rehuliuvannia spadkovoho dohovoru v Ukraini ta zarubizhnykh krainakh* [Peculiarities of the Legal Regulation of the Inheritance Agreement in Ukraine and Foreign Countries]. *Visnyk naukovoho tovarystva DonNU imeni Vasylia Stusa* 1 (13): 151–155.

Cherepakha, I. 2017. *Pravove rehuliuvannia poriadku vykorystannia imeni* [Legal Regulation of the Procedure for Using a Name]. *Spivdruzhnist' nauk: arkhitektura, ekonomika, pravo*, 350–354.

Cherevko, P. P. 2022. "The Legal Nature of the Author's Personal Non-Property Rights." *Analytical and Comparative Jurisprudence* 3: 335–339.

Chernohor, N. 2011. *Stroky ta terminy u spadkovomu pravi Ukrainy* [Time Limits and Terms in the Inheritance Law of Ukraine]. Abstract of a PhD dissertation, National University "Odesa Law Academy."

Chernohor, N. V. 2010. *Chas vidkryttia spadshchyny za zapovitom z umovoiu* [The Time of Opening of Inheritance under a Will with a Condition]. *Aktual'ni problemy derzhavy i prava* 53: 218–222.

Cherviatsova, A. O. 2013. *Pravo na zhyttia – pravo buty narodzhenym (pytannia pravovoho rehuliuvannia shtuchnoho pereryvannia vahitnosti za ukrains'kym zakonodavstvom)* [The Right to Life – The Right to Be Born (Issues of Legal Regulation of Artificial Termination of Pregnancy under Ukrainian Legislation)]. *Visnyk Kharkivs'koho natsional'noho universytetu imeni V. N. Karazina. Ser. "Pravo"* 15: 226–228.

Chornoochenko, S. 2000. *Osobysti nemainovi prava, yaki zabezpechuiut sotsial'ne isnuvannia fizychnykh osib v Ukraini* [Personal Non-property Rights That Ensure the Social Existence of Individuals in Ukraine]. Abstract of a PhD dissertation, Yaroslav Mudryi National Law University.

Chubokha, N. F. 2013. *Pryntsyp dyspozytyvnosti u tsyvil'nomu pravi Ukrainy* [The Principle of Dispositivity in the Civil Law of Ukraine]. *Naukovyi visnyk Uzhhorods'koho natsional'noho universytetu. Seriia "Pravo"* 1 (21, part 2): 299–302.

Cicero, Marcus Tullius. 1991. *On Fate*. Liverpool: Liverpool University Press.

Cicero, Marcus Tullius. 2010. *Cicero's Tusculan Disputations*. Kessinger Publishing.

Bernard of Clairvaux. 1987. *Selected Works*. Mahwah: Paulist Press.

Claraevallensis, Bernardus. 1620. *Opera omnia sancti*. Apud P. and I. Balleros.

Code civil [Civil Code]. n.d. (As amended). Legifrance. https://www.legifrance.gouv.fr/codes/texte_lc/LEGITEXT000006070721/.

Code rural et de la pêche maritime [Rural and Maritime Fishing Code]. 2026. Legifrance. https://www.legifrance.gouv.fr/codes/id/LEGITEXT000006071367/.

Cohen, Chapman. 1919. *Determinism or Free-Will?* London: The Pioneer Press.

Coleman, James S., Boris Frankel, and Derek L. Phillips. 1976. "Robert Nozick's *Anarchy, State, and Utopia.*" *Theory and Society* 3: 437–458.

"Compatibilism." 2024. In *Stanford Encyclopedia of Philosophy*. Retrieved October 4, 2025. https://plato.stanford.edu/entries/compatibilism/

Conditions of Patentability. 2010. 35 U.S.C. § 103.

"Conformism." 2023. In *Cambridge Dictionary*. Retrieved October 4, 2025. https://dictionary.cambridge.org/dictionary/english/conformism

Continental Casualty Co. v. Argentina. 2008. ICSID Case No. ARB/03/9. International Center for Settlement of Investment Disputes. September 5. https://www.italaw.com/cases/329.

Convention on the Grant of European Patents (European Patent Convention). 1973. October 5. 1065 U.N.T.S. 199.

Cooper, John M., ed. 1997. *Plato: Complete Works*. Indianapolis: Hackett Publishing.

Copenhaver, Brian P. 2022. *Pico della Mirandola on Trial*. Oxford: Oxford University Press.

Council Directive 93/13/EEC. 1993. "On Unfair Terms in Consumer Contracts." *Official Journal of the European Communities* L 95 (April 21).

Council of Europe. 1950. *European Convention for the Protection of Human Rights and Fundamental Freedoms*. ETS No. 005, November 4. https://www.echr.coe.int/documents/convention_eng.pdf.

Council of Europe. 2002. *European Convention for the Prevention of Torture and Inhuman or Degrading Treatment or Punishment*. December 20. https://rm.coe.int/16806dbaf0.

Council of Europe. 1983. *Protocol 6 to the European Convention for the Protection of Human Rights and Fundamental Freedoms concerning the Abolition of Death Penalty*. ETS No. 114, April 28.

Criddle, Evan J., Paul B. Miller, and Robert H. Sitkoff, eds. 2019. *The Oxford Handbook of Fiduciary Law*. Oxford: Oxford University Press.

Danylyan, O. 2009. *Filosofiia prava* [Philosophy of Law]. Kharkiv: *Pravo*.

Danylyan, O., ed. 2017. *Filosofiia prava* [Philosophy of Law]. Kharkiv: *Pravo*.

De Caro, Mario, and Hilary Putnam. 2020. "Free Will and Quantum Mechanics." *The Monist* 103 (4): 415–426.

De Tavernier, Johan. 2009. "The Historical Roots of Personalism." *Ethical Perspectives* 16 (3): 361–392.

Dennett, Daniel. 2007. *Die Erforschung des Bewußtseins und der Schlaf der Philosophie* [The Exploration of Consciousness and the Sleep of Philosophy]. Frankfurt am Main: Suhrkamp Verlag.

Denysov, S., and H. Zubov. 2016. *Rozuminnia "svobody" i "voli" v suchasnomu natsional'nomu pravi ta zakonodavstvi* [Understanding "Freedom" and "Will" in Modern National Law and Legislation]. *Yurydychna nauka* 64 (10): 4–15.

Descartes, René. 1985. *The Philosophical Writings of Descartes*. Cambridge: Cambridge University Press.

Dews, Peter. 2023. *Schelling's Late Philosophy in Confrontation with Hegel*. Oxford: OUP USA.

"Dialogue. The Critique: Sociobiology: Another Biological Determinism." 1976. *BioScience* 26 (3): 182–186.

Directive 2001/29/EC of the European Parliament and of the Council of 22 May 2001 on the harmonisation of certain aspects of copyright and related rights in the information society. 2001. *Official Journal of the European Communities* L 167. June 22.

Dodina, A. 2001. *Administratyvno-pravovyi status hromads'kykh orhanizatsii v Ukraini* [Administrative and Legal Status of Public Organizations in Ukraine]. PhD dissertation, Odesa National Academy of Law.

"*Doklad: Chislo smertnykh kaznei v 2018 godu snizilos' do minimuma za desiat' let*" [Report: The Number of Executions in 2018 Decreased to a Ten-Year Low]. 2019. Amnesty International. https://eurasia.amnesty.org/2019/04/10/doklad-amnesty-chislo-smertnyh-kaznej-v-2018-godu/.

Donchenko, O. 2010. *Svoboda yak katehoriia prava* [Freedom as a Category of Law]. Abstract of a PhD dissertation, National University "Odesa Law Academy."

Donchenko, O. P. 2009. *Svoboda yak katehoriia prava (hermenevtychnyi aspekt)* [Freedom as a Category of Law (a Hermeneutic Aspect)]. *Aktual'ni problemy derzhavy i prava* 45: 45–50.

Dosi, Giovanni, and Joseph E. Stiglitz. 2014. "The Role of Intellectual Property Rights in the Development Process, with Some Lessons from Developed Countries: An Introduction." In *Intellectual Property Rights*, 1–53. Oxford: Oxford University Press.

Dovhert, A., ed. 2000. *Kodyfikatsiia pryvatnoho (tsyvil'noho) prava Ukrainy* [Codification of Private (Civil) Law of Ukraine]. Kyiv: Ukrainian Center for Legal Studies.

Dreyfuss, Rochelle, and Justine Pila, eds. 2017. *The Oxford Handbook of Intellectual Property Law*. Oxford: Oxford University Press.

Drozdova, N. 2005. *Dohovir pro nadannia finansovykh posluh u tsyvil'nomu pravi Ukrainy* [The Contract for the Provision of Financial Services in the Civil Law of Ukraine]. Abstract of a PhD dissertation, Taras Shevchenko National University of Kyiv.

Duncan, Rebecca E., and Susan M. Sawyer. 2010. "Respecting Adolescents' Autonomy (as Long as They Make the Right Choice)." *Journal of Adolescent Health* 47 (2): 113–114.

Dutoit, Bernard. 2003. "Perspectives comparatives sur la succession ab intestat" [Comparative Perspectives on Ab Intestat Succession]. In *Le droit des successions en Europe : actes du colloque de Lausanne*, 13.

Dvornichenko, A. S. 2014. *Osoblyvosti medychnoho vtruchannia bez informovanoi zghody patsiienta* [Peculiarities of Medical Intervention without the Patient's Informed Consent]. *Naukovyi visnyk Mizhnarodnoho humanitarnoho universytetu. Seriia: "Yurysprudentsiia"* 2 (12): 31–37.

Dzera, O., et al. 2011. *Komentar do Tsyvil'noho kodeksu Ukrainy* [Commentary on the Civil Code of Ukraine]. Pravovyi portal "Yuryskonsult." Accessed October 4, 2025. https://legalexpert.in.ua/komkodeks/gk.html

Dzera, O. V., N. S. Kuznietsova, and V. V. Luts, eds. 2019. *Naukovo-praktychnyi komentar Tsyvil'noho kodeksu Ukrainy* [Scientific and Practical Commentary on the Civil Code of Ukraine]. Vol. 1. Kyiv: *Yurinkom Inter*.

Dzera, O. V., N. S. Kuznietsova, and R. A. Maidanyk, eds. 2017. *Tsyvil'ne pravo Ukrainy. Osoblyva chastyna* [Civil Law of Ukraine: Special Part]. 5th ed. Kyiv: *Yurinkom Inter*.

European Court of Human Rights. 1976. *Handyside v. United Kingdom*. Application No. 5493/72. December 7. https://hudoc.echr.coe.int/eng?i=001-57499.

European Court of Human Rights. 1979. *Marckx v. Belgium*. Application No. 6833/74. June 13. https://hudoc.echr.coe.int/eng?i=001-57534.

European Court of Human Rights. 1988. *Müller and Others v. Switzerland*. Application No. 10737/84. May 24. https://hudoc.echr.coe.int/eng?i=001-57543.

European Court of Human Rights. 1994. *Otto-Preminger-Institut v. Austria*. Application No. 13470/87. September 20. https://hudoc.echr.coe.int/eng?i=001-57897.

European Court of Human Rights. 2002. *Pretty v. United Kingdom*. Application No. 2346/02. April 29. https://hudoc.echr.coe.int/eng?i=001-60448.

European Court of Human Rights. 2005. *Gongadze v. Ukraine*. Application No. 34056/02. November 8. https://hudoc.echr.coe.int/eng?i=001-70964.

European Court of Human Rights. 2008. *Kats and Others v. Ukraine*. Application No. 29971/04. December 18. https://hudoc.echr.coe.int/eng?i=001-90345.

European Court of Human Rights. 2011a. *Haas v. Switzerland*. Application No. 31322/07. January 20. https://hudoc.echr.coe.int/eng?i=001-102940

European Court of Human Rights. 2011b. *Matushevskyi and Matushevska v. Ukraine*. Application No. 59461/08. June 23. https://hudoc.echr.coe.int/eng?i=001-105315.

European Court of Human Rights. 2012. *Gorovenky and Bugara v. Ukraine*. Application Nos. 36146/05 and 42418/05. January 12. https://hudoc.echr.coe.int/eng?i=001-108507.

European Court of Human Rights. 2013a. *Garnaga v. Ukraine*. Application No. 20390/07. May 16. https://hudoc.echr.coe.int/eng?i=001-119642.

European Court of Human Rights. 2013b. *Shchokin v. Ukraine*. Application Nos. 23759/03 and 37943/06. October 3. https://hudoc.echr.coe.int/eng?i=001-126532.

European Court of Human Rights. 2015. *Pryluts'kyi v. Ukraine*. Application No. 40429/08. February 26. https://hudoc.echr.coe.int/eng?i=001-152431.

Ehman, Robert R. 1961. "The Ideas of Reason." *The Review of Metaphysics* 15 (2): 225–235.

Eisenberg, Melvin Aron. 2018. *Foundational Principles of Contract Law*. Oxford: Oxford University Press.

Eleftheriadis, Pavlos. 2008. "The Right to Property." In *Legal Rights*, 129–148. Oxford: Oxford University Press.

Emerson, Caryl, George Pattison, and Randall A. Poole, eds. 2020. *The Oxford Handbook of Russian Religious Thought*. Oxford: OUP Oxford.

Energy Charter Treaty. 1994. December 17. https://www.energycharter.org/fileadmin/DocumentsMedia/Legal/ECTC-en.pdf.

Ennan, R. 2010. *Pravove rehuliuvannia vidnosyn intelektual'noi vlasnosti u Yevropeis'komu Soiuzi* [Legal Regulation of Intellectual Property Relations in the European Union]. Abstract of a PhD dissertation, National University "Odesa Law Academy."

Ennan, R. 2021. *Moral'ni (osobysti nemainovi) prava avtora: kontseptual'ni zasady ta yurydychna pryroda* [Moral (Personal Non-Property) Rights of the Author: Conceptual Foundations and Legal Nature]. *Aktual'ni problemy intelektual'noi, informatsiinoi, IT ta Internet prava*, 35–43.

Ergo Insurance SE v. If P&C Insurance AS. 2016. Case C-359/14. ECLI:EU:C:2016:40. January 21.

European Charter of Patients' Rights. 2002. November 15. Rome: Active Citizenship Network. https://www.activecitizenship.net/patients-rights/projects/29-european-charter-of-patients-rights.html.

Fedina, N. 2015. *Svoboda i rivnist' u pravovii diisnosti yak proiavy spravedlyvosti* [Freedom and Equality in Legal Reality as Manifestations of Justice]. *Naukovyi visnyk L'vivs'koho derzhavnoho universytetu vnutrishnikh sprav* 1: 71–79.

Fedorenko, T. 2017. *Problemy pravovoho rehuliuvannia spadkuvannia za zapovitom* [Problems of Legal Regulation of Inheritance by Will]. *Aktual'ni problemy vitchyznianoi yurysprudentsii* 3: 63–65.

Fedorych, I. 2018. *Zdiisnennia prava na spadkuvannia za tsyvilnym zakonodavstvom Ukrainy* [Exercise of the Right to Inheritance under the Civil Legislation of Ukraine]. PhD dissertation, Ivan Franko National University of Lviv.

Fediuk, L. 2006. *Systema osobystykh nemainovykh prav u tsyvilnym pravi* [The System of Personal Non-property Rights in Civil Law]. PhD dissertation, Vasyl Stefanyk Precarpathian National University.

Feinman, Jay M. 2018. *Law 101: Everything You Need to Know About American Law*. 5th ed. Oxford: Oxford University Press.

Feist Publications, Inc. v. Rural Telephone Service Co. 1991. 499 U.S. 340.

Feuerbach, Ludwig. 1986. *Principles of the Philosophy of the Future*. Indianapolis: Hackett Publishing Company.

Fleischer, Holger, Hideki Kanda, Kon-Sik Kim, and Peter Mülbert, eds. 2016. *German and Asian Perspectives on Company Law: Law and Policy Perspectives*. Tübingen: Mohr Siebeck. https://doi.org/10.1628/rabelsz-2018-0066.

Flume, Werner. 1979. *Allgemeiner Teil des Bürgerlichen Rechts. Band 2: Das Rechtsgeschäft* [General Part of the Civil Code. Volume 2: The Legal Transaction]. Berlin: Springer.

Fomichova, N. 2008. *Deiaki pytannia shchodo zdiisnennia protsedury pryiniattia spadshchyny* [Some Questions Regarding the Procedure for Accepting Inheritance]. *Aktual'ni problemy derzhavy i prava* 43: 211–215.

Fomichova, N. 2014. *Harantii zdiisnennia prava na vidmovu vid pryiniattia spadshchyny za Tsyvil'nym kodeksom Ukrainy* [Guarantees for Exercising the Right to Renounce Inheritance under the Civil Code of Ukraine]. *Chasopys tsyvilistyky* 17: 92–96.

Fried, Charles. 2014. "The Ambitions of Contract as Promise." In *Philosophical Foundations of Contract Law*, 17–41. Oxford: Oxford University Press.

Fromm, Erich. 2011. *Escape from Freedom*. New York: Ishi Press.

Gewirth, Alan. 1981. "Are There Any Absolute Rights?" *The Philosophical Quarterly* 31 (122): 1–16.

Gerber, M., A. Wittekind, G. Grote, and B. Staffelbach. 2009. "Exploring Types of Career Orientation: A Latent Class Analysis Approach." *Journal of Vocational Behavior* 75 (3): 303–18. https://doi.org/10.1016/j.jvb.2009.04.003.

Gertz v. Robert Welch, Inc. 1974. 418 U.S. 323.

Harasymiv, B. 2017. *Indyvidual'nist' u systemi sotsial'nykh zviazkiv: filosofs'ko-pravovyi aspekt* [Individuality in the System of Social Connections: A Philosophical and Legal Aspect]. *Visnyk Natsional'noho universytetu "L'vivs'ka politekhnika." Seriia: "Yurydychni nauky"* 865: 73–77.

Hasneziri, Luljeta. 2023. "The Principle of Autonomy of Contractual Will." *European Journal of Multidisciplinary Studies* 8 (1): 134–147.

Hehel', H. V. F. 2000. *Osnovy filosofii prava, abo pryrodne pravo i derzhavoznavstvo* [Elements of the Philosophy of Right, or Natural Law and Political Science]. Translated by R. Osadchuk and M. Kushnir. Kyiv: *Yunivers.*

Helych, Yu. 2010. *Informatsiino-pravovi harantii taiemnytsi osobystoho zhyttia liudyny* [Information and Legal Guarantees of the Secrecy of a Person's Private Life]. Abstract of a PhD dissertation, Taras Shevchenko National University of Kyiv.

Herman, K. Yu. 2015. *Rozvytok idei svobody u filosofs'kykh ta pravovykh doslidzhenniakh* [The Development of the Idea of Freedom in Philosophical and Legal Research]. *Pravo ta innovatsii* 11 (3): 115–123.

Herts, A. A. 2019. *Prychynnyi zviazok yak umova nastannia tsyvil'no-pravovoi vidpovidal'nosti pry nadanni medychnykh posluh* [Causal Connection as a Condition for Civil Liability in the Provision of Medical Services]. In *Pravovi problemy suchasnoi transformatsii okhorony zdorovia*, 39–41. Lviv: *Lvivs'kyi medychnyi forum.*

Hespanha, António Manuel. 2015. *Como os juristas viam o mundo. 1550-1750: direitos, estados, coisas, contratos, ações e crimes* [How Lawyers Saw the World. 1550-1750: Rights, States, Things, Contracts, Actions and Crimes]. CreateSpace Independent Publishing Platform.

Hobbes, Thomas. (1996). *Leviathan.* Edited by C. B. Macpherson. Penguin Books. (Original work published 1651).

Hoehner, P. J. 2003. "Ethical Aspects of Informed Consent in Obstetric Anesthesia - New Challenges and Solutions." *Journal of Clinical Anesthesia* 15 (8): 587–600.

Höffding, Harald. 1902. "Philosophy and Life." *The International Journal of Ethics* 12 (2): 137–151.

Hohol', B. M. 2010. *Pravo na informatsiiu u tsyvil'nomu pravi Ukrainy* [The Right to Information in the Civil Law of Ukraine]. Abstract of a PhD dissertation, Taras Shevchenko National University of Kyiv.

Holcomb, Justin S. 2018. *Christian Theologies of Salvation: A Comparative Introduction.* New York: NYU Press.

Holden, Thomas. 2023. *Hobbes's Philosophy of Religion.* Oxford: Oxford University Press.

Holubieva, N. 2008a. *Klasyfikatsiini kryterii dlia pobudovy systemy pryntsypiv tsyvil'noho prava Ukrainy* [Classification Criteria for Building the System of Principles of Civil Law of Ukraine]. *Aktual'ni problemy derzhavy i prava* 42: 20–24.

Holubieva, N. 2013. *Zobov'iazannia u tsyvil'nomu pravi Ukrainy: metodolohichni zasady pravovoho rehuliuvannia* [Obligations in the Civil Law of Ukraine: Methodological Foundations of Legal Regulation]. Abstract of a Dr. of Laws dissertation, National University "Odesa Law Academy."

Holubieva, N. Yu. 2007. *Zahal'na kharakterystyka pryntsypiv tsyvil'noho prava Ukrainy* [General Characteristics of the Principles of Civil Law of Ukraine]. *Aktual'ni problemy derzhavy i prava* 37: 282–286.

Holubieva, N. Yu. 2008b. *Pravova pryroda zahal'nykh zasad tsyvil'noho zakonodavstva Ukrainy* [The Legal Nature of the General Principles of Civil Legislation of Ukraine]. *Aktual'ni problemy derzhavy i prava* 43: 18–22.

Holubieva, N. Yu. 2008c. *Zakhyst prava vlasnosti pry pozbavlenni vlasnyka volodinnia (vindykatsiinyi pozov)* [Protection of Property Rights upon Deprivation of the Owner's Possession (Vindicatory Action)]. *Aktual'ni problemy derzhavy i prava* 41: 94–98.

Holubov, O. 2021. "Amnesty International: za rik u sviti zmenshylasia chyslo strat" [Amnesty International: The Number of Executions in the World has Decreased over the Year]. *DW,* April 21. https://www.dw.com/uk/amnesty-international-za-rik-u-sviti-zmenshylasia-kilkist-strat/a-57274654.

Hontar, M. 2017. *Pravo na indyvidual'nist' ta yoho mezhi* [The Right to Individuality and its Limits]. In *Rozvytok osvity, nauky, ekonomiky v umovakh intehratsiinykh protsesiv*, 94–96.

Honoré, Anthony Maurice. 1961. "Ownership." In *Oxford Essays in Jurisprudence,* edited by A. G. Guest, 107–147. Oxford: Oxford University Press.

Horobets', N. O. 2010. *Pravo na nedotorkannist' zhytla: tsyvil'no-pravovyi aspekt* [The Right to Inviolability of Housing: A Civil Law Aspect]. *Visnyk Kharkivs'koho natsional'noho universytetu vnutrishnikh sprav* 1: 19–52.

Horyslavs'kyi, K. O. 2003. *Pravo liudyny ta hromadianyna na samozakhyst zhyttia i zdorovia vid protypravnykh posiahan* [The Right of a Person and Citizen to Self-defense of Life and Health from Unlawful Encroachments]. PhD dissertation, Donetsk Law Institute of the Ministry of Internal Affairs of Ukraine.

Hospodars'kyi kodeks Ukrainy [Commercial Code of Ukraine]. 2003. Law of Ukraine No. 436-IV. Repealed August 28, 2025. https://zakon.rada.gov.ua/laws/show/436-15.

Howard, Rhoda E. 1993. "Cultural Absolutism and the Nostalgia for Community." *Human Rights Quarterly* 15 (2): 315–338.

Hrobova, V. P. 2009. *Shchodo vyznachennia zmistu katehorii "osobysta nedotorkannist'"* [Regarding the Definition of the Content of the Category "Personal Inviolability"]. *Forum prava* 2: 97–101.

Hrynko, S. 2010. *Prychynno-naslidkovyi zviazok yak ob'iektyvna mova vynyknennia deliktnykh zobov'iazan' Ukrainy* [Causation as an Objective Language for the Emergence of Tort Obligations in Ukraine]. *Universytets'ki naukovi zapysky* 34 (2): 66–78.

Hrynko, S. 2012. *Prostyi vypadok (casus) yak pidstava zvil'nennia vid deliktnoi vidpovidal'nosti za ryms'kym pryvatnym pravom i zakonodavstvom Ukrainy ta yevropeis'kykh krain* [A Simple Case (casus) as a Ground for Exemption from Tort Liability under Roman Private Law and the Legislation of Ukraine and European Countries]. *Pryvatne pravo i pidpryiemnytstvo* 11: 175–178.

Huivan, P. 2021. *Dobra sovist' okupanta yak odyn z osnovnykh chynnykiv utrymannia chuzhoho maina ta nabuttia prava vlasnosti za davnistiu volodinnia* [The Good Faith of the Occupant as One of the Main Factors in Retaining Another's Property and Acquiring Ownership by Acquisitive Prescription]. *Vcheni zapysky Tavriis'koho natsional'noho universytetu imeni V. I. Vernads'koho. Seriia: "Yurydychni nauky"* 32 (71), 4: 7–12.

Huivan, P. D. 2019. *Temporal'ni kharakterystyky volodinnia chuzhym mainom: posesornyi zakhyst* [Temporal Characteristics of Possession of Another's Property: Possessory Protection]. *Naukovi pratsi Natsional'noho universytetu "Odes'ka yurydychna akademiia"* 24.

Gunderman, Richard B. 2006. "Aristotle on Leadership." *Journal of the American College of Radiology* 3 (1): 64–66.

Hutsuliak, V. K. 2022. *Rozvytok konstruktsii dohovoru pro spil'nu diial'nist' u vitchyznianii pravovii systemi XX stolittia* [Development of the Joint Activity Agreement Structure in the Domestic Legal System of the 20th Century]. In *Rozvytok hromadians'koho suspil'stva yak neobkhidna skladova yevropeis'koi intehratsii Ukrainy*, 90–92.

Hague Convention for the Protection of Cultural Property in the Event of Armed Conflict. 1954. May 14.

Hannan, Barbara. 2009. *The Riddle of the World: A Reconsideration of Schopenhauer's Philosophy*. Oxford: Oxford University Press.

Iasechko, S. V. 2013. "Pravochyny, napravleni na perekhid prava na osobysti papery" [Transactions Aimed at the Transfer of the Right to Personal Papers]. *Forum Prava* [Forum of Law], no. 4: 432–436. http://nbuv.gov.ua/UJRN/FP_index.htm_2013_4_76

Ievinia, O. 2014. "Zapovit u nadzvychainykh obstavynakh" [A Will in Extraordinary Circumstances]. In *Spadkuvannia v Ukraini*, 15–17. Kyiv.

Ihnatenko, V. M. 2012. *Osoblyvosti vykonannia nedohovirnykh rehuliatyvnykh zobov'iazan'* [Peculiarities of the Performance of Non-contractual Regulatory Obligations]. *Visnyk Kharkivs'koho natsional'noho universytetu imeni V. N. Karazina. Seriia "Pravo"* 1028: 164–167.

Jansen, Nils. 2010. "The Concept of Non-Contractual Obligations: Rethinking the Divisions of Tort, Unjustified Enrichment, and Contract Law." *Journal of European Tort Law* 1 (1): 16–47.

Jaspers, Karl. 2000. *The Question of German Guilt*. New York: Fordham University Press.

Jaspers, Karl. 2011. *The Origin and Goal of History*. London: Routledge.

Jobbágyi, Gábor. 1994. *A méhmagzat életjoga – az abortuszlegalizáció konfliktusa* [The Right to Life of the Fetus - The Conflict of the Legalization of Abortion]. Budapest: Szent István Társulat.

Johnson, Laurie M. 2020. *Thucydides, Hobbes, and the Interpretations of Realism*. Ithaca: Cornell University Press.

Cambridge Dictionary. 2015. s.v. "Justice." Accessed October 4, 2025. https://dictionary.cambridge.org/dictionary/english/justice.

Oxford English Dictionary. 2014. s.v. "Justice." Accessed October 4, 2025. https://www.oed.com/viewdictionaryentry/Entry/102198.

Kachala, I. I. 2010. *Kryminal'na vidpovidal'nist' za vchynennia zlochyniv proty chesti ta hidnosti osoby* [Criminal Liability for Crimes against a Person's Honor and Dignity]. *Aktual'ni problemy derzhavy i prava* 55: 248–252.

Kalaur, I. 2016. *Dohovir u mekhanizmi pravovoho rehuliuvannia vidnosyn z peredannia maina v korystuvannia* [The Contract in the Mechanism of Legal Regulation of Relations for the Transfer of Property for Use]. *Aktual'ni problemy pravoznavstva* 1: 114–118.

Kant, Immanuel. 2007. *Critique of Pure Reason*. London: Penguin Classics.

Kant, Immanuel. 2017. *Critique of Practical Reason*. Cambridge: Cambridge University Press.

Kantzer Komline, Han-luen I. 2012. Review of *Mind, Text, and Commentary: Noetic Exegesis in Origen of Alexandria, Didymus the Blind, and Evagrius Ponticus*, by Blossom Stefaniw. *The Journal of Theological Studies* 63 (1): 310–312.

Karashchuk, O. O. 2019. *Mistse heohrafichnoho zaznachennia sered ob'iektiv prava intelektual'noi vlasnosti* [The Place of a Geographical Indication among Intellectual Property Objects]. *Prykarpats'kyi yurydychnyi visnyk* 1 (3, no. 28): 92–95.

Karnaukh, B. P. 2014. *Vyna yak umova tsyvil'no-pravovoi vidpovidal'nosti* [Fault as a Condition of Civil Liability]. Kharkiv: *Pravo*.

Karpenko, N. A. 2016. *Psykholohiia tvorchosti* [The Psychology of Creativity]. Lviv: *LvDUVS*.

Kasilova, D. Yu. 2012. *Pidstavy vynyknennia i prypynennia volodinnia* [Grounds for the Emergence and Termination of Possession]. *Pravova derzhava* 14: 35–40.

Kennedy, David, and Joseph E. Stiglitz, eds. 2013. *Law and Economics with Chinese Characteristics*. Oxford: Oxford University Press.

Khamula, D. S., and L. V. Kuznetsova. 2020. *Kharakterni osoblyvosti spadkovoho dohovoru* [Characteristic Features of the Inheritance Agreement]. *Travnevi pravovi chytannia*, 119–120.

Kharchenko, H. 2012. *Pryntsyp dobrosovisnoho nabuttia rechovoho prava* [The Principle of Good Faith Acquisition of a Real Right]. *Pidpryiemnytstvo, hospodarstvo i pravo* 193: 51–54.

Kharytonov, Ye. 2008. *Pryntsypy tsyvil'noho prava Ukrainy: do postanovky problemy* [Principles of the Civil Law of Ukraine: Toward Posing the Problem]. *Aktual'ni problemy derzhavy i prava* 42: 7–13.

Kharytonov, Ye. 2015. *Zobov'iazannia, shcho vynykaiut' vnaslidok vidvernennia shkody, u Tsyvil'nomu kodeksi Ukrainy* [Obligations Arising from the Aversion of Harm in the Civil Code of Ukraine]. *Pravo Ukrainy* 4: 26–34.

Kharytonov, Ye. O. 2011. *Zobov'iazannia, shcho vynykaiut' vnaslidok vidvernennia shkody, za tsyvil'nym zakonodavstvom Ukrainy* [Obligations Arising from the Aversion of Harm under the Civil Legislation of Ukraine]. In *Aktual'ni problemy tsyvil'noho prava ta protsesu*, 5–9.

Kharytonov, Ye. O., and O. I. Kharytonova. 2021. *Nedohovirni zobov'iazannia, shcho vynykaiut' iz dii, vchynenykh dlia zapobihannia shkodi v umovakh kovid-19* [Non-contractual Obligations Arising from Actions Taken to Prevent Harm in the Conditions of COVID-19]. *Chasopys tsyvilistyky* 39: 5–10. https://doi.org/10.32837/chc.v0i39.373.

Kharytonov, Ye. O., Yu. S. Chervonyi, and Yu. V. Bilousov. 2003. *Tsyvil'nyi kodeks Ukrainy: komentar* [Civil Code of Ukraine: A Commentary]. Edited by *Ye. O. Kharytonov* and *O. M. Kalitenko*. Odesa: *Yurydychna literatura*.

Kharytonov, Ye., O. Kharytonova, and K. Nekit. 2018. *Tsyvil'no-pravovyi zakhyst prava vlasnosti* [Civil Law Protection of Property Rights]. Odesa: *Feniks*.

Khomenko, V. 2017. *Prypynennia hospodars'koho tovarystva na pidstavi rishennia sudu* [Termination of a Business Company Based on a Court Decision]. *Yurydychna Ukraina* 11–12: 22–31.

Kieff, F. Scott. 2001. "Property Rights and Property Rules for Commercializing Inventions." *Minnesota Law Review* 85: 697–754.

Kim, J.-Y. 2004. "Good-faith Error and Intentional Trespassing in Adverse Possession." *International Review of Law and Economics* 24 (1): 1–13.

Kiriushyn, A. A. 2020. "Netsenzurna laika u bik spozhyvacha ye pidstavoiu dlia sudovoho zakhystu chesti, hidnosti ta stiahnennia moral'noi shkody" [Obscene Language toward a Consumer is Grounds for Judicial Protection of Honor, Dignity, and Recovery of Moral Damages]. *Protokol*, May 26. https://protocol.ua/ua/sud_netsenzurna_layka_1/.

Kivalova, T. 2008. *Zobov'iazannia z vidshkoduvannia shkody za tsyvil'nym zakonodavstvom Ukrainy: teoretychni problemy* [Obligations for Damages under the Civil Legislation of Ukraine: Theoretical Problems]. Abstract of a Dr. of Laws dissertation, National University "Odesa Law Academy."

Klimovs'kyi, S. 2013. *Poniattia osobystykh paperiv za tsyvil'nym zakonodavstvom Ukrainy* [The Concept of Personal Papers under the Civil Legislation of Ukraine]. *Naukovyi visnyk Uzhhorods'koho natsional'noho universytetu. Seriia "Pravo"* 1 (22): 154–157.

Kodynets', A. 2007. *Pravo na zasoby indyvidualizatsii uchasnykiv tsyvil'noho oborotu tovariv i posluh* [The Right to Means of Individualization of Participants in the Civil Circulation of Goods and Services]. Kyiv: *Kyiv University Publishing*.

Kodynets', A., and A. Sidorenko. 2020. *Pravova okhorona heohrafichnykh zaznachen': novely za zakonodavstvom Ukrainy* [Legal Protection of Geographical Indications: Novellas under Ukrainian Legislation]. *Teoriia i praktyka intelektual'noi vlasnosti* 1: 21–28.

Kokhanovs'ka, O. 2006. *Teoretychni problemy informatsiinykh vidnosyn u tsyvil'nomu pravi* [Theoretical Problems of Information Relations in Civil Law]. Kyiv: *Kyiv University Publishing*.

Kokhanovs'ka, O. 2011. *Osobysti nemainovi prava, shcho zabezpechuiut' pryrodne isnuvannia fizychnoi osoby yak uosoblennia zakhystu prav i osnovnykh svobod liudyny v suchasnii Ukraini* [Personal Non-property Rights Ensuring the Natural Existence of an Individual as an Embodiment of the Protection of Human Rights and Fundamental Freedoms in Modern Ukraine]. *Visnyk Kyivs'koho natsional'noho universytetu imeni Tarasa Shevchenka. Yurydychni nauky* 86: 7–10.

Kolber, Adam J. 2016. "Free Will as a Matter of Law." In *Philosophical Foundations of Law and Neuroscience*, 9–28. Oxford: Oxford University Press.

Kolodii, A. M. 1998. *Pryntsypy prava Ukrainy* [Principles of the Law of Ukraine]. Kyiv: *Yurinkom Inter*.

Kolodii, A. M. 1999. *Konstytutsiia i rozvytok pryntsypiv prava Ukrainy (metodolohichni pytannia)* [The Constitution and the Development of the Principles of Law of Ukraine (Methodological Issues)]. Abstract of a Dr. of Laws dissertation, National Academy of Internal Affairs of Ukraine.

Konstytutsiia Ukrainy [The Constitution of Ukraine]. 1996. Law of Ukraine No. 254k/96-VR, June 28. https://zakon.rada.gov.ua/laws/show/254к/96-вр.

Kopeichykov, V. V. 2003. *Pravoznavstvo* [Jurisprudence]. Kyiv: *Yurinkom Inter*.

Koroied, S. O., and A. I. Kryshtof. 2015. *Kontseptsiia zmistu prava na sudovyi zakhyst tsyvil'nykh prav v Ukraini: tsyvil'no-pravovyi ta protsesual'nyi aspekty* [The Concept of the Content of the Right to Judicial Protection of Civil Rights in Ukraine: Civil Law and Procedural Aspects]. *Sudova apeliatsiia* 4: 21–32.

Kortmann, Jeroen. 2005. "The Continental Doctrine of 'Negotiorum Gestio'." In *Altruism in Private Law*, 99–110. Oxford: Oxford University Press.

Kosenko, S. 2006. *Pryntsypy ta dzherela avtors'koho prava* [Principles and Sources of Copyright Law]. *Yurydychnyi zhurnal* 3: 57–60.

Kossak, V. M., ed. 2008. *Naukovo-praktychnyi komentar Tsyvil'noho kodeksu Ukrainy* [Scientific and Practical Commentary on the Civil Code of Ukraine]. Vols. 1–2. Kyiv: *Istyna*.

Kostruba, A. V. 2021. "Vdoskonalennia normatyvnoi rehlamentatsii mekhanizmu vidchuzhennia rechovykh prav" [Improving the Normative Regulation of the Mechanism for the Alienation of Real Rights]. In *Desiati yurydychni dysputy z aktual'nykh problem pryvatnoho prava*, 276.

Koval, I. F. 2013. *Hospodars'ko-pravove rehuliuvannia vidnosyn u sferi promyslovoi vlasnosti* [Economic and Legal Regulation of Relations in the Field of Industrial Property]. Donetsk: *Yuho-Vostok*.

Koval'chuk, O. 2014. *Sub'iekty prava intelektual'noi vlasnosti na heohrafichne zaznachennia* [Subjects of Intellectual Property Rights to a Geographical Indication]. *Nashe pravo* 3: 153–158.

Kovalchuk, Ya. 2016. *Pravo na skladannia zapovitu* [The Right to Make a Will]. *Yurydychnyi zhurnal* 52 (10): 32–35.

Kovalenko, O. O. 2017. *Volia i svoboda voli yak katehorii suchasnoho trudovoho prava* [Will and Free Will as Categories of Modern Labour Law]. In *Vid hromadians'koho suspil'stva – do pravovoi derzhavy*, 117–120.

Kovtun, N. 2018. *Kontseptual'ni pidkhody do sotsial'no-filosofs'koho analizu fenomena voli* [Conceptual Approaches to the Socio-philosophical Analysis of the Phenomenon of Will]. *Visnyk L'vivs'koho universytetu. Seriia filosofs'ko-politolohichni studii* 18: 99–106.

Kozhevnykova, V. 2018. *Mezhi ta obmezhennia zdiisnennia prava na vyznachennia ta zminu imeni dytyny* [Limits and Restrictions on the Exercise of the Right to Determine and Change a Child's Name]. *Chasopys Kyivs'koho universytetu prava* 3: 165–169.

Kozlovs'ka, L. 2014. *Pryiniattia ta vidmova vid spadshchyny yak zdiisnennia sub'iektivnoho prava spadkuvannia* [Acceptance and Renunciation of Inheritance as the Exercise of the Subjective Right of Inheritance]. *Pryvatne pravo i pidpryiemnytstvo* 13: 48–51.

Krasyts'ka, L. 2002. *Tsyvil'no-pravove rehuliuvannia osobystykh nemainovykh prav hromadian* [Civil Law Regulation of Personal Non-property Rights of Citizens]. Donetsk: *Donetsk Institute of Internal Affairs.*

Kravchyk, M. B. 2018. *Spadkovi pravovidnosyny yak mekhanizm zdiisnennia spadkovykh prav* [Inheritance Legal Relations as a Mechanism for Exercising Inheritance Rights]. *Naukovyi visnyk Mizhnarodnoho humanitarnoho universytetu. Ser.: "Yurysprudentsiia"* 33: 102–106.

Kryvenko, Yu. V. 2022. *Nepereborna syla – istoriia ta suchasnist'* [Force Majeure – History and Modernity]. In *Yevropeis'kyi vybir Ukrainy, rozvytok nauky ta natsional'na bezpeka v realiiakh masshtabnoi viis'kovoi ahresii ta hlobal'nykh vyklykiv XXI stolittia*, Vol. 2, 638–640.

Krylova, O. 2006. *Tsyvil'no-pravove rehuliuvannia vidnosyn po nadanniu medychnoi dopomohy* [Civil Law Regulation of Relations in the Provision of Medical Care]. PhD dissertation, Odesa National Academy of Law.

Kryminal'nyi kodeks Ukrainy [Criminal Code of Ukraine]. 1960. Law of the Ukrainian SSR No. 2001-05 (Repealed). https://zakon.rada.gov.ua/laws/show/2001-05.

Kryminal'nyi kodeks Ukrainy [Criminal Code of Ukraine]. 2001. Law of Ukraine No. 2341-III, April 5. https://zakon.rada.gov.ua/laws/show/2341-14.

Kryminal'nyi protsesual'nyi kodeks Ukrainy [Criminal Procedure Code of Ukraine]. 2012. Law of Ukraine No. 4651-VI. April 13. https://zakon.rada.gov.ua/laws/show/4651-17.

Kukhariev, O. 2021. "Regarding the Issue on Improving the Inheritance Agreement Institution in the Context of Recodification of Civil Legislation of Ukraine." *New Ukrainian Law* 3: 72–77.

Kukharev, O. 2016. *Vykonannia spadkovoho dohovoru: notarial'na ta sudova praktyka* [Performance of an Inheritance Agreement: Notarial and Judicial Practice]. *MEN* 5 (89): 140–149.

Kulinich, O. O. 2008. *Zasoby masovoi informatsii i pryvatne zhyttia "publichnykh" osib* [The Mass Media and the Private Lives of "Public" Figures]. *Aktual'ni problemy derzhavy i prava* 33: 33–37.

Kurakin, O., and M. Romanov. 2016. *Pravo na myrni zibrannia: vid avtorytaryzmu do demokratii* [The Right to Peaceful Assembly: From Authoritarianism to Democracy]. *Naukovyi visnyk Khersons'koho derzhavnoho universytetu. Seriia: "Yurydychni nauky"* 1 (1): 39–42.

Kurylo, L. 2017. *Pozytyvni obov'iazky derzhavy v konteksti prava liudyny na zhyttia (na osnovi praktyky YeSPL shchodo Ukrainy)* [The Positive Obligations of the State in the Context of the Human Right to Life (Based on the ECHR's Practice Regarding Ukraine)]. *Naukovyi visnyk L'vivs'koho derzhavnoho universytetu vnutrishnikh sprav. Seriia yurydychna* 2: 308–316.

Kuzmenko, K. 2023. "Good Faith as a Conceptual Basis for the Legitimate Implementation of Civil Procedural Rights and Obligations." *Uzhhorod National University Herald. Series: Law* 1 (75): 187–192.

Kuznietsova, N. 2003. *Pryntsypy suchasnoho zobov'iazal'noho prava Ukrainy* [Principles of Modern Law of Obligations of Ukraine]. *Ukrains'ke komertsiine pravo* 4: 9–15.

Larson, Carlton F. W. 2011. "Naming Baby: The Constitutional Dimensions of Naming Rights." *George Washington Law Review* 80 (1): 159–201.

Lashkul, Z., Yu. Sizintsova, and Ya. Fershal. 2013. *Informovana zghoda: poniattia, meta ta znachennia u protsesi realizatsii prav ta obov'iazkiv medychnykh pratsivnykiv i patsiientiv* [Informed Consent: Concept, Purpose, and Significance in the Process of Realising the Rights and Obligations of Medical Workers and Patients]. *Keramist.*

Lebid'-Hrebeniuk, Ye. 2009. *Svoboda voli: kontseptsiia u davnii ukrains'kii literaturi ta v liro-epichnii spadshchyni T. Shevchenka* [Free Will: The Concept in Old Ukrainian Literature and in the Lyrical-epic Heritage of T. Shevchenko]. *Literaturoznavchi studii* 24: 31–40.

Lee, K. Jane, Peter L. Havens, Thomas T. Sato, George M. Hoffman, and Steven R. Leuthner. 2006. "Assent for Treatment: Clinician Knowledge, Attitudes, and Practice." *Pediatrics* 118 (2): 723–730. https://doi.org/10.1542/peds.2005-2830.

Leff, Arthur Allen. 1967. "Unconscionability and the Code: The Emperor's New Clause." *University of Pennsylvania Law Review* 115 (4): 485–533.

Leibniz, Gottfried Wilhelm. 2017. *Theodicy: Essays on the Goodness of God, the Freedom of Man, and the Origin of Evil*. Pinnacle Press.

Lerner, Pablo. 2004. "Promises of Rewards in a Comparative Perspective." *Annual Survey of International and Comparative Law* 10 (1): 1–50.

Ligthart, Sjors, J. Christoph Bublitz, Elizabeth Richard, and Gerben Meynen. 2022. "Rethinking the Right to Freedom of Thought: A Multidisciplinary Analysis." *Human Rights Law Review* 22 (4): 1–25.

Lisnicha, T. 2007. *Zakhyst osobystykh nemainovykh prav, shcho zabezpechuiut' pryrodne isnuvannia fizychnoi osoby (pravo na zhyttia, zdorovia, svobodu ta osobystu nedotorkanist')* [Protection of Personal Non-property Rights Ensuring the Natural Existence of an Individual (Right to Life, Health, Freedom, and Personal Inviolability)]. Abstract of a PhD dissertation, Yaroslav Mudryi National Law University.

Lytovs'kyi statut [Statute of Lithuania]. 1529. Translated and edited by Karl von Loewe. Leiden: Brill, 1976. https://archive.org/details/lithuanianstatut0000lith.

Lokk, John. 2023. *Dva traktaty pro pravlinnia* [Two Treatises of Government]. Kyiv: *Nash Format*.

Locke, John. 1824. "An Essay Concerning Human Understanding Part 1." In *The Works in Nine Volumes*, 12th ed., vol. 1. London: C. Baldwin.

Lohvynenko, M. I., I. V. Karikh, and A. V. Dykovets'. 2019. "Problems of Protection of Copyright Objects in the Network Internet." *Legal Horizons* 15 (28): 21–25.

Look, Brandon C., ed. 2021. *Leibniz and Kant*. Oxford: Oxford University Press.

Loviak, O., and V. Perepichai. 2014. "Zapovit v tsyvil'nomu pravi zarubizhnykh krain" [The Will in the Civil Law of Foreign Countries]. In *Spadkuvannia v Ukraini*, 17–20.

Lucas, J. R. 1970. "Theological Determinism: Omniscience and Foreknowledge." In *The Freedom of the Will*, 71–77. Oxford: Oxford University Press.

Makhni, M. C., et al. 2018. "The Medicolegal Landscape of Spine Surgery: How Do Surgeons Fare?" *The Spine Journal* 18 (2): 209–215.

Makukh, O. 2016. *Dohovir u finansovo-pravovomu rehuliuvanni i yoho vplyv na dynamiku finansovykh pravovidnosyn* [The Contract in Financial and Legal Regulation and Its Influence on the Dynamics of Financial Legal Relations]. *Pravo ta innovatsii* 16 (4): 73–77.

Maliuha, L. V. 2004. *Osobysti nemainovi prava fizychnykh osib v tsyvil'nomu pravi: teoretychni osnovy ta problemy pravovoho zabezpechennia* [Personal Non-property Rights of Individuals in Civil Law: Theoretical Foundations and Problems of Legal Support]. PhD dissertation, Taras Shevchenko National University of Kyiv.

Mandryka, L. M. 2009. *Teorii prava vlasnosti* [Theories of Property Law]. *Pravo i Bezpeka* 2: 91–94.

Manzhosova, O. 2019. *Okremi aspekty realizatsii prava na povahu do chesti ta hidnosti v sotsial'nykh merezhakh* [Certain Aspects of the Realisation of the Right to Respect for Honor and Dignity in Social Networks]. *Chasopys tsyvilistyky* 32: 81–85.

Markov, Yu., and A. Zhezher. 2019. "Informovana zghoda v klinichnii praktytsi" [Informed Consent in Clinical Practice]. *Medytsyna nevidkladnykh staniv* 2 (97): 143–149.

Marushchak, N. V. 2016. "Deiaki problemni aspekty normatyvnoho vyznachennia ob'iekta prava na povahu do hidnosti" [Some Problematic Aspects of the Normative Definition of the Object of the Right to Respect for Dignity]. In *Ukraine-EU. Modern Technology, Business and Law*, vol. 2, 329–331.

Matsehorin, O. 2010. *Tsyvil'no-pravova okhorona prava na taiemnytsiu pro stan zdorov'ia* [Civil Legal Protection of the Right to Confidentiality of Health]. *Journal of the Kyiv University of Law* 4: 154–158.

Matveev, G. 1955. *Vina v sovetskom grazhdanskom prave* [Guilt in Soviet Civil Law]. Moscow: *Vyshcha shkola.*

Maidanyk, L. 2013. *Pravo na vykorystannia imeni vidomoi osoby post mortem: poniattia, pryroda, zakonodavche rehuliuvannia v Ukraini ta za kordonom* [The Right to Use the Name of a Famous Person Post Mortem: Concept, Nature, Legislative Regulation in Ukraine and Abroad]. *Teoriia i praktyka intelektual'noi vlasnosti* 4: 74–79.

Maidanyk, R., ed. 2007. *Anomalii v tsyvil'nomu pravi Ukrainy* [Anomalies in the Civil Law of Ukraine]. Kyiv: *Yustynian.*

Maidanyk, R. A. 2007. *Spadkovyi dohovir u tsyvil'nomu pravi Ukrainy* [The Inheritance Agreement in the Civil Law of Ukraine]. *Universytets'ki naukovi zapysky* 2: 90–105.

Maidanyk, R. A. 2012. *Tsyvil'ne pravo. Zahal'na chastyna. Vstup v tsyvil'ne pravo* [Civil Law. General Part. Introduction to Civil Law]. Vol. 1. Kyiv: *Alerta.*

Maidanyk, R. A. 2019a. *Modernizatsiia volodinnia u pravi Ukrainy: bazys i napriamy* [Modernisation of Possession in the Law of Ukraine: Basis and Directions]. *Problemy tsyvil'noho prava ta protsesu*, 53–59.

Maidanyk, R. A. 2019b. *Rechove pravo: priorytety ta perspektyvy* [Property Law: Priorities and Prospects]. In *Kyiv Law Readings*, 9–32.

Mazur, O. 2006. *Tsyvil'ne pravo Ukrainy* [Civil Law of Ukraine]. Kyiv: *Tsentr navchal'noi literatury.*

McCaffery, Edward J. 2000. "Must We Have the Right to Waste?" *SSRN Electronic Journal.* https://doi.org/10.2139/ssrn.246407.

McConnell, Michael W. 1988. "Contract Rights and Property Rights: A Case Study in the Relationship between Individual Liberties and Constitutional Structure." *California Law Review* 76 (2): 267–295.

Mele, Alfred R. 2017. *Aspects of Agency*. Oxford: Oxford University Press.

Mendzhul, M. V. 2020. *Teoretychni problemy dii pryntsypiv simeinoho prava* [Theoretical Problems of the Operation of the Principles of Family Law]. Dr. of Laws dissertation, National University "Odesa Law Academy."

Menell, Peter S. 2019. "Intellectual Property in the New Technological Age: 2019 – Chapters 1 and 2." *SSRN Electronic Journal.* https://doi.org/10.2139/ssrn.3415161.

Meng, Z. 2014. "Study on the Meaning of Lex Voluntaris: The Choice of Law in International Private Law." *Higher Education of Social Science* 7 (1): 41–45.

Merezhko, A. A. 2003. *Dohovor v chastnom prave* [The Contract in Private Law]. Kyiv: *Yustynian.*

Merrett, Louise, Paul Mitchell, and William Day. 2023. *Landmark Cases in Private International Law*. London: Bloomsbury Publishing.

Micklitz, Hans-Wolfgang. 2015. "On the Intellectual History of Freedom of Contract and Regulation." *Penn State Journal of Law and International Affairs* 4 (1).

Milova, T. 2008. *Konstytutsiine pravo liudyny i hromadianyna na svobodu naukovoi tvorchosti v Ukraini* [The Constitutional Right of a Person and Citizen to Freedom of Scientific Creativity in Ukraine]. Abstract of a PhD dissertation, Institute of State and Law of the National Academy of Sciences of Ukraine.

Ministry of Justice of Ukraine. 2011. *Deiaki aspekty nabuttia prava vlasnosti na ob'iekty bezkhaziainoho nerukhomoho maina* [Some Aspects of Acquiring Ownership of Ownerless Immovable Property]. Methodological Recommendations. October 13. https://zakon.rada.gov.ua/laws/show/n0065323-11#Text.

Ministry of Justice of Ukraine. 2022. *Perevazhne pravo orendaria na kupivliu zemel'noi dilianky sil'hospryznachennia* [The Tenant's Pre-emptive Right to Purchase a Plot of Agricultural Land]. November 1. Accessed October 4, 2025. https://minjust.gov.ua/m/perevajne-pravo-orendarya-na-kupivlyu-zemelnoi-dilyanki-silgosppriznachennya.

Miroshnychenko, O. 2005. *Pravo liudyny na zhyttia (teoriia ta praktyka mizhnarodnoho spivrobitnytstva)* [The Human Right to Life (Theory and Practice of International Cooperation)]. Abstract of a PhD dissertation, Yaroslav Mudryi National Law University.

Misiats', A. P. 2011. "Poniattia 'vidchuzhennia maina' u tsyvil'nomu pravi Ukrainy" [The Concept of "Alienation of Property" in the Civil Law of Ukraine]. In *Aktual'ni problemy yurydychnoi nauky*, 281–283.

Michurin, I. O. 2008. *Obmezhennia mainovykh prav fizychnykh osib (teoretyko-pravovyi aspekt)* [Restrictions on the Property Rights of Individuals (Theoretical and Legal Aspect)]. Kyiv: *Yur svit*.

Michurin, I. O. 2010. *Tsyvil'ne pravo Ukrainy. Al'bom skhem* [Civil Law of Ukraine. An Album of Schemes]. 3rd ed. Kyiv: *FOP Michurina N. O.*

Michurin, I. O. 2018. *Absoliutni ta vidnosni tsyvil'ni prava* [Absolute and Relative Civil Rights]. *Forum Prava* 1: 81–87.

Moccia, Luigi. 1994. "Promessa e Contratto" [Promise and Contract]. *Rivista di Diritto Civile* 40: 819.

Molchanov, R. Yu. 2009. *Zdiisnennia ta tsyvil'no-pravovyi zakhyst osobystoho nemainovoho prava na im'ia* [Exercise and Civil Law Protection of the Personal Non-property Right to a Name]. Abstract of a PhD dissertation, Yaroslav Mudryi National Law University.

Molchanov, R. Yu. 2014a. *Shchodo pravovykh pidstav zminy imeni* [Regarding the Legal Grounds for Changing a Name]. *Chasopys Kyivs'koho universytetu prava* 3: 153–156.

Molchanov, R. Yu. 2014b. *Zlovzhyvannia pravom na im'ia* [Abuse of the Right to a Name]. *Teoriia ta istoriia derzhavy i prava* 12: 22–27.

Mookerjee, Sulagna. 2019. "Gender-Neutral Inheritance Laws, Family Structure, and Women's Status in India." *The World Bank Economic Review* 33 (2): 498–515.

Moroz, V. P. 2014. *Pravo na im'ia fizychnoi osoby (psevdonim) yak ob'iekt prava intelektual'noi vlasnosti* [The Right to the Name of a Natural Person (Pseudonym) as an Object of Intellectual Property Law]. *Chasopys Kyivs'koho universytetu prava* 1: 243–246.

Morozova, S. 2011. *Pravove rehuliuvannia opiky ta pikluvannia za tsyvil'nym zakonodavstvom Ukrainy* [Legal Regulation of Guardianship and Custody under the Civil Legislation of Ukraine]. PhD dissertation, Taras Shevchenko National University of Kyiv.

Murphy, Liam. 2014. "The Practice of Promise and Contract." In *Philosophical Foundations of Contract Law*, 151–170. Oxford: Oxford University Press.

Murphy, Liam, and Thomas Nagel. 2002. *The Myth of Ownership: Taxes and Justice*. Oxford: Oxford University Press.

Mykhailenko, O. 2003. *Material'no-pravovi obmezhennia prava pryvatnoi vlasnosti za davn'oryms'kym ta suchasnym tsyvil'nym pravom Ukrainy* [Material and Legal Restrictions on the Right to Private Property under Ancient Roman and Modern Civil Law of Ukraine]. Abstract of a PhD dissertation, National University of Internal Affairs.

Nagel, Thomas. 1995. *Equality and Partiality*. Oxford: Oxford University Press.

Namnlag [Names Act] (SFS 1982:670). 1982. June 24. Stockholm: *Justitiedepartementet*.

Naumenko, K. S. 2014. *Poniattia ta vydy form tsyvil'no-pravovoho zakhystu osobystykh nemainovykh prav fizychnoi osoby, shcho zabezpechuiut' yii sotsial'ne buttia* [The Concept and Types of Forms of Civil Law Protection of Personal Non-property Rights of an Individual Ensuring Their Social Existence]. *Forum prava* 2: 296–300.

Naukovo-praktychnyi komentar do statti 96 Kryminal'noho kodeksu Ukrainy [Scientific and Practical Commentary on Article 96 of the Criminal Code of Ukraine]. 2009. Lihazakon.net. Accessed October 4, 2025. https://ips.ligazakon.net/document/KK004598

Naukovo-praktychnyi komentar st. 297 Tsyvil'noho kodeksu Ukrainy. Pravo na povahu do hidnosti ta chesti [Scientific and Practical Commentary on Art. 297 of the Civil Code of Ukraine. The Right to Respect for Dignity and Honor]. 2020. Protokol. Accessed October 4, 2025. https://protocol.ua/ru/tsivilniy_kodeks_ukraini_stattya_297/

Nekit, K. H. 2019. *Virtual'na vlasnist': poniattia ta sutnist'* [Virtual Property: Concept and Essence]. *Pravo i suspil'stvo* 2: 37–42.

Nekit, K. H. 2020. *Perevahy ta nedoliky smart-kontraktiv yak pidstav vynyknennia prava vlasnosti* [Advantages and Disadvantages of Smart Contracts as Grounds for the Emergence of Property Rights]. *Visnyk NTUU "KPI." Politolohiia. Sotsiolohiia. Pravo* 3 (47): 101–105.

Nestertsova-Sobakar, O., ed. 2017. *Spadkove pravo* [Inheritance Law]. Dnipro: *Dnipropetrovs'kyi derzhavnyi universytet vnutrishnikh sprav*.

NHS. 2023. "Euthanasia and Assisted Suicide." Accessed October 4, 2025. https://www.nhs.uk/conditions/euthanasia-and-assisted-suicide/.

Nicolaou, Nicos, and Scott Shane. 2010. "Entrepreneurship and Occupational Choice: Genetic and Environmental Influences." *Journal of Economic Behavior and Organization* 76 (1): 3–14.

Nikol's'ka, O., and I. Kirina. 2013. *Konstytutsiine pravo na myrni zibrannia: problemy realizatsii* [The Constitutional Right to Peaceful Assembly: Problems of Implementation]. *Yurydychna nauka* 3: 33–37.

Nordemann, Wilhelm, Kai Vinck, and Paul W. Hertin. 1990. *International Copyright and Neighboring Rights Law*. Weinheim: Wiley-VCH.

North American Free Trade Agreement. 1992. December 17.

Nosik, Yu. 2021. *Evoliutsiia vchennia pro pryntsypy tsyvil'noho prava Ukrainy* [The Evolution of the Doctrine of the Principles of Civil Law of Ukraine]. *Istoryko-pravovyi chasopys* 2 (14): 84–88.

Novak, David. 2007. *The Sanctity of Human Life*. Washington, DC: Georgetown University Press.

Novosolova, H., and A. Pedorenko. 2021. "Pravo vlasnosti na ob'iekt samochynnoho budivnytstva" [Ownership of an Object of Unauthorised Construction]. In *Teoriia i praktyka suchasnoi nauky ta osvity*, part II, 101–103.

O'Connor, Cailin. 2019. "The Evolution of Gender." In *The Origins of Unfairness*, 84–102. Oxford: Oxford University Press.

O'Connor, Niall. 2019. "Whose Autonomy is it Anyway? Freedom of Contract, the Right to Work and the General Principles of EU Law." *Industrial Law Journal* 49 (3): 285–317.

Ohneviuk, H. 2010. *Osoblyvosti pravovoho statusu patentnykh povirenykh za zakonodavstvom Ukrainy ta deiakykh zarubizhnykh krain: porivnial'no-pravovyi analiz* [Peculiarities of the Legal Status of Patent Attorneys under the Legislation of Ukraine and Some Foreign Countries: A Comparative Legal Analysis]. *Chasopys Kyivs'koho universytetu prava* 4: 227–232.

Okediji, Ruth L., and Margo A. Bagley, eds. 2014. Patent Law in Global Perspective. Oxford: Oxford University Press.

Oliinyk, V. S. 2006. *Konstytutsiine pravo liudyny na osobystu nedotorkannist' i yoho zabezpechennia orhanamy vnutrishnikh sprav Ukrainy* [The Constitutional Right of a Person to Personal Inviolability and Its Enforcement by the Internal Affairs Bodies of Ukraine]. PhD dissertation, National Academy of Internal Affairs of Ukraine.

On the Promotion of Patients' Rights in Europe, ICP/HLE 121. 1994. Amsterdam: WHO Regional Office for Europe.

Opols'ka, N. 2019. *Obmezhennia prava na svobodu tvorchosti v pretsedentnii praktytsi YeSPL* [Restrictions on the Right to Freedom of Creativity in the Precedent-based Practice of the ECHR]. *Ekonomika. Finansy. Menedzhment: aktual'ni pytannia nauky i praktyky* 1: 187–200.

Opols'ka, N. 2021. *Zabezpechennia prava na svobodu tvorchosti* [Ensuring the Right to Freedom of Creativity]. 2nd ed. Vinnytsia: *Tvory*.

Orzikh, Yu. 2013. *Spadkuvannia za zakonom: komentar do zakonodavstva Ukrainy* [Inheritance by Law: A Commentary on the Legislation of Ukraine]. *Yurydychnyi visnyk* 2: 98–104.

Osnovy zakonodavstva Ukrainy pro okhoronu zdorov'ia [Fundamentals of the Legislation of Ukraine on Health Care]. 1992. Law of Ukraine No. 2801-XII. https://zakon.rada.gov.ua/laws/show/2801-12.

Ostrovs'ka, B. V. 2016. *Pravo liudyny na zhyttia vid momentu yii zarodzhennia v konteksti prava ta morali* [The Human Right to Life from the Moment of Its Conception in the Context of Law and Morality]. *Filosofs'ki ta metodolohichni problemy prava* 2 (12): 140–148.

Otradnova, O. O. 2009a. *Nedohovirni zobov'iazannia v tsyvil'nomu pravi Ukrainy* [Non-contractual Obligations in the Civil Law of Ukraine]. Kyiv: *Yurinkom Inter*.

Otradnova, O. O. 2009b. *Printsipy spravedlivosti, razumnosti, dobrosovestnosti v nedogovornykh obyazatel'stvakh, voznikayushchikh iz naneseniya vreda, v grazhdanskom prave Ukraine* [The Principles of Justice, Reasonableness, and Good Faith in Non-contractual Obligations Arising from Harm in the Civil Law of Ukraine]. *Al'manakh tsivilistiki* 2: 370–383.

Oviedo Convention on Human Rights and Biomedicine. 1997. ETS No. 164, April 4. https://rm.coe.int/168007cf98.

Overkovs'kyi, K. V. 2019. *Shchodo vyznachennia poniattia "prava promyslovoi vlasnosti"* [Regarding the Definition of the Concept "Industrial Property Rights"]. *Pravnychyi chasopys Donets'koho universytetu* 1: 63–71. https://doi.org/10.31558/2518-7953.2019.1.8.

Owen, David G. 2007. "The Five Elements of Negligence." *Hofstra Law Review* 35 (4): 1671–1686.

Owens, David. 2012. *Shaping the Normative Landscape*. Oxford: Oxford University Press.

Palamarchuk, V., and O. Prystaiko. 2010. *Typolohiia form samozainiatosti* [A Typology of Forms of Self-employment]. *Problemy pidvyshchennia efektyvnosti infrastruktury* 25: 25.

Pankiv, O. M., and Yu. I. Petrovs'kyi. 2007. "Pravo liudyny na rozporiadzhennia zhyttiam: deiaki aspekty" [The Human Right to Dispose of One's Life: Some Aspects]. In *Medychnepravo Ukrainy: problemy stanovlennia ta rozvytku*, 210–215.

Parasiuk, V. M., M. V. Parasiuk, and N. Hrabar. 2014. *Tsyvil'ne pravo Ukrainy v skhemakh* [Civil Law of Ukraine in Schemes]. 2nd ed. Lviv: *Liha Pres.*

Paris Convention for the Protection of Industrial Property. 1883. March 20. 21 U.S.T. 1583, 828 U.N.T.S. 305.

Park, Ian. 2018. *The Right to Life in Armed Conflict*. Oxford: Oxford University Press.

Parkin, Jon, and Timothy Stanton, eds. 2013. *Natural Law and Toleration in the Early Enlightenment*. Oxford: OUP/British Academy.

Patten, Alan. 1995. "Hegel's Justification of Private Property." *History of Political Thought* 16 (4): 576–600.

Pavlenko, D. 2008. *Pryntsyp dobrosovisnosti v dohovirnykh zobov'iazanniakh* [The Principle of Good Faith in Contractual Obligations]. PhD dissertation, Taras Shevchenko National University of Kyiv.

Pavliuk, N., and A. Solomeniuk. 2021. "Osoblyvosti spadkuvannia za zakonom" [Peculiarities of Inheritance by Law]. In *Problemy derzhavotvorennia v Ukraini – 2021. Antykoruptsiina diialnist'*, 226–236.

Pechenyi, O. 2012. *Spadkove pravo* [Inheritance Law]. Kharkiv: *Faktor.*

Pereboom, Derk. 2001. *Living Without Free Will*. Cambridge: Cambridge University Press.

Pereboom, Derk. 2014. *Free Will, Agency, and Meaning in Life*. Oxford: Oxford University Press.

Peters, Thomas J. 1977. "Patterns of Winning and Losing: Effects on Approach and Avoidance by Friends and Enemies." Doctoral dissertation, Stanford University.

Petrenko, Yu., and Ye. Riabokon'. 2017. "Zakhyst prava yurydychnoi osoby na nedotorkannist' dilovoi reputatsii" [Protection of a Legal Entity's Right to the Inviolability of Its Business Reputation]. In *Aktual'ni naukovi problemy. Rozhliad, rishennia, praktyka*, 56–58.

Petriaiev, S. Yu., and N. D. Kohut. 2020. "Torhovel'ni marky i komertsiini naimenuvannia: problemni aspekty pravovoho rehuliuvannia" [Trademarks and Commercial Names: Problematic Aspects of Legal Regulation]. *Chasopys Kyivs'koho universytetu prava* 1: 237–243.

Piestruiev, D. 2020. *Zobov'iazannia, shcho vynykaiut' vnaslidok vchynennia dii v mainovykh interesakh inshoi osoby bez yii doruchennia, za zakonodavstvom Ukrainy ta Pol'shchi* [Obligations Arising from Actions Taken in the Property Interests of Another Person Without Their Authorisation, Under the Legislation of Ukraine and Poland]. PhD dissertation, National University "Odesa Law Academy."

Pidopryhora, O. O. 2003. *Rechovi prava na chuzhe maino za novym Tsyvil'nym kodeksom Ukrainy* [Real Rights to Another's Property under the New Civil Code of Ukraine]. *Visnyk Akademii pravovykh nauk Ukrainy* 35 (4): 149–156.

Pidopryhora, O. O. 2012. *Pravo na zasoby indyvidualizatsii uchasnykiv tsyvil'noho oborotu* [The Right to Means of Individualization for Participants in Civil Circulation]. *Chasopys tsyvilistyky* 13: 39–48.

Pikiner, K. V. 2002. *Svoboda na peresuvannia ta vybir mistsia prozhyvannia yak sub'iektivne tsyvil'ne pravo hromadian* [Freedom of Movement and Choice of Place of Residence as a Subjective Civil Right of Citizens]. *Visnyk Khmel'nyts'koho instytutu rehional'noho upravlinnia ta prava* 2: 97–99.

Pliatsko, U. 2015. *Pravova pryroda volodinnia* [The Legal Nature of Possession]. *Naukovyi visnyk Uzhhorods'koho natsional'noho universytetu. Seriia "Pravo"* 2 (35, part 1): 11–14.

Podatkovyi kodeks Ukrainy [Tax Code of Ukraine]. 2010. Law of Ukraine No. 2755-VI. December 2. https://zakon.rada.gov.ua/laws/show/2755-17.

Pohorets'ka, N. 2014. *Shchodo pytannia pro spivvidnoshennia instytutiv avtonomii voli storin ta obkhodu zakonu u mizhnarodnomu pryvatnomu pravi* [On the Issue of the Correlation between the Institutions of Party Autonomy and Evasion of the Law in Private International Law]. *Visnyk Chernivets'koho fakultetu Natsional'noho universytetu "Odes'ka yurydychna akademiia"* 2: 253–267.

Pohrebniak, V. 2020. *Mekhanizm vynyknennia prava vlasnosti na novostvorenyi ob'iekt nerukhomosti: analiz chynnoi normatyvnoi modeli* [The Mechanism of the Emergence of Ownership Rights to a Newly Created Real Estate Object: An Analysis of the Current Normative Model]. *Forum Prava* 1 (60): 67–74.

Pomaz, O., O. Tovkailo, and O. Stetsenko. 2015. *Kontseptsiia personal'noho brendu, yoho identyfikatsiia i pozytsiiuvannia* [The Concept of a Personal Brand, Its Identification and Positioning]. *Naukovi pratsi Poltavs'koi derzhavnoi ahrarnoi akademii. Ekonomichni nauky* 11 (2): 204–209.

Portnov, A. V., and O. V. Moskaliuk. 2012. *Shchodo absoliutnosti prava na im'ia fizychnoi osoby* [Regarding the Absoluteness of the Right to a Name of a Natural Person]. *Vydy kolizii u zakonodavstvi Ukrainy. Tsyvil'ne pravo ta protses* 18–19 (1–2): 41–45.

Postanova Cherkas'koho apeliatsiinoho sudu [Resolution of the Cherkasy Court of Appeal]. 2020. Case No. 692/452/17. January 22.

Postanova Kasatsiinoho hospodars'koho sudu u skladi Verkhovnoho Sudu [Resolution of the Cassation Economic Court within the Supreme Court]. 2019. Case No. 906/978/17. May 16.

Postanova Kasatsiinoho hospodars'koho sudu u skladi Verkhovnoho Sudu [Resolution of the Cassation Economic Court within the Supreme Court]. 2020. Case No. 910/11573/18. February 11.

Postanova Kharkivs'koho apelyatsiynoho sudu [Resolution of the Kharkiv Court of Appeal]. 2019. Case No. 615/1108/18. March 28.

Postanova Plenumu Verkhovnoho Sudu Ukrainy [Resolution of the Plenum of the Supreme Court of Ukraine]. 1995. No. 4., March 31. https://zakon.rada.gov.ua/laws/show/v0004700-95.

Postanova Plenumu Verkhovnoho Sudu Ukrainy [Resolution of the Plenum of the Supreme Court of Ukraine]. 2009. No. 1, February 27. https://zakon.rada.gov.ua/laws/show/v_001700-09.

Postanova Plenumu Verkhovnoho Sudu Ukrainy [Resolution of the Plenary of the Supreme Court of Ukraine]. 2009. No. 14. December 18. https://zakon.rada.gov.ua/laws/show/v0014700-09.

Postanova Velykoi Palaty Verkhovnoho Sudu Ukrainy [Resolution of the Grand Chamber of the Supreme Court of Ukraine]. 2018. Case No. 653/1096/16-ц. July 4.

Postanova Verkhovnoho Sudu Ukrainy [Resolution of the Supreme Court of Ukraine]. 2015. Case No. 3-39hs15. May 20.

Postanova Verkhovnoho Sudu Ukrainy [Resolution of the Supreme Court of Ukraine]. 2022. *Case No. 991/3401/21.*

Postanova Vyshchoho hospodars'koho sudu Ukrainy [Resolution of the High Commercial Court of Ukraine]. 2012. *Case No. 5021/1197/2011.*

Postanova Zakarpats'koho okruzhnoho administratyvnoho sudu [Resolution of the Zakarpattia District Administrative Court]. 2015. Case No. 807/1504/15. December 1.

Potsiurko, M. 2018. *Evoliutsiia idei pro svobodu voli i peredvyznachennia vid Antychnosti do Reformatsii* [The Evolution of Ideas about Free Will and Predestination from Antiquity to the Reformation]. *Svitohliad. Filosofiia. Relihiia* 13: 173–180.

Povar, P. 2009. *Pravove rehuliuvannia likvidatsii pidpryiemstv v Ukraini* [Legal Regulation of the Liquidation of Enterprises in Ukraine]. PhD dissertation, Taras Shevchenko National University of Kyiv.

Powell, Richard B. 1963. "The Relationship between Property Rights and Civil Rights." *Hastings Law Journal* 15: 135–152.

Predchuk, T. 2016. *Vydy servitutiv u konteksti zdiisnennia tsyvil'nykh pravovidnosyn* [Types of Easements in the Context of the Exercise of Civil Legal Relations]. *Naukovyi visnyk publichnoho ta pryvatnoho prava* 1 (1): 58–62.

Principles of European Contract Law (PECL). 2017. Trans-Lex.org. https://www.trans-lex.org/400200/_/pecl/

Hague Conference on Private International Law. (2015). "Principles on Choice of Law in International Commercial Contracts." *Uniform Law Review* 20 (2–3): 362–489. https://doi.org/10.1093/ulr/unv015.

Prince, Susan. 2020. "Antisthenes' Ethics." In *Early Greek Ethics*, 325–360. Oxford: Oxford University Press.

Pro advokaturu ta advokats'ku diial'nist' [On the Bar and Practice of Law]. 2012. Law of Ukraine No. 5076-VI. July 5. https://zakon.rada.gov.ua/laws/show/5076-17.

Pro aktsionerni tovarystva [On Joint-Stock Companies]. 2022. Law of Ukraine No. 2465-IX. July 27. https://zakon.rada.gov.ua/laws/show/2465-20.

Pro avtors'ke pravo i sumizhni prava [On Copyright and Related Rights]. 2022. Law of Ukraine No. 2811-IX. December 1. https://zakon.rada.gov.ua/laws/show/2811-20.

Pro banky i bankivs'ku diial'nist' [On Banks and Banking Activities]. 2000. Law of Ukraine No. 2121-III. December 7. https://zakon.rada.gov.ua/laws/show/2121-14.

Pro deiaki pytannia praktyky zastosuvannia hospodars'kymy sudamy zakonodavstva pro informatsiiu [On Some Issues of the Practice of Application by Commercial Courts of Legislation on Information]. 2007. Information Letter of the High Commercial Court of Ukraine No. 01-8/184, March 28. https://zakon.rada.gov.ua/laws/show/v_184600-07.

Pro derzhavne rehuliuvannia vyrobnytstva i obihu spyrtu etylovoho, koniachnoho i plodovoho, alkohol'nykh napoiv, tiutiunovykh vyrobiv, ridyn, shcho vykorystovuiut'sia v elektronnykh syharetakh, ta pal'noho [On State Regulation of the Production and Circulation of Ethyl, Cognac and Fruit Alcohol, Alcoholic Beverages, Tobacco Products, Liquids Used in Electronic Cigarettes, and Fuel]. 1995. Law of Ukraine No. 481/95-BP. December 19. https://zakon.rada.gov.ua/laws/show/481/95-вр.

Pro derzhavnu reiestratsiiu yurydychnykh osib, fizychnykh osib – pidpryiemtsiv ta hromads'kykh formuvan' [On State Registration of Legal Entities, Individual Entrepreneurs, and Public Formations]. 2003. Law of Ukraine No. 755-IV. May 15. https://zakon.rada.gov.ua/laws/show/755-15.

Pro derzhavnu sluzhbu [On the Civil Service]. 2015. Law of Ukraine No. 889-VIII, December 10. https://zakon.rada.gov.ua/laws/show/889-19.

Pro finansovi posluhy ta finansovi kompanii [On Financial Services and Financial Companies]. 2021. Law of Ukraine No. 1953-IX. December 14. https://zakon.rada.gov.ua/laws/show/1953-20.

Pro hromads'ki ob'iednannia [On Public Associations]. 2012. Law of Ukraine No. 4572-VI. March 22. https://zakon.rada.gov.ua/laws/show/4572-17#Text

Pro informatsiiu [On Information]. 1992. Law of Ukraine No. 2657-XII. https://zakon.rada.gov.ua/laws/show/2657-12.

Pro mizhnarodne pryvatne pravo [On Private International Law]. 2005. Law of Ukraine No. 2709-IV, June 23. https://zakon.rada.gov.ua/laws/show/2709-15.

Pro Natsional'nu politsiiu [On the National Police]. 2015. Law of Ukraine No. 580-VIII. https://zakon.rada.gov.ua/laws/show/580-19.

Pro nevidkladni zakhody shchodo zabezpechennia natsional'noi bezpeky v umovakh spalakhu hostroi respiratornoi khvoroby COVID-19... [On Urgent Measures to Ensure National Security in the Context of the Outbreak of the Acute Respiratory Disease COVID-19...]. 2020. Decision of the National Security and Defense Council of Ukraine, March 13. https://zakon.rada.gov.ua/laws/show/n0002525-20.

Pro notariat [On the Notariate]. 1993. Law of Ukraine No. 3425-XII. September 2. https://zakon.rada.gov.ua/laws/show/3425-12.

Pro ochyshchennia vlady [On Lustration]. 2014. Law of Ukraine No. 1682-VII. September 16. https://zakon.rada.gov.ua/laws/show/1682-18.

Pro orendu derzhavnoho ta komunalnoho maina [On the Lease of State and Municipal Property]. 2019. Law of Ukraine No. 157-IX. October 3. https://zakon.rada.gov.ua/laws/show/157-20.

Pro osnovni zasady molodizhnoi polityky [On the Basic Principles of Youth Policy]. 2021. Law of Ukraine No. 1414-IX. April 27. https://zakon.rada.gov.ua/laws/show/1414-20.

Pro osnovni zasady prymusovoho vyluchennia v Ukraini ob'iektiv prava vlasnosti Rosiis'koi Federatsii ta yii rezydentiv [On the Basic Principles of the Forcible Seizure in Ukraine of Property of the Russian Federation and its Residents]. 2022. Law of Ukraine No. 2116-IX. March 3. https://zakon.rada.gov.ua/laws/show/2116-20#Text

Pro okhoronu dytynstva [On the Protection of Childhood]. 2001. Law of Ukraine No. 2402-III. https://zakon.rada.gov.ua/laws/show/2402-14.

Pro okhoronu prav na promyslovi zrazky [On the Protection of Rights to Industrial Designs]. 1993. Law of Ukraine No. 3688-XII. December 15. https://zakon.rada.gov.ua/laws/show/3688-12.

Pro okhoronu prav na vynakhody i korysni modeli [On the Protection of Rights to Inventions and Utility Models]. 1993. Law of Ukraine No. 3687-XII. December 15. https://zakon.rada.gov.ua/laws/show/3687-12.

Pro politychni partii v Ukraini [On Political Parties in Ukraine]. 2001. Law of Ukraine No. 2365-III. April 5. https://zakon.rada.gov.ua/laws/show/2365-14.

Pro poriadok posvidchennia zapovitiv i dovirenostei, shcho pryrivniuiutsia do notarial'no posvidchenykh [On the Procedure for Certifying Wills and Powers of Attorney Equivalent to Notarially Certified Ones]. 1994. Resolution of the Cabinet of Ministers of Ukraine No. 419. June 15. https://zakon.rada.gov.ua/laws/show/419-94-п.

Pro pravovu okhoronu heohrafychnykh zaznachen [On the Legal Protection of Geographical Indications]. 1999. Law of Ukraine No. 752-XIV. June 16. https://zakon.rada.gov.ua/laws/show/752-14.

Pro profesiini spilky, yikh prava ta harantii diial'nosti [On Trade Unions, Their Rights and Guarantees of Activity]. 1999. Law of Ukraine No. 1045-XIV. September 15. https://zakon.rada.gov.ua/laws/show/1045-14.

Pro protydiu poshyrenniu khvorob, zumovlenykh virusom imunodefitsytu liudyny (VIL), ta pravovyi sotsial'nyi zakhyst liudei, yaki zhyvut' z VIL [On Countering the Spread of Diseases Caused by the Human Immunodeficiency Virus (HIV) and the Legal and Social Protection of People Living with HIV]. 1991. Law of Ukraine No. 1972-XII. https://zakon.rada.gov.ua/laws/show/1972-12.

Pro psykhiatrychnu dopomohu [On Psychiatric Care]. 2000. Law of Ukraine No. 1489-III. https://zakon.rada.gov.ua/laws/show/1489-14.

Pro sanktsii [On Sanctions]. 2014. Law of Ukraine No. 1644-VII, August 14. https://zakon.rada.gov.ua/laws/show/1644-18.

Pro sudovu praktyku u spravakh pro spadkuvannia [On Judicial Practice in Inheritance Cases]. 2008. Resolution of the Supreme Court of Ukraine No. 7. May 30. https://zakon.rada.gov.ua/laws/show/v0007700-08.

Pro sudovu praktyku u spravakh pro zakhyst hidnosti ta chesti fizychnoi osoby, a takozh dilovoi reputatsii fizychnoi ta yurydychnoi osoby [On Judicial Practice in Cases Concerning the Protection of the Dignity and Honor of an Individual, as well as the Business Reputation of an Individual and a Legal Entity]. 2009. Resolution of the Plenum of the Supreme Court of Ukraine No. 1, February 27. https://zakon.rada.gov.ua/laws/show/v0001700-09.

Pro sudoustrii i status suddiv [On the Judiciary and the Status of Judges]. 2016. Law of Ukraine No. 1402-VIII, June 2. https://zakon.rada.gov.ua/laws/show/1402-19.

Pro svobodu peresuvannia ta vil'nyi vybir mistsia prozhyvannia v Ukraini [On Freedom of Movement and Free Choice of Place of Residence in Ukraine]. 2003. Law of Ukraine No. 1382-IV. December 11. https://zakon.rada.gov.ua/laws/show/1382-15.

Pro vnesennia zminy do punktu 3 Poriadku rozhliadu zaiav pro zminu imeni (prizvyshcha, vlasnoho imeni, po batkovi) fizychnoi osoby [On Amending Paragraph 3 of the Procedure for Considering Applications for a Change of Name (Surname, Given Name, Patronymic) of a Natural Person]. 2021. Resolution of the Cabinet of Ministers of Ukraine No. 138, February 24. https://zakon.rada.gov.ua/laws/show/138-2021-%D0%BF.

Pro vykonavche provadzhennia [On Enforcement Proceedings]. 2016. Law of Ukraine No. 1404-VIII. June 2. https://zakon.rada.gov.ua/laws/show/1404-19.

Pro vyshchu osvitu [On Higher Education]. 2014. Law of Ukraine No. 1556-VII, July 1. https://zakon.rada.gov.ua/laws/show/1556-18.

Pro zakhody protydii nezakonnomu obihu narkotychnykh zasobiv, psykhotropnykh rechovyn i prekursoriv ta zlovzhyvanniu nymy [On Measures to Counter Illicit Traffic in Narcotic Drugs, Psychotropic Substances and Precursors and Their Abuse]. 1995. Law of Ukraine No. 62/95-ВР. https://zakon.rada.gov.ua/laws/show/62/95-вр.

Pro zapobihannia ta protydiiu domashn'omu nasyl'stvu [On Prevention and Counteraction to Domestic Violence]. 2017. Law of Ukraine No. 2229-VIII. https://zakon.rada.gov.ua/laws/show/2229-19.

Pro zastosuvannia transplantatsii anatomichnykh materialiv liudyni [On the Application of Transplantation of Anatomical Materials to Humans]. 2018. Law of Ukraine No. 2427-VIII. May 17. https://zakon.rada.gov.ua/laws/show/2427-19#Text

Pro zatverdzhennia Instruktsii z vyznachennia kryteriiv perynatalnoho periodu, zhyvonarodzhenosti ta mertvonarodzhenosti... [On the Approval of the Instruction for Determining the Criteria of the Perinatal Period, Live Birth and Stillbirth...]. 2006. Order of the Ministry of Health of Ukraine No. 179. https://zakon.rada.gov.ua/laws/show/z0427-06.

Pro zatverdzhennia Metodyky vyznachennia minimal'noi sumy orendnoho platezhu za nerukhome maino fizychnykh osib [On the Approval of the Methodology for Determining the Minimum Amount of Rent for Immovable Property of Individuals]. 2010. Resolution of the Cabinet of Ministers of Ukraine No. 1253. December 29. https://zakon.rada.gov.ua/laws/show/1253-2010-п.

Pro zatverdzhennia Metodychnykh rekomendatsii shchodo zapobihannia ta vrehuliuvannia konfliktu interesiv u diialnosti personalu orhaniv ta pidrozdiliv tsyvil'noho zakhystu [On the Approval of Methodological Recommendations for Preventing and Resolving Conflicts of Interest in the Activities of Personnel of Civil Protection Bodies and Units]. 2019. Order of the State Emergency Service of Ukraine No. 349. June 11. https://ips.ligakon.net/document/FN054200.

Pro zatverdzhennia Polozhennia pro predstavnykiv u spravakh intelektual'noi vlasnosti (patentnykh povirenykh) ta vnesennia zmin do polozhen' z pytan' atestatsii ta vedennia derzhavnoho reiestru predstavnykiv u spravakh intelektual'noi vlasnosti (patentnykh povirenykh) [On Approval of the Regulation on Representatives in Intellectual Property Matters (Patent Attorneys) and Amending the Regulations on Certification and Maintaining the State Register of Representatives in Intellectual Property Matters (Patent Attorneys)]. 2023. Order of the Ministry of Economy of Ukraine No. 20599. December 29. https://zakon.rada.gov.ua/laws/show/z0263-24.

Pro zatverdzhennia Polozhennia pro Spadkovyi reiestr [On Approval of the Regulation on the Inheritance Register]. 2011. Order of the Ministry of Justice of Ukraine No. 1810/5. July 7. https://zakon.rada.gov.ua/laws/show/z0831-11.

Pro zatverdzhennia Poriadku derzhavnoi reiestratsii zapovitiv i spadkovykh dohovoriv u Spadkovomu reiestri [On Approval of the Procedure for State Registration of Wills and Inheritance Agreements in the Inheritance Register]. 2011. Resolution of the Cabinet of Ministers of Ukraine No. 491, May 11. https://zakon.rada.gov.ua/laws/show/491-2011-п.

Pro zatverdzhennia Poriadku rozhliadu zaiav pro zminu imeni (prizvyshcha, vlasnoho imeni, po batkovi) fizychnoi osoby [On Approval of the Procedure for Considering Applications for a Change of Name (Surname, Given Name, Patronymic) of a Natural Person]. 2007. Resolution of the Cabinet of Ministers of Ukraine No. 915, July 11. https://zakon.rada.gov.ua/laws/show/915-2007-%D0%BF.

Pro zatverdzhennia Poriadku ukladannia dohovoriv servitutiv ta zrazku dohovoru servitutu u m. Zaporizhzhi [On Approval of the Procedure for Concluding Easement Agreements and a Sample Easement Agreement in the City of Zaporizhzhia]. 2012. Decision of the City Council No. 53. May 30. https://zp.gov.ua/upload/editor/rish_52_ob.pdf

Pro zatverdzhennia Pravyl derzhavnoi reiestratsii aktiv tsyvil'noho stanu v Ukraini [On Approval of the Rules for State Registration of Civil Status Acts in Ukraine]. 2000. Order of the Ministry of Justice of Ukraine No. 52/5, October 18. https://zakon.rada.gov.ua/laws/show/z0719-00.

Pro zatverdzhennia Pravyl skladannia, podannia ta provedennia ekspertyzy zaiavky na vynakhid i zaiavky na korysnu model' [On Approval of the Rules for Drafting, Filing, and Examining an Application for an Invention and an Application for a Utility Model]. 2024. Order of the Ministry of Economy of Ukraine No. 23301. September 9. https://zakon.rada.gov.ua/laws/show/z1411-24.

Pro zatverdzhennia Tymchasovykh standartiv nadannia medychnoi dopomohy pidlitkam ta molodi [On Approval of the Temporary Standards for Providing Medical Care to Adolescents and Youth]. 2009. Order of the Ministry of Health of Ukraine No. 382, June 2. https://zakon.rada.gov.ua/rada/show/v0382282-09.

Pro zovnishn'oekonomichnu diial'nist' [On Foreign Economic Activity]. 1991. Law of Ukraine No. 959-XII, April 16. https://zakon.rada.gov.ua/laws/show/959-12.

Proekt Tsyvil'noho kodeksu Ukrainy [Draft Civil Code of Ukraine]. 1996. August 25. https://w1.c1.rada.gov.ua/pls/zweb2/webproc34?id=&pf3511=12096&pf35401=21102.

Proskurka, N. 2009. *Profesiina kar'iera yak odyn iz aspektiv profesiinoho rozvytku osobystosti* [Professional Career as One of the Aspects of Personal Professional Development]. *Visnyk Natsional'noho aviatsiinoho universytetu. Seriia: Pedahohika. Psykholohiia* 2: 28–32.

Council of Europe. 1952. *Protocol to the Convention for the Protection of Human Rights and Fundamental Freedoms.* ETS No. 009, March 20. https://rm.coe.int/168006b0c7.

Prudka, T. 2019. *Svoboda voli u filosofii Artura Shopenhauera* [Free Will in the Philosophy of Arthur Schopenhauer]. *Visnyk Donbas'koho derzhavnoho pedahohichnoho universytetu. Seriia: sotsial'no-filosofs'ki problemy rozvytku liudyny i suspil'stva* 10 (1): 60–69.

Pryimenko, O. S. 2021. *Deiaki pytannia vil'noho vykorystannia tvoriv bez zghody avtora (na prykladi sudovykh sprav)* [Some Issues of Free Use of Works without the Author's Consent (on the Example of Court Cases)]. *Zbirnyk naukovykh prats' KhNPU imeni H. S. Skovorody "Pravo"* 33: 61–67. https://doi.org/10.34142/23121661.2021.33.08.

Punda, O. O. 2006. *Pravo na svobodu* [The Right to Freedom]. Khmel'nyts'kyi: *Evrika.*

Punda, O. O., and Ya. Yu. Kolobova. 2011. *Problemy zdiisnennia prava na svobodu tvorchosti* [Problems of Exercising the Right to Freedom of Creativity]. *Universytets'ki naukovi zapysky* 2: 81–86.

Quill, Eoin. 2014. *Torts in Ireland.* 4th ed. Dublin: Gill and Macmillan Ltd.

Rabinovych, P. M. 2001. *Osnovy zahal'noi teorii prava ta derzhavy* [Fundamentals of the General Theory of Law and State]. 5th ed. Kyiv: *Atika.*

Rabinovych, P., and M. Khavroniuk. 2004. *Prava liudyny i hromadianyna* [Human and Civil Rights]. Kyiv: *Atika.*

Raz, Joseph. 1982. "Promises in Morality and Law." *Harvard Law Review* 95 (4): 916–938.

Regulation (EC) No 864/2007 of the European Parliament and of the Council of 11 July 2007 on the law applicable to non-contractual obligations (Rome II). 2007. *Official Journal of the European Union* L 199. July 31. https://eur-lex.europa.eu/legal-content/EN/TXT/?uri=celex%3A32007R0864.

Reid, Kenneth G. C., Marius J. de Waal, and Reinhard Zimmermann. 2015. "Intestate Succession in Historical and Comparative Perspective." In *Comparative Succession Law*, 442–512. Oxford: Oxford University Press.

Reid, Kenneth G. C., George L. Gretton, and Andrew G. M. Duncan. 1996. *The Law of Property in Scotland*. London: Butterworths Law.

Report to the President of the Republic relating to Ordonnance no 2016–131 of 10 February 2016 On the reform of contract law, the general regime and proof of obligations. 2016. Norton Rose Fulbright. https://www.nortonrosefulbright.com/en/knowledge/publications/2a563f12/reform-of-the-french-civil-code-on-contract-law-and-the-general-regime-and-proof-of-obligations.

Rezvorovych, K. 2020. "Right to Personal Life vs Right to Private Life: Discussion of Relating Categories." *Naukovyi visnyk Dnipropetrovs'koho derzhavnoho universytetu vnutrishnikh sprav* 1 (1): 95–102.

Rieznikova, V. 2013. *Spil'na hospodars'ka diial'nist' v Ukraini: ekonomiko-pravova sutnist'* [Joint Economic Activity in Ukraine: Economic and Legal Essence]. *Publichne pravo* 10 (2): 269–273.

Rieznikova, V. V. 2010. *Pravove rehuliuvannia poserednytstva u sferi hospodariuvannia (teoretychni aspekty)* [Legal Regulation of Intermediation in the Sphere of Business (Theoretical Aspects)]. Khmel'nyts'kyi: *Vydavnytstvo Khmel'nyts'koho universytetu upravlinnia ta prava.*

Rishennia Frunzens'koho raionnoho sudu m. Kharkova [Decision of the Frunzenskyi District Court of Kharkiv]. 2013. Case No. 2033/2-2121/11. May 16.

Rishennia Halyts'koho raionnoho sudu m. L'vova [Decision of the Halytskyi District Court of Lviv]. 2021. *Case No. 461/10466/20.*

Rishennia Inhulets'koho raionnoho sudu m. Kryvoho Rohu Dnipropetrovs'koi oblasti [Decision of the Inhulets District Court of Kryvyi Rih, Dnipropetrovsk Oblast]. 2021. Case No. 213/405/21. May 19.

Rishennia Kirovs'koho raionnoho sudu m. Kirovohrada [Decision of the Kirovskyi District Court of Kirovohrad]. 2022. *Case No. 404/4420/20.*

Rishennia Konstytutsiinoho Sudu Ukrainy [Decision of the Constitutional Court of Ukraine]. 1999. Case No. 5-rp/99, May 19. https://zakon.rada.gov.ua/laws/show/v005p710-99.

Rishennia Konstytutsiinoho Sudu Ukrainy [Decision of the Constitutional Court of Ukraine]. 2001. Case No. 6-rp/2001, May 23. https://zakon.rada.gov.ua/laws/show/v006p710-01.

Rishennia Konstytutsiinoho Sudu Ukrainy [Decision of the Constitutional Court of Ukraine]. 2011a. Case No. 10-rp/2011, October 11. https://zakon.rada.gov.ua/laws/show/v010p710-11.

Rishennia Konstytutsiinoho Sudu Ukrainy [Decision of the Constitutional Court of Ukraine]. 2011b. *Case No. 1-rp/2011*, January 26. https://zakon.rada.gov.ua/laws/show/v001p710-11.

Rishennia Konstytutsiinoho Sudu Ukrainy [Decision of the Constitutional Court of Ukraine], Case No. 2-рп/2012 (2012). https://zakon.rada.gov.ua/laws/show/v001p710-11.

Rishennia Konstytutsiinoho Sudu Ukrainy [Decision of the Constitutional Court of Ukraine]. 2016. Case No. 2-rp/2016, June 1. https://zakon.rada.gov.ua/laws/show/v002p710-16.

Rishennia Konstytutsiinoho Sudu Ukrainy [Decision of the Constitutional Court of Ukraine]. 2019. Case No. 4-r/2019, June 13. https://zakon.rada.gov.ua/laws/show/v004p710-19.

Rishennia Malynovs'koho raionnoho sudu m. Odesy [Decision of the Malynovskyi District Court of Odesa]. 2021. *Case No. 521/8082/20*, March 24.

Rishennia Ternivs'koho mis'koho sudu Dnipropetrovs'koi oblasti [Decision of the Ternivka City Court of Dnipropetrovsk Oblast]. 2021. Case No. 194/1417/20. January 27.

Rishennia Tlumats'koho raionnoho sudu Ivano-Frankivs'koi oblasti [Decision of the Tlumach District Court of Ivano-Frankivsk Oblast]. 2014. Case No. 353/1768/13-ц. March 17.

Rishennia Truskavets'koho mis'koho sudu L'vivs'koi oblasti [Decision of the Truskavets City Court of Lviv Oblast]. 2021. Case No. 457/216/18. April 13.

Rishennia Velykoi palaty Konstytutsiinoho Sudu Ukrainy [Decision of the Grand Chamber of the Constitutional Court of Ukraine]. 2017. Case No. 1-r/2017, November 23. https://zakon.rada.gov.ua/laws/show/v001p710-17#Text.

Rishennia Velykoi palaty Konstytutsiinoho Sudu Ukrainy [Decision of the Grand Chamber of the Constitutional Court of Ukraine]. 2018. Case No. 5-r/2018, April 26. https://zakon.rada.gov.ua/laws/show/v005p710-18#Text

Rishennia Yenakiivs'koho mis'koho sudu Donets'koi oblasti [Decision of the Yenakiieve City Court of Donetsk Oblast]. 2013. Case No. 230/7096/13-ts. December 12.

Rishennia Zborivs'koho raionnoho sudu Ternopils'koi oblasti [Decision of the Zboriv District Court of Ternopil Oblast]. 2020. Case No. 2/599/11/2020. June 15.

Rishennia Zdolbunivs'koho raionnoho sudu Rivnens'koi oblasti [Decision of the Zdolbuniv District Court of Rivne Oblast]. 2020. Case No. 562/482/20.

Rogers, Daniel. 2007. "Exclusion from Patentability under Article 53(a) EPC upon 'Morality' Grounds." *Journal of Intellectual Property Law and Practice* 2 (2): 61–62.

Rohova, O. 2006. *Pravo na zhyttia v systemi prav liudyny* [The Right to Life in the Human Rights System]. Abstract of PhD dissertation, Yaroslav Mudryi National Law University.

Romovska, Z. V. 2003. *Problemy spadkovoho dohovoru* [Problems of the Inheritance Agreement]. *Yurydychna praktyka* 44 (306): 16.

Romovska, Z. V. 2009. *Ukrains'ke simeine pravo: akademichnyi kurs* [Ukrainian Family Law: An Academic Course]. Kyiv: *Pravova yednist'*.

Romovskaia, Z. 1968. *Lichnye neimushchestvennye prava grazhdan v SSSR* [Personal Non-Property Rights of Citizens in the USSR]. Abstract of PhD dissertation, Taras Shevchenko National University of Kyiv.

Rowan, Solène. 2012. *Remedies for Breach of Contract: A Comparative Analysis of the Protection of Performance*. Oxford: Oxford University Press.

Rowan, Solène. 2022. *The New French Law of Contract*. Oxford: Oxford University Press.

Rozhon, O. 2020. *Pervynni sub'iekty prava intelektual'noi vlasnosti u naukovomu parku* [Primary Subjects of Intellectual Property Law in a Science Park]. In *Modernizatsiia ta naukovi doslidzhennia: paradyhma innovatsiinoho rozvytku suspil'stva i tekhnolohii*, 176–179.

Rozhon, O. V. 2005. *Mezhi ta obmezhennia prava vlasnosti* [Limits and Restrictions on the Right of Ownership]. PhD dissertation, Yaroslav Mudryi National Law University.

Rudyi, N. 2011. *Instytut opiky i pikluvannia v Ukraini: istoryko-pravove doslidzhennia* [The Institution of Guardianship and Custody in Ukraine: A Historical and Legal Study]. PhD dissertation, Ivan Franko National University of Lviv.

Russell, Stephen T., and Stacey S. Horn. 2016. "Introduction." In *Sexual Orientation, Gender Identity, and Schooling*, edited by Stephen T. Russell and Stacey S. Horn, 1–12. Oxford: Oxford University Press. https://doi.org/10.1093/med:psych/9780199387656.003.0001.

Rusu, S., and M. Stefanchuk. 2003. *Problemy vyznachennia poniattia dobrosovisnosti ta rozumnosti u Tsyvil'nomu kodeksi Ukrainy* [Problems of Defining the Concepts of Good Faith and Reasonableness in the Civil Code of Ukraine]. *Visnyk Khmel'nyts'koho instytutu upravlinnia ta prava*: 53–57.

Saakov, V. 2020. *Smertna kara: u SShA rozshyryly perelik sposobiv straty* [The Death Penalty: The USA Has Expanded the List of Execution Methods]. *DW*, November 28. https://www.dw.com/uk/smertna-kara-u-ssha-rozshyryly-dozvoleni-sposoby-straty-zlochyntsiv/a-55757908.

Samoilova, I. 2021. *Spadkovyi dohovir: pravova pryroda za zakonodavstvom Ukrainy ta krain Yevropy* [The Inheritance Agreement: Legal Nature under the Legislation of Ukraine and European Countries]. *Pidpryiemnytstvo, hospodarstvo i pravo* 301 (3): 54–59. https://doi.org/10.32849/2663-5313/2021.3.09.

Samuel, Geoffrey. 1991. *The English Law of Obligations in Comparative Context*. Nijmegen: Ars Aequi Libri.

Sartre, Jean-Paul. 2021. *Being and Nothingness: An Essay in Phenomenological Ontology*. New York: Washington Square Press.

Saveliev, V. 2009. *Etyka. Korotkyi navchal'nyi slovnyk: terminy, poniattia, personalii* [Ethics. A Short Educational Dictionary: Terms, Concepts, Personalities]. L'viv: *Mahnoliia – 2006*.

Savchenko, V. 2014. *Medychni posluhy yak ob'iekt tsyvil'nykh pravovidnosyn* [Medical Services as an Object of Civil Legal Relations]. PhD dissertation, National Academy of Legal Sciences of Ukraine.

Savchenko, V. 2019. *Pravovyi status fotohrafa v Ukraini* [The Legal Status of a Photographer in Ukraine]. *Zhurnal skhidnoievropeis'koho prava* 62: 82–87. http://easternlaw.com.ua/wp-content/uploads/2019/04/savchenko_62.pdf.

Savchenko, V. 2022. "The Scope of Freedom of Will of a Juvenile." In *International Scientific Conference «New Approaches and Current Legal Research»*, 74–76. Riga: *Baltija Publishing*. https://doi.org/10.30525/978-9934-26-263-0-18.

Sax, Joseph L. 1971. "Takings, Private Property and Public Rights." *The Yale Law Journal* 81 (2): 149–186.

Schlechtriem, Peter. 2000. *Restitution und Bereicherungsausgleich in Europa. Band 1: Eine rechtsvergleichende Darstellung* [Restitution and Compensation for Enrichment in Europe: Volume 1: A Comparative Law Presentation]. Tübingen: Mohr Siebeck.

Schweizerisches Zivilgesetzbuch [Swiss Civil Code] (ZGB). 1907. December 10 (As amended). https://www.fedlex.admin.ch/eli/cc/24/233_245_233/de

Schmidt, J. P. 2015. "Intestate Succession in Latin America." In *Comparative Succession Law*, 118–158. Oxford: Oxford University Press.

Schneewind, J. B. 2002. *Moral Philosophy from Montaigne to Kant*. Cambridge: Cambridge University Press.

Schopenhauer, A. 1995. *The World as Will and Idea*. London: HardPress Publishing.

Seheniuk, A. 2016. *Osoblyvosti spadkuvannia za zakonom* [Peculiarities of Inheritance by Law]. *Chasopys tsyvilistyky* 20: 146–150.

Senin, Yu. 2013. *Novatsiia yak sposib prypynennia zobov'iazan' za tsyvil'nym zakonodavstvom Ukrainy* [Novation as a Way of Terminating Obligations under the Civil Legislation of Ukraine]. Abstract of PhD dissertation, National University "Odesa Law Academy."

Seniuta, I. (Ed.). 2010. *Medyko-pravovyi tlumachnyi slovnyk* [Medical and Legal Explanatory Dictionary]. L'viv: *Medytsyna i pravo*.

Seniuta, I. 2016. *Pravo na zghodu ta pravo na vidmovu vid medychnoi dopomohy: osoblyvosti ta mezhi zdiisnennia* [The Right to Consent and the Right to Refuse Medical Care: Features and Limits of Exercise]. *Tsyvil'ne pravo i protses* 10: 15–19.

Serohin, S., and N. Sorokina. 2016. *Poniattia «chest'», «hidnist'» u konteksti profesionalizatsii publichnoi sluzhby* [The Concepts of "Honor" and "Dignity" in the Context of the Professionalisation of Public Service]. *Aspekty publichnoho upravlinnia. Kadrova polityka ta publichna sluzhba* 34 (8): 57–64.

Sganga, C. 2021. "The Many Metamorphoses of Related Rights in EU Copyright Law: Unintended Consequences or Inevitable Developments?" *GRUR International* 70 (9): 821–833.

Shalyhanova, A. S. 2011. *Indyvidual'nist' yak filosofs'ko-pravova katehoriia* [Individuality as a Philosophical and Legal Category]. *Forum prava* 2: 972–980.

Shapiro, M., and A. S. Sweet. 2002. *On Law, Politics, And Judicialization*. Oxford: Oxford University Press.

Shapoval, L. 2021. *Shchodo neobkhidnosti vdoskonalennia polozhen' pro zapovit z umovoiu* [On the Need to Improve the Provisions on a Will with a Condition]. *Law. State. Technology* 3: 54–58.

Sharko, V. P. 2020. *Sytuatsiia z dotrymanniam prav patsiienta u narkolohichnykh statsionarakh (na prykladi Kyivs'koi mis'koi narkolohichnoi likarni «Sotsioterapiia»)* [The Situation with Patient Rights in Narcological Hospitals (on the Example of the Kyiv City Narcological Hospital "Sociotherapy")]. *Naukovi zapysky. Sotsiolohichni nauky* 18: 67–73.

Sharkova, H. 2014. *Rozmezhuvannia dohovoriv z nadannia posluh ta dohovoriv na vykonannia robit za predmetom dohovoru* [Distinguishing between Service Contracts and Work Contracts by Their Subject Matter]. In *Aktual'ni pytannia ta problemy yurydychnoi nauky*, 120–124.

Sheiko, S., and A. Ilchenko. 2023. *Problema vyznachennia svitohliadnoi paradyhmy u filosofii Hryhoriia Skovorody (krytychno-porivnial'nyi analiz)* [The Problem of Defining the Worldview Paradigm in the Philosophy of Hryhorii Skovoroda (a Critical-Comparative Analysis)]. *Filosofs'ki obrii* 47: 8–19.

Sheiko, S., and O. Kolodii. 2019. *Stanovlennia kontseptsii svobody voli liudyny u filosofii istorii P. Chaadaieva* [The Formation of the Concept of Human Free Will in the Philosophy of History of P. Chaadaev]. *Filosofs'ki obrii* 41: 19–33.

Sheiko, S., O. Kolodii, and A. Ilchenko. 2018. *Filosofs'ko-istorychni osnovy svobody voli liudyny v rosiis'komu zakhidnytstvi XIX stolittia* [Philosophical and Historical Foundations of Human Free Will in 19th-Century Russian Westernism]. *Filosofs'ki obrii* 40: 47–59.

Shemshuchenko, Yu. (Ed.). 2003. *Yurydychna entsyklopediia* [Legal Encyclopedia]. Vol. 1. Kyiv: *Ukrains'ka entsyklopediia.*

Shemshuchenko, Yu. S. (Ed.). 2004. *Yurydychna entsyklopediia* [Legal Encyclopedia]. Vol. 6. Kyiv: *Ukrains'ka entsyklopediia.*

Shevchenko, Ya. M. (Ed.). 2003. *Tsyvil'ne pravo Ukrainy: Navchal'nyi kurs: Pidruchnyk. T. 1: Zahal'na chastyna* [Civil Law of Ukraine: Academic Course: Textbook. Vol. 1]. Kyiv: *In Yure.*

Shcherbyna, B. 2015. *Okremi pytannia zdiisnennia prava na spadkuvannia* [Certain Issues of Exercising the Right to Inheritance]. *Yurydychnyi naukovyi elektronnyi zhurnal* 4: 93–96.

Shcherbyna, V. 2006. *Administratyvno-hospodars'ki sanktsii orhanizatsiino-pravovoho kharakteru: problemy zastosuvannia* [Administrative and Economic Sanctions of an Organizational and Legal Nature: Problems of Application]. *Universytets'ki naukovi zapysky* 17 (1): 138–144.

Shchyrba, M. 2018. *Donorstvo i transplantatsiia v aspekti prav patsiientiv* [Donation and Transplantation in the Aspect of Patients' Rights]. *Jurnalul juridic național: teorie şi practică* 29 (1–2): 25–28.

Shiffrin, Seana Valentine. 2007. "The Divergence of Contract and Promise." *Harvard Law Review* 120 (3): 708–753.

Shyshka, R. B. 2004. *Zasady tsyvil'noho zakonodavstva* [Foundations of Civil Legislation]. *Visnyk Zaporiz'koho derzhavnoho universytetu. Yurydychni nauky* 1: 94–98.

Shkoda, V. V. 1997. *Vstup do pravovoi filosofii* [Introduction to Legal Philosophy]. Kharkiv: *Folio.*

Shliakhtun, P. P. 2005. *Konstytutsiine pravo: slovnyk terminiv* [Constitutional Law: A Dictionary of Terms]. Kyiv: *Lybid'.*

Shtefan, O. 2023. *Piratstvo – riznovyd porushennia avtors'koho prava i sumizhnykh prav: novatsii zakonodavstva* [Piracy as a Type of Violation of Copyright and Related Rights: Legislative Innovations]. In *Materialy konferentsii*, 24–28.

Shuklina, N. H. 2005. *Konstytutsiino-pravove rehuliuvannia prav i svobod liudyny i hromadianyna v Ukraini (problemy teorii ta praktyky)* [Constitutional and Legal Regulation of Human and Civil Rights and Freedoms in Ukraine (Problems of Theory and Practice)]. Kyiv: *Tsentr navchal'noi literatury.*

Shvydkova, O. 2006. *Shchodo vyznachennia prava na svobodu ta osobystu nedotorkannist'* [Regarding the Definition of the Right to Liberty and Personal Inviolability]. *Pravo i bezpeka* 5 (4): 40–42.

Sibilov, M. M. 2014. *Spivvidnoshennia aktiv tsyvil'noho zakonodavstva i dohovoru ta bazovi modeli rehuliuvannia dohovirnykh vidnosyn za chynnym Tsyvil'nym kodeksom Ukrainy* [The Correlation of Acts of Civil Legislation and Contracts and the Basic Models of Regulation of Contractual Relations under the Current Civil Code of Ukraine]. *Visnyk Khmel'nyts'koho instytutu rehional'noho upravlinnia ta prava*: 56–61.

Sikach, I. V. 1999. *Pravova derzhava: kontseptsiia B. Kistiakivs'koho* [The Rule of Law State: The Concept of B. Kistiakivskyi]. *Naukovyi visnyk Dyplomatychnoi akademii Ukrainy* 2: 223–230.

Simeinyi kodeks Ukrainy [Family Code of Ukraine]. 2002. Law of Ukraine No. 2947-III. https://zakon.rada.gov.ua/laws/show/2947-14.

Simmonds, Nigel E. 2008. "Jurisprudence and the Nature of Law." In *Law as a Moral Idea*, 1–36. Oxford: Oxford University Press.

Simon, Albrecht. 2000. "A Right to Life for the Unborn? The Current Debate on Abortion in Germany and Norbert Hoerster's Legal-Philosophical Justification for the Right to Life." *The Journal of Medicine and Philosophy* 25 (2): 220–239.

Syvukhin, V. 2007. *Konstytutsiine pravo liudyny i hromadianyna na nevtruchannia v yikh osobyste i simeine zhyttia ta yoho zabezpechennia orhanamy vnutrishnikh sprav* [The Constitutional Right of a Person and a Citizen to Non-interference in Their Personal and Family Life and Its Provision by Internal Affairs Bodies]. PhD dissertation, Kyiv.

Syniehubov, O. V. 2013. *Zahal'ni polozhennia zdiisnennia prava dytyny na sim'iu* [General Provisions for the Exercise of the Child's Right to a Family]. *Forum prava* 4: 367–373.

Sychov, D. V. 2009. *Indyvidual'ni trudovi vidnosyny: teoretychno-pravovi aspekty* [Individual Labour Relations: Theoretical and Legal Aspects]. PhD dissertation, Luhansk State University of Internal Affairs.

Sizintsova, Yu. 2013. *Informovana zghoda na medychne vtruchannia: yurydychnyi zakhyst patsiientiv i medychnykh pratsivnykiv* [Informed Consent to Medical Intervention: Legal Protection of Patients and Medical Workers]. *Naukovyi visnyk Uzhhorods'koho natsional'noho universytetu. Seriia: «Pravo»* 1 (23): 266–269.

Skydanov, K. V. 2013. *Diisna volia osib u fiktyvnykh ta udavanykh pravochynakh* [The True Will of Persons in Fictitious and Sham Transactions]. *Teoriia i praktyka pravoznavstva* 2: 1–12.

Skydanov, K. V. 2015a. *Vyznannia oznak obmanu ta pomylky yak pidstava nediisnosti pravochynu* [Recognition of Signs of Deception and Mistake as a Ground for the Invalidity of a Transaction]. *Pravo ta innovatsiine suspil'stvo* 1: 99–106.

Skydanov, K. V. 2015b. *Znachennia volevyiavlennia dlia diisnosti pravochynu* [The Significance of the Expression of Will for the Validity of a Transaction]. *Yurydychna Ukraina* 2: 33–38.

Skopychenko, O. 2015. *Spadkovyi dohovir v systemi tsyvil'no-pravovykh dohovoriv* [The Inheritance Agreement in the System of Civil Law Contracts]. *Molodyi vchenyi* 5 (3): 79–82.

Slipchenko, S. 2005. *Deiaki pytannia kharakterystyky osobystykh nemainovykh prav, shcho zabezpechuiut' sotsial'ne buttia fizychnoi osoby* [Some Issues on the Characteristics of Personal Non-property Rights Ensuring the Social Existence of an Individual]. *Naukovi zapysky KhEPU* 1 (2): 11–17.

Slipchenko, S. 2012. *Osobysti nemainovi prava, shcho zabezpechuiut' sotsial'ne buttia fizychnoi osoby, yak riznovyd vykliuchnykh prav* [Personal Non-property Rights Ensuring the Social Existence of an Individual as a Type of Exclusive Rights]. *Teoriia i praktyka intelektual'noi vlasnosti* 4: 96–104.

Slipchenko, S. 2013. *Postanovka naukovoi problemy kvalifikatsii osobystykh nemainovykh pravovidnosyn* [Posing the Scientific Problem of the Qualification of Personal Non-property Legal Relations]. *Visnyk ONU im. I. I. Mechnykova. Pravoznavstvo* 18 (1): 7–15.

Slipchenko, S. O. 2014. *Ohliad teoretychnykh pidkhodiv do rozuminnia absoliutnoho prava* [A Review of Theoretical Approaches to Understanding Absolute Law]. *Pravo ta innovatsiine suspil'stvo* 2: 67–76.

Sloma, V. 2016. *Servitut yak vyd rechovykh prav na chuzhe maino* [Easement as a Type of Real Right to Another's Property]. *Aktual'ni problemy pravoznavstva* 2: 123–126.

Slovnyk ukrains'koi movy: v 11 t. [Dictionary of the Ukrainian Language: In 11 Vols.]. 1971. Vol. 2. Kyiv: Naukova dumka.

Slovnyk ukrains'koi movy: v 11 t. [Dictionary of the Ukrainian Language: In 11 Vols.]. 1977. Vol. 8. Kyiv: Naukova dumka.

Slovnyk ukrains'koi movy: v 11 t. [Dictionary of the Ukrainian Language: In 11 Vols.]. 1978. Vol. 9. Kyiv: Naukova dumka.

Slovnyk ukrains'koi movy: v 11 t. [Dictionary of the Ukrainian Language: In 11 Vols.]. 1979. Vol. 10. Kyiv: Naukova dumka.

Slovnyk ukrains'koi movy: v 11 t. [Dictionary of the Ukrainian Language: In 11 Vols.]. 1980. Vol. 11. Kyiv: Naukova dumka.

Soboliev, O. 2018. *Tsyvil'no-pravovi sposoby zakhystu prav na povahu do hidnosti y chesti ta na nedotorkannist' dilovoi reputatsii* [Civil Law Methods of Protecting the Rights to Respect for Dignity and Honor and to the Inviolability of Business Reputation]. *Porivnial'no-analitychne pravo* 2: 125–127.

Sofins'ka, I. 2014. *Pravo na im'ia v Ukraini: konstytutsiino-pravove rehuliuvannia* [The Right to a Name in Ukraine: Constitutional and Legal Regulation]. *Chasopys Kyivs'koho universytetu prava* 1: 95–99.

Sorabji, Richard. 2007. "Epictetus on *Proairesis* and Self." In *The Philosophy of Epictetus*, 87–98. Oxford: Oxford University Press.

Sprankling, John G. 2014. "The Right to Destroy." In *The International Law of Property*, 293–304. Oxford: Oxford University Press.

Statut politychnoi partii "Sluha Narodu" [Charter of the "Sluha Narodu" Political Party]. 2021. Sluha Narodu. Accessed October 4, 2025. https://sluga-narodu.com/wp-content/uploads/2021/03/Statut.pdf.

Statut politychnoi partii "Ievropeis'ka Solidarnist'" [Charter of the "European Solidarity" Political Party]. 2024. Ievropeis'ka Solidarnist'. Accessed October 4, 2025. Statut politychnoi partii "Ievropeis'ka Solidarnist'" [Charter of the "European Solidarity" Political Party]. n.d. Ievropeis'ka Solidarnist'. Accessed October 4, 2025. https://eurosolidarity.org/wp-content/uploads/2020/06/statut-politichnoyi-partiyi-yevropejska-solidarnist.pdf.

Stefanchuk, M., and L. Davyd. 2014. *Tsyvil'no-pravova okhorona ta zakhyst prav na komertsiine (firmove) naimenuvannia* [Civil Law Protection and Defense of Rights to a Commercial (Firm) Name]. *Pravo i suspil'stvo* 1–2: 51–52.

Stefanchuk, R. O. 2005a. *Pravo na im'ia* [The Right to a Name]. *Universytets'ki naukovi zapysky* 1–2: 83–92.

Stefanchuk, R. O. 2005b. *Tsyvil'ne pravo Ukrainy* [Civil Law of Ukraine]. Kyiv: *Pretsedent*.

Stefanchuk, R. O. 2008. *Osobysti nemainovi prava fizychnykh osib (poniattia, zmist, systema, osoblyvosti zdiisnennia ta zakhystu)* [Personal Non-property Rights of Individuals (Concept, Content, System, Features of Exercise and Protection)]. Kyiv: *KNT*.

Stetsenko, S. H., V. Yu. Stetsenko, and I. Ya. Seniuta. 2008. *Medychne pravo Ukrainy* [Medical Law of Ukraine]. Kyiv: *Pravova yednist'*.

Stockholm Declaration on the Human Environment. 1972. June 16.

Striker, Gisela. 2022. *From Aristotle to Cicero*. Oxford: Oxford University Press.

Suárez, Francisco. 2011. *De divina gratia*. Charleston: Nabu Press.

Sudebnyk Kazimira IV Iahailovycha 1468 roku [Sudebnyk of Casimir IV Jagiellon 1468]. 1468. In *Khrestomatiia z istorii derzhavy i prava Ukrainy* [Reader on the History of State and Law of Ukraine], edited by V. D. Honcharenko, 54–58. Kyiv: In Yure, 2000.

Supreme Court of New Hampshire. 1978. *Cheshire Oil Co. v. Springfield Realty Corp*. 7928.

Sus, Yu. S. 2022. *Do pytannia pro poniattia spadkovoho prava* [On the Question of the Concept of Inheritance Law]. In *Doktryna pryvatnoho prava: tradytsii ta suchasnist'*, 489–494.

Sviatoshniuk, A. 2019. *Pryntsypy dohovirnoho prava Ukrainy: poniattia, zmist ta systema* [Principles of Contract Law of Ukraine: Concept, Content, and System]. *Zhurnal skhidnoievropeis'koho prava* 59: 74–80.

Svitlychnyi, O. P. 2016. *Pravo intelektual'noi vlasnosti* [Intellectual Property Law]. 2nd ed. Kyiv: *NUBiP*.

Svitlov, S. 2015. *Zakriplennia prava na povahu do hidnosti u mizhnarodnomu ta vitchyznianomu zakonodavstvi* [Enshrinement of the Right to Respect for Dignity in International and Domestic Legislation]. In *Vid hromadians'koho suspil'stva – do pravovoi derzhavy*, 390–392.

"Svoboda" [Freedom]. (n.d.-a). In *Filosofskyi entsyklopedychnyi slovnyk*. Retrieved October 4, 2025. https://slovnyk.me/dict/fes/свобода.

"Svoboda" [Freedom]. (n.d.-b). In *Slovnyk synonimiv ukrainskoi movy*. Retrieved October 4, 2025. https://slovnyk.me/dict/synonyms/свобода.

"Svoboda" [Freedom]. (n.d.-c). In *Velykyi tlumachnyi slovnyk suchasnoi movy*. Retrieved October 4, 2025. https://slovnyk.me/dict/vts/свобода.

Sydorenko, M. 2012. *Sudovyi zakhyst tsyvil'noho prava ta interesu yak zahal'na zasada tsyvil'noho zakonodavstva Ukrainy* [Judicial Protection of Civil Law and Interests as a General Principle of the Civil Legislation of Ukraine]. Abstract of PhD dissertation, National University "Odesa Law Academy."

Taranenko, M., and T. Kolomiiets. 2018. *Henezys smertnoi kary na terytorii Ukrainy* [The Genesis of the Death Penalty on the Territory of Ukraine]. *Jurnalul juridic național: teorie şi practică* 3: 89–92.

Tarrant, Richard. 2020. *Horace's Odes*. Oxford: Oxford University Press.

Tatsiy, V. Ya., and O. V. Petryshyn (Eds.). 2011. *Konstytutsiia Ukrainy. Naukovo-praktychnyi komentar* [The Constitution of Ukraine. A Scientific and Practical Commentary]. 2nd ed. Kharkiv: *Pravo.*

Tedoradze, I. 2017. "The Principle of Freedom of Contract, Pre-Contractual Obligations Legal Review English, EU and US Law." *European Scientific Journal* 13 (4): 62.

Tedoradze, M. 2014. *Pidstavy vynyknennia nedohovirnykh zobov'iazan' za zakonodavstvom Ukrainy* [Grounds for the Emergence of Non-contractual Obligations under the Legislation of Ukraine]. *Mytna sprava* 95 (5): 104–108.

Tenenbaum, T., et al. 2004. "Oncological Management of Pediatric Cancer Patients Belonging to Jehovah's Witnesses: A Two-institutional Experience Report." *Oncology Research and Treatment* 27 (2): 131–137.

Terré, François, Yves Lequette, and Philippe Simler. 2002. *Droit civil: Les obligations* [Civil Law: Obligations]. 8th ed. Paris: Editions Dalloz - Sirey.

The Book of Genesis. 2001. Vatican. Accessed October 4, 2025. https://www.vatican.va/archive/bible/genesis/documents/bible_genesis_en.html.

The Editors of Encyclopaedia Britannica. 1998. "Entelechy | Definition, Example, Aristotle, and Leibniz." *Encyclopedia Britannica*. https://www.britannica.com/topic/entelechy.

The Oxford Handbook of Karl Marx. 2018. Oxford: Oxford University Press.

The Oxford Handbook of the Epistemology of Theology. 2017. Oxford: Oxford University Press.

Thomas de Aquino. n.d. *Opera omnia*. Corpus Thomisticum. Accessed October 4, 2025. https://www.corpusthomisticum.org/iopera.html.

Tiensuu, P. 2015. "Whose Right to What Life? Assisted Suicide and the Right to Life as a Fundamental Right." *Human Rights Law Review* 15 (2): 251–281.

Titko, E., and I. Bozhuk. 2020. *Pravo na zminu po bat'kovi: praktyka YeSPL ta dosvid Ukrainy* [The Right to Change a Patronymic: The Practice of the ECHR and the Experience of Ukraine]. *Porivnial'no-analitychne pravo* 1: 674–677.

Tkachuk, A. 2002. *Znachennia vyny u vidnosynakh vidpovidal'nosti za porushennia dohovirnykh zobov'iazan'* [The Significance of Fault in Relations of Liability for Breach of Contractual Obligations]. Abstract of PhD dissertation, Taras Shevchenko National University of Kyiv.

Tobota, Yu. A. 2020. *Pryntsyp spravedlyvosti, dobrosovisnosti i rozumnosti u tsyvil'nomu pravi* [The Principle of Justice, Good Faith, and Reasonableness in Civil Law]. Kharkiv: *H. S. Skovoroda Kharkiv National Pedagogical University.*

Toftul, M. H. 2014. *Suchasnyi slovnyk z etyky* [Modern Dictionary of Ethics]. Zhytomyr: *Zhytomyr Ivan Franko State University*.

Tomachyns'kyi, S. M. 2022. "Determination of Conformity of Inventions, Relating to the Compositions of Known Substances, Conditions of Patentability «Inventive Level."" *Expert: Paradigm of Law and Public Administration* 20 (2): 112–118.

Törnroos, Maria, Mikko Jokela, and Christian Hakulinen. 2019. "The Relationship between Personality and Job Satisfaction across Occupations." *Personality and Individual Differences* 145: 82–88.

Trishch, R., and S. Kuz. 2011. *Dohovir pro nadannia finansovykh posluh yak zmishanyi vyd dohovoru u tsyvil'nomu pravi Ukrainy* [The Contract for the Provision of Financial Services as a Mixed Type of Contract in the Civil Law of Ukraine]. *Universytets'ki naukovi zapysky* 3: 208–212.

Trots'ka, V. M. 2016. *Vil'ne vykorystannia tvoriv z metoiu zabezpechennia funktsionuvannia derzhavnoho mekhanizmu* [Free Use of Works for the Purpose of Ensuring the Functioning of the State Mechanism]. *Teoriia i praktyka intelektual'noi vlasnosti* 1: 32–41.

Trydub, A., and B. Osipov. 2020. *Vstanovlennia zemel'noho servitutu v sudovomu poriadku* [Establishment of a Land Easement by Court Order]. *Asotsiatsiia yurydychnykh klinik Ukrainy*. Accessed October 4, 2025. https://legalclinics.in.ua/consult/consultation-22-06-2020-2/.

Tserkovna, A. O., and A. S. Ellarian. 2014. *Dohovirna ta nedohovirna (deliktna) vidpovidal'nist': porivnial'no-pravovyi analiz* [Contractual and Non-contractual (Tort) Liability: A Comparative Legal Analysis]. In *Pravovi zasoby zabezpechennia ta zakhystu prav liudyny: vitchyznianyi ta zarubizhnyi dosvid*, Book 5, 242–246.

Tserkovna, O. 2008. *Pidstavy zvil'nennia vid tsyvil'no-pravovoi vidpovidal'nosti za zavdannia shkody* [Grounds for Exemption from Civil Liability for Causing Harm]. Abstract of PhD dissertation, National University "Odesa Law Academy."

Tserkovna, O. 2018. *Vyna yak element skladu tsyvil'no-pravovoho deliktu* [Fault as an Element of a Civil Law Tort]. In *Baltic International Academy*, 129–135.

Tsvihun, D. P. 2021. *Osoblyvosti zastosuvannia servitutu yak odnoho z vydiv rechovykh prav na chuzhe maino* [Peculiarities of the Application of an Easement as One of the Types of Real Rights to Another's Property]. *Naukovyi visnyk Mizhnarodnoho humanitarnoho universytetu. Ser.: «Yurysprudentsiia»* 51: 81–83.

Tsybul's'ka, O. Yu. 2012. *Vyznachennia ta sutnist' zapovidal'noho vidkazu yak pidstavy vynyknennia pravovidnosyn za tsyvil'nym zakonodavstvom Ukrainy* [Definition and Essence of a Testamentary Bequest as a Basis for the Emergence of Legal Relations under the Civil Legislation of Ukraine]. *Aktual'ni problemy derzhavy i prava* 68: 378–385.

Tymoshenko, V. I. 2007. *Problema svobody voli: vid mekhanistychnoho determinizmu do normatyvnoho idealizmu* [The Problem of Free Will: From Mechanistic Determinism to Normative Idealism]. *Problemy filosofii prava* IV–V: 232–235.

Tymoshenko, V. I. 2011. *Protypravna povedinka: vyznachennia ta motyvatsiia* [Unlawful Conduct: Definition and Motivation]. *Biuleten' Ministerstva yustytsii Ukrainy* 12: 61–67.

Tsyvil'ne pravo Ukrainy: Akademichnyi kurs [Civil Law of Ukraine: An Academic Course]. 2003. Vol. 1. *Ya. M. Shevchenko* (Ed.). Kyiv: *In Yure*.

Tsyvil'nyi kodeks Ukrainy [Civil Code of Ukraine]. 2003. Law of Ukraine No. 435-IV. https://zakon.rada.gov.ua/laws/show/435-15.

Tsyvil'nyi kodeks Ukrainy: Naukovo-praktychnyi komentar [Civil Code of Ukraine: Scientific and Practical Commentary]. 2004. Edited by the developers of the Draft Civil Code of Ukraine (*rozrobnykiv proektu Tsyvil'noho kodeksu Ukrainy*). Kyiv: Istyna. http://uristinfo.net/2010-12-27-04-58-59/76-komentar-tsivilnij-kodeks-ukrayini/.

Tsyvil'nyi protsesual'nyi kodeks Ukrainy [Civil Procedure Code of Ukraine]. 2004. Law of Ukraine No. 1618-IV. https://zakon.rada.gov.ua/laws/show/1618-15.

Ukr. Media. 2018. "*Imena, iakymy ne mozhna nazyvaty maliukiv v Ukraini ta riznykh krainakh svitu*" [Names that Cannot be Given to Babies in Ukraine and Various Countries of the World]. May 14. Accessed October 4, 2025. https://ukr.media/science/344284/.

UNESCO. 2003. *Declaration Concerning the Intentional Destruction of Cultural Heritage*. October 17.

Unintended Consequences: Twelve Years under the DMCA. 2010. San Francisco: Electronic Frontier Foundation. March 3. https://www.eff.org/wp/unintended-consequences-under-dmca.

United Nations General Assembly. 1948. *Universal Declaration of Human Rights*. Resolution 217 A (III), December 10. https://www.un.org/en/about-us/universal-declaration-human-rights.

United Nations General Assembly. 1959. *Declaration of the Rights of the Child*. Resolution 1386 (XIV), November 20. https://www.ohchr.org/en/instruments-mechanisms/instruments/declaration-rights-child.

United Nations General Assembly. 1966. *International Covenant on Civil and Political Rights*. December 16. https://www.ohchr.org/en/instruments-mechanisms/instruments/international-covenant-civil-and-political-rights.

United Nations General Assembly. 1989. *Convention on the Rights of the Child*. Treaty Series 1577, November 20. https://www.ohchr.org/en/instruments-mechanisms/instruments/convention-rights-child.

UNESCO. 1997. *Universal Declaration on the Human Genome and Human Rights*. November 11. https://www.unesco.org/en/legal-affairs/universal-declaration-human-genome-and-human-rights.

US. 1776. *The Declaration of Independence*. July 4. https://www.archives.gov/founding-docs/declaration-transcript.

Ustymenko, N. 2001. *Taiemnytsi osobystoho zhyttia liudyny ta yikh tsyvil'nopravova okhorona* [Secrets of a Person's Private Life and Their Civil Law Protection]. Abstract of PhD dissertation, Yaroslav Mudryi National Law University.

Uzhva, M. A., and O. O. Kruhlova. 2021. *Realizatsiia pryntsypu svobody dohovoru v nedohovirnykh zobov'iazanniakh* [Implementation of the Principle of Freedom of Contract in Non-contractual Obligations]. In *Suchasni aspekty ekonomiky, obliku, finansiv i prava*, 66–67.

Valihura, K. 2020a. *Pryntsyp dobrosovisnosti yak katehoriia tsyvil'noho prava* [The Principle of Good Faith as a Category of Civil Law]. *Entrepreneurship, Economy and Law* 4: 11–16. https://doi.org/10.32849/2663-5313/2020.4.02.

Valihura, K. 2020b. *Pryntsyp dobrosovisnosti yak moral'no-pravova osnova pryvatnykh vidnosyn* [The Principle of Good Faith as a Moral and Legal Basis for Private Relations]. In *Superechnosti vzaiemodii morali i prava v suchasnomu suspil'stvi*, 116–120. Kyiv: *Drukarnia Madryd*.

Varii, M. 2009. *Psykholohiia* [Psychology]. 2nd ed. Kyiv: *Tsentr uchbovoi literatury*.

Vasyl'chenko, V. 2003. *Yurydychna sutnist' instytutu spadkovoho dohovoru ta yoho mistse v systemi tsyvil'noho prava* [The Legal Essence of the Institution of the Inheritance Agreement and Its Place in the System of Civil Law]. *Pravo Ukrainy* 6: 115–119.

Vasyl'chenko, V. V. 2004. *Sutnist' ta kharakter synhuliarnoho nastupnytstva za zapovidal'nymy vidkazamy* [The Essence and Character of Singular Succession by Testamentary Bequests]. *Naukovyi visnyk yurydychnoi akademii Ministerstva vnutrishnikh sprav* 1: 321–324.

Vasyl'chenko, V. V. 2007. *Naukovo-praktychnyi komentar Zakonu Ukrainy «Pro mizhnarodne pryvatne pravo»* [Scientific and Practical Commentary on the Law of Ukraine "On Private International Law"]. Kyiv: *Istyna*.

Vashchuk, O. M. 2004. *Konstytutsiino-pravovyi status hromads'kykh orhanizatsii Ukrainy* [The Constitutional and Legal Status of Public Organizations in Ukraine]. Abstract of PhD dissertation, Taras Shevchenko National University of Kyiv.

Vdovychyn, I. Ya. 2013. *Realizatsiia svobody osoby v Starodavnii Hretsii (polityko-pravovi idei i derzhavno-pravovi mekhanizmy)* [The Realisation of Personal Freedom in Ancient Greece (Political-legal Ideas and State-legal Mechanisms)]. *Aktual'ni problemy polityky* 48: 419–431.

Velkley, Richard L. 2011. *Heidegger, Strauss, and the Premises of Philosophy.* Chicago: University of Chicago Press.

Venediktova, I. 2013. *Zakhyst okhoroniuvanykh zakonom interesiv u tsyvil'nomu pravi* [Protection of Legally Protected Interests in Civil Law]. Dr. of Laws dissertation, Taras Shevchenko National University of Kyiv.

Verbans'kyi, A., and R. Karpenko. 2019. *Dyskusiini pytannia pravovoi pryrody spadkovoho dohovoru* [Debatable Issues of the Legal Nature of the Inheritance Agreement]. *Aktual'ni problemy vitchyznianoi yurysprudentsii* 3: 39–44.

Veresha, R. 2010. *Umysel i yoho vydy (komentar do st. 24 KK Ukrainy)* [Intent and Its Types (Commentary on Art. 24 of the Criminal Code of Ukraine)]. *Visnyk Akademii advokatury Ukrainy* 19 (3): 73–82.

Veretel'nyk, L. 2007. *Systematyzatsiia dohovoriv u tsyvil'nomu pravi* [Systematization of Contracts in Civil Law]. Abstract of PhD dissertation, Yaroslav Mudryi National Law University.

Vidal, Matt, Tony Smith, Tiago Rotta, and Paul Prew (Eds.). 2018. *The Oxford Handbook of Karl Marx*. Oxford: Oxford University Press. https://doi.org/10.1093/oxfordhb/9780190695545.001.0001.

Vydryhan, M. 2019. *Rozdumy pro svobodu voli u filosofs'kykh traktatakh Tsytsenora* [Reflections on Free Will in Cicero's Philosophical Treatises]. *Visnyk Cherkas'koho universytetu* 1: 13–18.

Volkova, N. 2008. *Tsyvil'no-pravovi zasoby indyvidualizatsii fizychnykh osib* [Civil Law Means of Individualization of Natural Persons]. Abstract of PhD dissertation, National University "Odesa Law Academy."

Volkova, V. I., and H. O. Okhota. 2017. *Tsenzura v Ukraini* [Censorship in Ukraine]. In *Kiberbezpeka ta intelektual'na vlasnist': problemy pravovoho zabezpechennia*, 104–106.

Volodina, O. 2005. *Kryminal'na vidpovidal'nist' za vykradennia liudyny* [Criminal Liability for Kidnapping]. Kyiv: *SPD-FO Chalytsev O. V.*

"*Volia*" [Will]. 2019. In *Slovnyk ukrains'koi movy* [Dictionary of the Ukrainian Language]. Accessed October 4, 2025. https://slovnyk.ua/index.php?swrd=%D0%B2%D0%BE%D0%BB%D1%8F.

Vovk, M. 2021. *Zdiisnennia osobystoho nemainovoho prava dytyny na sim'iu* [Exercise of the Child's Personal Non-property Right to a Family]. In *Suchasnyi rukh nauky*, 336–337.

Waldron, Jeremy. 1991. *The Right to Private Property*. Oxford: Oxford University Press.

Waller, Bruce N. 2003. "A Metacompatibilist Account of Free Will: Making Compatibilists and Incompatibilists More Compatible." *Philosophical Studies* 112 (3): 209–224.

Walter, Lothar, and Frank-Christian Schnittker. 2016. *Patentmanagement: Recherche, Analyse, Strategie* [Patent Management: Research, Analysis, Strategy]. Berlin: *de Gruyter GmbH, Walter*.

Whittaker, Simon. 2011. "The Optional Instrument of European Contract Law and Freedom of Contract." *European Review of Contract Law* 7 (3): 371–398.

Wicks, Elizabeth. 2010. "The Right to Life and Prevention of Crime: Killing by the State as Punishment and/or Deterrence." In *The Right to Life and Conflicting Interests*, 102–150. Oxford: Oxford University Press.

Wicks, Elizabeth. 2012. "The Meaning of 'Life': Dignity and the Right to Life in International Human Rights Treaties." *Human Rights Law Review* 12 (2): 199–219.

WMA Declaration of Lisbon on the Rights of the Patient. 2015. (Originally published 1981). https://www.wma.net/policies-post/wma-declaration-of-lisbon-on-the-rights-of-the-patient/.

WMA Declaration of Oslo on Therapeutic Abortion. 1970. https://www.wma.net/policies-post/wma-declaration-of-oslo-on-therapeutic-abortion/.

WMA Declaration of Oslo on Therapeutic Abortion. 2018. Adopted by the 24th World Medical Assembly, Oslo, Norway, August 1970, and revised by 69th WMA General Assembly, Reykjavik, Iceland, October 2018. https://www.wma.net/policies-post/wma-declaration-on-therapeutic-abortion/.

WMA International Code of Medical Ethics. 2022. (Originally published 1949). https://www.wma.net/policies-post/wma-international-code-of-medical-ethics/.

Watt, H. M. G., P. W. Richardson, U. Klusmann, M. Kunter, B. Beyer, U. Trautwein, and J. Baumert. 2012. "Motivations for Choosing Teaching as a Career: An International Comparison Using the FIT-Choice Scale." *Teaching and Teacher Education* 28 (6): 791–805. https://doi.org/10.1016/j.tate.2012.03.003

Yakovenko, V., and N. Filyk. 2017. *Publichna obitsianka vynahorody: vyznachennia pravovoi pryrody* [Public Promise of a Reward: Determining the Legal Nature]. *Porivnial'no-analitychne pravo* 5: 136–140.

Yakubivs'kyi, I. Ye. 2021. *Pravo promyslovoi vlasnosti ta yoho ob'iekty* [Industrial Property Law and Its Objects]. *Aktual'ni problemy vdoskonalennia chynnoho zakonodavstva* 56: 103–116.

Yanovyts'ka, H., and V. Kuchera (Eds.). 2011. *Tsyvil'ne pravo Ukrainy: navchal'nyi posibnyk* [Civil Law of Ukraine: A Study Guide]. L'viv: *L'viv State University of Internal Affairs.*

Yanovyts'ka, H., and V. Kuchera (Eds.). 2014. *Tsyvil'ne pravo Ukrainy: pidruchnyk* [Civil Law of Ukraine: A Textbook]. Vol. 1. Kyiv: *Novyi Svit-2000.*

Yarema, A. H., et al. 2005. *Naukovo-praktychnyi komentar do tsyvil'noho zakonodavstva Ukrainy* [Scientific and Practical Commentary on the Civil Legislation of Ukraine]. Vol. 3. Kyiv: *A.S.K.*

Yarmol, L. V., and S. Vando. 2015. *Poniattia, znachennia svobody ta yii vzaiemozv'iazok iz pravom* [The Concept, Meaning of Freedom and Its Relationship with Law]. *Visnyk Natsional'noho universytetu «L'vivs'ka politekhnika." Seriia «Yurydychni nauky»* 825: 252–257.

Yaroshevs'ka, T. V. 2017. *Sub'iekty prava na ob'iekty promyslovoi vlasnosti* [Subjects of the Right to Objects of Industrial Property]. *Aktual'ni problemy vitchyznianoi yurysprudentsii* 1 (6): 90–95.

Yaruniv, M. 2018. *Aksiolohichno-normatyvna paradyhma svobody voli liudyny* [The Axiological-Normative Paradigm of Human Free Will]. PhD dissertation, Ivan Franko National University of Lviv.

Yefremova, I. 2011. *Svoboda yak moral'no-pravovyi fenomen: sotsial'no-filosofs'kyi aspekt problemy* [Freedom as a Moral and Legal Phenomenon: A Socio-philosophical Aspect of the Problem]. *Filosofiia nauky: tradytsii ta innovatsii* 3: 251–259.

Yemchuk, L. V. 2015. *Konstytutsiino-pravove rehuliuvannia osobystoho ta simeinoho zhyttia liudyny i hromadianyna* [Constitutional and Legal Regulation of the Personal and Family Life of a Person and Citizen]. Abstract of PhD dissertation, Uzhhorod National University.

Yeromenko, I. 2015. *Sutnist' pokarannia u vydi pozbavlennia prava obiimaty pevni posady abo zaimatysia pevnoiu diialnistiu* [The Essence of Punishment in the Form of Deprivation of the Right to Hold Certain Positions or Engage in Certain Activities]. In *Yurydychni nauky: problemy ta perspektyvy*, 120–123.

Yevstihnieiev, A. 2005. *Deiaki aspekty spadkovoho dohovoru* [Some Aspects of the Inheritance Agreement]. *Yurydychnyi zhurnal* 10: 38.

Yurynets', Yu., M. Bielkin, and L. Bielkin. 2019. *Pravova okhorona avtors'koho prava i sumizhnykh prav v Ukraini v konteksti mizhnarodnoho prava* [Legal Protection of Copyright and Related Rights in Ukraine in the Context of International Law]. *Nauka ta innovatsii* 15 (6): 62–75.

Zaborovs'kyi, V., and R. Popovych. 2015. *Pravochyny iz vadamy voli: osnovni teoretychni ta praktychni aspekty* [Transactions with Vitiated Will: Main Theoretical and Practical Aspects]. *Naukovyi visnyk Uzhhorods'koho natsional'noho universytetu* 31 (2): 18–22.

Zahorui, L. 2017. *Pryntsyp tsyvil'noho prava – forma vyrazhennia idei svobody fizychnoi osoby* [The Principle of Civil Law as a Form of Expressing the Idea of an Individual's Freedom]. *Visnyk LDUVS im. E. O. Didorenka* 2 (78): 222–230.

Zaika, Yu. 2014. *Zobov'iazannia, yaki vynykaiut' pry stvorenni zahrozy zhyttiu, zdorov'iu abo mainu, v systemi nedohovirnykh zobov'iazan'* [Obligations Arising from the Creation of a Threat to Life, Health, or Property in the System of Non-contractual Obligations]. *Yurydychna nauka* 7: 20–28.

Zaika, Yu. O. 2007. *Stanovlennia i rozvytok spadkovoho prava v Ukraini* [Formation and Development of Inheritance Law in Ukraine]. Abstract of Dr. of Laws dissertation, Taras Shevchenko National University of Kyiv.

Zaika, Yu. O. 2009. *Spadkove pravo* [Inheritance Law]. Kyiv: *Yurinkom Inter*.

Zaitsev, O. L. 2007. *Pravochyny z vadamy voli* [Transactions with Vitiated Will]. *Visnyk Kharkivs'koho natsional'noho universytetu vnutrishnikh sprav* 36: 364–369.

Zemel'nyi kodeks Ukrainy [Land Code of Ukraine]. 2001. Law of Ukraine No. 2768-III. October 25. https://zakon.rada.gov.ua/laws/show/2768-14.

Zhadko, V., and P. Bidzilia. 2019. *Rizni aspekty problemy svobody voli* [Different Aspects of the Problem of Free Will]. https://www.researchgate.net/publication/336679629_Rizni_aspekti_problemi_svobodi_voli.

Zhvaniia, L. 2009. *Ideia svobody v liro-epichnykh tvorakh T. Shevchenka ta Lesi Ukrainky* [The Idea of Freedom in the Lyrical and Epic Works of T. Shevchenko and Lesya Ukrainka]. *Literaturoznavchi studii* 23: 122–129.

Zhydkova, O. 2008. *Tsyvil'no-pravovyi mekhanizm zakhystu prava na nedotorkannist' dilovoi reputatsii* [The Civil Law Mechanism for Protecting the Right to the Inviolability of Business Reputation]. Abstract of PhD dissertation, Yaroslav Mudryi National Law University.

Zhuk, I. V. 2009. *Prymusovi zakhody medychnoho kharakteru ta prymusove likuvannia u kryminal'nomu pravi Ukrainy* [Compulsory Medical Measures and Compulsory Treatment in the Criminal Law of Ukraine]. Abstract of PhD dissertation, National Academy of Internal Affairs.

Zhukova, A. I. 2021. *Semantyka komertsiinoho naimenuvannia ta torhovel'noi marky yak zasib sotsial'noi komunikatsii u suspil'stvi spozhyvannia* [The Semantics of a Commercial Name and Trademark as a Means of Social Communication in a Consumer Society]. In *Studia Slobozhanica,* 128–135. Kharkiv: *DBT University.*

Zhylinkova, I. 2000. *Problemy pravovoho rezhymu maina chleniv sim'i* [Problems of the Legal Regime of Property of Family Members]. Abstract of Dr. of Laws dissertation, Yaroslav Mudryi National Law University.

Zimmermann, Reinhard. 2015. "Intestate Succession in Germany." In *Comparative Succession Law,* 181–223. Oxford: Oxford University Press.

Zudikhin, O. 2011a. *Tsyvil'no-pravovyi zakhyst korporatyvnykh prav uchasnykiv hospodars'kykh tovarystv* [Civil Law Protection of Corporate Rights of Participants in Business Companies]. Abstract of PhD dissertation, National University "Odesa Law Academy."

Zudikhin, O. 2011b. *Pravova pryroda prava na sudovyi zakhyst* [The Legal Nature of the Right to Judicial Protection]. *Aktual'ni problemy polityky* 42: 72–79.

Zudikhin, O. 2011c. *Zakhyst prava na otrymannia prybutku ta vyplatu dyvidendiv sub'iektiv korporatyvnykh vidnosyn za tsyvil'nym zakonodavstvom Ukrainy* [Protection of the Right to Receive Profit and Dividends for Subjects of Corporate Relations under the Civil Legislation of Ukraine]. *Aktual'ni problemy derzhavy i prava* 59: 406–410.

UKRAINIAN VOICES

Collected by Andreas Umland

1 *Mychailo Wynnyckyj*
Ukraine's Maidan, Russia's War
A Chronicle and Analysis of the Revolution of Dignity
With a foreword by Serhii Plokhy
ISBN 978-3-8382-1327-9

2 *Olexander Hryb*
Understanding Contemporary Ukrainian and Russian Nationalism
The Post-Soviet Cossack Revival and Ukraine's National Security
With a foreword by Vitali Vitaliev
ISBN 978-3-8382-1377-4

3 *Marko Bojcun*
Towards a Political Economy of Ukraine
Selected Essays 1990–2015
With a foreword by John-Paul Himka
ISBN 978-3-8382-1368-2

4 *Volodymyr Yermolenko (ed.)*
Ukraine in Histories and Stories
Essays by Ukrainian Intellectuals
With a preface by Peter Pomerantsev
ISBN 978-3-8382-1456-6

5 *Mykola Riabchuk*
At the Fence of Metternich's Garden
Essays on Europe, Ukraine, and Europeanization
ISBN 978-3-8382-1484-9

6 *Marta Dyczok*
Ukraine Calling
A Kaleidoscope from Hromadske Radio 2016–2019
With a foreword by Andriy Kulykov
ISBN 978-3-8382-1472-6

7 *Olexander Scherba*
Ukraine vs. Darkness
Undiplomatic Thoughts
With a foreword by Adrian Karatnycky
ISBN 978-3-8382-1501-3

8 *Olesya Yaremchuk*
Our Others
Stories of Ukrainian Diversity
With a foreword by Ostap Slyvynsky
Translated from the Ukrainian by Zenia Tompkins and Hanna Leliv
ISBN 978-3-8382-1475-7

9 *Nataliya Gumenyuk*
Die verlorene Insel
Geschichten von der besetzten Krim
Mit einem Vorwort von Alice Bota
Aus dem Ukrainischen übersetzt von Johann Zajaczkowski
ISBN 978-3-8382-1499-3

10 *Olena Stiazhkina*
Zero Point Ukraine
Four Essays on World War II
Translated from the Ukrainian by Svitlana Kulinska
ISBN 978-3-8382-1550-1

11 *Oleksii Sinchenko, Dmytro Stus, Leonid Finberg (compilers)*
Ukrainian Dissidents
An Anthology of Texts
ISBN 978-3-8382-1551-8

12 *John-Paul Himka*
Ukrainian Nationalists and the Holocaust
OUN and UPA's Participation in the Destruction of Ukrainian Jewry, 1941–1944
ISBN 978-3-8382-1548-8

13 *Andrey Demartino*
False Mirrors
The Weaponization of Social Media in Russia's Operation to Annex Crimea
With a foreword by Oleksiy Danilov
ISBN 978-3-8382-1533-4

14 *Svitlana Biedarieva (ed.)*
Contemporary Ukrainian and Baltic Art
Political and Social Perspectives, 1991–2021
ISBN 978-3-8382-1526-6

15 *Olesya Khromeychuk*
A Loss
The Story of a Dead Soldier Told by His Sister
With a foreword by Andrey Kurkov
ISBN 978-3-8382-1570-9

16 *Marieluise Beck (Hg.)*
Ukraine verstehen
Auf den Spuren von Terror und Gewalt
Mit einem Vorwort von Dmytro Kuleba
ISBN 978-3-8382-1653-9

17 *Stanislav Aseyev*
Heller Weg
Geschichte eines Konzentrationslagers im Donbass 2017–2019
Aus dem Russischen übersetzt von Martina Steis und Charis Haska
ISBN 978-3-8382-1620-1

18 *Mykola Davydiuk*
Wie funktioniert Putins Propaganda?
Anmerkungen zum Informationskrieg des Kremls
Aus dem Ukrainischen übersetzt von Christian Weise
ISBN 978-3-8382-1628-7

19 *Olesya Yaremchuk*
Unsere Anderen
Geschichten ukrainischer Vielfalt
Aus dem Ukrainischen übersetzt von Christian Weise
ISBN 978-3-8382-1635-5

20 *Oleksandr Mykhed*
„Dein Blut wird die Kohle tränken“
Über die Ostukraine
Aus dem Ukrainischen übersetzt von Simon Muschick und Dario Planert
ISBN 978-3-8382-1648-5

21 *Vakhtang Kipiani (Hg.)*
Der Zweite Weltkrieg in der Ukraine
Geschichte und Lebensgeschichten
Aus dem Ukrainischen übersetzt von Margarita Grinko
ISBN 978-3-8382-1622-5

22 *Vakhtang Kipiani (ed.)*
World War II, Uncontrived and Unredacted
Testimonies from Ukraine
Translated from the Ukrainian by Zenia Tompkins and Daisy Gibbons
ISBN 978-3-8382-1621-8

23 *Dmytro Stus*
Vasyl Stus
Life in Creativity
Translated from the Ukrainian by
Ludmila Bachurina
ISBN 978-3-8382-1631-7

24 *Vitalii Ogiienko (ed.)*
The Holodomor and the Origins of the Soviet Man
Reading the Testimony of Anastasia Lysyvets
With forewords by Natalka Bilotserkivets and Serhy Yekelchyk
Translated from the Ukrainian by Alla Parkhomenko and Alexander J. Motyl
ISBN 978-3-8382-1616-4

25 *Vladislav Davidzon*
Jewish-Ukrainian Relations and the Birth of a Political Nation
Selected Writings 2013-2021
With a foreword by Bernard-Henri Lévy
ISBN 978-3-8382-1509-9

26 *Serhy Yekelchyk*
Writing the Nation
The Ukrainian Historical Profession in Independent Ukraine and the Diaspora
ISBN 978-3-8382-1695-9

27 *Ildi Eperjesi, Oleksandr Kachura*
Shreds of War
Fates from the Donbas Frontline 2014-2019
With a foreword by Olexiy Haran
ISBN 978-3-8382-1680-5

28 *Oleksandr Melnyk*
World War II as an Identity Project
Historicism, Legitimacy Contests, and the (Re-)Construction of Political Communities in Ukraine, 1939–1946
With a foreword by David R. Marples
ISBN 978-3-8382-1704-8

29 *Olesya Khromeychuk*
Ein Verlust
Die Geschichte eines gefallenen ukrainischen Soldaten, erzählt von seiner Schwester
Mit einem Vorwort von Andrej Kurkow
Aus dem Englischen übersetzt von Lily Sophie
ISBN 978-3-8382-1770-3

30 *Tamara Martsenyuk, Tetiana Kostiuchenko (eds.)*
Russia's War in Ukraine During 2022
Personal Experiences of Ukrainian Scholars
ISBN 978-3-8382-1757-4

31 *Ildikó Eperjesi, Oleksandr Kachura*
Shreds of War. Vol. 2
Fates from Crimea 2015–2022
With an interview of Oleh Sentsov
ISBN 978-3-8382-1780-2

32 *Yuriy Lukanov*
The Press
How Russia Destroyed Media Freedom in Crimea
With a foreword by Taras Kuzio
ISBN 978-3-8382-1784-0

33 *Megan Buskey*
Ukraine Is Not Dead Yet
A Family Story of Exile and Return
ISBN 978-3-8382-1691-1

34 *Vira Ageyeva*
Behind the Scenes of the Empire
Essays on Cultural Relationships between Ukraine and Russia
With a foreword by Oksana Zabuzhko
ISBN 978-3-8382-1748-2

35 *Marieluise Beck (ed.)*
Understanding Ukraine
Tracing the Roots of Terror and Violence
With a foreword by Dmytro Kuleba
ISBN 978-3-8382-1773-4

36 *Olesya Khromeychuk*
A Loss
The Story of a Dead Soldier Told by His Sister, 2nd edn.
With a foreword by Philippe Sands
With a preface by Andrii Kurkov
ISBN 978-3-8382-1870-0

37 *Taras Kuzio, Stefan Jajecznyk-Kelman*
Fascism and Genocide
Russia's War Against Ukrainians
ISBN 978-3-8382-1791-8

38 *Alina Nychyk*
Ukraine Vis-à-Vis Russia and the EU
Misperceptions of Foreign Challenges in Times of War, 2014–2015
With a foreword by Paul D'Anieri
ISBN 978-3-8382-1767-3

39 *Sasha Dovzhyk (ed.)*
Ukraine Lab
Global Security, Environment, and Disinformation Through the Prism of Ukraine
With a foreword by Rory Finnin
ISBN 978-3-8382-1805-2

40 *Serhiy Kvit*
Media, History, and Education
Three Ways to Ukrainian Independence
With a preface by Diane Francis
ISBN 978-3-8382-1807-6

41 *Anna Romandash*
Women of Ukraine
Reportages from the War and Beyond
ISBN 978-3-8382-1819-9

42 *Dominika Rank*
Matzewe in meinem Garten
Abenteuer eines jüdischen Heritage-Touristen in der Ukraine
ISBN 978-3-8382-1810-6

43 *Myroslaw Marynowytsch*
Das Universum hinter dem Stacheldraht
Memoiren eines sowjet-ukrainischen Dissidenten
Mit einem Vorwort von Timothy Snyder und einem Nachwort von Max Hartmann
ISBN 978-3-8382-1806-9

44 *Konstantin Sigow*
Für Deine und meine Freiheit
Europäische Revolutions- und Kriegserfahrungen im heutigen Kyjiw
Mit einem Vorwort von Karl Schlögel
Herausgegeben von Regula M. Zwahlen
ISBN 978-3-8382-1755-0

45 *Kateryna Pylypchuk*
The War that Changed Us
Ukrainian Novellas, Poems, and Essays from 2022
With a foreword by Victor Yushchenko
Paperback
ISBN 978-3-8382-1859-5
Hardcover
ISBN 978-3-8382-1860-1

46 *Kyrylo Tkachenko*
Rechte Tür Links
Radikale Linke in Deutschland, die Revolution und der Krieg in der Ukraine, 2013-2018
ISBN 978-3-8382-1711-6

47 *Alexander Strashny*
The Ukrainian Mentality
An Ethno-Psychological, Historical and Comparative Exploration
With a foreword by Antonina Lovochkina
Translated from the Ukrainian by Michael M. Naydan and Olha Tytarenko
ISBN 978-3-8382-1886-1

48 *Alona Shestopalova*
From Screens to Battlefields
Tracing the Construction of Enemies on Russian Television
With a foreword by Nina Jankowicz
ISBN 978-3-8382-1884-7

49 *Iaroslav Petik*
Politics and Society in the Ukrainian People's Republic (1917–1921) and Contemporary Ukraine (2013–2022)
A Comparative Analysis
With a foreword by Mykola Doroshko
ISBN 978-3-8382-1817-5

50 *Serhii Plokhy*
Der Mann mit der Giftpistole
Eine Spionageschichte aus dem Kalten Krieg
ISBN 978-3-8382-1789-5

51 *Vakhtang Kipiani*
Ukrainische Dissidenten unter der Sowjetmacht
Im Kampf um Wahrheit und Freiheit
Aus dem Ukrainischen übersetzt von Christian Weise
ISBN 978-3-8382-1890-8

52 *Dmytro Shestakov*
When Businesses Test Hypotheses
A Four-Step Approach to Risk Management for Innovative Startups
With a foreword by Anthony J. Tether
ISBN 978-3-8382-1883-0

53 *Larissa Babij*
A Kind of Refugee
The Story of an American Who Refused to Leave Ukraine
With a foreword by Vladislav Davidzon
ISBN 978-3-8382-1898-4

54 *Julia Davis*
In Their Own Words
How Russian Propagandists Reveal Putin's Intentions
With a foreword by Timothy Snyder
ISBN 978-3-8382-1909-7

55 *Sonya Atlantova, Oleksandr Klymenko*
Icons on Ammo Boxes
Painting Life on the Remnants of Russia's War in Donbas, 2014-21
Translated from the Ukrainian by Anastasya Knyazhytska
ISBN 978-3-8382-1892-2

56 *Leonid Ushkalov*
Catching an Elusive Bird
The Life of Hryhorii Skovoroda
Translated from the Ukrainian by Natalia Komarova
ISBN 978-3-8382-1894-6

57 *Vakhtang Kipiani*
Ein Land weiblichen Geschlechts
Ukrainische Frauenschicksale im 20. und 21. Jahrhundert
Aus dem Ukrainischen übersetzt von Christian Weise
ISBN 978-3-8382-1891-5

58 *Petro Rychlo*
„Zerrissne Saiten einer überlauten Harfe ...“
Deutschjüdische Dichter der Bukowina
ISBN 978-3-8382-1893-9

59 *Volodymyr Paniotto*
Sociology in Jokes
An Entertaining Introduction
ISBN 978-3-8382-1857-1

60 *Josef Wallmannsberger (ed.)*
Executing Renaissances
The Poetological Nation of Ukraine
ISBN 978-3-8382-1741-3

61 *Pavlo Kazarin*
The Wild West of Eastern Europe
A Ukrainian Guide on Breaking Free from Empire
Translated from the Ukrainian by Dominique Hoffman
ISBN 978-3-8382-1842-7

62 *Ernest Gyidel*
Ukrainian Public Nationalism in the General Government
The Case of *Krakivski Visti*, 1940–1944
With a foreword by David R. Marples
ISBN 978-3-8382-1865-6

63 *Olexander Hryb*
Understanding Contemporary Russian Militarism
From Revolutionary to New Generation Warfare
With a foreword by Mark Laity
ISBN 978-3-8382-1927-1

64 *Orysia Hrudka, Bohdan Ben*
Dark Days, Determined People
Stories from Ukraine under Siege
With a foreword by Myroslav Marynovych
ISBN 978-3-8382-1958-5

65 *Oleksandr Pankieiev (ed.)*
Narratives of the Russo-Ukrainian War
A Look Within and Without
With a foreword by Natalia Khanenko-Friesen
ISBN 978-3-8382-1964-6

66 *Roman Sohn, Ariana Gic (eds.)*
Unrecognized War
The Fight for Truth about Russia's War on Ukraine
With a foreword by Viktor Yushchenko
ISBN 978-3-8382-1947-9

67 *Paul Robert Magocsi*
Ukraina Redux
Schon wieder die Ukraine ...
ISBN 978-3-8382-1942-4

68 *Paul Robert Magocsi*
L'Ucraina Ritrovata
Sullo Stato e l'Identità Nazionale
ISBN 978-3-8382-1982-0

69 *Max Hartmann*
Ein Schrei der Verzweiflung
Aquarelle von Danylo Movchan zu Russlands Krieg in der Ukraine
Mit einem Vorwort von Mateusz Sora
Paperback
ISBN 978-3-8382-2011-6
Hardcover
ISBN 978-3-8382-2012-3

70 *Vakhtang Kebuladze (Hg.)*
Die Zukunft, die wir uns wünschen
Essays aus der Ukraine
ISBN 978-3-8382-1531-0

71 *Marieluise Beck, Jan Claas Behrends, Gelinada Grinchenko und Oksana Mikheieva (Hgg.)*
Deutsch-ukrainische Geschichten
Bruchstücke aus einer gemeinsamen Vergangenheit
ISBN 978-3-8382-2053-6

72 *Pavlo Kazarin*
Der Wilde Westen Ost-Europas
Der ukrainische Weg aus dem Imperium
Aus dem Ukrainischen übersetzt von Christian Weise
ISBN 978-3-8382-1843-4

73 *Radomyr Mokryk*
Die ukrainischen »Sechziger«
Chronologie einer Revolte
ISBN 978-3-8382-1873-1

74 *Leonid Finberg*
My Ukraine
Rethinking the Past, Building the Present
ISBN 978-3-8382-1974-5

75 *Joseph Zissels*
Consider My Inmost Thoughts
Essays, Lectures, and Interviews on Ukrainian Matters at the Turn of the Century
ISBN 978-3-8382-1975-2

76 *Margarita Yehorchenko, Iryna Berlyand, Ihor Vinokurov (eds.)*
Jewish Addresses in Ukraine
A Guide-Book
With a foreword by Leonid Finberg
ISB 978-3-8382-1976-9

77 *Viktoriia Grivina*
Kharkiv—A War City
A Collection of Essays from 2022–23
ISBN 978-3-8382-1988-2

78 *Hjørdis Clemmensen, Viktoriia Grivina, Vasylysa Shchogoleva*
Kharkiv Is a Dream
Public Art and Activism 2013–2023
With a foreword by Bohdan Volynskyi
ISBN 978-3-8382-2005-5

79 *Olga Khomenko*
The Faraway Sky of Kyiv
Ukrainians in the War
With a foreword by Hiroaki Kuromiya
ISBN 978-3-8382-2006-2

80 *Daria Mattingly, John Vsetecka (eds.)*
The Holodomor in Global Perspective
How the Famine in Ukraine Shaped the World
With a foreword by Anne Applebaum
ISBN 978-3-8382-1953-0

81 *Olga Khomenko*
Ukrainians beyond Borders
Nine Life Journeys Through the History of Eastern Europe
With a foreword by Zbigniew Wojnowski
ISBN 978-3-8382-2007-9

82 *Mykhailo Minakov*
From Servant to Leader
Chronicles of Ukraine under the Zelensky Presidency, 2019–2024
With a foreword by John Lloyd
ISBN 978-3-8382-2002-4

83 *Volodymyr Hromov (ed.)*
A Ruined Home
Sketches of War, 2022–2023
ISBN 978-3-8382-2008-6

84 *Olha Tatokhina (ed.)*
Why Do They Kill Our People?
Russia's War Against Ukraine as Told by Ukrainians
With a foreword by Volodymyr Yermolenko
ISBN 978-3-8382-2056-7

85 *Mieste Hotopp-Riecke, Sarah Reinke (Hgg.)*
Die Krimtataren
Geschichte – Kultur – Politik
Mit einem Vorwort von Nariman Dschelal
ISBN 978-3-8382-1986-8

86 *Max Hartmann (ed.)*
A Cry of Despair
Danylo Movchan's Watercolors on the War in Ukraine
With a foreword by John A. Kohan and Matheusz Sora
ISBN 978-3-8382-2051-2

87 *Olha Marmilova, Yuliia Soroka (eds.)*
The Russian War Against Ukraine
Investigations of Its Social and Historical Context, 2014–2024
With a foreword by Ulrich Schmid
ISBN 978-3-8382-2035-2

88 *Mykola Davidyuk*
How Putin's Propaganda Works
Ukraine's Experience in Its War Against Russia since 2014
With a foreword by Roman Kostenko
ISBN 978-3-8382-1627-0

89 *Mikhail Minakov*
Der postsowjetische Mensch
Philosophische Betrachtungen zur Gesellschaftsgeschichte nach Ende der UdSSR
Mit einem Vorwort von Timm Beichelt
Aus dem Englischen übersetzt von Hermann Haushahn
ISBN 978-3-8382-2043-7

90 *Serhiy Kazimir, Vahur Laiapea*
This Is How It Was
A Ukrainian Officer's 691 Days In Russian Prisons
Translation by Tiiu Palumäe and Ott Palumäe
ISBN 978-3-8382-2077-2

91 *Anastasiia Simferovska (ed.)*
Confronting Catastrophes
The Art of Yohanan Petrovsky-Shtern
With an introduction by Andrew Horodysky
ISBN 978-3-8382-2163-2

92 *Сергій Казимир, Вагур Лайапеа*
Так Було
691 день українського офіцера в російських тюрмах
Переклад з російської на українську Тетяна Лач
ISBN 978-3-8382-2177-9

93 *Ilko-Sascha Kowalczuk*
Freedom Shock
A Different History of East Germany from 1989 to Today
ISBN 978-3-8382-2069-7

94 *Stephen Velychenko*
A Village in Revolutionary Ukraine
How Bolshevik Rule Changed a People
The Eyewitness Account of a Common Man, 1918–1928
With a foreword by Yaroslav Hrytsak
ISBN 978-3-8382-2065-9

95 *Katerina Sergatskova*
Occupation and Migration in Eastern Europe
How Citizens Are Forced into Exile and Shaped by New Realities—Reports, Essays, Articles, 2014–25
With a foreword by Christopher Miller
ISBN 978-3-8382-2060-4

96 *Olena Bogatyrenko (ed.)*
What Did Russia's Occupation of Crimea Mean?
Twelve Women Report How They Experienced the Start of the Russo-Ukrainian War in 2014
ISBN 978-3-8382-2092-5

97 *Larisa Kalik*
Dress Rehearsal
How Transnistria Became Russia's Roadmap for Hybrid Wars in Ukraine and Beyond
With a foreword by Francis Farrell
Translated from the Ukrainian by Kate Tsurkan
ISBN 978-3-8382-2074-1

98 *Petro Rychlo*
Regenbogen über der Donau
Studien zu deutsch-ukrainischen Literaturbeziehungen
Paperback
ISBN 978-3-8382-2093-2
Hardcover
ISBN 978-3-8382-2293-6

99 *Daria Antsybor, Michel Bouchard*
Memeing War
The Digital Folklore Memetic Mirror of Contemporary Ukrainian Culture and Society
ISBN 978-3-8382-2040-6

100 *Sergiy Korsunsky*
The Age of Revisionism
International Relations in Times of War, Uncertainty, and Insecurity
ISBN 978-3-8382-2023-9

101 *Olena Bogatyrenko (ed.)*
Was bedeutete Russlands Besetzung der Krim?
Zwölf Frauen berichten, wie sie 2014 den Beginn des Russisch-Ukrainischen Krieges erlebten
Übersetzt von Hermann Haushahn
ISBN 978-3-8382-2292-9

102 *Alla Prokhovnik-Raphique*
Whispers of Survival
War, Trauma, and the Making of Civilian Rescuers
With a foreword by Sarah Adams
ISBN 978-3-8382-2114-4

103 *Maryna Starodubska*
Ukraine Layer by Layer
Freedom and Friction in a Frontier Society
With a foreword by Natalka Cmoc
ISBN 978-3-8382-2117-5

104 *Viktor Savchenko*
Free Will in Civil Law
A Ukrainian Perspective
With a foreword by Thomas Douglas
ISBN 978-3-8382-2133-5

105 *Volodymyr Khandogiy*
Inside Ukrainian Diplomacy
Vol. 1: True Stories by a Career Diplomat, 1970–1994
ISBN 978-3-8382-2147-2

106 *Volodymyr Khandogiy*
Inside Ukrainian Diplomacy
Vol. 2: Reflections and Analyses, 1995–2016
ISBN 978-3-8382-2147-2

107 *Danylo Poliluev-Schmidt (ed.)*
The Armed Truth
What Germany and Europe Can Learn from Ukrainian Media, 1991–2026
With a foreword by Patrick Sensburg
ISBN 978-3-8382-2150-2

108 *Christian Fernández Huerta, Julia Sushytska, Alisa Slaughter (eds.)*
Borders de Todos Lados—Fronteras from all Directions—Кордони зусібіч
Vol. 1: Crossings, Elementals, Vigilances, Disborders
With a foreword by José Manuel Valenzuela Arce
ISBN 978-3-8382-2161-8

109 *Christian Fernández Huerta, Julia Sushytska, Alisa Slaughter (eds.)*
Borders de Todos Lados—Fronteras from all Directions—Кордони зусібіч
Vol. 2: Discourses, Reveries, Diasporas, Beyond Borders
With a foreword by Botakoz Kassymbekova
ISBN 978-3-8382-2162-5

110 *Amber French-Griette (ed.)*
Ukrainian Freedom
Collective Agency in National Defense
With a foreword by Oleksandra Matviichuk
ISBN 978-3-8382-2168-7

111 *Vadym Denysenko, Vitliy Pyrovych*
After Putin
The Russia We'll Have to Live with for the Next 50 Years
ISBN 978-3-8382-2113-7

112 *Iaroslav Petik*
Culture War
An Essay on the Origins of the Russo-Ukrainian Conflict
With a foreword by Iryna Grabovska
ISBN 978-3-8382-2017-8

113 *Anton Grushetsky, Volodymyr Paniotto*
Krieg und der Wandel der ukrainischen Gesellschaft
Eine soziologische Bestandsaufnahme der Jahre 2022-2025
Aus dem Englischen übersetzt von Hermann Haushahn
ISBN 978-3-8382-2144-1

114 *Max Hartmann (Hg.)*
Die verwundete Seele Europas
Stimmen aus der Ukraine über Krieg, Angst und Hoffnung
Mit einem Vorwort von Isa Alexander Zalitatsch
ISBN 978-3-8382-2251-6

Book series "Ukrainian Voices"

Sergiy Korsunsky, Kobe Gakuin University, Japan
Nadiia Koval, Kyiv School of Economics, Ukraine
Volodymyr Kravchenko, University of Alberta, Edmonton
Oleksiy Kresin, NAS Koretskiy Institute of State and Law, Kyiv
Anatoliy Kruglashov, Fedkovych National University, Chernivtsi
Andrey Kurkov, PEN Ukraine, Kyiv
Ostap Kushnir, Lazarski University, Warsaw
Taras Kuzio, National University of Kyiv-Mohyla Academy
Serhii Kvit, National University of Kyiv-Mohyla Academy
Yuliya Ladygina, The Pennsylvania State University, USA
Yevhen Mahda, Institute of World Policy, Kyiv
Victoria Malko, California State University, Fresno, USA
Yulia Marushevska, Security and Defense Center (SAND), Kyiv
Myroslav Marynovych, Ukrainian Catholic University, Lviv
Oleksandra Matviichuk, Center for Civil Liberties, Kyiv
Mykhailo Minakov, Kennan Institute, Washington, USA
Anton Moiseienko, The Australian National University, Canberra
Alexander Motyl, Rutgers University-Newark, USA
Vlad Mykhnenko, University of Oxford, United Kingdom
Vitalii Ogiienko, Ukrainian Institute of National Remembrance, Kyiv
Olga Onuch, University of Manchester, United Kingdom
Olesya Ostrovska, Museum "Mystetskyi Arsenal," Kyiv
Anna Osypchuk, National University of Kyiv-Mohyla Academy
Oleksandr Pankieiev, University of Alberta, Edmonton
Oleksiy Panych, Publishing House "Dukh i Litera," Kyiv
Valerii Pekar, Kyiv-Mohyla Business School, Ukraine
Yohanan Petrovsky-Shtern, Northwestern University, Chicago
Serhii Plokhy, Harvard University, Cambridge, USA
Andrii Portnov, Viadrina University, Frankfurt-Oder, Germany
Maryna Rabinovych, Kyiv School of Economics, Ukraine
Valentyna Romanova, Institute of Developing Economies, Tokyo
Natalya Ryabinska, Collegium Civitas, Warsaw, Poland
Darya Tsymbalyk, University of Oxford, United Kingdom
Vsevolod Samokhvalov, University of Liege, Belgium
Orest Semotiuk, Franko National University, Lviv
Viktoriya Sereda, NAS Institute of Ethnology, Lviv
Anton Shekhovtsov, University of Vienna, Austria
Andriy Shevchenko, Media Center Ukraine, Kyiv
Oxana Shevel, Tufts University, Medford, USA
Pavlo Shopin, National Pedagogical Dragomanov University, Kyiv
Karina Shyrokykh, Stockholm University, Sweden
Nadja Simon, freelance interpreter, Cologne, Germany
Olena Snigova, NAS Institute for Economics and Forecasting, Kyiv
Ilona Solohub, Analytical Platform "VoxUkraine," Kyiv
Iryna Solonenko, LibMod - Center for Liberal Modernity, Berlin
Galyna Solovei, National University of Kyiv-Mohyla Academy
Sergiy Stelmakh, NAS Institute of World History, Kyiv
Olena Stiazhkina, NAS Institute of the History of Ukraine, Kyiv
Dmitri Stratievski, Osteuropa Zentrum (OEZB), Berlin
Dmytro Stus, National Taras Shevchenko Museum, Kyiv
Frank Sysyn, University of Toronto, Canada
Olha Tokariuk, Center for European Policy Analysis, Washington
Olena Tregub, Independent Anti-Corruption Commission, Kyiv
Hlib Vyshlinsky, Centre for Economic Strategy, Kyiv
Mychailo Wynnyckyj, National University of Kyiv-Mohyla Academy
Yelyzaveta Yasko, NGO "Yellow Blue Strategy," Kyiv
Serhy Yekelchyk, University of Victoria, Canada
Victor Yushchenko, President of Ukraine 2005-2010, Kyiv
Oleksandr Zaitsev, Ukrainian Catholic University, Lviv
Kateryna Zarembo, National University of Kyiv-Mohyla Academy
Yaroslav Zhalilo, National Institute for Strategic Studies, Kyiv
Sergei Zhuk, Ball State University at Muncie, USA
Alina Zubkovych, Nordic Ukraine Forum, Stockholm
Liudmyla Zubrytska, National University of Kyiv-Mohyla Academy

Friends of the Series

Ana Maria Abulescu, University of Bucharest, Romania
Łukasz Adamski, Centrum Mieroszewskiego, Warsaw
Marieluise Beck, LibMod—Center for Liberal Modernity, Berlin
Marc Berensen, King's College London, United Kingdom
Johannes Bohnen, BOHNEN Public Affairs, Berlin
Karsten Brüggemann, University of Tallinn, Estonia
Ulf Brunnbauer, Leibniz Institute (IOS), Regensburg
Martin Dietze, German-Ukrainian Culture Society, Hamburg
Gergana Dimova, Florida State University, Tallahassee/London
Caroline von Gall, Goethe University, Frankfurt-Main
Zaur Gasimov, Rhenish Friedrich Wilhelm University, Bonn
Armand Gosu, University of Bucharest, Romania
Thomas Grant, University of Cambridge, United Kingdom
Gustav Gressel, European Council on Foreign Relations, Berlin
Rebecca Harms, European Centre for Press & Media Freedom, Leipzig
André Härtel, Stiftung Wissenschaft und Politik, Berlin/Brussels
Marcel Van Herpen, The Cicero Foundation, Maastricht
Richard Herzinger, freelance analyst, Berlin
Mieste Hotopp-Riecke, ICATAT, Magdeburg
Nico Lange, Munich Security Conference, Berlin
Martin Malek, freelance analyst, Vienna
Ingo Mannteufel, Broadcaster "Deutsche Welle," Bonn
Carlo Masala, Bundeswehr University, Munich
Wolfgang Mueller, University of Vienna, Austria
Dietmar Neutatz, Albert Ludwigs University, Freiburg
Torsten Oppelland, Friedrich Schiller University, Jena
Niccolò Pianciola, University of Padua, Italy
Gerald Praschl, German-Ukrainian Forum (DUF), Berlin
Felix Riefer, Think Tank Ideenagentur-Ost, Düsseldorf
Stefan Rohdewald, University of Leipzig, Germany
Sebastian Schäffer, Institute for the Danube Region (IDM), Vienna
Felix Schimansky-Geier, Friedrich Schiller University, Jena
Ulrich Schneckener, University of Osnabrück, Germany
Winfried Schneider-Deters, freelance analyst, Heidelberg/Kyiv
Gerhard Simon, University of Cologne, Germany
Kai Struve, Martin Luther University, Halle/Wittenberg
David Stulik, European Values Center for Security Policy, Prague
Andrzej Szeptycki, University of Warsaw, Poland
Philipp Ther, University of Vienna, Austria
Stefan Troebst, University of Leipzig, Germany

[Please send requests for changes in, corrections of, and additions to, this list to andreas.umland@ukma.edu.ua.]

***ibidem**.eu*